THE
EVERYDAY
TORAH

Also by Rabbi Bradley Shavit Artson

Gift of Soul, Gift of Wisdom: A Spiritual Resource for Mentoring and Leadership
The Bedside Torah: Wisdom, Visions, and Dreams
It's a Mitzvah! Jewish Living Step by Step
Making a Difference: Putting Jewish Spirituality into Action, One Mitzvah at a Time
Love Peace & Pursue Peace: A Jewish Response to War and Nuclear Annihilation
Jewish Answers to Real-Life Questions

THE
EVERYDAY
TORAH

Weekly Reflections and Inspirations

RABBI BRADLEY SHAVIT ARTSON

New York   Chicago   San Francisco   Lisbon   London   Madrid   Mexico City
Milan   New Delhi   San Juan   Seoul   Singapore   Sydney   Toronto

The McGraw·Hill Companies

Library of Congress Cataloging-in-Publication Data

Artson, Bradley Shavit.
    The everyday Torah : weekly reflections and inspirations / Bradley Shavit Artson. —
1st ed.
        p.   cm.
    Includes index.
    ISBN-13: 978-0-07-154619-5 (alk. paper)
    ISBN-10:   0-07-154619-7 (alk. paper)
    1. Bible. O.T. Pentateuch—Meditations.   I. Title.

    BS1225.54.A78   2008
    222'.107—dc22   2007052926

1 2 3 4 5 6 7 8 9 10 11 12 13 14 15 16 17 18 19 20 21 22 23 24   FGR/FGR   0 9 8

ISBN 978-0-07-154619-5
MHID   0-07-154619-7

Interior design by Lovedog Studios

McGraw-Hill books are available at special quantity discounts to use as premiums and sales promotions or for use in corporate training programs. To contact a representative, please visit the Contact Us pages at www.mhprofessional.com.

This book is printed on acid-free paper.

For
Elana

For
Jacob and Shira

For
My Students

Contents

Leviticus: *Va-Yikra*/He Called

Numbers: *Be-Midbar*/In the Desert

Deuteronomy: *Devarim*/Words

Foreword

For decades now, Bradley Artson has been one of America's leading rabbis for laymen—and a rabbi's rabbi. As Dean of the Ziegler School of Rabbinic Studies, he has upgraded rabbinic education—intellectually, spiritually, and ethically. Simultaneously, through the causes he advocated as rabbi—upholding and welcoming the excluded, the handicapped, the poor—he has stimulated and elevated his peers. Throughout his career, he has reached out beyond his denomination to Jews and Gentiles alike, serving as teacher, role model, and coworker in the sacred work of the Lord. He is a national leader in every sense of the word.

In this book, Rabbi Artson turns his wisdom and teaching to the layperson, the intelligent reader, the seeker who wishes to understand the Five Books of Moses and apply their teaching for the improvement of everyday life. Artson offers a three-way path into Jewry's eternal message as he goes through the weekly Torah portion for a whole year. First he gives a summary of the theme(s), narrative, and content of the weekly reading. The summary gives us the heart of the message. (Fellow rabbis will learn from a master what to include, what to omit.) Then he reflects on a theme or themes in the section that are worthy of further attention. In developing this second insight, he never goes for the obvious or the clichéd. For example, in the opening of Genesis, instead of focusing on the Creation, or the Adam and Eve story, Artson turns the account into an opportunity to show that the Torah is not "a shoddy science text or a sloppy history" (which is what fundamentalists turn it into when they insist that it must be taken literally). Rather, as he shows throughout this volume, the Torah is a body of teaching about the values of existence and the purpose of life. In the same portion, the story of Hanokh (who walked with God but died young) is highlighted to rebuke those who justify God's ways by insisting that sickness, suffering, or premature death reflects God's judgment or punishment. He sees the text with a fresh eye every week. His keen vision and quick insights give him a high batting average for hits.

The third path consists of Artson's applications of the themes to personal life and today's issues. Examples include: to love God through helping those who need help, the courage to defy the world, the need to dare to dream, the legitimacy of questioning God, discovering hope in going through a life situation full of despair, and the idolatry in self-centeredness. Other teachings include: equality is not to be equated with identicality, true power is expressed in compassion and restraint, the need to be yourself, when a rabbi (or other major leader) sins. The list goes on and on. Read this volume and have the pleasure of making your own selection!

There are foundational themes running through this book that are classic expressions of Brad Artson's values—sometimes they are articulated, sometimes they are communicated through the structure of his writing. This book is a living proof of the Talmudic teaching *hafach ba, va'hafach ba, d'kula bah* (turn it [the text] over and turn it over [meaning: dig into the Torah] for all [wisdom] is in it) [Ethics of the Fathers, Chapter 5, Mishnah 25]. Artson believes that the ongoing study of the text shapes our lives for the good and makes up the strongest fabric of our Jewish identity. By his treatment of the text, Artson shows us the way to be continuously engaged with the Torah—every day and in every situation in our lives. His repeated explanations of the power of tradition *and* change, his constant evocation of the ethical dimension of the Torah, his conviction that the relationship of God and Israel is one of covenantal love (= marriage), and his never-failing tendency to be *melamed zchus* (seeking out the best possible understanding of people's behavior) run as leitmotifs through this book, and they teach us values that we all need to learn and practice.

Artson is a powerful teacher and a dialectical one. He develops important messages and metaphors, but he portrays their limits as well. He develops the theme of God's unqualified love for us out of the Torah's description of the Tabernacle. Yet just as he communicates the power of holy space, he insists on the limits of sacred buildings. He explicates the commandments and the importance of halakhah, yet he calls us to understand and practice Judaism "beyond the letter of the law." Artson brings the reader closer to the Jewish way of life without preaching or judgmentalism. Rather, all through this book, he explains and puts the best light on primary mitzvot of the Torah—circumcision, Shabbat, kashrut, tefillin. Yet he includes a defense of the identity-building power of the *hukkim* (the laws that defy logic). As he puts it, "Nothing Jewish is irrelevant." He proves this dictum with his explications and applications on every page. All this is done without hectoring or condescending. Instead, he weaves a thread of humor that runs throughout. For example, in "Human Dignity: For the Birds?," he shows how cheaper (bird) sacrifices were established so the poor would not be shut out of the Temple worship; "Come on, Baby, Light My Fire" on the menorah; and "Seek Though You Won't Find" about the importance of a spiritual quest although we can never know God or God's self.

In everything that Rabbi Artson does in this book and in his life's work, he behaves like the tzaddik (truly righteous person) that he is. He comforts the afflicted and challenges the comfortable, and his compassion is over all of God's creatures. Like a tzaddik, he says "a little but does [deliver] a lot." In this book, too, he delivers what he promises. *The Everyday Torah* has messages, teachings, and inspirations for every day in our lives. It remains only for you, the reader, to pick up this book and, in reading, bring a great teacher and spiritual guide into your life. The life you enrich will be your own!

—Rabbi Irving Greenberg,
  Past President, Jewish Life Network;
  Past President, CLAL: National
  Jewish Center for Learning and
  Leadership

Acknowledgments

As with the writing of any book, there are many people to thank.

Thanks to Rena J. Copperman, who linked me to my editor, Sarah Pelz, a consummate professional and a delightful partner in this work. Thanks also to the many skilled people at McGraw-Hill who have produced such a beautiful book.

Thanks to my friend and mentor, Sam Smotrich, of blessed memory, who first encouraged me to write a weekly column reflecting on the Torah; to his sons and their wives—Marvin and Mehry, Thomas and Iris—and their families, whose goodness and caring extends their father's legacy and perpetuates his worthy values.

While writing this book, it has been my delight to serve as Dean of the Ziegler School of Rabbinic Studies and Vice President of the American Jewish University (formerly the University of Judaism) in Bel-Air, California. I am reminded daily of the blessing of working with an outstanding group of people: students, faculty, administration, and lay leaders. My deepest thanks go to the university's president, Rabbi Dr. Robert Wexler, who is both a mentor and a friend; to Rabbi Cheryl Peretz, Rabbi Aaron Alexander, and Reb Mimi Feigelson—partners in building a world-class rabbinical school in the context of holiness, goodness, and friendship; and to my beloved students—rabbis and soon-to-be rabbis. I also wish to express my gratitude to Blanca Jensen and Lorri Gums for their professionalism and devotion to our school. It is a privilege and a joy to work at such a *makom* Torah.

My continuing thanks and affection also go to the Jewish Theological Seminary, where I was ordained as a rabbi and where I still cherish friendships and many close ties, and to the Hebrew Union College–Jewish Institute of Religion, where I am granted the privilege of doctoral studies under the scholarly and humane supervision of my teacher and friend, Rabbi Dr. David Ellenson.

I owe gratitude also to the Wexner Heritage Foundation.

My deepest thanks to Maria Lara for all the care and assistance she extends to me and my family—especially my children.

Of course, my beloved family has provided a constant backdrop of love and support. I am deeply grateful to my mother, Barbara Friedman Artson; my father, David Artson, and his partner, Jeanne Markson; my sister and sister-in-law, Tracy and Dawn Osterweil-Artson; my niece, Sydney, and my nephew, Benjamin; my brother, Matthew Artson; and Grace Mayeda, my beloved childhood nanny.

The ancient rabbis spoke wisely (yet again) when they commented that as much as they learned from their teachers and colleagues, they learned even more from their students. Certainly my students have been a great source of learning for me, as well as a great source of joy. Seeing the future sparkle in their eyes, soar in their hopes, and dance in their resolve, I know that the future of Torah is in good hands. To all of my students—former congregants, rabbis, rabbinical students, seeking men and women across North America—I dedicate this book as a token of my love and my gratitude that you allow me the privilege of bringing Torah to your lives.

My children, Jacob and Shira, fill my life with profound joy and purpose. They are both heroic in their ability to face the challenges that life brings and to meet those challenges with courage, depth, compassion, and success. The twins fill me with pride and illumine my life with the deepest joy.

My beloved wife, Elana, is my partner as we journey together along the path of Torah. To have the privilege of sharing my life with my lifelong best friend is a true blessing and an abiding joy. She is indefatigable on behalf of our children and our family and of all children with special needs. I know of no one who better exemplifies the values of Torah than she, and I love her with all my heart.

To my students, and to Elana, Shira, and Jacob, I lovingly dedicate this book. *Aharon, aharon haviv*—I am grateful beyond words to the Holy Blessing One. You have allowed me the privilege of studying, teaching, and observing Your Torah; of glimpsing, from time to time, the shimmering light; and of rejoicing to mold the warmth of that light into words. I pray that this book will in some small way refract Your divine love and to allow others to grow with Your word.

Tam ve-Nishlam Shevach Le-El Borei Olam.

Introduction

Rabbinic law exhorts Jews to read the parashah (weekly Bible portion) at least three times each week. To accommodate that expectation, it has become a custom to call worshippers to thank God for the gift of the Torah (the first five books of the Bible) and to publicly chant from the scroll during the morning minyan, or prayer service, on Monday, Thursday, and Saturday mornings. This commonsense approach ensures regular exposure to Israel's most sacred writings, permitting no more than a two-day interval between each new encounter with the holy scripture.

The reflections in this collection take advantage of that same schedule. Offered here is one year's worth of perspectives on the Torah. Three essays for each parashah explore different insights (ancient, medieval, and modern), blending them together to allow readers to gain insights helpful for daily living and spiritual growth.

It is my hope that the discipline of reading three essays each week (along with the Torah portion itself, of course) will enrich and deepen the impact of the words of Torah for every seeking soul. As the common inheritance of Jews and Christians, greater immersion in the sea of Torah and its commentaries can only strengthen a sense of God's presence and a level of comfort with one's own religious traditions and insight.

For Jews, these reflections will provide an exposure to the classical Talmudic and medieval commentaries viewed through the lenses of contemporary issues and perspectives. For Christians, often educated in the Israel of biblical antiquity alone, these words will demonstrate the continuing vitality of a venerable people. For all, these meditations provide a forum for wrestling with questions of ultimate worth and perennial concern.

I pray that these thoughts will inspire and enrich the religious lives of all who read them. They seek to reveal a contemporary application of each parashah, utilizing the insights of ancient rabbis and sages, medieval commentators and philosophers, and modern scholars and religious leaders. My writing was guided by the conviction that—in the words of my teacher, Rabbi Alan Miller—the Torah is a "high-voltage book," still giving off sparks, still enlightening those who make themselves channels for its power.

Like any classic, the Torah appears in different guises with each rereading. Its infinite layers of meaning and depth offer the opportunity to harvest anew, without any fear of exhausting its supply of wisdom, counsel, and *kedushah* (holiness). To encounter Torah is to encounter God. I pray that these meditations are worthy of that awesome responsibility and that they, in some small way, provide a glimpse beneath the sacred canopy where Israel and the Holy One first consecrated a love relationship, one that retains its ability to startle, to excite, to soothe, and to sanctify.

genesis

B'raisheet

———◄►◄►———

In the Beginning

B'raisheet/In the Beginning
Genesis 1:1–6:8

B'raisheet ("beginnings") is the concern of this parashah, as it is of the book known in English as Genesis. Like many ancient religious narratives, the Bible begins with the creation of everything, culminating in life on earth. Distinct to this telling, however, are two significant variations. Instead of creation as the result of a cosmic battle requiring great effort, the God of the Torah creates simply by issuing an effortless verbal command: "Let there be." The incomparable ease with which God summons the sun, moon, stars, water, sky, earth, and life into existence and that God does so without the aid or counsel of any other being marks this God as incomparable and unique.

The second distinctive feature of the Torah's creation account is that it culminates not with the creation of humanity as the servants of the deity, but with the cessation of all labor, hence there is a day of rest—the Shabbat (Sabbath). That God's efforts should culminate in the gift of rest establishes a radical new reality. Made in God's image, human beings are free. And the fullest expression of their humanity is to be found in their freedom, demonstrated by putting aside their chores and returning to their God, Torah, and community.

At the end of the process of creation, God declares the cosmos, the world, and living things to be very good. In the Garden, humanity is given one solitary commandment—to not eat from the fruit of the tree of knowledge of good and evil. Enticed by the snake, first Eve and later Adam eat of the fruit, resulting in their moral responsibility, their expulsion from paradise, and their mortality. That mortality is immediately apparent as one of their sons, Cain, murders his brother Abel and is doomed to wander. The parashah closes with the record of Adam's genealogy to Noah and the foreboding recognition that God saw how great was humanity's wickedness on earth and how every plan devised by the human mind was evil.

Beginnings

A good deal of debate goes into the nature of the truth of Torah. Is it chronological—is it true the way a reliable history book is true? Or is the Torah's truth factual—is it true the way a comprehensive science textbook is true? Or is there, perhaps, a third way, in which the level of meaning and purpose that is the truth of Torah can be found? As we begin the year's cycle of Torah readings, it may be fitting to return to beginnings, to reexamine what the Torah seeks to convey.

B'raisheet bara—the opening words of the book of Genesis—have invited a complex range of translations. The most well-known English translation, the King James Version, understands that "In the beginning God created the heaven and the earth." The language itself relates to creation as a matter of history—this came first, then that. This way of accepting creation is popular among more orthodox (within Judaism) and more fundamentalist (within Christianity) approaches. It affirms a simple faith—if the Torah says it, then it is true. End of story.

But it is not the end of the story. To read this first sentence as simple history creates an immediate problem, one recognized by no less traditional a giant than Rashi (Rabbi Shlomo Yitzhaki, the greatest of the medieval Bible commentators). For reasons theological, textual, and grammatical, Rashi insists that the true meaning of the very first sentence of Torah cannot be taken on the level of *p'shat* (history or fact). The grammatical challenge is that the noun *B'raisheet* is in the construct, requiring another noun to complete the phrase. That other noun is missing. The weightier theological problem is that the concern can't be a chronological description of the order God used to create, since the waters already exist. Rashi says, "The verse does not come to teach the order of creation by telling us that these preceded those."

When we force Hebrew school students to memorize what was created on which days, when we engage in sterile arguments about how long the seven days actually were, we are missing the truth that is before our eyes. Not chronological information, but religious truth is the purview of this (and every) biblical insight.

And what is that truth?

Rashi proposes that the verse comes to teach purpose, not history. He argues that the first letter in *B'raisheet* means "for the sake of," and he looks elsewhere in the Torah to see what is described as *resheet*. He finds two objects described by that term: the Torah itself, and the people Israel. Accordingly, Rashi understands the verse to be saying that heaven and earth were created for the sake of Torah and Israel. We locate meaning and purpose in the facts of existence and the cosmos by discovering layers of belonging and holiness in text and community. Coming together as the children of Israel, locating our story in the narrative of Torah, setting our actions in the context of *mitzvot* (commandments) and *gemillut hasadim* (good deeds)—this purposefulness is what gives meaning to our lives.

Read the Torah, and come to savor its truth. It is not intended as a shoddy science text or a sloppy history book. No, says Rashi and the weight of Jewish thinkers throughout the ages. The truth of Torah is of a higher sort—the kind that lends life a pervasive and elevating purpose that can carry us through our days in joy and can link the generations to one another and to God.

Why Walk with God?

In recording the ten generations separating Adam and Noah, the Torah provides brief encapsulations of their lives. By far the most intriguing on the list is Hanokh (in English, he is referred to as Enoch), the seventh generation of humanity. Here is the complete record of what the Torah reveals about him:

> When Jared had lived 162 years, he begot Hanokh. . . . When Hanokh had lived 65 years, he begot Methuselah. After the birth of Methuselah, Hanokh walked with God 300 years; and he begot sons and daughters. All the days of Hanokh came to 365 years. Hanokh walked with God; then he was no more, for God took him.

With the other people in the list of generations, we are simply told that they lived. Only Hanokh merits this superlative description of having "walked with God" during his lifetime. On the level of *p'shat*, it appears that Hanokh was a righteous man who lived his life in full accord with divine will and great intimacy with God. The phrase appears on only two other occasions, for Noah and for the ideal priest described by the prophet Malachi. High praise indeed!

The curious nature of his end also attracts our attention. The phrase "he was no more" replaces the more frequent expression "then he died." It suggests some sudden, unexpected, unexplained disappearance that was different from the deaths of the other figures. This unusual end is linked to two other oddities. First, Hanokh died very young, relatively speaking. His father lived for 800 years, and his son for 969 years; he only lived a third as long as they did. Second, the Torah specifies that "God took him." Biblical scholar Nahum Sarna explains this as a euphemism for death, and Rashi explains it as premature death. Yet one could also read this odd passage as suggesting that Hanokh didn't die at all, that like Elijah, he was simply transported to heaven.

In fact, several midrashim make that suggestion. Derekh Eretz Zuta observes that he was one of only nine tzaddikim (righteous people) who entered paradise without having died first. Another legend says that God took him to heaven to become the chief of the angels. God transformed him into the angel Metatron, altering his fleshly body into one of purest fire.

Whether he died a natural death or was carried to heaven, the greatest curiosity linked to Hanokh is that he walked with God *and* died an early death. How is that possible? Shouldn't his righteousness have been rewarded with longevity? Isn't his premature death a religious scandal?

The rabbis of the Talmud were acutely aware of this problem, and they resolved it by stating that Hanokh wasn't really righteous after all. They observe that the second, superfluous "he walked with God" is followed immediately by "he was no more," and they connect the two: "Hanokh was a hypocrite, acting sometimes as a tzaddik, sometimes as a *rasha* (wicked person). Therefore the Holy Blessing One said, 'While he is righteous, I will remove him.'" His early death, then, is really an act of divine mercy—dying in a state of righteousness allows him to enjoy a greater reward in the coming world.

This "solution" as to why a good man would die an early death has clear connotations of how these rabbis perceived the world and

God's justice. However much we may admire their faith and their confidence, most moderns cannot accept the notion that reality and the ideal are identical. We have a hard time reading a message from a just and loving God in an early death.

So what can this biblical paradox mean for us? What do we do with the idea that one can "walk with God" during his lifetime and still suffer disappointment, misfortune, illness, and death? In fact, rabbinic opinion itself suggests another way to read God's message in this story. The *Bekhor Shor* suggests that the second "he walked with God" was repeated specifically to ensure that we *not* read the brevity of Hanokh's life as a punishment for sin. Whatever the reason for Hanokh's early death, it is not a condemnation of the worth of his life.

Today, we still suffer from those who would abuse religion as a cudgel to denigrate other human beings and castigate their opponents. How many have suggested that AIDS, for example, is the payment for sin? Some prominent ministers even suggested that the L.A. earthquake was a punishment for what they judged to be Hollywood's lifestyle.

The example of Hanokh repudiates such smug judgments. The righteous suffer and die just as the rest of us do. Whether one is rich or poor, whether one survives to a ripe old age or not is not necessarily a measure of divine favor or wrath. Hanokh reminds us that one can be a tzaddik and still suffer, that bad things do happen to good people.

God is to be found, not in the punishment, not in the suffering, not in self-righteous condemnation, but in those who reach out to help, to mitigate each other's pain, to comfort each other's sorrow, and to enhance each other's joy.

Walking with God is not an investment for a better tomorrow; it is the expression of a righteous today. It is no mere tool for amassing reward; walking with God is the way to infuse whatever time we do have with profundity and purpose.

Anyone care for a stroll?

The World Created for You

It is certainly easy enough to become disheartened by humanity and the mess we have made of God's creation. Everywhere we choose to look, signs of human cruelty, abuse, and decay abound. Our cities, once the alabaster pride of American modernity, now suggest primarily danger, violence, and poverty. Our suburbs, once models for how middle-class communities could provide the amenities of bounteous living while still offering access to the cultural riches of our age, are simply shopping malls and planned developments for people fleeing the cities and each other. And rural America, for years the breadbasket of the world, is now often a dead end for those unable to move away.

In the beginning of our nation's history, America was seen as a great experiment, or in John F. Kennedy's words, as the "last, greatest hope of mankind." What happened to that hope? Would Washington, Adams, and Jefferson have invested their lives, their minds, and their hearts in establishing the Republic if they had known where we would wind up more than two hundred years later?

Even more to the point, if God had known how humanity's history would progress, would the Holy One have created us?

That question is addressed explicitly in the rabbinic commentaries to today's parashah. After the expulsion from the Garden of Eden, the generations of humanity come and go, and it soon becomes clear that "the wickedness of humanity was great in the earth and every impulse and thought was evil all the time." God's response to the disappointing reality that people turned into was not surprising: "God regretted having made people on the earth, and it grieved God's heart."

Rashi raises the issue in the context of a religious debate between Rabbi Joshua ben Korhah and a heretic. The heretic establishes that Rabbi Joshua does believe that God can see into the future. In that case, argues the heretic, if God knew in advance that humanity would turn out to be so rotten, why did God later "regret" having created us?

In typical Jewish fashion, Rabbi Joshua answers his challenge with a rhetorical question: "Did you ever have a child?"

The heretic answered, "Yes."

"What did you do when the infant was born?"

The heretic responded, "I rejoiced and made others rejoice with me."

"Didn't you know at the time," Rabbi Korhah asked, "that the fate of that child was to die one day?"

"Yes," said the heretic, "but I felt that at the time of joy, there should be joy, and mourning at the time of mourning."

At that point, Rabbi Korhah presented his defense, "So are the works of the Holy Blessing One. Even though God knew that humanity's destiny was to sin and be destroyed, God did not refrain from creating them for the sake of the tzaddikim who are destined to arise from those first generations."

Rabbi Joshua's response imposes a sacred obligation on each one of us. If God created the world only for the sake of future tzaddikim, then we have the power to vindicate God's decision or to render it untenable. If we choose to act like tzaddikim—by performing deeds of loving-kindness, by caring for each other and for creation, by living lives of mitzvot, and by delighting in the Torah—we can, retroactively, justify God's creation. Each act of *tzedek* (righteousness) proves God right.

And by the same token, each time an opportunity to do a mitzvah slips through our grasp, each time we could perform a compassionate deed or help another human being but refrain, we belie God's justification for making the world.

Rabbi Joshua's argument, you see, is that God needs tzaddikim to make creation worthwhile. The time is now, and who better to be that tzaddik than you?

Noah/Noah

Genesis 6:9–11:32

God turns to the one righteous person on earth, Noah, and instructs him to build an ark of gopher wood to save his family and representatives of every species of every land-dwelling animal. God also tells Noah to store enough vegetables to feed the ark's passengers. Foretelling the institution of temple sacrifice and kashrut (dietary laws), Noah takes seven of each tahor (ritually permissible) species and only two each from the tamei (ritually impermissible). He gathers this menagerie into the ark. Then it rains for forty days and forty nights, submerging even the highest mountains. The waters cover the earth for 150 days and then begin to recede as the ark settles on the summit of Mount Ararat. For three more months, the waters continue to diminish; at the end of forty days, Noah sends out first a raven, then a dove, each of which is unable to find enough dry land to rest. After another seven days, Noah sends out the dove again. This time, it returns clutching an olive branch. After yet another seven days, the dove flies out and never returns. God instructs Noah and his family to replenish life on land. As his first act after the flood, Noah builds an altar and sacrifices every kind of tahor animal. God is pleased with the offering, pledging, "Never again will I doom the earth because of humanity, since the devisings of the human mind are evil from their youth." As a sign of this covenantal promise, God sets the rainbow in the sky. In recognition of human nature, God makes animals fear humans and permits eating meat, provided that the blood is separated from the flesh (as is still performed during kosher meat preparation). Noah's three sons, Ham, Shem, and Japhet, emerge with him from the ark. Noah becomes a vintner and gets drunk. Ham sees his father's nakedness, which his brothers cover without looking. As a result of this incident, Ham (Canaan) is cursed; Shem, ancestor of the Semites, is blessed; and Japhet prospers.

After tracing the record of the descendants of Noah through his three sons, the Torah recounts how a homogeneous humanity attempts to build a tower to make a name for itself. God responds to this arrogant overreaching by dividing and multiplying the language of humans and by scattering them over the face of the whole earth. The parashah ends by tracing Shem's descendants through Terah to Abram and Sarai.

Floods and Children

Precisely what sin was responsible for the Flood? Different authorities have proposed a variety of possible explanations, but the one that I would like to explore is that of *Sefer Ha-Yashar*, a pseudepigraphic work of mythic history from Creation through the Exodus, dated to the eleventh or twelfth century. The *Sefer Ha-Yashar* suggests that the reason for the Flood was the universal failure to value children.

Even Noah refrained from having children until he was five hundred years old. He rationalized his choice by saying, "Why should I bring children into a world that will likely be destroyed?"

Think of the striking parallels between Noah's generation and our own: a lack of role models, of righteous men and women for young people to aspire to imitate. Violence was rampant and random. Sexual depravity—pleasure taken through force or through anonymity—appeared normal. And in that horrible world, there were sensitive souls like Noah who felt it would be an act of cruelty to bring an innocent baby into such a world.

There is certainly some merit to his feelings. By no means should everyone have children, nor is life empty and valueless for those who do not bear children. Yet the bias in favor of having children is so firmly rooted in the Torah and the biblical tradition that participating in child rearing in some way virtually defines happiness. Certainly everyone should encourage and support the raising of children, even if they are not one's own offspring. As a society, we ought to facilitate willing adults raising children to be healthy and compassionate adults.

Like the generation of Noah, ours seems not to value children very highly. A serious commitment to children requires a serious commitment to providing parents with the knowledge and skills they need and to equipping schools, synagogues, and other public institutions with the resources necessary to be truly helpful to the families themselves.

Is that the kind of society America has become? Rather than truly providing for our young people, we have millions of homeless children on the streets (many of them runaways). We make decent child care unaffordable, thus making it difficult for parents to afford the children they are supposed to rear. We don't provide sufficient family leave time for illness nor adequate health security for kids (or their parents). We throw ideological hoops in the paths of our public schools, doing everything in our power to prevent our teachers from educating their students. And we bombard our children—through television, music, and movies—with a glorification of ignorance, addiction, and violence; precisely those values least capable of nurturing their better selves or providing a better future.

In contrast to Noah's age, in which children were so insufficiently cherished, Jewish tradition offers another model as well: that of the generation who deserved to leave Egyptian slavery. There, too, violence and poverty abounded. Yet the midrash tells us that the women of Israel refused to abandon the bearing and raising of children, regardless of any other factor. For them, children came first. And because of their stalwart advocacy for their offspring, we merited freedom from slavery, we were given a promised land—a gift that counts on children and forthcoming generations. Otherwise, it's not worth very much, is it?

A Comfort to Ourselves, a Comfort to the World

We all know people who blame their every misfortune on their parents. Long after their teen years are over, well into their thirties, forties, and beyond, they continue to lay their own problems and personal shortcomings at their parents' doorstep.

There may well be justification for their disappointment. None of us are perfect, and raising a child is, after all, one of the few jobs for which there is no lengthy training, no job application, no interview process, and no continuing education requirements along the way. Becoming a gardener requires more preparation than parenting.

Given our own imperfections, it is only natural that we pass them along (with a few extras) to our children. So blaming our parents for our own problems has its roots in the reality that parents probably do stack the deck against their children in some crucial ways.

While our parents may have, indeed, passed on their imperfections, most parents also try to do their best, to provide a reasonably stable environment in which their children can mature. While they may not be ideal nurturers, most of the time they are good enough parents.

In many cases, then, blaming parents is simply a way to dodge the responsibility of being an adult. No longer is there some all knowing person to clean up after our mess, to straighten out a problem we have created, or to soothe away our fears in the dark of a lonely night. In a harsh world of competition and disappointment, we are very much on our own. Small wonder that we often continue to condemn the previous generation, since the act of accusing implies that we can still look to them to set things right.

Rabbinic tradition offers an interesting alternative to this flight from responsibility. The rabbis of *B'raisheet Rabbah*, the ancient midrash on the book of Genesis, noticed a strange sentence in this Torah portion, "This is the line of Noah: Noah . . . Shem, Ham, and Japheth." Why, they wonder, in a verse that claims to list Noah's sons, does the Torah begin by repeating Noah's own name first?

The midrash asks and then answers its own question: "Surely Scripture should have written, 'These are the offspring of Noah: Shem, etc.?' It teaches, however, that he was a comfort to himself and a comfort to the world, a comfort to his parents and a comfort to his children." In other words, Noah took responsibility for parenting himself.

No longer willing to cower in the shadow of his parents' supposed power or their failings, Noah knew that being an adult meant directing his own life, for better or for worse. Guided by the voice of God and his own sacred traditions, Noah could not avoid making his own decisions, living his own life. The midrash reminds us that Noah became his own third (and final) parent.

That same challenge faces all of us. It wasn't so long ago that we ourselves were children. The distance we have traveled professionally, geographically, and emotionally may seem so large as to be unreal. Simultaneously, we may also feel that childhood was simply yesterday.

No longer able to count on our parents to generate the right answers, no longer able to solve our problems by shifting responsibility to our forebears, we must turn to ourselves, consult our hearts, and seek guidance from ourselves. Just as Noah was "a comfort to himself" we too must learn to provide our own balance, wisdom, and direction.

None of us need do our self-parenting alone. Psalm 27 wisely observes, "Though my father and my mother leave me, the Lord will care for me." No Jew is ever alone. In the company of other Jews at prayer, at study, or while performing a mitzvah, we stand in the presence of God. Holiness bursts into our lives through the deeds and words of our sacred tradition—guidance and companionship are but a mitzvah away.

"A comfort to ourselves and a comfort to the world." Like Noah, we too can learn to hear God's word in a world gone mad and to embody that calming wisdom in the path of our own lives, in the security of our own ark.

Tender Mercies Over All

After the floodwaters storm, Noah, his family, and his herds float across the undifferentiated surface of the water for weeks, until, says the Torah, "God remembered Noah and every living thing, and all the beasts that were with him in the ark. And God made a wind to pass over the earth and the waters subsided."

Rabbinic Judaism wasn't troubled by the philosophical issues raised by the claim that God remembered (as though God had previously forgotten). The sages of the Talmud and Midrash weren't even bothered by the claim that God remembered Noah. After all, it was commonplace to assert that God heard the prayers of the righteous. Indeed, Rashi summarizes both sides of this assertion when he explains that God remembering implies that God transformed his *middat ha-din* (virtue of judgment) into the *middat ha-rachamim* (virtue of mercy) through the prayer of the righteous. "And the wickedness of the wicked turns the virtue of mercy into the virtue of judgment."

What really drew the attention of the ancient rabbis was the Torah's insistence that God remembered not only Noah, but also every living thing. God remembers cows?!

In exploring this daring assertion, the ancient midrash *B'raisheet Rabbah* quotes the book of Psalms: "The Lord is good to all, and God's tender mercies are over all" (Ps. 145:9). Yes, indeed, say the ancient rabbis, there is biblical precedent to support that God does care for all living things, not just for humans. But then the rabbis take an interesting and paradigmatically Jewish twist: "Rabbi Joshua said in the name of Rabbi Levi: The Lord is good to all, and God inspires mankind with his compassion." In other words, what matters most is not God's objective traits, not God's essence, but how God's essence takes form in human behavior. God's goodness channels through human hands. We perceive a religious obligation to model God's virtues in the world. Human beings are the ones who must make manifest God's compassion. When we allow ourselves to be inspired and directed by God's mercy, then—and only then—is it true that God's mercies are over all.

What is it, then, that God "remembered"? According to the midrash, God didn't remember Noah (the person) or even the living things (the animals). God remembered ethical action: "What did God remember in Noah's favor? That he provided for the animals the whole 12 months in the Ark. . . . 'God remembered Noah' and the spirit of justice approved it."

One of the distortions of human mortality is that our eyes see things but do not see deeds. God's "eyes," as it were, don't suffer from our blindness. Instead, God's vision focuses not on status, but on doing—acts of care, acts of kindness, acts of justice—these are the data that fill divine vision and stimulate divine memory.

If you want to be recalled to God's memory, then lift up your hands and do. Reach out to heal the sick, to feed the hungry, to clothe the homeless. By caring for each other, for humanity, and for all of God's creatures, we make ourselves worthy to come to God's attention, and we give substance and form to the claim that God is, after all, merciful.

Lekh Lekha/Take Yourself, Go Forth
Genesis 12:1–17:27

God commands Abram, "Go forth from your native land and from your father's house to the land that I will show you." Promised that he will become a great nation, Abram leaves Haran with his wife, Sarai, his nephew, Lot, and their entourage, and they journey to the city of Shechem in Canaan. God promises this land to Abram's descendants, and Abram builds an altar to God at Beth El. A famine forces Abram and Sarai down to Egypt, where Pharaoh lusts after Sarai, thinking she is Abram's sister. God prevents Pharaoh from touching her. Instead, Pharaoh gives Abram great wealth and expels the group to Canaan.

There the servants of Lot and Abram quarrel; the two agree to separate, with Lot choosing the cities of Sodom and Gomorrah in the well-watered plains of Jordan. God reiterates the promise that the land will belong to Abram's heirs, who will number as the dust of the earth. Four kings battle five kings and, in the process, capture Lot. When Abram hears of this, he musters 318 fighters, routing them near Damascus and rescuing Lot and the residents and wealth of Sodom. In gratitude, King Melchizedek of Salem—later Jerusalem—blesses Abram in the name of God Most High.

God tells Hagar that her son, Ishmael, will become a great nation, and that she must, in the meantime, return to Abram and Sarai. God changes Abram's name to Abraham ("father of a multitude") and Sarai's name to Sarah ("princess"), ordaining the mitzvah of brit milah, *the ritual circumcision binding on all Jewish males throughout the generations. God promises that Sarah will bear a son—despite being ninety years old—and that the boy will be called Isaac. Abraham circumcises himself and all his followers. Responding to Abraham's complaint that he is still childless, God tells him to look toward heaven and count the stars: "So shall be your offspring." God tells Abraham to sacri-*

fice a heifer, a goat, a ram, a turtledove, and a bird. Abraham sleeps between the split carcasses, and God says that his descendants will be enslaved for four hundred years but that God will liberate them with great wealth and Abraham will die in peace. Sarah takes matters into her own hands and has Abraham sleep with her servant, the Egyptian handmaid Hagar. Hagar conceives and thereafter disdains her barren mistress. In response, Sarah treats her harshly; Hagar runs away. An angel tells her to return.

For the Common Good

In a society that values rugged individuals and go-it-alone types above all others, it is often hard to fathom the biblical-rabbinic commitment to the community and the people as a whole. We moderns are so used to elevating our own concerns over society's, to pursuing our private happiness, even at the expense of others and our planet, that we look with horror on any assertions of the priority of the communal.

It's not hard to see why we cherish the individual so highly. American democracy is founded on the ideal of each individual retaining a wide range of freedoms through which to blossom in a unique way, untrammeled by governmental edict or ideological tyranny. Thinking for ourselves, acting on our own—the vitality of our country and its cultures attest to the rich reward that individual liberty can bestow.

Yet we also pay a cost for this "me first" mentality. Our pursuit of private gain has produced a deep rift between those who have and those who don't, creating great animosity from those whose ancestors immigrated to America toward those bold souls who have the courage and vision to come here now. We no longer cultivate civic-mindedness and volunteerism, since time spent on others is deemed time wasted. Our planet is battered by our selfishness, our skies and our waters filthy and assaulted by our greed.

Today's parashah addresses putting the self first. God offers a reward to Abram, our first patriarch, because of his devotion to God and mitzvot. And Abram's response is "Lord God, what can You give me, seeing that I shall die childless?" In response to Abram's cry that he is without child, God arranges for him to sire a child through his wife's handmaid, Hagar.

Almost immediately, we are told, trouble breaks out in Abram's household. Sarai, his wife, is lowered in Hagar's esteem. In her bitterness and humiliation, Sarai turns on her husband: "The wrong done me is your fault! I myself put my maid in your bosom; now that she sees that she is pregnant, I am lowered in her esteem."

Careful readers of Torah will have trouble understanding Sarai's response. How is it Abram's fault that Hagar became pregnant, when it was Sarai who proposed that he should consort with her maid in the first place? All Abram did was to go along with his wife's suggestion for a way to bear a child. So how is he to blame?

The ancient rabbis of *Midrash B'raisheet Rabbah*, scrupulous and sensitive readers of Torah, explain this verse through the words of Rabbi Judah: "You wrong me with words, since you heard me be insulted and you were silent." Abram should have spoken out on his wife's behalf. His silence is his responsibility and his culpability.

The rabbis compare this case to two imprisoned men. The king passes their cell, and one of them cries out, "Spare me!" upon which the king orders that man released from incarceration. As he leaves, the other prisoner shouts to him, "I have a grievance against you, for had you just said, 'Spare *us*,' I would be released too. But since you didn't, he released you but not me." In precisely the same way, when God made a generous offer to Abram, the patriarch of our people could have said, "What can You give to *us*, seeing that *we* shall die childless?" Then God might have acted to assist Sarai along with Abram. Instead, great spiritual force that he was, Abram's focus on his own misery—exclusive of his wife's sorrow—resulted in a solution of only his childlessness. And getting what he thought he wanted, as opposed to getting what his family needed, turned out to be a disaster for everyone.

Abram, we are told, was a righteous man, noted for his goodness, compassion, and generosity. Yet even he slipped into the solipsism of thinking only of himself. He and his community paid a terrible price for that self-centeredness. How much the more so must we, lacking Abram's moral greatness, accustomed to selfishness and autonomy, wonder what legacy our training in the pursuit of our own happiness will leave for those we love.

Sarai's cry accuses us all: "My lack is yours!" In defining our happiness too narrowly, in seeing our own interests in too small a circle, we confine ourselves within walls too constraining for comfort or security. Unless we learn to see "us" in "me" and "them," there won't be much happiness for anyone at all. *Al tifrosh min ha-tzibbur*, don't separate yourself from the community. Ultimately, it's all we have.

Timing Isn't Everything

One of the most passionate divides separating today's Jews is the question of the authorship of Torah. According to some groups, God dictated each and every word of the Torah through Moses. Yet others see the Torah as inspired by God's vision and presence, but with a significant contribution by the people through whom the Torah percolated. Still others see it as purely a human work—glorious and deep, but human through and through.

This parashah includes one of the passages that serves as a magnet for this debate. The narrative picks up with the great move of Abraham and his retinue from his home to the Land of Israel. Following God's wondrous summons, Abraham picks up and passes through the land as far as the site of Shechem, at the terebinth of Moreh. "The Canaanites were then in the land" (Gen. 12:6).

What does the Torah imply when it notes that *"ha-K'naani az ba-Aretz"* ("the Canaanites were then in the land")? It certainly seems to mean that they were in the land *then* (when the tale took place) but not *now* (when the book was being written). The challenge to those who hold that Moses literally wrote each and every word of the Bible is that there were Canaanites in the land during his entire lifetime. So what does the word *then* reveal?

According to Rashi, the word comes to teach us that the Canaanites were in the process of conquering the land from the sons of Shem, who had been given the land lawfully. Because the Canaanites took the land from its rightful owners, it was only proper that descendents of Shem should come and reclaim it from the Canaanites. Thus, for Rashi, the *az* is an assertion of the propriety of the Israelite conquest in the time of Joshua.

The Radak, Rabbi David Kimhi (twelfth-century France), acknowledges Rashi's interpretation, but he suggests a very different take. He says that the surprising word is to teach us "how God deals with those whom God loves." In other words, the Canaanites were in the land while Abraham was, and they would have destroyed him if not for the miraculous protection extended to him by God. As Radak notes, the *az* signifies that "this was proof that God was with him."

The most suggestive comment is offered by that towering medieval sage Rabbi Abraham Ibn Ezra (eleventh-century Spain and Italy), who agrees with Rashi: "It is possible that the Canaanites seized the land of Canaan from some other tribe at that time" (i.e., then, but not prior to this). Then he drops his bombshell: "Should this interpretation be incorrect, then this text has a great secret. Let the one who understands it remain silent."

What secret would be so great that those who understood its meaning were duty-bound to maintain silence? Could it be that Ibn Ezra understood that Moses could not have written that verse, so that the dogma of attributing the specific words of the entire Torah to Moses could not possibly be true? That insight would certainly shake the foundations of faith, and one can easily imagine a medieval sage counseling silence in its wake. Another medieval scholar, Joseph Bonfils, commenting on Ibn Ezra's words, breaks the silence: "Joshua or another of the other prophets wrote it."

But Bonfils's shocking revelation simultaneously opens the door to a reconciliation between those whose faith in Torah is dependent on its Mosaic authorship and those whose love of truth prevents them from embracing that claim. He goes on to write, "Since we are to have trust in the words of tradition and the prophets, what should I care whether it was Moses or another prophet who wrote it, since the words of all of them are true and inspired?"

What difference indeed? The wisdom intrinsic to the Torah is the best proof of its divinity. While those who do accept Moses as (human) author may argue with those who accept the documentary hypothesis, with its claim of generations of Israelite schools and sages as the (human) authors, both groups affirm that there has never been a book with the wisdom, depth, insight, and power of the Torah. Capable of inspiring humanity in every corner of the earth, able to mobilize national liberation movements and inspire slaves to reach for freedom, the Torah has been humanity's link to God from the moment ancient Israel presented it to mankind.

Ultimately, Bonfils (and Ibn Ezra) offer us a way to link arms across our respective understandings of who wrote the Bible. The authenticity of the Torah's contents and the revolutionary assertions of human dignity, of the sanctity of the Sabbath, of a God who liberates slaves, all join to reveal the sweep of God just under the surface.

Whether God handed that book to us through a single man on a single mountain on a single day, or whether God handed that book to us through schools of sages and prophets, the Torah that we have in our hands is none other than the word of God. On that we can agree and celebrate.

Moral Misers—Let It Shine!

Notice how it's easier to criticize from a distance than it is to make a positive difference? Sitting in a comfortable chair in the safety of our homes, we peruse the newspapers and comment on the "obvious" solution to a problem, even though that solution seems to have escaped the attention of everyone else in the world.

Almost everyone succumbs to the temptation to solve the world's troubles over coffee or while watching the nightly news. But notice how few are the numbers of people who volunteer at the local hospital, for the AIDS walk, or at a nearby synagogue.

In that regard, Abraham was not so different from the rest of us. In *Parashat Lekh Lekha*, we pick up his life in the middle, so to speak. Abram is a comfortably well-off gentleman. He is married and seems to be at the center of a thriving clan.

Probably he sounded off at festival gatherings about what was wrong with Ur and how it should be fixed but minded his own business and spent his precious leisure time privately. In *Midrash B'raisheet Rabbah*, Rabbi Berekiah compares him to "a vial of myrrh closed with a tight-fitting lid and lying in a corner, so that its fragrance was not disseminated."

It isn't hard to guess what Rabbi Berekiah thinks of a bottle of perfume that is so tightly sealed that no one can smell it. And it isn't hard to extrapolate his opinion of people who are well-off, well educated, and full of opinions but somehow never seem to find the time to try out their opinions in a practical way. Good advice on how to live, if sealed into a cozy corner, doesn't do the world any good.

In the midst of Abram's comfort and self-absorption, God shattered Abram's complacency forever. With one forceful call, God nudged him to abandon his posturing and lectures, and to apply his wisdom to helping his fellow human beings: "Go forth from your native land, and from your father's house, to the land that I will show you."

Without even knowing where his involvement would lead, Abraham shifted his focus from editorializing to acting—working on behalf of morality, God, and other people. Rabbi Berekiah shrewdly notes that the sealed perfume, "once it was taken up, disseminated its fragrance. Similarly, the Holy Blessed One said to Abraham, 'Travel from place to place and your name will become great in the world.'"

Perfume gains value by sharing its rich fragrance with all who can smell it. A wise education, moral balance, or physical strength are worthwhile to the extent that they inspire action on behalf of a better world. When we use the innate gifts that God has given us, when we harness the education and guidance that our parents, teachers, and friends have provided, then we do them and ourselves credit. Rather than hoarding our viewpoints and our energy, we become rich to the extent that we share them with others.

That same wisdom shines in the aphorism of Rabbi Tarfon, when he observes that "the day is short, the task is great, the workers indolent, the reward bountiful, and the Master insistent." We are the indolent workers. Our onerous and glorious task, as always, is repairing the world to wholeness, to health, and to peace. As have past generations, we shy away from our sacred calling, preferring instead to simply bottle up our fragrance, terrified to really encounter each other and ourselves.

Yet there is nothing so glorious, nothing so rewarding, and nothing so needed as reaching out to a needy stranger. In caring for an anonymous creature in the image of God, we uncover a new reflection of God's precious love, and we illumine our own lives by the light of that beauty.

Va-Yera/He Saw

Genesis 18:1–22:24

As Abraham sits in the opening of his tent, he sees three men coming toward him. He offers them hospitality, they accept, and as the food is prepared, they inquire after Sarah. One of the guests tells Abraham that when he returns a year later, Abraham will have a son. Overhearing this, Sarah laughs. "Is anything too wondrous for God?" God—who is apparently one of the guests—responds. The focus of the scene abruptly changes, as God tells Abraham that he intends to destroy Sodom and Gomorrah. Rather than resign himself to God's announcement, Abraham argues against such collective punishment. God listens and agrees not to destroy the cities if there are ten righteous people there. Two angels go to Sodom to warn Lot of the impending catastrophe; he invites them to stay as the townspeople surround his house and demand that he surrender the guests to them for abuse and humiliation. Pleading with them not to violate his hospitality, Lot offers his daughters to the mob instead. But the angels pull Lot back inside, blinding the townspeople and protecting the girls. Lot and his family flee as the cities are annihilated—Lot's wife turns back and by doing so becomes a pillar of salt. The plains are destroyed. Convinced that they are the only humans to survive the destruction of the planet, Lot's daughters sleep with their intoxicated father to perpetuate the human race. One conceives Moab—ancestor of the Moabites (and later of Ruth)—and the other, Ben Ammi, ancestor of the Ammonites.

Once again, Abraham tries to pass his wife off as his sister, this time to King Abimelech of Gerar. Again God protects her, and Abraham and the king part amicably. As promised, Sarah conceives and bears Isaac. After an ambiguous incident, she insists that Abraham expel Hagar and Ishmael, a demand that God instructs Abraham to meet. Hagar and her son move to the wilderness of Paran. Abraham and Abimelech sign a friendship pact.

God tests Abraham, telling him to sacrifice his son, "Isaac, whom you love." The two proceed in silence for three days until they arrive at Mount Moriah. At the top of the mountain, Abraham builds an altar, straps his son to it, and lifts the knife to slay him. "Abraham, Abraham," calls an angel, interrupting him. "Hineni (here I am)," responds the patriarch. The angel tells him not to harm the boy. Looking up, Abraham sees a ram caught in a nearby bush and slaughters the animal in Isaac's stead. In response to Abraham's obedience to a commandment, God again promises to multiply Abraham's descendants and to give them Eretz Yisrael (the Land of Israel). "All the nations of the earth shall bless themselves by your descendants, because you have obeyed My commands," God tells him.

Through Circumcision We Still See God

One of the difficulties in perpetuating Jewish practices is their striking dissimilarity from any American custom. That divergence shouldn't be surprising. After all, Jewish traditions are rooted in ages past, in millennia long gone. What might have seemed natural and common thousands of years ago now seems forced, strange, and difficult.

Few customs are more difficult for some Jews to understand than that of brit milah, or ritual circumcision on the eighth day after birth. We have no problem with surgery for the sake of health or even for the sake of appearance and vanity. But the idea of surgery as a form of ritual is often labeled barbaric. Few parents relish the idea of submitting a newborn boy to the knife of a mohel—even when she is a physician—if they don't have to. And few participants enjoy the suffering of a baby during the circumcision itself.

Here, more than in many other deeds, traditional Judaism and American sensibilities part ways. For Judaism, brit milah is the sine qua non, the essential beginning, for any male entering the covenant between God and the Jewish people. Yet for a loud minority of Americans, circumcision reflects only superstitious violence against a defenseless child. Between these extremes, there is no room for compromise.

All of which makes today's parashah so noteworthy. Immediately after commanding Abraham to circumcise himself and his son, the Torah reports, "the Lord appeared to him by the terebinths of Mamre." For the ancient rabbis, the proximity of these verses is deliberate: God appeared to Abraham because he was willing to undergo brit milah. For support, they quote from the book of Job: "Then through my flesh shall I see God." *Midrash B'raisheet Rabbah* explains, "Had I [Abraham] not done so, why should God become revealed to me?"

Even in antiquity, the courage to perform brit milah evoked praise and wonder. Thus Rabbi Isaac exclaimed, on God's behalf, "If I reveal Myself to bless one who builds an altar in My name, how much the more to Abraham who circumcised himself for My sake!"

What a remarkable claim. That it is precisely in mutilating our bodies and those of our male children that we will come to see God.

Yet the claim is not as outlandish as it appears. It takes tremendous dedication and determination to go through with this ancient and powerful ritual. It takes courage and devotion to see it as a mitzvah rather than an ordeal. And its very antiquity and bloodiness give it a depth and a profundity that few other practices can ever match.

The whole point of a brit milah is to shake people up. That queasy feeling is the sense of standing in the presence of something awesome, frightening, and compelling—in fact, of standing in the presence of God. During brit milah, we bend our will and our preferences to that of our ancient faith and the ways of those who have come before us.

For almost four thousand years, every boy or man who entered the covenant between God and the Jews did so through brit milah. And each generation had to choose anew to (literally) spill blood for the sake of that relationship.

Brit milah reminds us that we are but flesh and blood. It highlights our mortality by showing the frailty of the successors and the vacillation of the parents. It imposes a symbolic restraint on our drive for unlimited sex, our pledge to harness our sexuality to building a covenant community that can weather the storms of time and of desire.

Yet brit milah also highlights what is eternal about Jews: the link between the generations that spans the ages. Just as those before us underwent this mysterious and imposing rite, so too do we. Just as parents and children wish for each other a life free from pain, so we also remind ourselves that some things are worth suffering for—first and foremost our sacred bond with God and our people.

This uncomfortable rite is indispensable; it reminds us of our sacred mission on God's behalf. Awe, fear, majesty, piety, sorrow, and joy—the range of feelings that brit milah engenders are the sure signs that the midrash was right. Brit milah brings us face-to-face with God.

May we never shy away from that continuing encounter.

The Heart of a Mother, the Heart of a Father

I am puzzled by the same question each time I read the story of the destruction of Sodom and Gomorrah: Why did Lot delay leaving the city, why did Lot's wife look back, and why did she turn into a pillar of salt?

Almost every traditional and modern commentary offers the same explanation for these events: Lot was a relatively pious man (he is called a tzaddik once), as shown by his insistence on hosting the two mysterious guests. He is favorably contrasted with his two sons-in-law, who refuse to heed his warning and choose to stay in Sodom. And his fidelity is also contrasted with the behavior of his wife, who disobeys the angels' explicit orders. While taking Lot and his family from the condemned city, the angels issue the order, "Do not look behind you, nor stop anywhere in the plain; flee to the hills, lest you be swept away!" Lot, obedient servant that he is, marches resolutely forward. Lot's wife, an anonymous rebel, looks back and suffers the consequences.

The rabbis of *Midrash B'raisheet Rabbah* extend the contrast between the two spouses even further. They claim that while Lot was pleading with the two men to become his guests so he could fulfill the mitzvah of *hakh'nasat orehim* (welcoming guests), his wife tried to frustrate his generosity. But she had to rely on a ploy, so she went to all her neighbors asking to borrow some salt because there were some guests in her house. She appeared to be on a mission of generosity, but in reality she was alerting her neighbors with the hope that they would intervene. In the words of Rabbi Isaac, she was turned into a pillar of salt "because she sinned through salt."

We know virtually nothing about Lot's wife—we don't know her name, her family, her personality. All we have is this story of her looking back, her transformation into salt, and the rabbinic justification of that punishment through a midrash recounting her act of treason and inhospitability. Yet Christian and Muslim tradition both seem to accept that rabbinic reading, viewing this nameless woman as a foil for her husband's goodness and generosity, a woman who paid the just penalty for rebellion against the will of God.

Actually, we know one other fact about Lot's wife: she was the mother of four daughters. Two were married, and their husbands refused to take Lot's warning seriously. In addition to those two married daughters were two others, the "two remaining daughters." When the angels came to take Lot and his family out of the condemned city, they actually left two of Lot's daughters behind with their husbands.

That tragic family rupture allows us to account for the story in a way that diverges from the traditional account. After Lot tried to convince his sons-in-law that he wasn't joking, after he realized that they would compel his married daughters to remain in Sodom, he must have been despondent. It isn't hard to imagine that Lot's wife would have shared his horror. The next morning, when the fatal rain of sulfurous fire and brimstone was about to engulf the city, the Torah recounts, "The angels urged Lot on, saying, 'Up, take your wife and your two remaining daughters, lest you be swept away because of the iniquity of the city.' Still, he delayed."

The only traditional explanation for his delay, in *Midrash B'raisheet Rabbah*, is that "he kept on delaying, exclaiming, 'What a loss of gold and silver and precious stones!'" I prefer a different motivation. Lot was slow in leaving because he could not make his peace with leaving his married daughters behind. The angels had to physically take him from Sodom; he couldn't abandon his own children voluntarily.

Once he had left the city and the fire and sulfur began to pour down, he must have decided that the survival of his remaining two daughters was primary, so he purposely marched them forward toward safety.

But the mother's heart could not let go. Mrs. Lot couldn't choose between her children, couldn't bear that two of her daughters were trapped in the flames. Her head knew it had to fight to live for her surviving children, but her mother's heart tugged her toward Sodom, toward the children left behind.

"Just one more look, maybe it's not too late to help them," she might have reasoned. And so, imperiling her own life like countless mothers have done for their children throughout the ages, she stopped and looked back, desperately trying to see her children one last time. And that moment of turning cost her her life—the advancing sulfur, the streaming lava, immediately engulfed her.

Which parent was right: the father who loved his daughters so much that he delayed leaving and then loved his surviving daughters so much that all he thought about was their survival? Or the mother whose love could not be severed in two, whose connection to her married daughters cost her her life?

On that point, the Torah is silent. Perhaps we should be too.

Who Would Dare?

It's one of the most poignant moments in the Torah's earliest narratives: angels visit Lot to announce the impending destruction of Sodom, but before they even have a chance to inform their host of the heavenly intention, the local townsmen, intent on dragging out Lot's guests and causing them severe bodily harm, besiege his home.

In desperation, Lot pleads with his fellow townsmen to refrain from harming his guests. He reminds them what a serious violation of morality such an assault would be, and he tries to offer them a desperate distraction, all with an eye to getting them to leave his visitors in peace.

What is most striking, and most revealing, is the nature of the Sodomites' response. They reject Lot's plea, and in doing so, they declare, "This one came here as a sojourner, and already he acts the ruler!" Not only do the local residents reject Lot's commitment to *hakhnasat orehim*, but they also reject his claim to be part of their community. After all, he isn't a real citizen; he is merely an alien, a sojourner. As such, his attempt to give them any advice whatsoever amounts to sheer effrontery. How dare this stranger tell them what to do?

There are so many levels to unpack in this troubling moment. Rashi understands their exclamation as a rejection of outsiders, a xenophobic response to difference: "You are alien, alone, and among us. You came to sojourn and now you become the one to rule us!?!" As Rashi portrays the scene, the Sodomites will only listen to their own, and they see any attempt by Lot to share his opinion as an unpardonable intrusion into their local affairs. Stay invisible or get out—that's the only way they tolerate outsiders.

Midrash B'raisheet Rabbah sees the locals' words not as questioning Lot's right to participate, but as rejecting his right to change their local custom in any way: "You wish to destroy the judgments of your predecessors." In other words, the real Sodomites, those who were born there, uphold the local custom of torturing guests. No outsider, however prosperous, however long he's lived in town, has the right to try to modify their social norms.

Finally, Ovadiah ben Jacob Sforno takes the words of the Sodomites as an expression of shock—"Would anyone dare do such a thing?" Would someone from the outside risk making himself visible as an outsider? Would he not only make his identity visible but also speak out against injustice, even when hallowed by custom?

Apparently Lot would. In refusing to be invisible as the price of acceptance, he crossed a line that enraged the local men. Yet he went even further than publicly affirming his identity as a Hebrew, as one with a distinct identity from that of Sodom. He also affirmed that part of his identity is a calling to make the world a better place, to bring an element of welcome, of haven, to those who wander without a home of their own. What really made Lot's action intolerable was its implication that those in need of shelter have a claim on all of us; that every human being is a sojourner on this earth, and we are all in need of each other's care and protection.

Who would dare do such a thing? Good question. Would you?

Hayei Sarah/The Life of Sarah
Genesis 23:1–25:18

Despite the name of this parashah, it opens with the death of Sarah in Hebron and Abraham's need to acquire a burial site for her remains. He purchases the Cave of Machpelah, marking the first time a Hebrew owns land in Eretz Yisrael. Recognizing the need to ensure the transmission of the covenant, he then arranges for her servant to return to his homeland and find a wife for his son, Isaac, from among his extended family. The servant discovers Rebekah, of Abraham's family line, at the well in the oasis, fulfilling exactly the signs for which the servant had prayed. Returning to her home with her, he meets the rest of the family; both her brother, Laban, and her father, Bethuel, recognize the handiwork of God in this fortuitous connection and ask Rebekah if she wants to return with the servant and marry Isaac. She does.

As the caravan with Rebekah approaches, Isaac is out walking—or meditating—in the fields. They see one another, and in a powerfully moving moment, the Torah tells us that as she alights, Isaac takes her into the tent that had been his mother's, loves her, and is comforted for his mother's death.

Abraham marries again, this time to Keturah, and though he provides for all his progeny, only his son Isaac inherits his blessing, remaining wealth, and land. By now 125 years old, Abraham dies and, like Sarah, is buried in the Cave of Machpelah.

A New Generation

It is a truism of human nature that we often denigrate our own abilities while extolling those of the generations before us. Our grandparents appear to us as giants, perhaps as a reflection of our size relative to them when we were infants, but also because we are able to look back on the challenges of their age from the perspective of the passage of time. Events in the past look bigger, more romantic, more heroic than the puny happenings of the present. It is no surprise, then, that ancestor worship is so common to the peoples of the earth and that even secular America treats the generation of its "founding fathers" with a reverence bordering on the religious.

That reverence is to be found in Judaism too. At the beginning of the *Amidah* (the standing, silent prayer that marks the liturgical pinnacle of every Jewish worship service), we speak to God as "God of our ancestors, God of Abraham, of Isaac, and of Jacob. . . . You remember the pious deeds of our ancestors and will send a redeemer to their children's children because of Your loving nature." The greatness of each preceding generation only increases with the passage of time, as each new age imputes ever-loftier levels of perfection to the ones who have come before.

The natural urge to see earlier generations as more wise, more good, or more sacred finds embodiment in the ruling of Mishnah Eduyot (a volume in the Mishnah dealing with testimony) that "a beit din (court) has not got the power to nullify the opinion of another beit din unless it is greater than it in wisdom and in numbers," which some commentators have interpreted to mean that the rulings of earlier battei din are binding on later generations. That same impulse lies behind the practice of most Orthodox *poskim* (legal decisors) to treat the rulings of the Talmud as no longer open to refutation or reversal.

That same temptation must have faced Isaac and his generation as well. Imagine how they revered Abraham, the man who introduced the world to ethical monotheism, the one whom God consulted before acting in the world, the one who passed every test God posed to him. Abraham was a giant among men, a leader and a tzaddik. There had been no Judaism before him; was it possible for Judaism to survive after his death?

The Torah reports the transmission of the mantle of leadership in the following words: "And it came to pass after the death of Abraham, that God blessed his son Isaac." The sages of *Midrash B'raisheet Rabbah* note that each time the Torah uses the phrase "And it came to pass," subsequent events reveal that "the world relapsed into its former state." Each great leader struggled valiantly to elevate the morality and godliness of the times, but as soon as the leader's efforts ceased, the world returned to its troubling ways.

It must have looked to Isaac and his contemporaries that without the shining example of Abraham and Sarah, it would be impossible to maintain adherence to the lofty values and holiness of the newly founded faith. How could the son possibly hope to fill his father's shoes? And how could his wife possibly live up to the sterling example of the matriarch Sarah?

We have every right to doubt our own abilities and to recognize our own flaws. But to surrender to that sense of inadequacy is a form of atheism, a denial of God's ability to give us the strength, wisdom, and courage to carry on. Even as the world reverted to its former condition, even then God "blessed his son Isaac," assuring a new generation of leadership to maintain and transmit the ways of Abraham and Sarah. As Rabbi Judan notes in the ancient midrash: "Had not God set up others in their stead, the world would have relapsed into its former state."

Whatever doubts we may have of our own ability, even in comparison with earlier generations, we are not allowed to give in to despair. Even if the leaders of our generation are as small as Jephtah and Samson, the Talmud instructs that we must treat them with the same reverence we would reserve for Moses. God gives each generation the wisdom and skill needed for the tasks at hand, but it is we who must supply the courage and the resolve.

Yes, there is a tradition within Judaism of venerating and deferring to earlier generations. But there is also a halakhic principle that *hil'kheta ke-vatrai* (the law follows the most recent ruling) and that later battei din do have the authority to overturn precedent when necessary. That is why most Conservative *poskim* claim the same level of authority as our Talmudic forebears.

We will never escape the tension between our childlike perception of earlier generations as greater than we are and our adult assertion of the need to act with equal authority. But that tension can be a fruitful and a beneficial one if it creates a balance between reverence for tradition and our ancestors with a commitment to hear the still-living voice of God and treat the insights of each new age and the needs of our children no less reverentially.

God does provide for a new generation of leaders. Are we willing to lead?

Sunrise, Sunset

Almost every Jew who is involved in communal Jewish living can recall an older Jewish relative (or neighbor) who provided precious memories of Jewish holy days, Sabbaths, and festivals. Whether we were born Jewish or have chosen to be Jewish, we have all been touched by a grandparent, an in-law, or a dear friend and mentor who invited us over for a Pesach seder (Passover service), showed us how to bake a challah, or took the time to explain and share the lighting of Hanukkah candles.

The stands of Jewish belonging are built one-on-one. Or in the words of the Talmud, "What comes from the heart enters the heart." However large our classes on Judaism, however magnificent our central institutions, the key component for transmitting a love of *yiddishkeit* (Jewish learning) and Torah is one Jew willing to lavish time, caring, and wisdom on a single seeking soul. The personal touch of *rav* (teacher) and *talmid* (student) has been the vehicle for the transmission of Torah and Jewish identity from its inception.

That person-to-person transmission makes good psychological sense, as we are drawn to communities in which we feel loved, welcomed, and valued. Particularly if the community also offers profundity and beauty to enhance our lives and goodness and values to enrich our morality and our families, we are more likely to respond by drawing near. Such is surely the case for Judaism.

But the individual connection makes theological sense too, and this parashah speaks of that human linkage. It begins with the statement that "Sarah's lifetime—the span of Sarah's life—came to 127 years. Sarah died in Kiryat-Arba." The previous parashah ended by providing the seemingly unconnected information that "Milkah too has borne children to your brother Nahor . . . [including Bethuel,] Bethuel being the father of Rebekah."

Why did the Torah tell us about the birth of Rebekah prior to informing us of the death of Sarah? The sages of *Midrash B'raisheet Rabbah* explained this juxtaposition by referring to the curious line from the biblical book *Kohelet* (Ecclesiastes): "The sun also rises and the sun sets." Rabbi Abba said, "Do we then not know that the sun rises and the sun sets? But the meaning is that before the Holy Blessing One causes the sun of one righteous person to set, God causes the sun of another tzaddik to rise. . . . Before the Holy Blessing One allowed Sarah's sun to set, God caused that of Rebekah to rise."

Before allowing the righteous Sarah to die, God had already assured the rise of another righteous matriarch through the birth of Rebekah. Knowing that the health of the Jewish community could not continue without a loving embodiment of its warmth and wisdom, God made sure that a new matriarch was ready before allowing the old one to journey on.

So it is in our journeys through life. We are Jewish today because of the loving Jews we encountered along the way: grandparents, rabbis, parents, siblings, family friends, neighbors, and acquaintances. With their willingness to reach out to us, to include us in their holy day celebrations, to seat us inside their sukkah, to feed us at their seder, and to teach us the fundamentals of Torah and its values, they are the reason we know from the inside how wonderful it is to be a Jew. Because someone cared enough to give us the experiences of Jewish living, our hearts can resonate to the sacred cycles of the seasons and of the Sabbaths.

How can we ever repay them? How can we show our deep gratitude and appreciation for those feelings and festivities that add so much to our lives, providing comfort in our grief and adding form to our joy? By passing their gift on to someone else.

Perhaps you know someone who is interested in becoming Jewish. Maybe you know a Jew who has never experienced the warmth and beauty of a Shabbat service and meal afterward. We were all involved by someone reaching out to us; now it's our turn to reach out to someone else.

Before the sun sets, the new sun rises. Now, today, it is your light that shines. And now is the time to reach out to someone younger, someone new, someone estranged from their Jewish heritage. Your warmth can yet light their path.

Blessed with All

Just after concluding his mourning for Sarah, Abraham turns to the task of finding a wife for his son, Isaac, as though the impact of his loss has made him realize what is still missing from his son's life. The

Torah lets us know that this will be the last act of the patriarch, introducing this topic with the words, "Abraham was old, well along in days, and the Lord had blessed Abraham in all (*ba-kol*)" (Gen. 24:1).

This is surely a lovely tribute, to receive God's blessing in every area of your life, but it raises problems for a careful reader. Over the past few parashiyot, we have witnessed Abraham leaving his father's house; smuggling his wife under Pharaoh's nose; participating in the animosity of his wife, Sarah, and her servant, Hagar; expelling Hagar and his son Ishmael; suffering the feuds between his own servants and the servants of his nephew Lot; waging war with a victorious coalition of kings to save his nephew; arguing with God about the destruction of Sodom and Gomorrah; and being ordered to kill his beloved son, Isaac. That's an awful lot of struggling, loss, and suffering for a man who is described as "blessed in all."

Our tradition does not lack for insightful responses to the nature of Abraham's blessings. Rashi notes that the numerical value of the word *ba-kol* is the same as the numerical value of the word *son*, reminding us of what an immense blessing a child brings to one's life. Connected to that understanding, Rabbi David Kimhi says that at the end of one's life, "the years when a person thinks about his departure from this earth, [Abraham] lacked nothing, and did not need anything in this life except to see his son well married." For Radak, the fullness of Abraham's life impels him to seek that same fullness for Isaac. Rabbi Abraham Ibn Ezra observes that the blessings that constitute human richness are riches, possessions, honor, longevity, and children. Abraham was blessed in all of these areas.

A second stream of insight sees the blessing in a more radical light. According to Rabbi Judah in the ancient midrash *B'raisheet Rabbah*, "it means that God gave him a daughter." What a surprising concept—even though the Torah is silent on this point, Rabbi Judah notes what a special blessing a daughter is and tells us that this is a reference to the unknown girl who blessed Abraham.

There is a third path alluded to by some of our sages and worthy of our reflection. Ramban tells us that the reference to *ba-kol* is an allusion to "one of the secrets of the Torah, a great matter, namely that the Holy Blessing One has an attribute called 'kol/all,' so-called because it is the foundation of everything." Instead of seeing Abraham's blessings only in the abundance in his life, in the good things he owned, can't we learn to see blessings in the fullness of his life, the sheer "allness" of it.

Life doesn't come in sweetness and light. It erupts with an irrepressible mixture of joy and sorrow, achievement and defeat, vitality and illness, connection and isolation. To focus only on part of that mix would be to produce a caricature of the fullness of life, and God is not found in caricature. The energy that it takes to edit out the unpleasant aspects of life can only suck out our passion and our ability to live enthusiastically. Such denial requires ever-greater amounts of energy to sustain the illusion yet still results eventually in defeat. Only by embracing the totality of life's experiences can we truly live. By allowing ourselves to dwell in the suffering and the ecstasy, to embrace the disappointment and the hurt along with the delight, we can experience the fullness of being alive, the holiness of being itself.

Seeing blessing in "all" shifts our focus away from possessions and toward our inner response to what life brings. All living beings suffer. But remaining open to see the blessings amid the suffering is the key inner work that allows us to be with God and each other even in our pain. The *Midrash Tanhuma* notes that "the Holy Blessing One only elevates a person after testing and trying him first." Echoing that broad view of blessing, Rabbi Ya'akov Yitzhak, the Seer of Lublin, reminds us that God blessed Abraham with the qualities of "with all," or as the Torah states, "with all your heart, with all your soul, and with all your might" (Dt. 6:3).

To be able to see blessings in "all," to be able to release his inner energy to embrace everything that life brought him, that is indeed the blessing that Abraham was able to reveal. To see blessing *ba-kol* is the task of a lifetime and the opportunity of every moment.

Toldot/Generations

Genesis 25:19–28:9

Toldot *tells the story of the second generation of patriarchs and matri-*
archs, and it begins the dramatic story of the third. Scenes from this
parashah are among the most famous in the Bible. The saga begins
when Isaac is forty and Rebekah is experiencing a difficult pregnancy.
Learning from God that she is pregnant with twins who will become
ancestors of different peoples, Rebekah is also told by the Divine that
the older of the twins will someday serve the younger. Esau and Jacob
are born—the first famously red and hairy, and thus named "Esau," the
second emerging clutching the heel of his brother, and hence named
"Jacob." In a poignant line, the Torah tells us that Isaac loves Esau
because he brought him food, but Rebekah loves Jacob.

Impetuous from birth, Esau, a hunter, returns one day from a hunt
so hungry that he agrees to sell his birthright to his younger brother in
exchange for a bowl of the lentil stew that Jacob is preparing.

The scene changes, and what follows is a series of incidents that
echo nearly identical ones from the life of Abraham, again involv-
ing Abimelech and the attempt to pretend his wife is his sister; once
more the Hebrew patriarch is protected by the king and grows rich.
Then forced from place to place by avaricious Philistines, Isaac leads a
nomadic life. As God once blessed his father, Abraham, in Beersheba,
so God blesses Isaac there.

Next comes one of the most powerful incidents in all of Torah. Blind
and frail, Isaac decides the time has come to bless his elder son, and
so he sends him out to hunt game and to prepare a dish for Isaac to
eat before he bestows the blessing. At Rebekah's behest and with her
help, Jacob masquerades as his brother, approaches his blind father,
offers him food, and asks for the blessing. In words that have resounded
through history, Isaac responds, "The voice is the voice of Jacob, but
the hands are the hands of Esau," and blesses his son.

Esau returns and discovers that his younger brother has stolen his blessing; distraught, he begs his father for a blessing as well and plans to kill Jacob as soon as Isaac dies. Rebekah sends Jacob away to safety with her brother Laban, telling her husband that Jacob needs to find a non-Canaanite bride. Isaac agrees and now, in a blessing intended for his younger son, says, "May God grant the blessing of Abraham to you and your offspring, that you may possess the land where you are sojourning, and which God bequeathed to Abraham."

When Eternity Opens Beneath You

Ours is an age of busy people scurrying around to accomplish more at work, at play, and at home. Agendas filled to bursting keep us bustling from one activity to another, always on the run, always a little late. Our public activities—involving our image and our reputation—consume the better part of our attention and the lion's share of our energy.

And yet, there is always a price to be paid for the choice of how we spend our time. If we occupy ourselves with too much work or with too much public service, then the ones who pay the price are often our families and our friends. Absentee fathers, distracted mothers, and latchkey children are the silent sufferers in our struggle for attention, prestige, and status. All of us pay a price for our misguided priorities.

Ours is not the first generation to realize that our children and our relationships require more time than we have allotted to them. As is often the case, problems we think are new reverberate across the ages, finding consummate expression in the pages of our holy Torah.

The first father too busy to notice his children was Isaac, and our patriarch paid a heavy price for his public commitments, however laudable they might have been.

At the end of his life, Isaac becomes blind—perhaps the outward sign of his own inability to perceive his children's needs. Through Rebekah's ruse, he bestows his paternal blessing—the *brit* (the covenant between the Jewish people and God)—to Jacob, the unintended, younger son.

When Esau shows up with the meal, Isaac is horrified to realize that he must have blessed the wrong son. He asks his son, "Who are you?" and Esau exclaims, "I am your son, Esau, your firstborn." At that point, the Torah recounts, "Isaac was seized with very violent trembling."

The extremity of Isaac's response attracted rabbinic attention. Why did he tremble so? *Midrash B'raisheet Rabbah* records the viewpoint of Rabbi Yohanan: "When a man has two sons, and one goes out and the other comes in, does he tremble? Surely not! The reason, however, was that when Esau went in, Gehinnom (the rabbinic equivalent of hell) went in with him." In other words, Esau was such a difficult and troubled boy that disaster followed in his wake. His father was quaking, recoiling from his disappointing son.

Another intriguing midrash recounts a similar reason for Isaac's reaction with one slight variation. *Midrash Tanhuma* records, "When Esau entered, Gehinnom opened for him." Along that same line, Rashi says that "he saw Gehinnom opened beneath him." This version of the midrash may refer not to Esau, but to Isaac himself. Perhaps it is saying that when he saw the misery of his son, it felt as though Gehinnom itself were opening up underneath him. That bottomless turmoil was the sense of the father, too late, that his own inattention had contributed decisively to his son's delinquency.

Perhaps if Isaac had taken some of the time he devoted to his public leadership and used it to be a more involved father, his son would have grown up in a very different way. It is striking that this is the first recorded conversation between the two of them—and Esau is already an adult!

While Isaac was focusing on tribal matters and issues of religious leadership, his two boys grew up without a father's care and guidance. Small wonder, then, that Isaac felt Gehinnom open up beneath him. Our chance at repairing the world comes only once, through the kind of care, teaching, and examples we provide for our children. While they are living with us, while they still turn to us for approval and instruction, that is the time to erect a legacy, to touch tomorrow.

Time is short. The task is great. And the children are waiting.

True Friendship Is Reliable

In this parashah, we encounter a false friend: our ancestor Isaac faces a famine in the Land of Israel. Rather than leave his beloved homeland, he settles in the region of Avimelekh, the king of the Philistines, who pretends to befriend Isaac, even going so far as to protect Isaac's wife, Rebekah, from the lust of his immoral countrymen. Isaac settles in the land and prospers. Soon he is a wealthy man with large herds and a bounteous household. His newfound happiness, however, threatens his friendship with Avimelekh. Once it becomes clear that their relationship will no longer be based on dependency or adulation, Avimelekh terminates the association, sending Isaac a painful note: "Go away from us, for you have become far too big for us." Imagine how devastated Isaac must have been to receive Avimelekh's abrupt termination of their friendship.

Later on, when it again becomes clear that Isaac has God's blessing and Avimelekh sees the possibility of benefit from an association with Isaac, the king again approaches the patriarch to formalize a friendly relationship. Avimelekh is the kind of friend the Talmudic rabbis warned of when they said, "There are many persons who eat and drink together, yet they pierce each other with the sword of their tongues."

This secular notion of friendship denigrates people by viewing them as tools to be used, rather than hearts to be esteemed. Contrast that with a lovely midrash (found in Adolph Jellinek's *Bet Ha-Midrash*) that speaks of the Jewish view of friendship—one that recognizes human beings as infinitely precious, worthy of our deepest loyalty and love:

> The outcome of a war parted two friends who had previously lived in the same country. . . . One of them, visiting his friend by stealth, was captured and sentenced to die as a spy. But the man implored the king who had decreed his death: "Your majesty, give me a month's respite so I may place my affairs in order. At the end of a month, I will return to pay the penalty." The king said, "Who will be your surety?" The man answered, "Call in my friend, and he will pay for my life with his in the event I don't

return." To the king's amazement, the friend accepted the condition. On the last day when the sword was about to descend, the first friend returned and placed the sword at his own neck. The second friend begged him, "Let me die in your place." The king was touched and pardoned them both, asking them to include him as a third in their remarkable friendship.

True friendship is not a utilitarian tool—friends are not objects to be used and then abandoned when they no longer serve our needs. A friend is a treasure to be cherished and guarded, requiring a level of fidelity that takes constant effort. As *Yalkut Shimoni* understands, "it is difficult to acquire a friend."

To offer the unconditional caring and love that one human being can bestow upon another, to see the chance to know someone else as an opportunity to witness God's steadfast and reliable love is a great gift, both to the recipient and to the giver. Those who see friendship as a series of functional connections to be used and then abandoned can never know the joy, peace, and depth that comes with unconditional love.

True friendship is a form of *hesed* (love that need not be continually earned, caring that is its own justification). Only in the context of that *hesed* can we risk exposing our souls and our hearts to each other's insight, only then can we risk healing each other's wounds, and only then can we in turn allow ourselves to be healed.

True friendship is reliable—and the only kind worth sharing.

Released from Responsibility

How involved should parents and children be in each other's lives? Is there a graceful way of allowing those we love and live with to be responsible for their own lives while still offering whatever support and nurturance lies within our power?

The issue of where parental responsibility ends and a child's begins is hardly new to our own age. In every generation, parents have struggled with their appropriate role as their children reach adulthood and begin to live independent lives.

As much as we might like to think of children as extensions of ourselves, the truth is that they are born with their own personalities, preferences, and dislikes. Parents may be able to mold their children, even to fine-tune their character, but the essence of each child is there in the little bundle taken home from the hospital.

This parashah speaks of the individuality of children and the consequence of that autonomy for the parents. In speaking of Jacob and his brother, Esau, the Torah comments on their distinct appearance and interests. In *Midrash B'raisheet Rabbah*, Rabbi Pinhas repeated the words of Rabbi Levi: "They were like a myrtle and a wild rose growing side by side; once they attained maturity, one yielded its fragrance and the other its thorns."

What Rabbi Levi observed is that children can be molded and directed in their infancy and their youth, but with diminishing returns as they approach puberty. In preschool, everyone can play together. By high school, cliques become the rule. As the midrash notes of Jacob and his brother, "For thirteen years both went to school and came home from school. After this age, one went to the house of study and the other to idolatrous shrines."

After becoming *b'nai mitzvah* (responsible for the commandments), Jacob's personality asserted itself through an interest in Jewish pursuits: study, prayer, good deeds. Similarly, Esau treated becoming a bar mitzvah as the end of any Jewish involvement—now he was free to leave Hebrew school behind him, to squander his time in the boastful vanities of young manhood.

Our midrash confirms what we know from life itself: that try as they might, parents cannot make children in their own image. Those children will be themselves, and their own inner selves will filter our best efforts in their own ways.

The consequence of this timeless truth is that we do not own our children, nor do we bear total responsibility for their personalities. While parents can indeed make a huge impact on a child, the child will engage the parental advice and example in his or her own way. Perhaps for that reason, the *berakhah* (blessing) traditionally recited at a child's bar/bat mitzvah birthday and recorded in our midrash is "Blessed is the One who has now released me from legal culpability for this child."

One can only take responsibility for the consequences of one's own actions. While parents cast a giant shadow over children's perceptions and actions, their maturation entails a retreat of the parents' ability to impose their own preferences.

Ultimately, children learn to become responsible for themselves and their own behavior. We, as parents, need to learn to let our children take charge.

Va-Yetze/He Went Out

Genesis 28:10–32:3

On his way to his uncle's house, in the middle of the wilderness between Paran and Beersheba, Jacob prepares to sleep, a stone for a pillow under his head. He dreams of a stairway reaching from the ground to the heavens, with angels at once ascending and descending, and of God standing by his sleeping form and repeating the promise made to his ancestors: "Your descendants shall be as the dust of the earth, and you shall spread out to the west and to the east, to the north and to the south; all the families of the earth shall bless themselves by you and your descendants."

When Jacob awakes, he recognizes that God had surely been present, and he had not known it. He vows that if God protects him along his way, the Lord will be his God. Jacob reaches his destination and, in the town center, sees Rachel. He rolls the stone from off of the well to which she has brought her flocks to be watered. Thus begins the story of their romance. Jacob works for her father, Laban, for seven years in order to marry her, but Laban substitutes his older daughter, Leah, in disguise for Rachel in the nuptial bed. Angered by the deception, Jacob nevertheless agrees to labor another seven years for Rachel.

Over the years, Leah and Rachel compete with one another for children. Leah bears many sons and one daughter for Jacob, hoping with each birth that her husband will love her. Desperate for a child too, Rachel (like Sarah before her) arranges for Jacob to sleep with her handmaid, Bilhah, who in turn thus becomes the mother first of Dan and then of Naphtali. Leah responds by having Jacob sleep with her handmaid, Zilpah, who bears Asher. She then, with Rachel's assent, sleeps with Jacob and bears him another two sons and a daughter. Finally, Rachel herself gives birth to Joseph. Later she will bear the family's youngest son, Benjamin.

Having amassed significant wealth, Jacob wants to return home, despite Laban's protests. As Jacob and his family are leaving, however,

Rachel steals her father's household gods. Discovering that his daugh-
ters and their family are missing and that his idols have been stolen as
well, Laban pursues them and accuses them of the theft of his gods.
Having no idea at all that it is his beloved Rachel who has stolen the
idols, Jacob tells Laban that the one who has the idols shall not live,
thus tragically foreshadowing his wife's early death. Rachel, pretend-
ing to be menstruating, hides the idols underneath her and blames her
inability to rise and greet her father on her "condition."

The parashah ends with Jacob and Laban agreeing to separate per-
manently, and Jacob continues on the road home.

Comfort for the Ages

One of the truisms of formal Jewish prayer is that we recite our
prayers in the plural: we ask God to save *us*, to redeem *us*, to heal *us*.
The prayers don't speak from the heart of the individual alone, but
rather recognize us as members of a covenantal people, a nation in
prayer to God.

That strong sense of community is one of the great strengths of
rabbinic Judaism—a bond that links one Jew to another, across time
and space. No Jew need ever feel completely alone, precisely because
we are so thoroughly integrated into the entire Jewish people that our
very spirituality is a collective outpouring, the souls of each person
merging into a larger whole that is Am Yisrael (the Jewish people).

Yet there are moments when our sense of belonging is strained,
when events in life or in our community dissipate our urge to belong.
There are times for all of us when we stand as isolated individuals,
alone in the dark.

At times of extreme individuality, accompanied by either the high
of exultation or the low of despondency, there is a helpful Jewish aid
that can walk with us even on those occasions of relentless solipsism.
That guide is the book of Psalms. Traditionally attributed to King
David, these unparalleled outpourings of soul speak from the perspective of the solitary individual communing intimately with God.
One hundred and fifty poems that come straight from the heart and
therefore—as the Talmud points out—go straight to the heart. So
important are the psalms for any living Jewish spirituality that it was

impossible for the rabbinic tradition to imagine an age untouched by their wonder, spontaneity, and power.

When Jacob finally summons the courage to leave Laban, he faces his cruel father-in-law, telling Laban that he had worked so hard that "sleep fled from my eyes." The rabbis of *Midrash B'raisheet Rabbah* notice that our third patriarch apparently spent many sleepless nights. Surely the way he chose to spend those nights would be of interest and instruction for his descendants as well. What did Jacob do during those unhappy nights when he felt distant from his beloved parents, isolated from any loving community, alone with only his wiles and his wives?

Obviously, someone of the spiritual stature of Jacob wouldn't simply waste precious evening hours, even in the depths of depression. One of the religious giants of all time, Jacob must have used his time wisely. What precisely did he do?

According to Rabbi Joshua Ben Levi, he recited the fifteen Song of Ascent psalms. Rabbi Samuel Bar Nahman claimed that Jacob recited the entire book of Psalms, his evidence being the line in the twenty-second psalm that says that God is "enthroned upon the praises of Israel." Since Israel is one of Jacob's names, it follows that God is enthroned on Jacob's words—that is, his recitation of psalms.

Now what is particularly striking about these midrashic claims is that the rabbis knew full well that the context of the psalms of ascent was the Holy Temple in Jerusalem, a structure that wouldn't be built for another eight hundred years! And if King David was understood to be the author of the book of Psalms, how could his distant ancestor Jacob recite them in advance?

This bold midrash correctly understands that Torah stands outside of the categories of history, that religious truth spans the ages and parts company from the canons of chronology or objective analysis.

Jacob, the symbol of the entire Jewish people, had moments when he felt ultimately alone. In the depth of his pain and his sorrow, cut off from any sense of *brit*, of *kehillah* (community, congregation), or of purpose, he turned to the same sacred songs that have sustained us in such moments ever since.

The book of Psalms is the essential accompaniment to the siddur. Just as the siddur speaks on our behalf as a people to God, so the Psalms provide structure and words for the mute longings of our solitary souls. Together, they provide a path of expression for the range of our inner needs and our communal hopes. Together, they are the building blocks of our passionate love affair with God.

Spend some time getting to know the book of Psalms. It worked for Jacob, and it can work for you too.

Lulei: What Keeps Us Going

Jacob wasn't someone who was born with a silver spoon in his mouth. Instead, he worked—hard—for everything that came his way. The birthright, his father's blessing, his beloved wife, Rachel—all of these accomplishments and relationships came to him as the result of long, arduous toil. Looking back on his life, it isn't hard to understand why Jacob paused to consider what the source of strength was that enabled him to persevere. How, despite the difficulties and the disappointments, did our ancestor manage to keep on keeping on?

For Jacob, that question became especially poignant as he left the home of his father-in-law, Laban. Having worked for fourteen years for his two wives, Leah and Rachel, and another six years for a share in Laban's flocks of sheep, Jacob spent twenty years living in a foreign land, away from his cherished Israel and away from his family and his childhood haunts. Only after the fact could Jacob allow himself to see the enormity of his struggle and the extent of his own inner exile and transformation.

In response to Laban's claim that Jacob owed his success to him, his father-in-law, Jacob insisted that it was "*lulei*, were it not for the God of my ancestors, the God of Abraham and the fear of Isaac who was with me." God, not Laban, was Jacob's sustaining rock throughout his years of turmoil and deprivation.

The rabbis of *Midrash B'raisheet Rabbah* noticed the odd Hebrew word *lulei*, which is generally translated as "were it not" or "had not." Coming as it does at the beginning of the sentence, the word seemed sufficiently superfluous to warrant the insertion of ingenious rabbinic interpretation.

Zavdi Ben Levi understood *lulei* to be an appeal to ancestral merit, *zekhut avot*. He understood Jacob to say that had it not been for the good deeds and the role model of his grandparents, Abraham and Sarah, and his parents, Isaac and Rebekah, he would have lacked the clear sense of right and wrong and the inner strength to hew to the proper path. As the Talmud notes, *"Ma'aseh avot siman la-banim* (The deeds of the parents become signs for the children)." The goodness of his ancestors gave him his sense of purpose, his vision of what could be, and the ability to work toward that distant goal.

Rabbi Yohanan has a different *drash* (inventive commentary) for *lulei*, seeing it as devotion "for the sake of the sanctity of God's name," or *kiddush ha-Shem*. Jacob knew that his behavior would either reflect credit on the God of Israel or would make God and Jacob's religion seem hypocritical and foolish. How he behaved would affect God's reputation among the people who knew him. *Kiddush ha-Shem*, acting in a way that reflects positively on God, motivated our patriarch to live up to his ideals, to walk in God's ways even during times of sorrow, want, and fear.

Finally, Rabbi Levi asserted that *lulei* implied being motivated by "the merit of faith and the merit of Torah." As he understood Jacob, the patriarch was inspired by his sense of God's presence in his life, the pervasive holiness made concrete through the mitzvot, the sacred commandments that link Jews and God.

These three interpretations—ancestral merit, sanctification of God, and Torah and mitzvot—form the three legs of Judaism:

- Ancestral merit is an awareness of being connected to those who preceded us. It is found in cherishing our traditions by living them in our daily lives and by transmitting them to our children and to their children. It is a sense of identity that involves the continuing stream of Jewish people, starting with Abraham and Sarah, continuing through ourselves, and extending to each new generation of Jews.
- *Kiddush ha-Shem* is an awareness of spirituality and the importance of making God's presence and love a pervasive part of our consciousness and our lives. Through prayer, contemplation, song, dance, meditation, and study, we sanctify God by focusing our minds, hearts, and souls on our sacred source.
- Faith and Torah translate into a devotion to the mitzvot, the 613 commandments of the Torah as understood, amplified, and defined through rabbinic *drashot* (interpretation) and *takkanot* (legislation). By teaching how to enact the deep wisdom of Jewish values through concrete actions, Judaism provides a pedagogy of hands and feet, a

spirituality of pots and pans, a sense of fidelity to God that extends to every aspect of our lives.

On these three legs, Jewish life is assured and our Jewish lives are enriched. Holiness, wisdom, and belonging are within our grasp, able to sustain and nurture us through life's trials, even as they did for our patriarch Jacob.

Marriage: The Greatest Miracle

Life can be painfully lonely. Even with the best health, an adequate income, friends, and a fulfilling career, it is still possible to succumb to a sense of the futility and isolation of life.

It isn't difficult to imagine why loneliness is so pervasive. As we proceed through our own life journeys, we experience the gradual relinquishment of our strength, vigor, and abilities. As we proceed in our careers, we enjoy our attainments but note the increasing gap between our accomplishments and the excitement and drive of our younger colleagues. Friends drop out of touch; older relatives move away or die. Given our constant effort to hold our lives and ourselves together, coupled with the ever-present necessity of giving up relationships, abilities, and dreams, it is no surprise that so many people go through life feeling alone.

It is also no surprise, therefore, that the Torah places such a premium on a good marriage. It is the way of the world for parents to precede us in death and for children to move off to live their own lives. But a spouse can be a partner and friend for every phase of our time on earth.

Imagine what a miracle it is that two people can come together in love. I sometimes feel amazed that I can live with myself all the time. That my wife chooses to do so is altogether remarkable. Yet that same miracle is replicated in household after household, as countless couples offer solace, comfort, care, and guidance through the rigors and the disappointments that society and nature dish out.

This parashah speaks about the miracle of marriage. It begins by noting that "Jacob left Beersheba and set out for Paran." Why was he going to Paran? According to *Parashat Toldot*, his parents sent him to Beersheba to "take a wife there from among the daughters of Laban, your mother's brother." Jacob went from his home to seek the comfort of love and marriage.

What is remarkable about that marital voyage is that his father did the opposite, a fact that did not escape the attention of the rabbis of *Midrash B'raisheet Rabbah*: "Sometimes a man goes to his spouse, and sometimes it is the reverse. In the case of Isaac, his spouse came to him. . . . Jacob, however, went out to his spouse."

Even more remarkable than the issue of who goes to whom is the mere fact that relationships happen at all. That two people—two entire universes of ideas, experiences, preferences, and quirks—can share their lives as one is astounding. In fact, the rabbis considered the existence of good marriages to be one of the most astounding of God's miracles on our behalf.

They tell the story of a wealthy Roman matron who asked Rabbi Yosi what exactly God had been doing ever since the completion of Creation. Rabbi Yosi answered that since the creation of the world, God "sits and makes matches, assigning this person to that one, and that one to this."

The matron scoffed, thinking that this was merely a case of matching one from column A and one from column B. So to demonstrate her parity with God, she matched all her slaves, one to another. After a few days, her household was pure pandemonium, as fights were constantly erupting among ill-matched couples. She then returned to Rabbi Yosi and conceded that "there is no god like your God; it is true, your Torah is indeed beautiful and praiseworthy." Rabbi Yosi's response was that creating loving couples is "as difficult before the Holy Blessed One as was splitting the Red Sea."

Creating a loving, nurturing relationship of love is how God has spent the intervening time since the Creation. And the existence of loving couples is a miracle no less taxing or stupendous than any reported in the Torah. We look for miracles in the wrong places. Rather than waiting for special effects from the sky, the strongest evidence of God's love for each one of us is sitting in the chair next to us or in the next room. In the love of another human being, we can come to know the love of God.

Va-Yishlach/He Sent

Genesis 32:4–36:43

Jacob prepares to face his brother at Seir. Attempting to assuage his brother, Jacob sends servants in advance, who report that Esau is with four hundred men. Fearing violence, Jacob divides his retinue into two separate camps, hoping that at least one of them may survive. After praying to God for safety, Jacob sends a large selection of animals from his herd to his brother as a gift. These he sends in droves, hoping to propitiate Esau. Then Jacob spends the night alone by the river Jabbok. A mysterious man wrestles with him all night, wrenching Jacob's hip at the socket. Jacob refuses to release the stranger without a blessing, and the other renames Jacob as Israel, "for you have striven with beings divine and human, and have prevailed." From that day on, Jacob limps, and the children of Israel do not eat the meat around the sciatic nerve. When the brothers reunite, Jacob and Esau embrace and weep. Jacob tells his brother, "Seeing your face is like seeing the face of God." Esau invites Jacob to travel with him, but Jacob and his retinue venture alone to Succoth and then to Shechem, purchasing land from the local ruler.

Dinah, Jacob's daughter, visits with the local women, attracting the attention of Shechem, son of Hamor the Hivite, who rapes Dinah and then asks his father to arrange a marriage. Hamor invites the Israelites to intermarry with the Hivites, and he asks for Dinah for his son. Jacob and his sons are outraged by the assault. Speaking with guile, the sons insist that the Hivite men must be circumcised, to which they agree. While the Hivite men are still in pain, the Israelites attack, killing the males, taking the women and children captive, and gathering the livestock as booty.

Jacob is outraged by his sons' behavior, and he moves on to Beth El, instructing the members of his household to purge themselves of any idols. Jacob builds an altar at the very site where God was first revealed to Jacob. At Beth El, Rebekah's nurse, Deborah, dies, and God confirms Jacob's new name, promising, "The land that I assigned to Abraham and Isaac I assign to you; and to your offspring to come will I assign the land."

Rachel struggles in labor and dies giving birth to a second son whom she names Ben-oni ("son of my suffering"). Jacob renames him Benjamin ("son of my right hand"). Rachel is buried on the road to Ephrat, near Bethlehem.

Reuben, Jacob's son, sleeps with Bilhah, his father's concubine, and Jacob discovers the betrayal but does nothing about it. Isaac dies at the age of 180, and Jacob and Esau bury him. The parashah ends by listing Esau's descendants, including Edom.

Jacob's Compromise for Peace

Dignity and honor are important attributes for most people. We zealously guard our own dignity, often overreacting to perceived slights delivered by others. We recoil with horror from moments that compromise our dignity, and we respond with rage when we feel belittled.

At the same time that we assert our own honor, we also cherish a conflicting virtue—a willingness to make peace and to appease enemies. Even when that reconciliation requires some compromise of our own standing, we often consider waiving our "right" to respect to be a praiseworthy act. If we feel the strain of that tension—the desire to maintain our dignity and the desire to live harmoniously with others—for ourselves, how much greater will it be when it involves compromising the dignity of a tradition or an institution we venerate?

It is precisely that conflict that this parashah explores in the reunification of our patriarch Jacob and his brother, Esau. According to both biblical and rabbinic accounts, Esau was a wicked man—impulsive, immoral, violent, and ignorant. Jacob, to the contrary, is esteemed as the ancestor of the entire Jewish people, a role model for moral development and the acquisition of wisdom.

After a long estrangement, Jacob and his brother are about to meet again. Fearful for his life and for the safety of his beloved family,

Jacob instructs his servants to approach his explosive brother and say, "Thus says your servant Jacob."

Your servant!? How can Jacob, patriarch of the Jewish people, devoted follower of God, grandson of Abraham, allow himself to stoop so low? How can he describe himself as the servant of a thug?

With indignation, *Midrash B'raisheet Rabbah* records the view of Rabbi Judah Ben Shimon: "As a troubled fountain and a corrupted spring, so is a tzaddik who abases himself before the wicked." Rabbi Judah asserts that Jacob's act of self-abasement also constitutes the degradation of what Jacob stands for—the Torah and the service of God. As a tzaddik, Jacob stands for something beyond his own personal identity. Therefore, he cannot allow himself to be slighted, since to do so causes the Torah itself to be diminished.

This view is reflected in the Talmudic dictate prohibiting a Torah scholar from waiving the appropriate honor paid him or her by others. As an individual, that choice might be an option, but as a walking symbol of Torah and of God, such a slight would encourage disdain for the sacred.

In opposition to this view, the midrash relates the time that Rabbi Judah Ha-Nasi, the compiler of the Mishnah itself, sent a letter to Antoninus, the emperor of Rome. His salutation was "From your servant Judah to our Sovereign, the Emperor Antoninus." When his scribe saw Rabbi's salutation, he was horrified and exclaimed, "My master, why do you treat your honor so lightly?" To which the rabbi responded, "Am I better than my ancestor Jacob?"

Rabbi Judah Ha-Nasi understood the wisdom and depth of Jacob's precedent. In the interests of human harmony, in pursuit of peace, a willingness to compromise our own dignity may indeed constitute the highest service of God, the most powerful assertion of the dignity of all humankind.

Not that dignity is so cheap, but that peace is so precious.

Who Owns Dinah?

One of the stumbling blocks that often makes it difficult for contemporary Jews to embrace Jewish tradition fully is the perception that women are treated as second-class citizens, as somehow less than equal within Judaism. Indeed, that perception is not limited to a few uneducated Jews, but is shared by many leading scholars as well. The founders of the Conservative, Reform, and Reconstructionist movements within Judaism all saw a part of their task to be to elevate the role and status of the Jewish woman, seeing her place within contemporary Orthodoxy as a denigration of her true worth and a denial of her true potential. Even the spokesmen of contemporary Orthodoxy speak about the woman's elevated status today, and it is no longer uncommon to see women studying and teaching biblical and rabbinic literature within each of the denominations.

Somehow coming to terms with the perception of women as "less than" men, as the voice that was silenced or repressed within our traditions, is an essential task if we hope to be able to invite and include today's Jews. So the story of the rape of Dinah, troubling even in past ages, is particularly perplexing today.

The plot is quite simple—Dinah, Jacob's daughter, goes out and meets Shechem, a prince of a guy and a Canaanite to boot. He rapes her and then falls in love with her, so he asks his father, Hamor, to arrange for their wedding. When Dinah's brothers hear of their sister's rape, they are "distressed and very angry" because "Shechem has committed an outrage in Israel by lying with Jacob's daughter—a thing not to be done." Apparently, what most concerned the brothers was the affront to their honor (after all, *their sister* was raped) and that a Canaanite man had slept with a Jewish woman, violating the mandate to marry only another Jew.

In a ruse, the brothers "agreed" to the marriage, provided that Hamor, Shechem, and their men all became circumcised. Then, while the men were still healing, Shimon and Levi killed all the men of the village. Additionally, "they put Hamor and his son Shechem to the sword, took Dinah out of Shechem's house, and went away."

When Jacob challenged his sons for their behavior, their response was, "Should our sister be treated like a whore?" Again, it sounds like their primary concern was that she should be treated a certain way because she was their sister, not simply because no one should be treated that way. Her connection to them meant that they were affronted by her mistreatment. For them, this was an issue of their reputation, not of her pain.

Strikingly, Jewish tradition denounces the brothers. After all, the Torah itself condemns their macho display, as the patriarch Jacob upbraids them, "You have brought trouble on me, making me odious among the inhabitants of the land." Similarly, the rabbis of *Midrash B'raisheet Rabbah* put the following words into Jacob's mouth: "The vat was clear, and you have muddied it." Jacob reminds his sons that in a contest of male power and dominance, his small band would lose. There has to be another way, a way that transcends male displays and possessiveness.

Important strands within Judaism, from the time of the Torah on, have disdained the way the brothers treated their sister as simply an extension of their own reputation and as their possession to be kept from other men. Would that the rest of the world had a similar attitude. Many are United States court cases in which a husband comes home to find his wife making love to another man. He attacks the two with some sort of weapon and is brought to court on charges of assault with a deadly weapon. In many instances, the judge gives the husband a token penalty, commenting that any man in his position would have felt the need to inflict a corporeal revenge.

For such a benighted judge, the rash actions of Shimon and Levi make perfect sense. How we treat a woman reflects badly on the men to whom she belongs—if she is unmarried, then her father and brothers; if she is married, then her husband. These men have the right to defend their proprietary interest and to beat the woman into submission for the sake of their own pride and honor. Women, in this view, are little more than pets that can talk, clean, and cook.

How refreshing then, in the light of this persistent chauvinism, that our ancestor Jacob more than thirty-five hundred years ago condemned that mentality. Jacob stood in the traditions of his ancestors, a tradition that loudly proclaims that all human beings are made in God's image. When we act as though we own another person, or that we have some proprietary interest over that person, we deny the divine image within. When we strike another person, we are committing an assault against God.

Outside of immediate self-defense, no human being has the right to beat another. Other than in a defensive war or to protect against immediate attack, no human being has the right to shoot another.

Jacob knew that in antiquity, and Jewish tradition established it as a matter of law between nations.

It remains our task to apply that law to our closest relationships, to cherish the divine image in each other through acts of love and kindness and justice.

Once a Jacob, Always a Jacob

Upon his arrival at Paddan-Aram, having wrestled with the angel, pacified his brother, survived the trauma of his daughter's rape and his sons' revenge on the men of Shechem, and built an altar to God at the ancestral home base of Beth El, Jacob receives a surprising message from God. God appears again to Jacob and blesses him. God says to him, "You whose name is Jacob, you shall be called Jacob no more, but 'Israel' shall be your name." Thus, God names him Israel.

Perhaps because of all Jacob had experienced in his lifetime, perhaps because of the spiritual growth that transformed a scheming, manipulative adolescent into a sage and a spiritual giant, God gave him a new name to signify that new, enhanced identity.

Indeed, Rashi seems to reflect that understanding when he comments that the name Jacob "means a man who comes as a lurker and a trickster, but 'Israel shall be your name' signifies a prince and a chief." Jacob was the name that implied his former identity. The Torah itself tells us that Yaakov refers to the baby Jacob's attempt to supplant his brother by grabbing Esau's heel during birth. That willful attempt to wrest destiny from his elder sibling and to force the world to bow to his strategies and his plotting typify Jacob as a youth. But in a remarkable transformation, Jacob in his prime learns to listen to the world, learns that not all efforts can be crowned with success. By wrestling with the angel and learning to be satisfied merely with holding on (rather than with a clear victory), Jacob learns the wisdom of patience and modesty, he acquires the ability to put God at the center and to surrender the doomed need to control everyone and everything. At the end of that transforming moment, the angel acknowledges Jacob's new, more mature nature by bestowing on him the new name Israel.

In this parashah, God confirms that new, enlightened identity. Not only does the name Israel signify a spiritual transformation, but it gives a political and social stature as well. As the Radak (Rabbi David Kimhi) tells us, that new name, Israel, embraces the nation—it recognizes Jacob as the ancestor of the entire Jewish people and links our identity to his. He is now truly the father of the nation, the heir of his grandfather Abraham.

But the Torah throws a problem our way when it persists in calling Israel "Jacob" from time to time throughout his life. If God has given him a new name, why doesn't that name replace the old one forever?

The Talmud (*Massekhet Berakhot*) notes that "Jacob is not to be entirely eliminated, but 'Israel' is to be primary and 'Jacob' secondary." And the great medieval sage Rabbi Sa'adia Gaon wrote that "you will no longer be called by your name Jacob only, but also you will be called by the name Israel." That understanding is supported by Rabbi Abraham Ibn Ezra.

Why does the third patriarch retain his earlier, somewhat embarrassing name?

The reality of human life is that we never eradicate our earlier identities. Rather than living solely in the present, each person's identity is a blend of all previous embodiments—the infant, the child, the adolescent, the young adult, and so on throughout life. With each new phase of existence, we grow and add new aspects of an emerging self. But we are never simple, never single layered. Instead, just as a thriving tree adds new rings but always around the earliest core, so too do we humans add new modifications and identities to the increasingly complex and layered history of who we are. The little child within never goes away, but simply lies underneath the surface. The right smell or place can reawaken feelings we didn't remember having or can excite memories long forgotten. Interactions with parents or situations that reenact childhood struggles can summon up the passions and helplessness that childhood once imposed.

No matter how much our surface radiates the placid wisdom, profundity, and tranquillity of an Israel, the chaos, passion, and turbulence of our earlier identities as a Jacob never lurk very far beneath the surface.

Who we were, we are. But the glory of human growth is that we too, like our ancient ancestor, need not accept our shortcomings as defining. Instead, we can struggle with our own angels and wrestle with the demons that we retain from our youth.

While we will never obliterate the Jacob within, it is within our power to transcend him. We too can grow to become Israel.

Va-Yeshev/He Dwelt
Genesis 37:1–40:23

We meet Joseph as a seventeen-year-old who tattles on his brothers. Jacob favors Joseph, presenting him with an ornate, colored coat. This contributes to his brothers' jealousy, as do Jacob's recurrent dreams in which his entire family bows down to Joseph. Oblivious to the fraternal hostility, Jacob sends Joseph to report on how his brothers are faring while shepherding the flocks. A mysterious man directs Joseph to Dothan, where the brothers are gathered. When they see him approach, they plan to kill him, but Reuben persuades them to throw him into a pit instead. They strip Joseph of his coat and throw him into the pit. Then, sitting to eat, they spy a band of Ishmaelite and Midianite traders passing by. Judah suggests selling Joseph into slavery rather than letting him die, and Joseph is sold for twenty pieces of silver. Jacob refuses to be comforted over the supposed "death" of his son, saying, "No, I will go down mourning to my son in Sheol [the realm of the dead]." In Egypt, the Midianites sell Joseph to Potiphar, the chief steward of the pharaoh.

Meanwhile, back in Canaan, Judah marries a Canaanite woman, Shua, and they have three sons—Er, Onan, and Shelah. Judah marries his eldest son to Tamar, and when Er dies childless, marries Tamar to the next son, Onan. God kills Onan too, and Judah hesitates before giving up son number three. He tells Tamar to return to her parents' home and wait. Some years later, Judah's wife having died, he goes to Timna. Tamar dresses like a prostitute and sleeps with him, demanding his staff and his ring in lieu of payment. Months later, when he hears that she is pregnant, he orders her execution, but she presents his own emblems to him. He realizes that she is more in the right than he is, and she gives birth to twins, naming one Perez (the ancestor of King David and the Messiah) and the other Zerah.

In Egypt, Joseph quickly gains the favor of his new master, becoming his assistant in the house. There, Potiphar's wife lusts after Joseph, trying to force herself on him. When she fails, she accuses him of trying to rape her. Potiphar imprisons Joseph, but even there the chief jailer favors him.

Some time later, Pharaoh's baker and cupbearer are imprisoned. Each has perplexing dreams that trouble them. Joseph says to them, "Surely the Eternal One can interpret dreams," and when they recount their dreams, he informs the cupbearer that Pharaoh will soon pardon him. He then tells the baker that Pharaoh will find him guilty and execute him.

Events occur exactly as Joseph has predicted, but the cupbearer forgets about Joseph and his abilities as soon as he is restored to high office.

The Power of *Teshuvah*

Every year, during the Days of Awe, rabbis urge their congregants to repent of their wrongdoings of the previous year. This process of taking stock in ourselves, of examining our actions and our motivation, and of recognizing and regretting where we have gone astray is called *teshuvah* in Hebrew and "repentance" in English. It is the single most important value within rabbinic Judaism, the key to the entire system of mitzvot. Small wonder, then, that our holiest days are devoted to its pursuit.

How is *teshuvah* the key to Judaism? God and the Jewish people are linked through the *brit*, the covenant in which God promises to be our God and we promise to be God's people. That *brit* is concretized in the Torah and made real through the mitzvot. The 613 commandments of the Torah, with all the amplifications and interpretations of the rabbis, are obligatory on each and every Jew for all time. Yet even the most pious Jew cannot perform them all perfectly, and many of us are unable to always do even those mitzvot we find personally compelling. So what happens when a Jew fails to perform a mitzvah or violates a prohibition? Are we then always in a state of sinfulness? Are we forever barred from God's love?

For the system of commandments to work, there has to be a provision for how to wipe the slate clean in the case of an error or even an intentional sin. That corrective is *teshuvah*. God's love is bigger than any sin we might commit. After making it up to the person we have wronged, after attaining their absolution, all it takes to get God's forgiveness is a simple act of contrition; all it takes is *teshuvah*.

Teshuvah, then, is the linchpin that keeps Jews connected to God and engaged in mitzvot. Without it, our sins would simply mount irreversibly, and there would be no correction within the system. *Teshuvah* is the oil that keeps the machinery of Torah humming.

Paradoxically, however, there are few biblical embodiments of the act of *teshuvah*, few biblical figures who repent their sins and then are forgiven by God. Even the command to repent, while understood by the rabbis to come from the Torah, is itself a little murky. True, the book of Numbers records that "when a man or woman commit any sin . . . then they shall confess their sin." But this sentence, in context, goes on to mandate the making of a sin offering, a sacrifice to atone for the sin that was committed. Ever-careful readers of the Torah, the rabbis note that offering the sacrifice is preceded by an awareness that a sin was committed and implies a remorse about having erred. But separating *teshuvah* from sacrifice isn't explicitly mentioned until the prophets.

This parashah is understood to contain one of the few cases of *teshuvah* in the Torah. Reuben watches as his brothers decide to kill Joseph by leaving him in a pit. When he returns to the scene, they have already sold Joseph to the Midianites as a slave. Describing his return, the Torah says, "And Reuben returned to the pit." The verb used for "return" is *va-yashav*, the same verb as "to repent." One can translate the verse as "When Reuben repented at the pit."

Unlike his brothers, Reuben is filled with remorse. He realizes that he has allowed his brother to be wronged, and he returns to the pit to try to correct his sinful act, to restore his brother to freedom. Yet he arrives too late. Anguished, he turns to God. While the Torah never tells us where Reuben had gone, the rabbis fill in that lacuna through their powerful imaginations: "Where had he been? Rabbi Eleazar said, Reuben was taken up with his fasting and sackcloth, and when he became free he went and looked into the pit." Reuben did *teshuvah* and sat with sackcloth and ashes to mourn his tragic lapse.

In reward for that act of repentance, according to *Midrash B'raisheet Rabbah*, God said, " 'No one has ever repented after sinning before Me, and you are the first who has repented. As you live, your descendant will stand forth and be the first to urge repentance.' To whom does this allude, to Hosea, who cried out, 'Return, O Israel, to Adonai your God.'"

Because Reuben "discovered" *teshuvah*, he was rewarded by having that mitzvah expounded through one of his descendants, the prophet Hosea. Such is the greatness of *teshuvah*.

As the *Sefer Ha-Hinnukh*, a thirteenth-century Spanish listing of the mitzvot, explains, "The essence of *teshuvah* is sincere remorse in the heart over the past, and one must resolve not to do such a thing ever again. This confession is the essential part of repentance."

By offering himself as a model of *teshuvah*, Reuben cleansed his family name and gave a precious gift to his children and to us, his distant relations. Let us pray that we can use his model to stimulate our own introspection, repentance, and resolve.

Living Through Our Dreams

Human life is fleeting. We are born, we age, we busy ourselves, and we die. Viewed from the perspective of biology and materialism, our frenetic pace simply provides distraction before an inevitable doom. In that constricted space, our hearts yearn for something more—something significant and beautiful that can give life meaning and hope. Our lives are made full by our dreams.

Aspirations for a better tomorrow, hopes for a world of peace and plenty, of inclusion and freedom, of spirit and dance—these hopes keep us alive and help us to live our lives with purpose. Were it not for our dreams, the world would be too narrow and too cold to contain us. As Theodor Herzl observed, "Every creed of man was once a dream." Or to use more religious language, Rabbi Yehudah Ha-Levi exults, "A dream brought me into the sanctuaries of God."

Through our dreams, we imagine a world worthy of our efforts and responsive to our needs. Through our dreams, we preview ourselves as heroic, as larger than life in bringing that better tomorrow today. "A person's dreams are an index to their greatness," claimed the Hasidic sage Rabbi Z. Rabinowitz in the *Pri Tzaddik*. Dreams offer dress rehearsals for the reality yet to be.

Yet precisely because dreams provide a chance to see ourselves as significant, to view our contributions as substantial, they can also become vessels for our ambition and sources of jealousy to those in whom we confide. Such was the case for Joseph and his brothers. Naturally gifted, ebullient, and driven, young Joseph dreamed a dream in which his brothers and his parents bowed down to him, while he, standing tall and beautiful, received their adoration in the center of their circle. Small wonder that they became enraged, exclaiming to him, "'Do you mean to reign over us? Do you mean to rule over us?' And they hated him even more for his talk about his dreams" (Gen. 37:8).

Joseph was so captivated by the power of his dreams that he couldn't stop himself from sharing them with his family, couldn't stop to see his dreams from their perspective. And the brothers couldn't help but read those dreams as reflections of Joseph's vast ambition. Rabbi Ovadiah Sforno notes that "the details he told them proved to the brothers that Joseph was hoping that his dreams would be realized." Filtered through the prism of Joseph's pride and his brothers' fear, the dreams weren't beautiful at all; they were unbridled expressions of raw ambition. As Rabbi David Kimhi teaches, "If you have dreams of this kind, this only reflects dreams of power you entertain during the day."

The challenge to Joseph—and to us—is to take the time to see our dreams through the eyes of others. What may appear to us as a glorious future can seem to other parties involved as conquest, exploitation, or marginalization. We need to strive for a "God's-eye view," in which how our dreams appear to everybody can be factored into the unfolding of the dream into a more welcoming reality embracing the best for other people as well.

A world without dreams is too small for the human soul. But a world in which our dreams are projected onto the world without making room for each other is too brutal. Ultimately, Joseph and his brothers learned to bring each other into their dreams, recognizing that the greatest dream of all is the one God dreams for us: "On that day, all will be one, and God's name: One."

From Pride Comes Loneliness

In the development of Joseph's character and the events of his life, the Torah portrays a bittersweet lesson about the loneliness of pride.

On the surface, there is no reason for Joseph to be lonely. He is, after all, the favorite child of his father surrounded by eleven brothers in the midst of a bustling and energetic family. Joseph has the potential to fill his life with friendship, family, and love. Yet his need to be pre-eminent, his need to belittle the gifts and experiences of this family in order to glorify his own talents, isolate him from his own kin.

We get a clue about the extent of Joseph's pride from the very start. The Torah tells us, "Joseph, being seventeen years old, was still a lad." The rabbis of *B'raisheet Rabbah* struggle with that sentence. After all, if he is seventeen, he is no longer a mere lad. They suggest that the Torah is telling us that he behaves like a boy, "penciling his eyes, curling his hair, and lifting his heel." Like many people today, Joseph thinks he must invent a false and glamorous image in order to show his worth to himself and the world. As if that weren't sufficiently piti-ful, he also feels compelled to put others down in order to be noticed and appreciated.

His desire to be better than everyone else expresses itself even in his dreams. Twice Joseph dreams about his family bowing down before him, and twice he tells his family about his visions of his own superi-ority. His brothers, hurt and enraged by their sibling's arrogance, sell Joseph into slavery. Joseph experiences the depths of despair as an Egyptian slave and as a prisoner in an Egyptian jail.

In that prison, Joseph learns how to sympathize. He learns that prisoners at the bottom are still human beings and that one can excel without having to minimize the talents or interests of other people. In prison, Joseph accepts a basic principle of Jewish living: *Yisrael areivim zeh ba-zeh* (all of us are responsible for each other).

In prison, Joseph shows an interest in the dreams of a deposed but-ler and baker, and in caring for such "lowly people," he in fact plants the seeds of his own restoration and future glory. He learns that his own talent can thrive best with other people's well-being. Far from being a threat, the happiness of acquaintances, friends, and relatives form a supportive environment in which each of us can blossom.

Arrogance isolates, not skill. Ruthlessness, not drive, leads to loneliness.

By living in community, we can support each other to be the best that we can be. And in this way, we all serve to hasten the rule of God on earth.

Miketz/At the End

Genesis 41:1–44:17

Pharaoh dreams that seven sturdy cows are grazing by the banks of the Nile when they are swallowed by seven thin cows. He has a second dream in which seven healthy ears of grain are consumed by a stalk of seven parched grains. In a panic, Pharaoh seeks the meaning of his dreams, though none of his magicians or wise men can decipher them. It is then that the cupbearer remembers Joseph and tells Pharaoh of the Hebrew youth who can explain dreams. Pharaoh summons Joseph from jail and relates his two disturbing dreams.

Joseph explains that both dreams are one, foretelling seven years of abundance followed by seven years of famine. Joseph then offers some unsolicited advice to Pharaoh: find a man of discernment and wisdom to administer Egypt, so that the people can survive the next fourteen years. Pharaoh likes the plan and realizes that he won't be able to find another like Joseph, in whom Pharaoh senses the spirit of God, so he appoints Joseph as his prime administrator, giving him the name Zafenath-Paneah and a wife, Asenath. During the years of plenty, Joseph and Asenath have two sons, Manasseh and Ephraim.

The famine begins and is no less severe in Canaan, so Jacob sends his sons to procure food from the new vizier in Egypt. Joseph, now aged thirty, recognizes his brothers, although they do not seem to know him. He accuses them of being spies, and he tells them that to prove their innocence they must bring their youngest brother, Benjamin, to Egypt. He imprisons the brothers and then offers to let them all go free if one remains in the meantime. The brothers realize that they are being punished for their treatment of Joseph, and Joseph, overhearing their acknowledgment, goes off to cry in private. He keeps Shimon in prison, and the rest go home, discovering the money they had paid for the grain in the sacks of grain on the way.

At first, Jacob refuses to let them take Benjamin, but the severity of the famine forces him to relent. When they arrive in Egypt, Joseph takes them into his house and gives them a lavish feast, offering double portions to Benjamin. Again Joseph cries in private.

He then has his servants place his silver goblet in Benjamin's sack of grain. Once they set out for home, Joseph instructs his soldiers to pursue them, to accuse them of stealing the cup, and to search the sacks. Benjamin is caught, and Joseph threatens to enslave him, despite Judah, who steps forward to plead on Benjamin's behalf.

Dedication, Transformation, and Cleansing

We read *Parashat Miketz* during the celebration of Hanukkah, the commemoration of the rededication of the Holy Temple in Jerusalem almost two thousand years ago. In history, this period marks the assertion of Jewish national and religious freedom, a period of quasi independence that made it possible for Judaism to survive the onslaught of Roman rule in the centuries that followed. Spiritually, the image of a Temple rededicated invites introspection about our own internal rededication to our highest ideals, to correlate our ways with God's aspirations and mandate.

The miracle of the human capacity to refocus, to begin anew, to reconsecrate our deeds to a path of mindful compassion is a cause for wonder and for real celebration, and we can see that same remarkable burst of insight and vision in this parashah. Pharaoh has a dream: seven sturdy, healthy cows are grazing by the banks of the Nile, when seven sickly cows consume them. The monarch's official interpreters are befuddled and cannot correctly uncover the meaning of the dream, but God provides insight to Joseph, the righteous prisoner, who is then able to reveal the proper interpretation.

I often marvel at the miracle of the Hanukkah and Shabbat lights and just how different they are. The lights of Shabbat stretch into Jewish antiquity, a biblical commandment that links the generations, one candle "guarding" and the other "remembering" the Creation and the Exodus. These two candles reflect a lofty light, the elevated holiness of Shabbat. In contrast, the lights of Hanukkah are of relatively recent vintage, reflecting the practice of the rabbis of old, rather than the Torah itself. The Talmud records that these lights are to be placed where they can be viewed from the street, illumining the world and proclaiming the miracle of the Hanukkah story.

In his marvelous Torah commentary, *Ma'or Eynayim*, the Hassidic master Rabbi Menachem Nahum of Chernobyl (eighteenth-century Ukraine) reflects on this contrast between the elevated nature of Shabbat's holiness and the accessible warmth of Hanukkah's glow when he says,

> [T]he holiness of Sabbath is difficult to enter; Shabbat is very high and sublime, the name of God itself. How can a person enter into something so high as Shabbat? On Hanukkah, however, God is willing to come down, right down to where the person is, in order to draw the person near.

On Shabbat, our job is to elevate our thoughts and deeds to a level so lofty that we lift ourselves into the courtyards of the Divine. Through the ancient words of prayer, through study, through the mitzvot unique to Shabbat (including refraining from prohibited labors), we refine ourselves sufficiently to rise in holiness. But such an elevated holiness is difficult to maintain. Taken by itself, it can be a rigorous and forbidding path. Hanukkah offers a complementary path, one in which holiness descends to meet us at our level, welcoming us from the place we are at. As the *Ma'or Eynayim* continues:

> On Hanukkah, God descends to the people; God gives them light by which they may come back to God, a light that may even lead them to the high and most ecstatic form of God's service.

What is that "high and most ecstatic" way of integrating God's presence? The *Ma'or Eynayim* contrasts people who merely go through the motions (mitzvah observance without consideration of the deeper meaning or ethical purpose of the practice, Torah study without reflection on how those teachings mandate a practice of compassion and justice) with those who lead a more mindful religious life:

> There are people who perform mitzvot without any awareness of mind or understanding. . . . Such performance, however, cannot bring forth wisdom from above.

Hanukkah is the time to reconcile our religious observance with our moral vision, to light the world with the glow of goodness. The Festival of Lights is an opportunity to rededicate our hearts and minds to a consciousness of each other's needs, of our human connection, of our links to all of creation. By bringing awareness to our behavior, compassion to our ritual, and justice to our observance, we open a path for divine wisdom to bathe our world in light, as the *Ma'or Eynayim* affirms:

> Hanukkah is the time for a person to return to God by means of the Torah, just as happened in the days of Mattathias, the high priest. The Hellenists had defiled all the oil; all of wisdom had been corrupted. There remained but a single container of wisdom, that of Torah. . . . The oil of the candles refers to wisdom . . . teaching man how to serve God in a higher contemplative way.

May your lights burn bright, your service be wholehearted and mindful, and your illumination become a source for true liberation and joy!

Dare to Dream

When we speak of dreams, we mean two different things. On the most literal level, dreams are what we do in our sleep. Psychologists tell us that our dreams reflect the workings of our unconscious mind sorting through our fears, wishes, and desires, attempting to resolve whatever wasn't clarified during the preceding day. Our dreams often take the forms of weird narratives and juxtaposed images, all of which seem bizarre to our waking mind but adhere to a logic of their own. Dreaming is something that virtually all people do, and the vast preponderance of us can remember some of what we have dreamt the night before.

But to dream has a higher meaning as well. To dream can imply a sense of a larger vision of life, a sense that things could somehow be better than they are at present, and a direction for how to advance toward that goal. One mark of leadership is the ability to dream in this second, more profound way and to be able to persuade others to share in that dream, to make it their own.

After tracing the arrival of the new slave, Joseph, in the land of Egypt, the Torah tells us that he winds up in the house of Potiphar, where the illicit lusts of Potiphar's wife trap him. Condemned to prison, Joseph is more than just a model prisoner; he is also an inspired interpreter of dreams. Eventually, he gains quite a reputation for the accuracy of his interpretations, which always materialize with the passage of time.

Then the Torah relates, "Pharaoh dreamed." The Torah could have said that Pharaoh was puzzled by his most recent dream—that would tell us something we don't already know. But to simply tell us that Pharaoh dreamed? As the rabbis of *Midrash B'raisheet Rabbah* comment, "And don't all people dream?" So why does the Torah waste precious words to tell us something we could guess from common experience?

Obviously, it must be hinting at some deeper meaning, telling us something unique about the nature of his dream. In the words of the midrash, it is "true [that everyone dreams] but a king's dream embraces the whole world." The dreams of a monarch are different than the dreams of most of us, because the sovereign dreams about matters that affect entire populations. In our sleep, we may dream about a fight with our boss, an upcoming *simcha* (celebration), or someone we find attractive. But the dreams of kings are their visions, and their visions transform our lives and our world.

When the late Reverend Dr. Martin Luther King, Jr., wanted to train us to see the world through his visionary eyes, he told us, "I have a dream." His dream was of an America in which children of all races and creeds were free to make friendships and to nurture each other without regard to the color of their skin or the contours of their faith. By using the biblical language of dreams, Dr. King made it impossible not to be infected by his enthusiasm, his faith, and his righteousness.

The Torah uses dreams to give us new visions, to broaden our horizons beyond the limits of habit, convention, and expectation. The Torah trains us, through its *aggadah* (stories) and its *halakhah* (law), to see the world not merely as a place where different species wage an endless war for evolutionary supremacy, but also as a place where humanity, as God's messengers, brings all of creation closer to a time of universal harmony, security, and love.

In the transforming vision of another of the great men of the Torah, Moses, we learn that the rituals of Judaism are the essential tools for integrating the moral expectations of our tradition. The rituals teach us to remember to redeem the world and to love our fellow human beings. The stories teach us who we are and where we have come from. They connect us to our most distant ancestors and unite us with them and each other in a common cause and a shared destiny.

If great men and women have great dreams, then imagine just how grand God's dream must be. Perhaps we can also read the Torah and the words of the prophets as the expression of God's great dream— an age in which all humanity unites in the service of God, the inauguration of an age of justice and peace, using our minds to heal the sick and comfort the bereaved, to feed the hungry and shelter the homeless. Perhaps God's great dream, of a humanity that reflects God's image, not merely in potential but in actuality, is within our grasp. If we but dare to dream.

The Path to Perfection Isn't Perfect

One of the abiding truths of human nature is that we delight in discovering each other's faults and hate to reveal our own shortcomings. While we know in our hearts that "to err is human," none of us likes to acknowledge our own humanity, our own propensity to make mistakes, even to sin.

Yet error is the inevitable result of finite creatures doing their best, and sin is the unavoidable result of finite creatures giving in to their own finitude. There is simply no way for human beings to be perfect, and the very attempt to embody perfection can itself lead to the sin of arrogance and false pride.

This parashah focuses on one human being who is able to grow to accept his own humanity. After spending time in an Egyptian jail, Pharaoh's chief cupbearer had a dream that only Joseph, the lonely Hebrew slave, was able to interpret. Joseph told him that his dream was a portent of good tidings that he would soon be liberated from jail and that Pharaoh would restore him to his position of prominence at court. In exchange for bringing such good news, all Joseph asked in return was "to think of me when all is well with you again, and do me the kindness of mentioning me to Pharaoh, so as to free me from this place."

Of course, once he was liberated, the cupbearer was so taken with his own good fortune that he forgot Joseph and his jailhouse promise. Perhaps the memories of the jail were too painful to face; perhaps the cupbearer simply felt he had his good fortune coming to him anyway. For whatever reason, he didn't fulfill his promise to Joseph, with the result that Joseph continued to languish in prison.

Then one day in court, Pharaoh had a dream that filled him with fright. None of the magicians or sages of Egypt were able to interpret it; none could tell the king what his vision meant. As he saw the anguish on his sovereign's face, the desperate cupbearer suddenly remembered his own brush with dream interpretation and suddenly recalled the Hebrew boy in jail: "The cupbearer then spoke up and said to Pharaoh, 'I must make mention today of my offenses. Once Pharaoh was angry with his servants and placed me in custody in the house of the chief steward. . . . We had dreams . . . A Hebrew youth was there with us . . . and when we told him our dreams, he interpreted them for us.'"

Now the story proceeds to relate the encounter between Pharaoh and Joseph, with ponderous consequences for subsequent Jewish history. But for the moment, let's focus on the remarkable insight of the cupbearer. In a rare moment of honesty and insight, he recognizes his own ingratitude, his own sin in forgetting his promise to Joseph.

Midrash B'raisheet Rabbah understands his mentioning his own offenses as "'I have been guilty of two faults,' he confessed. 'One, that I did not deal kindly with Joseph and mention him to you; the other, that I saw you troubled about the interpretation of a dream, yet did not reveal to you that he knows its interpretation.'" From the perspective of the midrash, the cupbearer had sinned in neglecting his obligation to help Joseph out of his desperate straits. But he had also sinned in seeing Pharaoh's anguish and standing silently by when he was in a position to offer help. His silence when he could speak was an offense in itself.

Imagine his courage, when he could have simply continued his silence, in speaking out to Pharaoh, in confessing his own shortcoming. In doing so, he took a tremendous risk—the anger of Pharaoh, the scorn of the court. Yet his courageous stand, admitting his own fault publicly, was the necessary first step in correcting his error.

That first step is necessary for every one of us. Covering up our own sins can only perpetuate them. Only after we acknowledge our errors and denounce them can we hope to transcend and correct them.

Our salvation, as always, lies in honestly admitting our imperfections and then seeking the assistance of God, our families, our friends, and our communities in overcoming those flaws. The path to perfection begins with the admission that we are not perfect.

Va-Yigash/He Came Near
Genesis 44:18–47:27

In an act of great integrity, Judah steps forward and explains that he will allow himself to become a slave so that Benjamin will not have to do so, because their father so loves Benjamin that losing his favorite son, to whom his soul is bound, would kill him. Joseph is so moved by this clear evidence of Judah's repentance that he reveals himself to his brothers, crying so loudly that it can be heard even in Pharaoh's palace. Joseph explains that it was God's plan to send him to Egypt to make sure the family wouldn't starve during the famine, "so it was not you who sent me here, but God." He tells his brothers to hurry back to get their father and invites them to all live in Egypt, in the region of Goshen.

Pharaoh is pleased to learn of the reunion of Joseph's family, and he too invites them to move to Egypt. The brothers prepare to fetch Jacob, and Joseph instructs them to not be quarrelsome on the way.

Jacob and his family sleep in Beersheva overnight, and God visits Jacob one more time, assuring him that he need not fear going down to Egypt, for "I Myself will go down with you to Egypt, and I Myself will also bring you back." Jacob descends into Egypt with a party of seventy people. Joseph rides his chariot to greet his father, and the two men embrace and weep, as Jacob says, "Now I can die, having seen for myself that you are still alive."

Joseph instructs his family to claim that they are shepherds, whom the Egyptians abhor, since this will allow the Israelites to dwell apart in Goshen. Indeed, when Pharaoh has an audience with the brothers and Jacob, he grants them the region of Goshen. When Jacob appears before Pharaoh, he tells the ruler, "the years of my sojourn [on earth] are 130. Few and hard have been the years of my life, nor do they come up to the life spans of my fathers during their sojourns."

During the remainder of the famine, Joseph sustains his family and manages Egypt for Pharaoh. Under his guidance, Pharaoh acquires all the land in Egypt, as well as its people, who sell first their real estate and then themselves in exchange for sustenance.

What Are We?

If contemporary America were to pick a motto, it might well be "What have you done for me lately?" Each of us pursues individual happiness as we understand it. When the agenda of some outside organization intersects our own, we are willing to belong. But our belonging is usually pretty fragile—we belong on our own terms, for our own interests. If we're unhappy with a rabbi's sermon, we quit the synagogue; if we don't have time to attend their meetings, we quit the organization. In both instances, we rarely pause to ask whether or not the group does worthy work that requires our support. If we aren't getting gratification at that moment, we take our marbles and go home.

It wasn't always that way. In *Parashat Va-Yigash*, Jacob hears the joyous and unpredictable news that his son Joseph is still alive. He prepares to join him in Egypt and stops on his way at the ancestral worship site, at Beersheba. Once there, the Torah tells us, "he offered sacrifices to the God of his father Isaac."

I'm struck by Jacob's willingness to make sacrifices for his father's God. Jacob doesn't ask, "What's in it for me?" Instead, his guiding question is "What do I owe God? What does God expect of me?"

Judaism cannot survive unless Jews are willing to make sacrifices on its behalf. God can't make a difference in this world unless we are willing to maintain our posts regardless of personal gain. Needy Jews (and non-Jews too) won't be helped unless we provide the resources and energy necessary to ensure the presence and health of Jewish institutions and charities.

Once upon a time, Jews understood that communal institutions deserved their support and affiliation—not for what each individual got out of them at the moment, but because those institutions allowed us to take care of each other and to serve God. *Bikkur holim* committees visited the sick and made sure that no ill Jew was neglected or abandoned. *Hevra kadisha* committees ensured the proper and loving care for the remains of deceased Jews. *Menachem aveilim* committees provided shiva minyanim and comforted mourners while making sure they ate and maintained their health despite their sorrow. And, of course, minyanim ensured that a sizable company of Jews was always on hand to pray, to study, and to provide community to all who needed it.

Once upon a time, Jews gave to charities—both Jewish and non-Jewish—at a far higher rate than their Gentile neighbors. Members of those organizations didn't give of their time and their money because it felt good. They did so because that was what a mensch does. They, like Jacob, were prepared to make a sacrifice for the greater good of their fellow Jews, their fellow human beings, and their *brit* with God.

We're very good at part of Hillel's wisdom, recorded in the Mishnah: "If I am not for myself, who will be?" We're less attentive to his next line: "If I am only for myself, what am I?"

The problem with only staying involved when it serves our own interests is that we can no longer count on each other during our own moments of need. If we don't support synagogues, federations, and charities for the sake of others, why should others stay involved for us?

In a world in which everybody looks out for number one, we never add up to much. One plus one plus one equals one, the loneliest number of all. Perhaps making a sacrifice is a good investment after all.

The Depths of the Heart

Every human being is a mystery that never fully unfolds. Think for a moment about your own depths, how little about you actually makes it to the surface. How many of your desires, fears, quirks, and interests are subterranean—some known to a few, some known only to yourself, and a few hidden even from your own conscious thought? Like an eddy of water that the current passes by, the human soul has unplumbed depths that never fail to astonish, to delight, and to dismay.

The manifold layers of human personality are nothing new. They extend back to the earliest beginnings of humankind and find expression in our biblical heritage as well. In this parashah, Joseph is one whose hidden depths drive an entire story. At the pinnacle of his power and fame, when he was the second most powerful man in all of Egypt, his brothers appeared before him, although they were unaware of his true identity.

Imagine the *razim* (secrets) of Joseph. On the surface, he appeared to have everything—a wife, children, wealth, power, and good health. Who could know the secrets of his heart—his pining for his aged father, his desire for his brothers' love, his anger at how he had been treated, his regret for his own childhood arrogance? Perhaps it was that welter of hidden emotions that led him to devise the trap for his brothers. He planted a cup in Benjamin's sack, forcing the brothers to expect that Benjamin would be imprisoned, perhaps even executed, and that they would have to go to their father and witness his pain and sorrow at discovering the loss of another child.

Only someone very wise and very deep could attempt to speak to the surface and the depth of Joseph's heart. Speaking only to the surface risked ignoring the deeper causes that moved the surface. Addressing only the depths risked trivializing the very real threat of what appeared on the surface. The life of young Benjamin was at stake, as was the life of the great patriarch Israel. That wise someone, who had himself experienced sorrow, loss, and suffering, was Joseph's brother Judah.

And so, the Torah tells us, "Judah went up to his brother." The rabbis of antiquity, careful readers of Torah, understood the verb *va-yiggash* to mean that he drew close to Joseph, not just physically, but by speaking to his depth.

Thinking of the encounter between Joseph and Judah, *Midrash B'raisheet Rabbah* applies the proverb "The designs in someone's mind are deep waters, but a person of understanding can draw them out" (Gen. 20:5). The midrash explains that "this may be compared to a deep well full of cold and excellent water, yet none could drink of it. Then came one who tied cord to cord and thread to thread, drew up its water and drank, whereupon all drew water in that way and drank from it. In the same way, Judah did not cease from answering Joseph word for word until he penetrated to his very heart."

As the midrash portrays their encounter, Joseph had locked up all his pain, regret, shame, rage, and sorrow behind an impenetrable wall. No frontal assault could hope to release all his repressed feelings and grant him some peace, no superficial conversation could hope to handle his depths. Judah, made wise by his lifetime of living, made responsible by what had befallen him and his family, was able to speak to Joseph patiently, slowly, and persistently. As layer upon layer was peeled back, Judah was able to gain sight of the hidden Joseph within and was able to allow that true Joseph to come to the surface. Just as the one who gained access to the deep water made it possible for all who came later to drink, so Judah's patient listening and gentle encouragement allowed the true Joseph to surface and to remain on the surface.

Each of us can provide attentive listening and persistent questioning to those around us. All of us have our wounds, our secrets, our shame, our sorrow, and our rage. Often those scars feel so threatening that we wrap ourselves behind them and trap ourselves within, even as we distance ourselves from our friends and our families.

Judah allowed Joseph to emerge into the sunlight by giving him the most precious gift of all, the gift of soul. Through a willingness to truly listen, to truly care, and to truly be present, we too can give such a gift.

Enough Is Enough

An ancient midrash portrays Alexander III of Macedon, conqueror of the known world, standing at the gate of the Garden of Eden. He demands admission and is told that only the tzaddikim may enter there. Alexander becomes indignant; no one has treated this monarch with such indifference before. To try to save face, he insists that, at the very least, the angel guarding the gate should offer him something of great worth. So the angel gives him a human eyeball.

Puzzled, Alexander places the eyeball on a scale, and in order to determine its worth, he begins to load gold and silver on the other scale. No matter how much of the precious metal he adds, the eyeball outweighs it. Finally, the angel intervenes by covering the eyeball with a layer of dust. Unable to see the gold, the eyeball immediately and finally resumes its normal weight.

The explanation offered by the midrash is that the human eye always covets more than it has. No matter how much we possess, enough is never enough.

The infinite desire of humanity is the cornerstone of the harsh philosophy of Thomas Hobbes, who posited that life is "nasty, brutish, and short" because of the inevitability of human greed and the consequent violence that infinite desire will always generate.

What a difference, then, to see a Jewish role model who teaches the indispensability of setting limits to our own desires and simultaneously demonstrates that restraint is indeed within our reach.

Through all the long years of Joseph's servitude to Potiphar, his imprisonment in an Egyptian jail, his appearance in Pharaoh's court, and his elevation to the position of head minister during years of drought and famine, Jacob mourns the death of his beloved son. Inconsolable, Jacob knows the pain of loss—a suffering that has no end, no bottom.

Then comes miraculous news. His remaining sons return from Egypt loaded down with food, provisions, and gifts. Thrilled, they report to their father that Joseph is still alive, still in Egypt. After fainting, Jacob says, "It is enough. Joseph, my son, is still alive." Those brief words, "it is enough," stand in articulate dissent from the Hobbesian lust for more, more, more.

There is such a thing as enough. The restoration of love—between parent and child, between spouses, between friends—that is surely enough. A life lived with morality and purpose is surely enough. A community passionate in the service of God, that is clearly enough. As the Mishnah insists, "Who is rich? One who is happy with his portion."

Contentment is the only source of peace of mind. Satisfaction is still our only wealth. Love, after all, is the only possession. It is enough.

Va-Yehi/He Lived

Genesis 47:28–50:26

Jacob is ill, and Joseph takes his two sons and visits his ailing father. Jacob tells Joseph that he wants to claim Joseph's two sons, Ephraim and Manasseh, as his own, because of Rachel's early demise. Joseph takes them to his father's bedside, and Jacob embraces the boys, telling Joseph, "I never expected to see you again, and here God has let me see your children as well."

He then crosses his arms, blessing the eldest with his left hand and the younger with the right. When Joseph tries to correct him, Jacob insists, saying that the younger brother shall be greater than his sibling. Jacob blesses the boys, saying, "By you shall Israel invoke blessings, saying: God make you like Ephraim and Manasseh." Jewish parents use this same blessing for their sons to this day.

Jacob then summons his sons and offers them each a blessing in one of the Bible's finest poems. In his blessing, he does not omit areas of disappointment, such as Reuben sleeping with his concubine, or Shimon and Levi's violence against the residents of Shechem. Jacob assigns sovereignty to Judah—"the scepter shall not depart from Judah"—and interrupts his message to his sons to exclaim, "I wait for your deliverance, Eternal One."

Jacob concludes by asking to be buried with Abraham and Isaac in the Cave of Machpelah. When he dies, Joseph gets permission from Pharaoh to bury his father in Canaan, which he does with the entire court, and there he observes Shiva, the traditional seven days of mourning. Afterward, the brothers fear that Joseph will seek retribution, but he tells them, "Am I a substitute for God?" and assures them that they need not fear him.

Joseph lives to be 110 years old. Prior to his death, he extracts a promise from the Israelites that they are to carry his bones from Egypt and bury him in Eretz Yisrael when God brings them up from Egypt to the land promised to them.

Unlike the patriarchs (Abraham, Isaac, and Jacob), Joseph is buried in a coffin, following Egyptian custom.

Who You Gonna Call?

Ours is a society that almost worships titles. When foreign royalty visits the United States, the newscasters televise the thousands of Americans who wait for hours to fall on their knees for a king, a queen, or a prince. When the talking heads of radio or television want an authoritative fix on a current issue, they interview someone with a Ph.D., trusting the title to give the comments added weight and authority. When we need advice about children, we tend to ask people with letters after their name, whether or not they have ever been personally involved in raising children. The idea of asking actual parents rarely crosses our mind. After all, what could they possibly know?

So stymied are we by the challenges of life, that we are willing to put an almost blind faith in total strangers as long as some institution of higher learning will attest that they sat in classrooms, read the right books, and wrote a long and technical piece of research.

Now, far be it from me to seek to belittle the real value of education and the opportunity to grow in wisdom that added knowledge can provide. But I do want us to question the way we fall like lapdogs around the feet of anyone with a graduate degree, as though technical knowledge or professional skill always implies moral depth, compassion, or wisdom.

There are smart and dumb people with and without degrees; there are wise and benighted people with and without degrees. Erudition doesn't automatically correlate with common sense. What is needed, then, is the ability to discern who is truly wise, who is empathic, who is able to help. Those traits are essential today, and they were essential in the past too.

When the patriarch Jacob was about to die, "he called his son Joseph." Why Joseph? Joseph wasn't the eldest, nor was he the one destined to become the head of the Jewish people. So why did Jacob call Joseph to his deathbed?

We are hardly the first to ask that question. In fact, the sages of *Midrash B'raisheet Rabbah* asked the same question around fifteen hundred years ago. "Why did he [Jacob] not call Reuben or Judah? Reuben was the firstborn and Judah was king, yet he disregarded them and called Joseph. Why was this?"

Apparently ours isn't the only age to equate worth and social status. Reuben was the *bekhor* (firstborn). In biblical society, that was a mark of the favorite son who was entitled to inherit more than his younger brothers, the true heir to his father. Judah, as the ruler of the household, also had a claim to Jacob's attention at the fateful moment that his soul was to leave his body. Yet Jacob turned to Joseph, who was neither the eldest nor the head of the brothers. Why did the aged Jacob behave in such a strange way?

Answers the midrash, "Because Joseph had the means of fulfilling [his wishes]." Jacob called Joseph because he was simply the most suited for the purpose Jacob had in mind. Never mind that he lacked the title (of *bekhor*). Forget that he didn't have the position of leader of the family. What Joseph did have was the precise ability required to meet Jacob's needs at that crucial moment.

Joseph was able to see that Jacob adopted Ephraim and Manasseh, and Joseph was able to arrange for Jacob's burial in his beloved homeland, the Land of Israel. More than that, Jacob didn't need.

Perhaps this can serve as a role model for us as well. When we have a need, we should find the person with the attributes of soul, wisdom, and concern suitable to help us solve our problem or to achieve our goal. That doesn't always require a title.

I remember my first day in rabbinical school. Nervous beginning students, we met with the then-dean, Rabbi Joel Roth. Rabbi Roth told us to look around the room, saying that the people with whom we were studying were the greatest spiritual resource we would find during our studies and later on in life. I remember how struck I was by his wisdom, how true it has remained to this day. My peers, people who were going through what I was experiencing, were among the most helpful then and have remained lifelong friends since. Rather than letting us expect help only from our professors (many of whom were also wise and compassionate), Rabbi Roth was reminding us, as does the example of Jacob calling Joseph, to look to any available source for help, not simply to the favored few with titles, degrees, or status.

Comfort

Each of us is a greater theologian than we can possibly know. In the ways neighbors treat each other, in the ways parents raise children, in the ways lovers protect their beloved, we transmit profound and intangible lessons about the reality of the world. Take, for example, the baby who wakes up screaming. The parent who gets up in the dark to cradle the child teaches—without words—that when we cry out, there will be someone to cradle us. Most children have the luxury of parents and relatives who can offer them comfort. But who is there to comfort the adults? Who will comfort the comforter?

That same issue emerges with poignant power at the death of the great patriarch Jacob. Despite the fact that Joseph and his brothers had been reunited and lived in peace in Egypt together during Jacob's declining years, the brothers always shared a lurking suspicion that Joseph's forgiveness of them was false, that in reality he still bore a grudge against them. Perhaps Joseph was simply biding his time, not wanting to upset his aged father by adding yet another tragedy—total fratricide—to the long list of sufferings that poor Jacob had endured in his lifetime. Maybe Joseph, the second most powerful man in all of Egypt, was simply waiting for his father's death before wreaking revenge on his vulnerable brothers.

Up to this time, the vitality of their father had shielded them from the terror of life and of their imperious brother. But now that Jacob was dead, what was to become of them? The Torah tells us that Joseph hastened to reassure his terrified siblings: "He comforted them and spoke to their hearts."

Rabbinic tradition focused on that peculiar and striking phrase, speaking to their hearts. Whatever does that mean? Rashi, basing his commentary on *Midrash B'raisheet Rabbah*, explains that these were "words which were accepted by the heart." Joseph was able to put himself in his brothers' shoes, to imagine their terror and their weakness. Rather than exploiting their panic, rather than giving a lecture, he chose his words so that his brothers would be able to understand what he wanted to say, so that the comfort he intended would be received.

So often, we speak without considering how our listeners might hear our words. In getting it off our chest, we don't pause to reflect on what we have now dumped on the chests of others. Not so Joseph. He knew that his brothers needed assurance that he understood their fears and needed to know that he shared their estimation of what ought to happen. In English, we call that ability *empathy*. The rabbinic phrase is "what comes from the heart goes straight to the heart."

The only comfort Joseph could offer was to open his heart to his brothers. He truly listened to their concerns, and then he, in turn, shared his heart with them. From the depths of his heart to the depths of theirs, no misunderstanding, no distortion, no animosity could intrude.

In acting the way he did, Joseph offered a role model for us all to follow. We too can speak "heart to heart," trusting each other sufficiently to share the deepest parts of our souls, caring for each other enough to treat that revelation like the fragile treasure it is.

That lesson, like the caring parent in the dark of night, also points to a reality beyond the physical. Parents cradling a screaming infant demonstrate a trustability that will gird the child throughout his or her life. Reliable parents create *emunah* (the ability to trust). Ultimately, that ability to trust is a religious posture, an ability to feel at home in the cosmos, to feel at one with creation.

By demonstrating trustworthiness to his brothers, Joseph offered testimony to the trustworthiness of God as he had in jail. As *Midrash B'raisheet Rabbah* notes, "If Joseph could thus comfort our ancestors, . . . how much the more so will the Holy Blessing One comfort us, as it says, 'Comfort, O comfort, My people, says your God.'"

Parents pave the path for God, showing the little child that there is reason to trust. And the child in each of us need never feel abandoned, because there is still a Parent who loves us, every one.

True Love for a Patriarch

Put yourself in Jacob's place. Lying on his deathbed, he was filled with apprehensions about the special way of understanding God and the world that his grandfather Abraham established. It wasn't so long ago, he must have mused, that everyone worshiped a multiplicity of deities, that people sacrificed children to their gods, that they gashed themselves with knives as part of a religious fervor, that cultic prostitution was an integral part of worship.

Abraham's insight changed all that. By recognizing that the diversity of nature is only apparent, that beneath that variety is an underlying unity, Abraham was able to recognize that all things are linked to that one source of life and that the Source—God—demands justice, morality, and compassion. He and Sarah were able to transmit that heritage to only one of their sons, Isaac. Isaac and Rebekah were able to pass this vital truth on to only one of their sons, Jacob, who was also known as Israel. And now, nearing the end of his life, the weary patriarch must have feared for the future of this precious insight.

His twelve sons were an unlikely source of religious heroes. Marred by their propensity toward violence, their explosive tempers, and their jealousy, they had given Israel abundant cause for alarm throughout their young adulthood. Could he trust them to hold fast to the central legacy of Judaism—to one God who is passionate about ethics, who infuses moral fervor with ritual profundity?

Just before he was about to die, Jacob summoned his children to gather around his bed. He told his sons, "Come together that I may tell you what is to befall you in days to come." Then, rather than beginning his list of predictions, he interposed the comment "Assemble and hearken, O sons of Jacob; *ve-shim'u el Yisrael avikhem* (hearken to Israel, your father)."

The rabbis were struck by the unexpected disruption. Why didn't Israel simply continue with his predictions for each son? They also noticed that the language of this digression sounded very much like one of Judaism's most famous declarations: *Sh'ma Yisrael* ("Hear, O, Israel"). That had to be more than coincidence.

Midrash Devarim Rabbah makes explicit why Israel digresses and why this verse echoes the lines of the *Sh'ma*. From where did the Jewish people gain merit to recite the *Sh'ma*? From the death of Jacob, who called all the tribes and said to them, "Perhaps after I perish from the world you will worship other deities?" The sons responded to their father, "Hear, O Israel, Adonai is our God, Adonai alone."

The rabbis used the fact that the third patriarch, Jacob, was also called Israel. Thus, the *Sh'ma* could be understood as an address not to the Jewish people, but to Jacob himself. The use of similar language between the *Sh'ma* and what Jacob said to his sons confirms that reading. So the midrash develops a dialogue between the patriarch and his descendants. Fearful that they maintained a superficial loyalty to Judaism out of deference to him, Israel asked them whether they would turn from Judaism once he died. In unison, the sons responded, "Listen, Dad, Adonai—the God our great-grandfather recognized as the exclusive sovereign of the world—is our only God. We'll stick with it, not for your sake, but for our own and for God's."

In response to his sons' fidelity and conviction, Jacob exclaimed, "*Barukh Shem Kevodo l'olam va-ed* (praised be God's glorious sovereignty throughout all time)."

The *Sh'ma*, then, becomes a living drama in which the latest generation of Jews promises those who have come before us that our loyalty is undimmed by years, that our faithfulness to the covenant of Abraham and Sarah; Isaac and Rebekah; Jacob, Rachel, and Leah still motivates our deeds and informs our identity.

How many Jews remember keeping a kosher home to care for an observant grandparent or parent? And how many have allowed those precious practices to evaporate, the inheritance of millennia past vanishing in the short space of a single lifetime?

Isn't it time to stand with the children of Jacob, swearing our renewed loyalty to the Jewish calendar and the sacred deeds and practices of our ancient heritage, to renew our loyalty to the God of Israel? Can we, in all honesty, conjure the memories of *bubbes* (grandmothers) and *zeydes* (grandfathers), of childhood rabbis and great scholars, of martyrs and leaders of our people throughout history and tell them that their God is still our God, that their legacy is apparent in the food we eat, the rituals we observe, and the deeds of loving-kindness that we practice?

Can we give Jacob the same assurance and comfort that his sons were able to provide?

Exodus

Sh'mot

———⟶►◄⟵———

Names

Sh'mot/Names

Exodus 1:1–6:1

A new king arises over Egypt who does not know Joseph and fears that the Israelites pose a threat to his power. The new pharaoh forces them to perform brutal labor, building the garrison cities Pithom and Rameses. Despite the bitterness of slavery, the Israelites continue to thrive, so Pharaoh orders the Hebrew midwives, Shiphrah and Puah, to kill any Jewish boy at birth. The midwives are pious, however, and they don't follow Pharaoh's order. Pharaoh then orders every Egyptian to throw the Israelite boys into the Nile to drown them.

A Levite woman, Yocheved, bears a son and hides him for three months. She then fashions a wicker basket to float her son down the Nile, hoping that he might survive. The baby's sister, Miriam, follows on the shore and sees Pharaoh's daughter take the child as her own. Miriam offers the services of her mother as wet nurse. Pharaoh's daughter names the child Moses.

When Moses is an adult, he walks among the slaves, seeing their oppression. He is so outraged by the sight of a taskmaster beating a slave that he kills the Egyptian. The next day, he tries to stop two Hebrews from fighting, and one accuses him, "Who made you chief and ruler over us?" Pharaoh tries to kill Moses, who flees to Midian. By a well, he defends the seven daughters of Jethro, the priest of Midian, against other shepherds, and the women invite him home. He stays and marries one of the daughters, Zipporah. They have a son whom Moses names Gershom, meaning, "I was a stranger in a strange land."

Pharaoh dies, and God determines to free the Israelites. Moses sees a bush that burns but is not consumed. God calls from the bush, commanding Moses to remove his shoes, since he is standing on holy ground. Then God tells Moses that he is to go to the new Pharaoh and insist that he let the Israelites go. To bolster Moses's credibility, God reveals the special divine name, Ehyeh-Asher-Ehyeh (I will be *what/that I will be). God instructs Moses to turn his rod into a snake to convince the people of his authenticity.*

As Moses sets out for Egypt, God tells Aaron, his brother, to meet him in the wilderness. They assemble the elders of Israel, and the people, who are now convinced to follow Moses. Moses and Aaron then appear before Pharaoh, demanding in the voice of the Holy One that Pharaoh "Let My people go that they may celebrate a festival for Me in the wilderness." Pharaoh refuses and orders the taskmasters to make the Israelites' labor even more onerous.

Who Are the Elders for Our Time?

One of the most moving speeches I have ever heard was a Kol Nidre appeal of Sherry Miller, a past president of Congregation Eilat. She spoke lovingly of her childhood memories of her *bubbe* (grandmother) and *zayde* (grandfather) and of the many beautiful Shabbat meals she had enjoyed with them in her youth.

She recalled helping her *bubbe* set out the candlesticks and the white candles for the Sabbath, and she spoke of napping with her *zayde* on Friday afternoon and then watching him pour the glistening red wine into the kiddush cup as he prepared to intone the blessings that would commence their weekly, sacred celebration.

As my eyes (and those of other congregants) filled with tears at the force of her emotions and the beauty of her memories, she then asked us who would make the Jewish memories for our children and our grandchildren now. Who would be the elders of today, so that tomorrow our children and grandchildren might know Judaism?

One of the great insights of historical Judaism is the recognition that a healthy faith tradition requires the active involvement and leadership of its elders. Only they can transmit the life-wisdom and the depth of experience necessary to provide insight into the challenges of every day, and only they can muster the unconditional love necessary to persuade their children and grandchildren to keep our sacred covenant alive.

No one can take the place of elders, and the degree to which they are willing to lead by love and example and to which they are granted dignity and respect is the measure of the vitality of their Jewish community.

This parashah highlights the importance of elders in a particularly dramatic fashion. Thrilled and frightened by the call of God, Moses wastes no time in inducting his brother, Aaron, as his ally. The first official action of these two leaders is that they "went and gathered together *kol ziknei b'nei Yisrael* (all the elders of the children of Israel)." Moses and Aaron knew that the only way a project of such magnitude—to persuade the Jewish people to trust in God and work toward their own liberation—could hope to succeed was if they could enlist the support and participation of Israel's elders.

In *Midrash Sh'mot Rabbah*, Rabbi Akiva (second-century Israel) presents the importance of elders in a beautiful metaphor: "Why is the people Israel compared to a bird? Just as a bird can only fly with its wings, so Israel can only survive with the help of its elders." Rabbi Akiva recognized that only when children grow up in a Jewish home will they come to transfer the love they feel for their parents and grandparents to their heritage as well. But his metaphor suggests something more. Wings are not only the bird's indispensable mode of transportation, they are the essence of what it means to be a bird (imagine a bird without wings). So too, elders are the essence of what it means to be Jewish (imagine Judaism without grandma and grandpa, or without sages!). Rabbi Akiva is telling us that if we want Judaism to survive, then we must act as though we are its elders, so that our youth see Judaism as a priority in our deeds.

Let our children and grandchildren see our eyes occupied with studying Torah, with reading a Jewish book, so their vision will be trained for lifelong learning. Let them see our hands occupied with mitzvot—building sukkot, feeding the hungry, binding tefillin, wearing *tallitot*, and visiting the sick—so their hands will be strengthened for the task ahead. Let their tongues repeat our own Shabbat *zemirot* (songs) and our passionate debates so their voices will one day be joined in the age-old dialogue that unites the generations. And let their hearts fill with joy as we celebrate the holy days and festivals, travel with them to Israel, drive them to Jewish camps, and create Jewish memories within our own homes.

In doing those things, we make ourselves worthy elders, regardless of our age, and earn the tribute of the midrash: "Great is eldership, for if the elders are old, they are beloved before God, and if they are young, their youth is but of secondary consequence."

Can a Good Jew Question God?

We all expect religious leaders to stand up for God and for the world as it is, to justify God's ways to a questioning and troubled congregation. After all, if God is the greatest possible being, then God's creation should be the best of all possible worlds. Jews who would like to believe in a loving and powerful God, a God who is just and good, often come to their rabbi hoping that this spiritual leader will make sense of tragedy and show how what appears unjust is really part of a higher order.

We don't expect our leadership to question (and challenge) God's order. If rabbis question God, then how can the rest of us have faith? If they don't see the world as orderly and loving, then how can the rest of us know peace?

Just as we expect our rabbis to demonstrate untroubled devotion to point the way for us all, the rabbis of antiquity turned to the rabbi of all rabbis, Moshe Rabbenu (Moses our Rabbi), as the embodiment of all that a spiritual leader should be. Inspired by his remarkable infancy, by his miraculous encounter with the burning bush, and his courageous confrontation with Pharaoh, Moses certainly seems to exemplify all the characteristics a rabbi should have. But then the Torah recounts a most troubling accusation.

After appearing before Pharaoh, Moses and Aaron are appalled to learn that Pharaoh has responded to their demands for freedom by increasing the slaves' suffering. Of course, the Israelites blame Moses for their new agonies, telling him, "May Adonai look upon you and punish you for making us loathsome to Pharaoh and his courtiers." Moses is so tormented by their rage that he turns to God and says, "Adonai, why did You bring harm upon this people? Why did You send me? Ever since I came to Pharaoh to speak in Your name, he has dealt worse with this people; and still You have not delivered them."

The rabbis of *Midrash Sh'mot Rabbah* found that outburst shocking: "It is usual that when one person asks another, 'Why have you done this?' the question is asked out of anger, yet Moses says it to God!?!"

In fact, they develop Moses's short exclamation into a cogent and forceful use of logic against the Holy One:

> I have perused the book of Genesis and read the doings of the generation of the Flood and how they were punished, and that was deserved; also how the generation of Sodom, which witnessed the separation of the races, was punished, and that it deserved its punishment too. But this people, what has it done to be more enslaved than all preceding generations? Is it because of [the doubts expressed by] our father Abraham? . . . Then Esau and Ishmael, being his descendants also, should have been subjected to slavery too; moreover, the generation of Isaac or Jacob should have been the ones subjected, rather than my own generation!

Moses finds God's treatment of Israel unjust: not only does God let the people suffer unfairly, but God still hasn't brought about their deliverance. Moses poses the challenge directly, expecting God to meet his high expectations and his own understanding of what constitutes justice.

In the midrash, Moses even responds to the answer offered by too many theologians that God's salvation is just around the corner: "I know that you will one day deliver Israel, but what about those who have been immured in the buildings?" In other words, those who have already suffered and died at the hands of the cruel taskmasters won't derive comfort from a salvation yet to come. Future redemption does not justify past or current oppression.

In response to this, God's "attribute of justice sought to strike Moses." Why did God allow him to air such heretical thoughts? "After God saw that Moses argued this way only because of his devotion to the people Israel, God did not allow the attribute of justice to strike him."

Questioning God's justice is actually an assertion of love and loyalty to those who are suffering; it shows an inner passion for justice and goodness. Because of that passion, questioning God's justice is really a form of loyalty; only someone with a commitment to morality and ethics could have an ethical problem with the way the world works. We don't question the ethics of a spider eating a fly, because we don't expect morality there. But we do expect morality from God, out of our loyalty to God and our loyalty to the Torah as an expression of God's morality.

Questioning God's ways, even expressing disappointment or anger at the pain of living, shows the expectation that the universe is morally accountable, which only makes sense in the context of religious faith. Questioning God is, in fact, an affirmation of loyalty to the Torah, an act of loyalty to God and to humanity.

Yirat Shamayim: Fear of Heaven

With the opening of *Sefer Sh'mot* (the book of Exodus), the Torah moves from cosmic origins to the role of God in salvation and history. As the Israelites find themselves in a descending spiral of servitude and suffering, their call to God unleashes the ultimate conflict between the very wellsprings of life and liberation that we recognize as God and the embodiment of tyranny and pointlessness epitomized by Pharaoh. This is not merely a contest between two unequal rivals, but the steady opposition of two incompatible ways of organizing one's life, of structuring a society, of moving through time. Life versus death, freedom versus tyranny, ultimate meaning versus personal pleasure—these are the archetypal poles between which human destiny plays out.

Into that explosive struggle, the Torah shines a light with the bold courage of the most unlikely of sources: two Hebrew midwives. Birth and death are never far removed from the contest over competing values, and Pharaoh escalates his forces of death by ordering the midwives to murder the Israelite boys. Despite these instructions from the world's most powerful despot, "The midwives, fearing God, did not do as the king of Egypt had told them; they let the boys live."

What is the nature of this "fear" that could motivate such courageous dissent? Jewish tradition steps in to make the chasm of Pharaoh's edict and the midwives' stance all the more impressive. Says the Talmud, keeping the boys alive meant that the midwives "supplied them with water and food." The medieval sage Rabbi Abraham

Ibn Ezra explains, "Even more than at first, they now worked with all their strength to save the children." How can we explain their daring and their disobedience?

There are two ways to understand the *yira* (fear) the Torah mentions. Later Jewish traditions understood a lesser fear to be the fear of God's punishments. Such a motivation was viewed with some disdain, as not really worthy of the realm of faith and holiness.

What the *Zohar* calls "holy fear" and Rabbi Yosef Albo calls "noble fear" is not the fear of consequences. It is awe that emerges from the contemplation of God's incomparability, greatness, and magnificence. *Yira* involves marvel, wonder, and awe—that is, for David Ibn Daud, the "awe of greatness" as opposed to a mere "fear of harm." It was this holy fear that moved these two brave women.

Such awe is different than our common fears. The Hasidic commentary *Mei ha-Shiloach* notes, "When one fears a person, one cannot remain calm, because fear is the opposite of being calm. However, awe of heaven brings calm to the soul. . . . As the midwives were calm because of their awe of heaven, they did not have any fear of Pharaoh's decrees."

Fear of heaven is a step toward liberation of the soul. A soul that trembles before human displays of might, power, or influence is one that has not really apprehended the vastness of the cosmos, the frailty of even the most imposing personage, the sheer wonder of life and being—the greatness of God. To focus the mind on that greatness, to mold one's consciousness around the radical majesty of God's presence—that is the spur that faith offers toward freedom. As the medieval compendium *Orhot Tzaddikim* realizes, "This fear is really love."

Small wonder, then that this virtue, *yirat shamayim*, is so basic. Rabbi Bahya Ben Asher tells us that fear of heaven is "the foundation of the entire Torah," and the *Orhot Tzaddikim* insists that "the Torah is of no use to an individual but for *yirat shamayim*, for it is the very peg upon which everything hangs." The contemporary sage Rabbi Louis Jacobs insists, "Religion without *yirat shamayim* is no more than a sentimental attachment to ancient forms from which the spirit has departed."

Yirat shamayim is the beginning of an inner liberation from the tyranny of human opinion and coercion. Imagining the sublimity and dignity of God, the pressures of conformity or social consensus pale to insignificance. For the Hebrew midwives, fear of God was a way of seeing Pharaoh for who he was—simply another human being, seeking to silence his own fear and fragility by bullying the weak. It was their awe and wonder at God's greatness that imbued these women with clarity about their own real greatness—the opportunity to shine God's light in a murky and hurting world.

Va-Era/He Appeared
Exodus 6:2–9:35

God summons Moses to demand that Pharaoh free the Israelites and to establish a unique relationship: "I will take you to be My people, and I will be your God." Moses objects that he has a speech impediment, so God appoints Aaron to be the spokesman. God explains that Pharaoh's heart will be hardened to demonstrate the extent of God's might to the Egyptians. Moses and Aaron appear before Pharaoh and cast down Moses's rod, turning it into a snake. Pharaoh's magicians are able to replicate this wonder, although Moses's snake swallows theirs. Pharaoh still refuses to listen. The next morning, Aaron and Moses go to the banks of the Nile. They strike the water with the rod, the Nile turns to blood, and all the fish in it die. Again Pharaoh's magicians replicate this wonder, and Pharaoh refuses to concede.

After seven days, God tells Moses to threaten Pharaoh with a plague of frogs. There come to be so many of them that they cover the entire land, and Pharaoh asks Moses to plead with God to remove them. Moses agrees to do so in order to show Pharaoh that there is none like the Lord our God. The frogs die, yet Pharaoh still refuses to heed God's will. Aaron holds out his arm, striking the dust with his rod, and a plague of lice swarms throughout Egypt. The magicians' attempt to replicate this action fails completely, and they recognize that it is indeed the finger of God.

Pharaoh still refuses to relent.

Moses threatens a plague of locusts, which devour the crops. Pharaoh summons Moses and Aaron, permitting the people to leave and sacrifice to God if they will but plead with God to remove the insects. Once this is done, however, Pharaoh reneges on his agreement to let the Israelites go.

The next day, the plague of pestilence wipes out the Egyptian livestock, while the livestock of the Israelites remain healthy. Pharaoh still refuses to free the slaves.

Moses and Aaron throw up handfuls of soot, which become a fine dust throughout Egypt, causing boils on the people and the remaining animals. This inflammation is so severe that it strikes the magicians themselves, but Pharaoh's heart remains hard.

Moses announces that the next plague will be hail, and those Egyptians who revere God take their slaves and livestock inside. The hail is so heavy, fire flashing in its midst, that it wreaks widespread devastation.

There is no hail in Goshen. Pharaoh asks Moses to intervene, but once the hail stops, he again refuses to liberate the slaves.

Compassion Is a Jewish Value

Having enslaved the Jewish people, Pharaoh sought to destroy their spirit by exhausting their bodies. Desiring total control over their hearts and souls, the idolatry that Pharaoh wanted to impose came at a very high cost; his insistence that true power is ruthless, that supremacy is something to be imposed continued to rear its ugly head, continued to assault the biblical tradition and those who loved it. No mere relic from antiquity, our century has more than its share of those who believed that their lofty visions could justify any cruelty they needed to inflict to cement their hold on power.

The alternative—to suggest that true power must be wedded to kindness, that abiding strength is that which offers solidarity and nurturance—risks making one look weak. Now, as in the past, those whose convictions impel them to reach out to the outcast and the despised are themselves cast out with scorn. Then, as now, Pharaoh knew that cultivated ruthlessness would please the "realists" of the court and would instill fear and obedience in the hearts of the people.

Pity poor Moses, who had to stand up not merely against this particular pharaoh, but against the kind of heartless, self-serving power that this pharaoh (and all pharaohs of every age) embodied. Moses could rely on no armies to enforce his edicts, no chariots to defend his people. Instead, in seeking the liberation of the slaves, all Moses could utilize were his stirring words and the power of an idea so pure that it has reshaped the world: "Let my people go!" Over and over, Moses repeated this incantation of freedom to the Egyptian king, confronting Pharaoh with a witness to power based on the dignity of each human being and the holiness of all living things.

Compassion was not very persuasive in Pharaoh's court, just as it is pretty unpersuasive in today's court of public opinion. Yet compassion was at the very core of Moses's mission to fashion a sacred and just community in the service of God.

When words failed, Moses turned to a more conventional sort of persuasion, unleashing the plagues that afflicted Pharaoh and his courtiers and eventually resulted in the Israelites' liberation. Yet even within that display of a clearly intimidating and coercive power, God continued to show a caring and concern for humanity and for creation.

God told Moses to appear before Pharaoh and to say, "I will rain down a very heavy hail, such as has not been in Egypt from the day it was founded until now. Therefore, order your livestock and everything you have in the open brought under shelter; every man and beast that is found outside, not having been brought indoors, shall perish when the hail comes down upon them!"

Even at the very height of this divine display of power against evil, God still sought to protect the innocent and to care for the animals. As the rabbis of the ancient midrash *Sh'mot Rabbah* commented, "See the extent of God's compassion: even in a moment of anger, God has compassion on the wicked and on animals."

True, there are occasions when compassion alone will not suffice. Such a conflict motivated God to strike against Pharaoh and his legions. Yet even in such a conflict, the victory emerges from being able to retain what is distinctive and moral and better. To completely abandon compassion would be to become just a bigger Pharaoh. Rather than a victory, this would be a loss.

God bests Pharaoh while expressing compassion. Egyptians who were willing to break with Pharaoh's cruelty and see the humanity of their Israelite slaves and the holiness of Israel's God earned God's protection and love.

In our day too, that distinction needs to be reiterated time and time again. Compassion need not entail weakness, nor does empathy require abandonment of traditional values. From the time that Moses stepped into Pharaoh's court, compassion has been a traditional value, and care of the suffering a biblical mandate.

Fanning the Flames of Freedom

There are striking parallels between Moses and Reverend Dr. Martin Luther King, Jr., the great African-American civil rights leader. Both were remarkably courageous leaders who had the courage to insist on nothing less than liberty and justice for their oppressed people. Both suffered the initial derision of powerful leaders who belittled their mission. And both lived to see their oppressors forced to concede respect and deference to their noble efforts. Moses and Dr. King had a lot in common.

The same is true of another great black leader of an earlier time, one who has been explicitly compared to Moses—Harriet Tubman. A remarkable woman, she was a former slave who escaped and then returned to the South many times to assist other men and women to find freedom. Like Moses, she led her people out of slavery. Walking into a classroom of the religious school at a local synagogue, I spotted a book about Harriet Tubman that the children were reading. I opened it and noticed that it spoke about her in glowing terms, even mentioning that she met the president of the United States. What caught my attention, however, was not the praise lavished on her, but that the textbook didn't mention the name of the president!

Today, we all know the name Harriet Tubman. But how many people know about the lives of Franklin Pierce or James Buchanan? In their time, these men were the leaders of the nation—powerful and wealthy, heads of state, known throughout the land. Today, only true history buffs know their life stories. But the former slave woman inspires schoolchildren everywhere with her simple decency and her tenacious courage.

These reflections pertain to *Parashat Va-Era* as well. Moses is known and loved throughout the world. Liberation movements the world over recall Moses as inspiration for their own struggles against oppression. Yet the name of the Egyptian king who opposed him is completely unknown. The Torah tells us his title (pharaoh) just as the textbook told us the title of the nation's leader (president). But the name isn't significant enough to mention.

Isn't it odd that the most powerful potentate of his age is now unknown—a foil for the heroic former slave, Moses. And James Buchanan is simply a backdrop to the reflected glory of Harriet Tubman. Power may be fun, and prominence may thrill the heart, but what lasts across the ages is loftier stuff: justice, compassion, courage, and a willingness to fight for the dignity and freedom of one's fellow human beings.

Want to be famous? Enlist as a soldier in the struggle against human suffering and oppression. In standing up for his people, Moses cast a glow that will inspire generations until the end of time, and in liberating her people, Harriet Tubman lit a torch that will blaze in human hearts forever. Got a match, anybody?

The Hope Discovered in Despair

We live in trying times—terror around the globe, freedom under siege, poverty and starvation throughout the world, persistent ignorance and bigotry despite great efforts. It is easy to despair of a better tomorrow, to throw up our hands in hopelessness against the entrenched resilience of evil, of suffering, of hate.

We are surely not the first to feel the urge to surrender. *Parashat Va-Era* recounts our ancestors' brush with despair. Having survived centuries of slavery in Egypt, they were shocked and elated by the good news brought to them by Moses. God had heard their cry. Liberation was at hand! The Torah recounts that they believed in Moses, and yet the awaited liberation did not come. Having their hopes raised to almost unimaginable heights and then dashed down as the painful reality of their enslavement continued, the Israelites abandoned their dreams of freedom. The Torah recounts, "They would not listen to Moses, their spirits crushed by cruel bondage" (Exod. 6:9).

Many of the great Torah commentators of the medieval period worked to explain the nature of the Israelites' despair. Rashi recognized that "they did not accept consolation." He noticed that the Hebrew expression for "crushed spirits" is the same as for "shortness of breath." Using that similarity as his springboard, Rashi taught, "Anyone who is under stress is short of wind and breath and is unable to breathe deeply." The weight of slavery was so onerous, the pain of lost hope so searing, that the Israelites' very breath was constricted.

Abraham Ibn Ezra noticed that the Hebrew expression could also mean "impatience." He tells us, "Israel did not hearken nor pay attention to the words of Moses, as their spirit was impatient because of the length of their exile and the hard labor." For Ovadiah Ben Jacob Sforno, the gap between their expectation and reality was too great for hope to exist: "It did not appear believable to their present state of mind, so that their hearts could not assimilate such a promise."

Most intriguing of all, perhaps, is the psychological insight offered by Rabbi Hayim Ben Attar (seventeenth-century Morocco, Italy, and Israel). He understands that new hope can make suffering even harder to tolerate. The closer liberation comes, the more difficult it is to tolerate one's oppression: "The people had good reason for becoming impatient at their fate, because when Moses had come, he had given them hope that their liberation was close at hand. This had given them a new and broader perspective on life."

These insights illumine the nature of despair: it can be physically devastating; it can preclude the acceptance of good news; and hope itself can make a bad reality even less acceptable. There is yet one more comment to make about despair. There are insights that can only be accessed from a place of despair. There are times when only by hitting rock bottom, by being forced to abandon our own self-centeredness or sense of control, that we can become open to help from beyond. Only when we despair of ourselves can we then reach beyond ourselves for consolation and help. In the brilliant words of Rabbi Abraham Joshua Heschel,

> Only those who have gone through days on which words were of no avail, on which the most brilliant theories jarred the ear like mere slang; only those who have experienced ultimate not-knowing, the voicelessness of a soul struck by wonder, total muteness, are able to enter the meaning of God, a meaning greater than the mind. There is a loneliness in us that hears. When the soul parts from the company of the ego and its retinue of petty conceits; when we cease to exploit all things but instead pray the world's cry, the world's sigh, our loneliness may hear the living grace beyond all power.

Abandoning the pretense of our own self-sufficiency can open doors to a deeper sustenance. Releasing our own delusions of power and control can permit us to flow with currents far more profound than our own. Turning our destiny back to the One who actually writes the script can be both liberating and a source of deep illumination.

By feeling the fullness of despair, the Israelites became open to the possibility of liberation. Perhaps we too need to invest less energy in distracting ourselves from our sorrows and open ourselves to their embrace, to our consequent transformation.

Bo/Go
Exodus 10:1–13:16

Sending Moses to Pharaoh again, God clarifies the pedagogy behind the plagues: "that you may know that I am the Lord." Moses and Aaron tell Pharaoh to free the Israelites or face a another plague of locusts. Pharaoh's courtiers are disheartened, and they too entreat Pharaoh to relent. Pharaoh is willing to let the men go to worship God but insists on keeping the women and children. Moses responds, "We will go, young and old. We will go with our sons and daughters." Pharaoh refuses to permit the entire people to go.

Moses holds out his rod, and God brings an east wind, which covers the land with locusts. They devour every remaining plant, fruit, grass, and tree in Egypt. Pharaoh summons Moses and Aaron, admits his guilt before God, and asks Moses to intercede. When Moses does, God removes the locusts, but Pharaoh's heart is hardened, and he refuses to let the Israelites go.

Moses stretches out his arm, and God brings a plague of darkness so thick it can be touched. It covers the land for three days, while all the Israelites enjoy light in their dwellings. In a panic, Pharaoh is willing to permit the people to go but insists that the flocks and herds remain behind. Moses refuses, and Pharaoh kicks him out, saying that if he sees Moses again, the Israelite will die. Moses responds that his words are confirmed above; the two will never again meet. God turns the hearts of the Egyptians to the Israelites, and Moses is highly esteemed by the Egyptian people. The Israelites "borrow" objects of silver and gold from the Egyptians, who willingly give them over.

The final plague is the death of the firstborn.

The establishment of the festival of Pesach (Passover) interrupts the progression of plagues. On the tenth day, each household selects a lamb (or joins with other families and shares a lamb). When the lamb is slaughtered, its blood is spread on the doorposts, and its flesh is roasted and eaten in its entirety that same night, with matzo (unleavened bread) and marror (bitter herbs). Throughout the week of Pesach, the Israelites are to eat only unleavened bread and remove all traces of hametz (leaven) from their possession. This celebration is for all generations: "When your children ask you, 'What do you mean by this rite?' you shall say, 'It is the Passover sacrifice to the Eternal One, because God passed over the houses of the Israelites in Egypt when God smote the Egyptians, but saved our houses.'"

In the middle of the night, God strikes down the firstborn Egyptian boys. The outcry of the Egyptians is so great that even Pharaoh awakes. He summons Moses and Aaron and tells them to leave with the entire Israelite people and their flocks and herds. Along with the Israelites, other peoples also flee to freedom.

Tefillin: Bound for Greatness

Ask anyone in a Jewish audience to create a mental image of a "pious Jew" and chances are good that the vision will be male and wear a head covering; a tallith; and tefillin, the leather boxes containing four biblical passages that are worn on the forehead and wrapped around the arm.

The first reference to these holy items is found in this parashah. Speaking about the miraculous liberation of the Israelite slaves, the Torah recounts God's instruction to "explain to your child on that day, 'it is because of what Adonai did for me when I went free from Egypt.'" Each of us is to view this act of freedom as a direct gift to us from the Creator of the Universe.

The Torah then relates, "And this shall serve you as a sign on your hand and as a reminder on your forehead—in order that the teaching of Adonai may be in your mouth—that with a mighty hand Adonai freed you from Egypt. You shall keep this institution at its set times from year to year." The Torah continues by insisting that the celebration of Pesach continue after the wandering in the wilderness has concluded with the conquest of the Land of Israel, then again reiterates, "And so it shall be a sign upon your hand and as a symbol on your forehead that with a mighty hand Adonai freed us from Egypt."

It might seem that the Torah is using metaphorical language to say that the Pesach story is fundamental to Jewish identity, but rabbinic tradition expanded its meaning in a rather literal direction. *Targum Onkelos*, the ancient Aramaic translation of the Torah, renders the Hebrew word for symbol (*totafot*) as "tefillin." The Talmud (*Massekhet Menahot*) quotes the rabbinic sage Mar, saying that the first reference to a sign refers to the tefillin placed on the head and the second refers to the tefillin worn on the arm.

Hezekiah Ben Rabbi Manoah Hizkuni, a great medieval rabbi, specifies that the tefillin of the head "memorializes the signs and wonders which the Holy Blessing One did in our sight" and the tefillin of the arm "memorializes God's strength." Others have understood that wearing the tefillin on forehead and arm represents our pledge to use both mind and strength in the service of God.

Why have tefillin remained as such lasting symbols of Jewish piety and Jewish identity itself? To answer that question moves us beyond the words of Torah, causing us to look at what the practice creates.

Each morning (other than a Shabbat or festival), after waking, dressing, and washing, I go downstairs and wrap myself in my tallith and bind myself with my tefillin. As I perform these mitzvot, I say the ancient words that have regularly accompanied the deed: I speak of God being wrapped in a tallith of light and then close with the stirring words of our prophet Hosea: "I will betroth you to Me forever. I will betroth you with righteousness, with justice, with love, and with compassion. I will betroth you to Me with faithfulness, and you shall love Adonai." The combination of the words and the deed create a sacred space—both physically, by devoting the space within the tallith and bound by the tefillin to prayer, and mentally, by focusing my mind and soul on God's loving betrothal of the Jewish people, of which I am a part and an embodiment.

There is an awe and a strangeness about the tefillin. I can see that by the way my two-year-old twins look at them and ask to touch them, by the way they like to be in the room watching as I *davven* (pray), by the way they call out, "Bye-bye, tefillin," as I pack them away. And I know that those tefillin will be etched into their young minds as a powerful symbol of Jewish wholeness. Morning, in their experience, is tefillin time. The rising of the sun and its setting are linked, inextricably, to the rhythms of Jewish ritual, to the faithful response to a mitzvah.

For thousands of years, we have worn those tefillin to testify to our liberation from slavery and our betrothal to God. Generations of

Jewish children have learned to love their heritage and to revere their God by watching their fathers wearing tefillin to start the new day. Do we owe our children any less? Don't we also deserve as much?

Hard-Hearted

God instructs his servant Moses, "Go to Pharaoh. For I have hardened his heart and the hearts of his courtiers in order that I may display these My signs among them." Throughout the years, as Jews gather to recount the exodus from Egyptian slavery, that passage causes puzzlement, resentment, and embarrassment. It sounds like God purposely makes it impossible for Pharaoh to do the right thing. Perhaps Pharaoh could have come to see the justice for which Moses was asking. Or perhaps he wasn't really such an evil person and only acted the way he did because under God's heavy-handed influence, Pharaoh's heart turned heavy too.

As if we don't have enough problems with what God does to Pharaoh, there's also the issue of God's justification for making Pharaoh so irresponsible. The reason God provides is that Pharaoh's refusal to let the Jews go will permit a display of divine power that will make a big impression.

The problem is that all this makes it sound like divine ego prevents Pharaoh from being a mensch. That hardly reflects the lofty ethics that we expect from the Torah. It hardly corresponds to the selfless love we expect from God.

As unpleasant as this intrusion of divine power may be, as morally questionable as it seems, it is nonetheless true that it reflects the reality of human psychology and behavior. A wonderful story in *Midrash Sh'mot Rabbah* affirms that the process that Pharaoh went through is very much like the process of desensitization that we all require to endure life's unpleasant situations.

Rabbi Yohanan shares our moral discomfort with God's role. He asks, "Doesn't this [heart-hardening] provide skeptics with the grounds for arguing that Pharaoh had no possibility of repenting?"

Rabbi Shimon Ben Lakish responds that "when God warns someone once, twice, and even a third time, and that person doesn't repent, then and only then does God close his heart against repentance and exact vengeance from his sins. Thus it was with wicked Pharaoh. Since God sent five times to him and he sent no notice, God then said, 'You have stiffened your neck and hardened your heart on your own; well, I will add to your uncleanness. . . .' So it was that the heart of Pharaoh did not receive the words of God."

Isn't that how the human heart always works: At first, we are strong enough to say no to temptation. The first time we give in to an illegitimate urge, we do so only moderately and with great guilt and anxiety. With each succeeding indulgence, our guilt is a little less, and our participation a little more sweeping and wholehearted. After a few exposures to the lust of the moment, we are soon enjoying it without even recalling our initial discomfort.

In short, our hearts, like Pharaoh's, become hardened. Passing a beggar on the street without responding to his need is impossible for children because they aren't used to it. But hardened residents of any American city get to a point where they no longer even see the humanity of the hungry person before them, no longer hear the sorrow or despair in the voice that calls out to them.

In so many ways, our hearts have become hard too. Are we really willing to live in a country teeming with homeless people, with hunger as an ever-present affliction, with illness and illiteracy and bigotry rampant in our midst?

Open your hearts, once again, to outrage. Our brothers and our sisters are suffering among us. Our indifference permits their pain. Our hardened hearts allow their disgrace. Pharaoh wasn't evil; he was apathetic. Indifference is all it takes for evil to triumph.

Who Do You See? Your Brother and Sister!

Of all the plagues, the one that strikes me as most curious is the ninth: the plague of darkness. The Torah recounts that the darkness is so thick that "a person could not see his brother, and for three days no one could rise from where he was. But all the Israelites enjoyed light in their dwellings" (Exod. 10:23).

What a curious darkness this is. Egyptians are literally weighed down by it; they sink to the ground and cannot get up for a full three days. The darkness is so oppressive that they cannot even recognize their nearest and dearest. Yet the Israelites walk in light. How are we to understand this weird and tangible darkness? Explanations that seek to rely on natural phenomena fall short, precisely because the Torah sees the plagues as extraordinary and unique—signs of God's vast power in the war against Pharaoh's tyranny.

So if we are not to view the plagues through the filter of natural occurrences, how are we to see them? What is the darkness if not the literal, smothering absence of all light?

Rabbinic tradition offers a radical way of construing this darkness. When the Torah says, "But all the Israelites enjoyed light in their dwellings," the rabbis take the dwellings to be Egyptian dwellings, as if the Torah is telling us that even when the Israelites venture into the homes of the Egyptians, they take the light with them. I find this fact staggering. Why would Israelites go into Egyptian houses in the midst of the plagues?

Here I would like to offer a solution of my own. What makes the Israelites sources of illumination is precisely their willingness to enter the homes of their oppressors. Seeing the suffering the Egyptians endure, the Israelites are able to see the Egyptians for who they truly are: a people also oppressed by Pharaoh, deserving of visits to alleviate their loneliness and fear. As the Egyptians suffer from the blindness of the darkness, the Israelites are able to truly see.

Indeed, so blinded are the Egyptians that they cannot even see each other as brothers (*lo ra'u ish et-ahiv*, "a man couldn't see his brother"). This is a devastating darkness indeed. So accustomed are the Egyptians to living in a society that views human beings only in terms of what they can produce, how they can benefit the system, that they have forgotten how to see the beauty and uniqueness of every human being; they literally couldn't "see" their brothers.

The *Or Ha-Hayim*, a seventeenth-century commentary to the Torah, recognizes the psychological nature of this crippling darkness: "Our sages tell us that the wicked envelop themselves in darkness. Accordingly we can understand the darkness as something subjective—the Egyptians who were evil experienced darkness, whereas the Jews who were good experienced light in the very places the Egyptians experienced darkness."

The contrast could not be clearer: the inability of the Egyptians to see another human being as a "brother" or "sister" is precisely the darkness that keeps them down. The insistence of the Israelites to enter even the homes of suffering Egyptians, to affirm their humanity, is a powerful blast of light into the darkness.

And their light works. The Egyptians cannot rise because of the darkness. But if the darkness is subjective and internal, then the "rising" isn't physical either. It too refers to an inner state—the lowliness of denying the humanity of others, of belittling one's own. The next time we hear of the Egyptians, the Torah relates, "The Lord disposed the Egyptians favorably toward the [Israelite] people. Moreover, Moses himself was much esteemed in the land of Egypt, among Pharaoh's courtiers and among the people."

Previously, the Egyptians had been unable to acknowledge the humanity of other people—their brothers. Then the Israelites, through the mitzvah of visiting, illuminate the homes and hearts of the Egyptians. Now, enough light is shed for the Egyptians to "rise" to the occasion—to recognize the Israelites as kin, to identify with their passion for freedom and their affirmation of life. The Egyptians "rise" morally—standing in solidarity with the people of Israel and with Moses on the side of freedom and enlightenment.

So may we, in an age of darkness, gather the light so that we too may turn to each other and recognize only brothers and sisters when we gaze into the eyes of our fellow human beings. All human beings: our brothers and sisters. Let us rise.

Be-Shalah/He Sent

Exodus 13:17–17:16

The Israelites begin their march toward their own land. God leads the people to the Sea of Reeds (the Red Sea). Marching with the bones of Joseph, the Israelites follow a pillar of cloud by day and a pillar of fire by night.

God tells Moses that Pharaoh will pursue the former slaves. The king regrets freeing the Hebrews. He orders his chariot and soldiers to go after the Israelites, and they overtake the terrified fugitives by the sea. Crying out to God, the people panic, but Moses calms them with the promise that they will see God's work that same day. God scolds Moses, telling him not to cry to God, but to tell the Israelites to go forward. Moses then lifts up his rod, and the sea splits, so that the Israelites may march through on dry land. Behind the fleeing people, a cloud of darkness settles on the Egyptians, preventing them from moving ahead.

The next morning, the Egyptians are able to give chase, but a pillar of fire creates panic among the soldiers. The chariot wheels become bogged in the mud, and the Egyptians finally realize that God is fighting for the Israelites. God instructs Moses to extend his rod once more, and the sea crashes over the Egyptian army, drowning every one of the soldiers. So great is their joy at seeing this miracle of liberation that Moses and the Israelites sing to God, "Who is like You, O Lord, among the mighty?" Miriam takes up a timbrel, and she and the women dance and sing in celebration.

From the sea, the Israelites move on into the wilderness. For three days, they find no water and begin to criticize Moses. With another miracle, Moses is able to make bitter water sweet, until they finally arrive at an oasis at Elim. A few days later, the Israelites again grumble, this time complaining of hunger. God responds by making manna and quail fall from the sky. The Israelites are commanded to gather the manna and quail each day, and on the sixth day to collect double so they won't need to violate the Sabbath by working. The people are instructed to remain in their places, inactive, for that holy day.

From the wilderness of Sin, the Israelites move on to Massah and Meribah, again quarreling with Moses over water. God tells Moses to strike a rock with his rod, and when he does, water shoots forth.

Finally, the evil Amalekites launch an attack on the Israelites at Rephidim. Moses sits between Aaron and Hur. They hold up his arms, and Israel prevails under the military leadership of Joshua.

Know Your Place!

Ours is probably the wealthiest society in the history of humanity and, at the same time, the poorest. We are rich in the possession of things and impoverished in the possession of time. Contemporary life is so frenetic that rather than being in control of our schedules and our obligations, it is more accurate to say that time controls us.

This pathetic rushing about has infected even our leisure time (which may now be an oxymoron). A recent article related that a group of bird-watchers traveled to a rustic and beautiful place, and there they set up a contest for who could sight the most birds in a set period of time. Even our leisure is pressured by the need for achievement.

Our generation is not the first to feel the iron grip of productivity. After being liberated from slavery, the Israelites wander in the desert and complain to Moses that they lack adequate food. In gracious response, God provides for their hunger with manna—a white, flaky substance that comes from the sky every day of the week except for Shabbat. On Friday, the Israelites are told to collect a double portion so they don't have to do any work on Shabbat.

But the ability to enjoy leisure time is an acquired skill, something that requires a sense of inner peace and clear priorities. Most of us are too insecure to give up the need to be doing something productive. So even though they had been ordered not to work, a group of Israelites set out to collect manna on Shabbat. When they found nothing to gather, God asked them, "How long will you people refuse to obey My commandments and My teachings? Mark that Adonai has given you the Sabbath; therefore God gives you two days' food on the sixth day. Let everyone remain where they are; let no one leave their place on the seventh day."

Note that prior to the giving of the Torah at Mount Sinai, God and the Israelites were already developing the laws of Shabbat. Linked to the very structure of the cosmos (God rested on the seventh day), "its blessed and sacred character is a cosmic reality wholly independent of human initiative" (Professor Nahum Sarna). Sacred rest, claims the Torah, is built into the structure of the universe and into the soul of every human being. In order to be fully human, we must give way before the mitzvah of rest.

Shabbat offers a unique kind of rest, a rest that is physically easy yet spiritually challenging, a time for replenishing the soul, for restoring community, and for renewing love. One key part of the Shabbat offering is the restriction on travel: "Let everyone remain where they are; let no one leave their place on the seventh day." Paradoxically, it is a restriction of freedom that liberates our deepest nature. Rather than focusing on getting somewhere or seeing something new, the prohibition against travel forces us to simply be.

Within Orthodoxy, that prohibition is understood as literally restricting the distance one may travel. Within Conservative Judaism, permission to drive to the synagogue has the effect of including the congregation in the definition of one's "place." And for all expressions of Judaism, there is a sense that Shabbat observance requires a kind of physical centering to allow for a spiritual flowering.

No surprise, then, that one pre-Sinaitic law about Shabbat, a spiritual enterprise unique to the people Israel, emerges from the context of providing for the people's food. As the Mishnah teaches, "Without sustenance, there can be no Torah."

The interdependent nature of what we perceive as the physical and the spiritual informs the biblical institution of Shabbat, one that has refreshed and renewed the Jewish people throughout the ages. In our overly busy and pressured age, Shabbat is needed not less but more.

In the sanctuary of the synagogue, in the company of loved ones and friends, around a festive Shabbat meal, make the time to reintroduce yourself to Judaism, to yourself, and to God. Today, now, figure out where your "place" is, and then give yourself the time to enjoy it.

Jewish Vocational Service (Tenure Assured)

You can imagine the fear of the former slaves as they fled toward the wilderness, toward the desert of Sinai. Risking what little they had in Egypt, facing a precarious and dangerous future, these brave men, women, and children were driven by desperation, by a faith in God, and by a passionate rejection of human domination. Determined to meet their destiny with dignity, they packed their belongings and proceeded to flee from Egypt.

Of course, the Egyptians pursued them. The traditional commentators notice that the Torah uses a peculiar verb form to describe the mobilization of the Egyptians, saying that "the Egyptians marched [singular] after them." According to Rashi, the reason the verb is in its singular form is to tell us that they marched "with one heart, like one man."

The Egyptians were united in their purpose—to maintain the power and supremacy of Egyptian might and wealth. That purpose continues to motivate many of the nations of the world to this day, lending unity and purpose to the pursuit of national interest.

What provided unity and purpose to Israel, our ancestors, fleeing toward freedom?

The Torah records that they faced this Egyptian ruthlessness with an approach quite distinct from their oppressors' reliance on military might: "Greatly frightened, the Israelites cried out to the Lord." Lest you think this recourse to prayer was merely panic, a spontaneous surrender to terror, Rashi clarifies that "they seized upon the occupation of their ancestors. Regarding Abraham, the Torah records, 'to the place where he stood [in prayer]'(Gen. 10:27), of Isaac, it says: 'to pray in the field' (Gen. 24:63), and for Jacob, it says: 'he entreated in that place' (Gen. 28:11)."

Rashi understood that the Jews cried out to God not as some blind act of terror, but as a return to their essence, their true calling in the world. He pointed out that each of the three patriarchs were exceptionally precise in their attention to matters of spirit, piety, and faith. All three ancestors turned to God as their center and their core.

In Egyptian slavery, the Jews had forgotten their own true purpose, thinking instead that they were to be a people like any other.

But in their liberation, they rediscovered what it has always meant to be a Jew: a people who can cry out to God, a people emotionally oriented toward heaven.

Throughout the millennia, Jews survived not by ignoring the reality of life, not by escaping from the often cruel and disappointing events of everyday. Instead, our ancestors were able to endure and thrive by tapping into wells of supernal strength, linking themselves to God by elevating their own perspective beyond their own limitations. Jews learned to measure their lives with a divine yardstick, to seek comfort by living in accordance with God's way.

We too have forgotten our true vocation, have grown indifferent to the stunning task handed to us in days of old. To be a Jew, according to Rabbi Abraham Joshua Heschel, is to be a messenger. To be a Jew is to cry out to God.

God Wants a Little Atheism

A story is told of a man who possessed a deep faith in God. He was traveling on an ocean liner when the ship sank. The frenzied crew offered him a life vest, which he declined, saying, "God will save me." They offered him a seat in a life raft, and he said no, insisting, "God will save me." The ocean liner sank, and the passengers who could departed on the life raft. As he paddled in the water, he was approached first by a navy frigate, then by a submarine, and finally by a fishing vessel. In each case, he refused their help, insisting, "I trust in God, and God will save me." Ultimately, he drowned. Standing before the Throne of Glory at the gates of heaven, he finally faced his Maker and said, "I have just one question: why didn't you save me?" And a great voice boomed, "Who do you think sent all those ships?"

We laugh at the tale of a man whose faith was so misplaced that he failed to recognize his own important role in his salvation. Passively waiting for God, his foolishness blinded him to the miraculous opportunities that came his way.

Parashat Be-Shalah contains a similar insight from God directly. After ten plagues finally force Pharaoh to free the Israelites, our ancestors find themselves trapped at the shore of the sea with the Egyptian soldiers and chariots hurling down upon them. Terrified, the people turn to God and Moses, and Moses himself turns to God in prayer. Instead of acting pleased that the people are pious and trusting, God rebukes them: "Why do you cry out to Me? Tell the Israelites to go forward!" (Exod. 14:15).

God's intent is clear and shocking: religious people should not become passive in the face of crisis, injustice, or peril. The great commentator Rashi understands God to say, "Now isn't the time to prolong prayer, because the people Israel are in distress." In other words, stop with the acts of piety and do something!

Rabbi Bahya Ben Asher goes even further: "According to the plain meaning of these words, the word *elai* (to Me) means that the matter does not depend on God at all, but upon Israel." Rashi doesn't dispute that God could be the one to act here, but Bahya reads the Torah as insisting that it is the people who must act, and God will act through them.

Jewish tradition is quite clear on this point: loving God and turning to God with *emunah* (faith, trust) is a high Jewish virtue. But that *emunah* doesn't remove our need to be the vessels for God's actions in the world. God acts, quite often, through us. We become God's hands in carrying caring to those in need. We become God's feet in standing with those oppressed and weighed down. We are God's heart, moved to share the sorrow and burdens of our brothers and sisters, whoever they are.

Kabbalistic tradition offers a beautiful reading of the word *elai* to highlight the interconnection of faith and action. The mystics note that it is made of three Hebrew letters. The first two spell "to" or "toward" (*el*, "*alef-lamed*"). The last is a *yud*, which is the first letter in God's holiest (and ineffable) name. Bahya relates the kabbalistic tradition that the Israelites were summoned to rise to a higher level of being, a level in which faith is made real through action, to rise to the level of "*yud*."

Indeed, Bahya makes that implication clear by telling us that "God hinted that as soon as the Israelites would move forward, the sea would part for them to let them through. They only needed to demonstrate a little faith by moving forward."

Demonstrating a little faith—not a great grand gesture, nothing dramatic or momentous—was all that Israel needed to do, all that God needed to see. Rabbi Abraham Ibn Ezra understands the holiness of little, gradual acts of faithfulness: "little by little until they reach the edge of the sea." Indeed, Judaism links our initiative to God's ability to act, as it were: "God advised Moses to perform an act of faith such as entering the sea, so I [God] can activate My attribute of mercy and perform the miracle I have in mind."

Our initiative can unleash God's liberation in the world, and God waits for our leadership, our vision, our resolve. Judaism recognizes the cosmic power of human action. Indeed, when it comes to social action and social justice, a little atheism may well be in order. Perhaps we should act as though there were no God, as if justice were solely dependent on us (trusting that God will indeed support our efforts). As Rabbi Yisrael Salanter (nineteenth-century Lithuania), the great Musar rabbi, remarked, "When it is at the expense of the Jewish people, one should not live on faith."

We have the tools, the talent, and the ability to heal this broken world—to feed the hungry, to clothe the naked, to educate and employ the poor with dignity, to repair the world's oceans and air, to bring security and peace to the world's people. Those abilities are God's gift to us—and God's hope.

Do something already!

Yitro/Jethro

Exodus 18:1–20:26

Jethro, Moses's father-in-law, hears of the miracle of Israel's liberation and brings Moses's wife, Zipporah, and their two sons, Gershom and Eliezer, to the Israelites' encampment. Moses goes out to greet his family, escorts them into his tent, and recounts the many wonders that God performed against Pharaoh for the sake of the Israelites. In joy, Jethro blesses God and offers a burnt offering, joined by Aaron and the elders.

The next morning, Moses works as judge for the people from early morning until late at night. Jethro is horrified, telling Moses that this seeming act of kindness is actually an imposition on the people and that he will wear himself out. Jethro organizes a hierarchy of judges, culminating in Moses as chief judge, allowing the people to have access to justice and letting Moses rest. Once Moses establishes this judicial order, Jethro bids him farewell and returns home.

Three months after the Exodus, the Israelites arrive at the wilderness of Sinai. God offers a special covenant that confirms the unique relationship between God and the Jewish people: "If you obey Me faithfully and keep My covenant, you shall be My treasured possession among all the peoples."

When Moses reports this offer to the people, they respond in unison, "All that God has spoken, we will do!" For three days, the Israelites purify themselves. On the morning of the third day, they hear thunder and lightning, see a dense cloud on the mountain, and hear a loud blast of the shofar. Moses ascends to the mountaintop as God descends. God tells Moses to return to the people, and when he and they are together, God speaks the words of the Ten Commandments:

1. I am the Lord your God.
2. Worship no idolatrous images.
3. Do not swear falsely by the name of God.
4. Remember the Sabbath and keep it holy.

5. *Honor your father and mother.*
6. *You shall not murder.*
7. *You shall not commit adultery.*
8. *You shall not steal.*
9. *You shall not bear false witness.*
10. *You shall not covet.*

The people are so awed by this revelation that they ask Moses to record the rest of God's word while they remain at a distance. God concludes by prohibiting idolatry, establishing animal sacrifice in "the place where I cause My name to be mentioned," and prohibiting the use of hewn stones in the altar.

God Speaks with Many Voices

One of the debates raging through the various contemporary trends within Judaism is the issue of revelation: in what way did God make divine will known at Mount Sinai, and in what way do we come to know God's will for today?

At one extreme are those who claim that each and every word in the Torah is literally God's word. The words of the Torah, subsequent prophecies by Israel's prophets, and subsequent rulings by rabbinic sages are all understood as being given by God at Mount Sinai to Moses and the Israelites.

At the other extreme are those who see revelation as so pervasive as to become almost meaningless. This view sees the will of God in everything that happens, in all literature, art, music. If everything emerges from the will of God, then no single path to God can serve as a reliable vehicle for piety and obedience.

Traditional Judaism has always been somewhere in the middle of these two views, asserting that the Torah and subsequent traditions do embody the will of God, without necessarily insisting that each and every word is literally God's own. To the contrary, Judaism affirms the essential role that human beings play in bringing God's revelation to light.

Just before the beginning of the Ten Commandments, the Torah records that "God spoke all these words, saying." The rabbis of *Midrash Sh'mot Rabbah* notice an apparently unnecessary word: *all.* Wouldn't the sentence have worked just as well without it? And if so, what was intended by its insertion? What additional lesson is the Torah trying to teach?

The midrash explains that this phrase indicates that every generation has a voice in how God's word is translated into life in each new age: "these are the souls that will one day be created, . . . Although they did not yet exist, still each one received his share of the Torah. . . . Not only did all the prophets receive their prophecy from Sinai, but also each of the sages that arose in every generation received his wisdom from Sinai."

Now we know from the Tanakh that the prophecies to Isaiah and the other prophets were not articulated at Sinai but were given during their lifetimes. So what this midrash is saying is that each new application of the original revelation, each new understanding of what God wants of us or of how to develop and apply the Jewish tradition—that new understanding itself acquires the force of Sinai.

Even though rabbinic tradition developed thousands of years after Sinai, even though we know names and lifetimes of the sages whose words and rulings built Talmudic Judaism, still we assert that the authority for their wisdom is Sinai itself. When a human being speaks, the words issue forth, are heard, and then die away. But not so the word of God. In interpreting the biblical verse "The voice of the Lord is with power," the midrash understood that to mean "it was with the power of all voices."

The power of God's voice resonates whenever Jews study and live our sacred traditions, whenever rabbinic sages argue about new phenomena or seek to apply Judaism in new ways. In all of these instances, we realize again the mysterious power of encountering God afresh, a new Sinai that recurs over and over again whenever Jews harvest their heritage anew.

The voice of God is with the power of all voices. In new readings of our ancient writings, we hear that voice as if for the very first time.

The Greatest Wedding of All

Recognizing a gap between new ways of expressing Jewish commitment and a cogent way of expressing that commitment in words, scholars and writers of every part of the Jewish spectrum put forth different metaphors to describe how God and the Jewish people relate.

Surely the most repeated metaphor is that of sovereign or ruler. In fact, that's how almost every *berakhah* (blessing) begins, addressing God as "*melekh ha-olam*" (the Monarch of Space and Time). The power of this image of God reminds us of the awesome power undergirding both the cosmos and life. We didn't choose to be born or to die, as the Mishnah tells us, and referring to God as a monarch reminds us of our obligation to gratitude and obedience.

Another popular image of God is as a teacher. According to one Talmudic understanding of the afterlife, the souls of the righteous study Talmud directly from God. God is *honen da'at* (the One who bestows understanding and confers knowledge). The power of that metaphor—God as teacher and rabbi—is that it recognizes the use of the mind as part of serving God and encourages us to cultivate clear and precise thought as a way to learn about the universe and improve the quality of life.

Yet another venerable metaphor for God is that of a warrior—the Torah speaks of God as a "man of war" who strikes out at Pharaoh and the oppressors of Israel with an outstretched arm and a mighty hand. Judaism understands that a passion for justice involves a willingness to fight against evil and against suffering. As the true judge (another traditional metaphor characterizing our relationship with God), God hates evil and intervenes to oppose it. To be like God implies a similar willingness to stand up and fight evil.

Literally hundreds of different metaphors are invoked by the Torah, the Talmud, the Midrash, philosophical writings, and modern thinkers. Because God eludes ultimate understanding, because God is unique, there is no perfect way to describe God absolutely. To talk about God requires the use of metaphors, since all talk about God is at best an approximation.

That having been said, my favorite metaphor for our relationship with God comes from this parashah. The Torah recounts the thrilling moment when the Jewish people gather at the foot of Mount Sinai to receive the Torah. Atop the mountain, clouds spread out amid thunder and lightning. With the people behind him, Moses walks to the summit of the mountain and enters the canopy of clouds. There, alone with God, he receives the engraved tablets bearing the Ten Commandments.

The *Midrash Mekhilta* comments, "This teaches that the Divine Presence went forth to meet them like a bridegroom who goes forth to meet the bride." According to this rabbinic understanding, God married the Jewish people at Mount Sinai. Moses stood there as the best man, the clouds were the huppah (wedding canopy), and the Ten Commandments were the *ketubbah* (wedding contract) binding God and the Jews in a public commitment of love and mutual caring.

What a remarkable idea! The metaphor of Sinai as marriage conveys that the core of our relationship with God is the consequence of a mutual love affair. God loves us, and we respond by loving God in return. Because of this passion between the Jews and God, God offers a *brit*, an eternal covenant that will link us through the ages. The terms of our relationship are spelled out in great detail in the Ten Commandments and the other 603 mitzvot found in the rest of the Torah.

Every good marriage hearkens back to the courtship that established the core of the relationship. And every good marriage requires that both parties make a commitment to respond to each other's needs and to grow with each other. As spouse, each agrees to take responsibility for the other and to offer care and succor in times of need. And always at the core of a strong marriage is a love that grows ever stronger over the years.

So it is with the Jewish people and God. The initial commitments and responsibilities that formalized our relationship are codified in the Torah. But openness to growth and new experience has resulted in a dynamic and vibrant relationship—just as it would for any loving couple. Judaism continues to grow and develop as we and God continue to discover more and more about each other.

At the core of any marriage is something that remains constant—the mutual obligation to care and respond, a willingness to receive the needs of the other as commandments. Because I love my wife, I respond to her priorities and her needs by making them my own.

Because we are in a marriage with God, we take on God's needs and priorities—the mitzvot—as our own.

This age-old love affair sustained our ancestors in the past, and it continues to motivate and nurture us in the present day. Happy anniversary.

The Naked and the Nude

In *Parashat Yitro*, the Torah turns from the foundational stories of Western civilization—the Creation and the Exodus—to the rich legislative legacy that implements the biblical vision of holiness, justice, and peace. Gathering around the base of Mount Sinai, the Jewish people receive *Aseret Ha-Dibrot* (the Ten Commandments) and pledge their loyalty to the covenant offered by God. After unveiling these magisterial tablets—distillations, really, for the entire Torah—Moses closes with a consideration of the rituals through which our awareness of God and cultivation of gratitude may be expressed.

The core mode of biblical public worship is to be the altar, where sacrifices will atone for sins, express thanks, celebrate the passage of time and the observance of holy days, and allow for the fulfillment of vows. Prior to the establishment of the Holy Temple in Jerusalem, Israelites are permitted to erect altars wherever they dwell. During the period of the First Temple (1000–586 B.C.E.), some Israelites continue that practice, despite the restriction imposed in the book of Deuteronomy limiting sacrifice to the Temple on Mount Zion. Only the members of the *kahunah* are permitted to offer sacrifice on the Temple's altar.

Many contemporaries turn away from the sacrificial laws, certain that these rituals are devoid of value. Yet the perspective of the Torah (amplified by later generations of Jewish sages) reveals that the sacrificial system is the concrete embodiment of profound moral and theological convictions, helping us to both express and affirm timeless values. Take, for example, the final verse in this parashah: "Do not ascend My altar by steps, that your nakedness may not be exposed upon it" (Exod. 20:23).

On the surface, this verse appears quite silly. Worried about the exposed buttocks of some ancient clergy, it hardly rises to the realm of moral rigor and visionary insight we would want from divine revelation!

Let's look again, shall we? Professor Nahum Sarna (twentieth-century United States) comments that this verse is speaking about private altars, because only *kohanim* (priests) officiated at the public altar in the Temple, and they were mandated to wear linen breeches; their nakedness would never have been exposed. This contemporary insight is anticipated by the great medieval scholar Rabbi Abraham Ibn Ezra, who writes, "The law prohibiting the use of steps to go up to the altar takes in all altars of earth, stone, or copper. The phrase 'My altar' implies all altars made for the Lord." Ritual nudity was not uncommon in the ancient Near East, yet the Torah fuses bodily modesty with divine service.

What is the connection between insisting on a ramp (an architectural/structural requirement) and the concern not to expose one's nakedness (a human/ethical concern)?

Nakedness is different than nudity. Nudity is a state of personal intimacy and trust, without pretense or artifice. The nudity of a baby is beautiful and simple, lacking all guile. The nudity of a married couple is equally beautiful and trusting. Nakedness, on the other hand, entails more than an absence of clothing—it is a mental state (both for the person lacking garments and for those observing the undressed body). To be naked is to lack an element of protection, to be stripped of dignity or decency. Nakedness is about objectification, reducing a person to a mere object to be appraised and used. In the Garden, Adam and Eve were nude and complete. Outcast and with a consciousness of having sinned, they became naked.

Nakedness can also be an assault on those forced to view another person undressed. Only someone very powerful, arrogant, or angry is in a position to impose their nakedness on others. To be forced to confront someone's nakedness can be jarring. To endure someone's exhibitionism is to have one's own privacy and modesty shredded.

Rashi realizes this verse is all about human dignity. He recognizes that if there are large steps leading to the altar, the only view that would catch the person's nakedness would be from the steps themselves. Yet stones don't see, so what's the problem? "If the Torah says, 'Do not treat them in a humiliating way since there is need for them,' of these stones, which do not have awareness to care about their humiliation, how much the more so in the case of your fellow human being, who is in the image of your Creator and who does care about humiliation!" According to Rashi, the Torah goes out of its way to cultivate modesty and restraint for inanimate objects so as to heighten our awareness of how our unwanted exposure might constitute an imposition and an assault on another person's human dignity.

A later guide, *Sefer Ha-Hinnukh,* also recognizes that this law creates a context to express joy, gratitude, and wonder. The author explains that the purpose of this law is "to implant a conception in our heart of reverent awe for the location, its eminence, and its supreme majesty. For out of one's action is the heart acted upon."

According to this second interpretation, the issue isn't human dignity, but decency. Human emotion requires physical expression ("Out of one's action is the heart acted upon"). If we wish to improve ourselves, then we need a place that encourages us to restrain our own insecurities and aggression. We need a space consecrated to majesty and decorum. The Torah's requirement creates a physical space that allows us to experience awe and tranquillity.

Ultimately, then, this law isn't just about clothing (or the lack thereof) or about steps (or ramps). God's vision fixes on the establishment of human dignity and on the need to create physical havens for healing, regeneration, and quiet joy. Just as a ramp offers a gradual means for steady elevation, so do all God's mitzvot—lifting us up to heights previously unattainable to reside in the realm of the holy and the good.

Mishpatim/Ordinances

Exodus 21:1–24:18

This parashah is known in Hebrew as Sefer Ha-Brit *(the book of the covenant). It contains the first body of laws in the Torah. These rules— a combination of moral imperatives, social standards, civil and criminal injunctions, and rules for proper worship—are all recognized as the will of God, the embodied consequence of the distinct relationship between God and the people Israel.*

Beginning with laws concerning slaves, the Torah establishes a kind of indentured servitude for a fellow Hebrew, who must go free after seven years of enslavement. If the eved Ivri *(Hebrew slave) wishes to remain with master, wife, and children, he is taken to a door and his ear is pierced with an awl, after which he is a slave for life. The Torah also establishes procedures for the* amah *(female slave).*

In a section on criminal legislation, the Torah lays out three capital offenses: murder, physically injuring parents, and kidnapping. The punishment for crimes of bodily injury caused by human attack is limited to no more than an equivalent loss: "an eye for an eye." A homicidal beast is to be killed. A thief is to repay the lost object and four (for an ox) or three (for a sheep) more animals as restitution. Responsibility to care for loaned items is enforced, whether these items are fixed property or an animal. Seducing an unmarried woman forces the seducer to pay her bride price or to marry her.

A second section of Mishpatim *lays out a variety of categorical laws known as apodictic laws: prohibition of sorcery and idolatry; justice for foreigners, widows, and orphans; extending loans to the poor; respect for God; honesty in courts; humane treatment of one's enemy; and a series of agricultural laws.* Mishpatim *then lays out the calendar of the three festivals of Passover, Shavuot (the Festival of Weeks), and Sukkoth (the Festival of Booths). God reiterates a promise to protect the Israelites during their wanderings and commands them to remain distinct and true to their covenant.*

Finally, Moses and the elders repeat all the commands and rules of the Lord aloud, and the people affirm their loyalty to the covenant and its commandments with one voice. As the elders and people celebrate the new partnership with God, Moses goes up to the mountaintop to receive the stone tablets containing God's inscription of the laws and rules.

Moses remains hidden in the clouds for forty days and nights.

Religious Ritual at the Service of Human Dignity

"Great is human dignity, for it overrides a prohibition in the Torah" is a famous assertion found over and over again in the Talmud, holding out a challenge and an opportunity for all of us to prioritize people over rules and to elevate human dignity over systemic consistency. How easy it is to allow ideology to obliterate human worth, to permit devotion to an ideal to render invisible the individual in front of us.

Generations of sages have asked a structural question about *Parashat Mishpatim*: why is it that the listing of rules ("These are the rules that you must set before them") follows immediately on the conclusion of the parashah dealing with the proper treatment of the altar in the Tabernacle? The final verses of that parashah read, "Do not ascend My altar by steps, that your nakedness may not be exposed upon it." What is the logical connection between rules of deportment at the altar and the social rules of *Parashat Mishpatim*?

Rashi reflects an earlier Midrashic understanding when he sees the connection as telling us "to place the Sanhedrin adjacent to the Temple." There is to be a connection between social priorities and religious observance. Rather than two separate realms that have nothing to do with each other, this confluence of verses reminds us that religion has everything to do with justice, compassion, and decency, and that how we behave should reflect our spiritual and religious convictions.

The Talmud offers another interpretation that supports Rashi's point. Rabbi Elazar says, "Where can it be derived that a judge should not trample on the heads of holy people? Because the Torah says, 'Do not ascend My altar by steps,' and adjacent to that it says, 'And these are the laws' (Sanhedrin 7b)."

Rabbi Elazar tells us that the connection between the end of the previous parashah (about the rules of the altar) and the beginning of this one (about social and ethical conduct) is to be found in the religious value of human dignity. Rashi makes the implicit logic clear:

> Isn't the matter of not ascending on steps a *kal va-homer* [inference from a minor matter to a major conclusion]? If the Torah says regarding the stones of the altar, which are not sentient and are not particular about their disgrace, "do not ascend My altar by steps"—meaning do not treat them in a disrespectful manner—then your colleague who is made in the image of your Creator and who is particular about being disgraced, how much more so should you treat that person with respect!

It is too easy to let ideology blind us to the humanity and the need of the individual in front of us. On the Right and the Left, our systemic commitments can erase the humanity of a person, the simple reality of pain and sorrow, need that calls out for an equally human response. Rather than indulging that erasure, Judaism confronts it. Even a commitment to Torah cannot remove the priority of human dignity.

In an age of ideological rigidity, in a time when too many put ideas or systems ahead of actual people, the Torah demands that we remember systems that are there to serve human betterment, that ideology is a tool for justice, righteousness, and love. And that rules must defer to those abiding Torah goals.

For God So Loved the Jews

One of the charges most frequently leveled against Judaism is that of excessive legalism. According to this accusation, Judaism is obsessed with the petty and restrictive rules that make Jewish life onerous and irrelevant. By focusing on endless regulations, Judaism misses the bigger picture.

This accusation, repeated throughout the centuries, has resulted in two general Jewish responses. The first, offered by apologists for traditional Judaism, was to put together collections of rabbinic "theology," culling the vast tractates of rabbinic law and lore to compile the more obviously spiritual and "religious" quotations. The most famous (and successful) of these compilations was *Aspects of Rabbinic Theology* by Solomon Schechter, great scholar and founding figure of Conservative Judaism in North America.

A more recent response to the charge that Judaism misses the forest for the trees is to insist that the overarching splendor of Jewish theology is to be found precisely in the details of its halakhot. Led by scholars such as Jacob Neusner and Abraham Joshua Heschel, this approach abandons the attempt to construct a Jewish theology along the same lines as Christian theologies. Instead, it looks at Judaism from the same perspective as the rabbis of the Talmud, appreciating Judaism from its own vantage point rather than judging it by the external standards of another faith.

In this approach, modern scholars and rabbis are actually walking in the footsteps of the great sages of classical Judaism. In *Parashat Mishpatim* is found a great list of detailed biblical law. The attention to each possible development and the formulation of a law to match each occasion is magisterial and raised the same questions for our ancestors that it does for us today—why is there so much law; so many rules; and so few grand statements about God, faith, death, the purpose of life, punishment and reward, the afterlife, and all the other "spiritual" concerns of most other religions?

Midrash Sh'mot Rabbah answers that question with a parable: "It can be compared to a prince whom his father exhorted to be careful not to stumble over anything and hurt himself because he was as dear to him as the apple of his eye. God, likewise, exhorted Israel concerning the mitzvot, because the Jews are more beloved to God than the angels, as the Torah says, 'You are the children of the Lord your God.'"

Just as a parent shows love to a child by providing detailed guidance for every aspect of the child's life, so God shows love for the Jewish people by bestowing a myriad of mitzvot to guide our steps along paths of righteousness and wisdom. Just as a good parent knows that reasonable and consistent rules are the clearest demonstration of caring possible, allowing the child to internalize a sense of right and wrong, so God—our heavenly parent—continues to provide for our training in a life of goodness and meaning.

For God so loved the Jews that God gave us many, many mitzvot. What a gift! What a romance!

Don't Tell Me What to Do!

We live in an age of radical autonomy. Each individual zealously guards his or her own independence. We resent when someone presumes to tell us what is right or wrong, or seeks to impose external limitations to our discretion or our behavior. There is much to be said in praise of this enthusiasm for independence. America has succeeded in molding a population that cherishes individuality and free thought. Art, democracy, science, and spirituality all blossom with thousands of different faces. Surely that pluralism of expression is a precious heritage.

Yet we also pay a price for our autonomy. All this freedom and lack of direction or discipline also produces tremendous loneliness, drifting, and superficiality. Pop psychology has taken the place of true understanding, and pop spirituality has replaced true religion. Rather than letting God into our hearts, rather than molding our behavior to conform to God's will, we prefer instead to construe God after our own image, to expect God to accede to our own preferences or whims.

Small wonder, then, that Judaism has such a difficult time in contemporary life. Based on the premise that all human beings must become slaves to something, Judaism asserts that we are either slaves to the Holy Blessing One or else slaves to some lesser tyrant—our drives, our work, our guilt, or another human being. Only in the service of God, in the yoke of the mitzvot, are we able to find the antidote to human bondage.

Parashat Mishpatim is the expression of that assertion. It lists a variety of laws and guidelines meant to shape Israelite life to conform to the lofty ethics and pervasive holiness of God's will. Rather than perceiving these laws as oppressive restrictions and burdensome obligations, our ancestors exulted in their newfound ability to grow spiritually and morally as God's agents in the world.

Judaism celebrates the love between God and the Jewish people, viewing the myriad laws and mitzvot as confirmation of that abiding passion and devotion. Parents who don't tell their children what to eat, what to wear, and when to sleep don't really love their children, regardless of how often they speak of their affection. True love, the kind that nurtures independence of soul and depth of personality, requires attention to detail.

True love requires guiding the young child on the paths of goodness, restraint, intelligence, and persistence. Each of us has a young child inside, some part of ourselves still in need of guidance and caring. The mitzvot speak to that deeper part of our personalities, summoning us to a life of holiness and belonging, shaping our communities to reflect God's love and concern for all of creation. Rather than being shackled by these laws, Jews have celebrated the opportunity to use them to infuse our lives with spirit, passion, and depth. The mitzvot remain a source of growth, discipline, and identity. They remain our pathway to our truer selves. And to God.

Terumah/Offering
Exodus 25:1–27:19

The Torah records the instructions for the building of the Mishkan *(Tabernacle), which will house the* Aron *(Ark of the Covenant) holding the tablets of the Ten Commandments. The Tabernacle becomes a symbol of God's presence among the Israelites, and its mobility allows that presence to follow the Israelites throughout their wanderings. It is stationed at the center of the encampment, a token of national unity for the entire people.*

It is striking that, just as the story of the Creation unfolded in six days, each of which began, "And the Lord said . . . ," so the instructions for building the Tabernacle are found in six sections, each of which begins, "The Lord spoke to Moses." The seventh section deals with the laws of Shabbat. What this suggests to us is that building the Tabernacle marks a second creation—this time, the creation of the Jewish people.

The people are to bring gifts for the construction of the Mishkan *voluntarily. God shows Moses the pattern of the building and commands that the Israelites build it so "that I may dwell among them."*

They are to fashion an ark to house the two tablets of the Decalogue and to make poles so the ark can be transported as the people themselves move. Above the ark is the kapporet *(a slab of gold with a cherub on each end of the top). God promises to speak to Moses from between the two cherubim. These are the contents of the most sacred space, the holy of holies.*

In the second region, the holy place is a table of acacia wood overlaid with gold. This table will be used to hold the lechem panim *(showbread). Near the table is the* menorah, *the seven-branched candlestick. Permeated with plantlike traits (cups, calyxes, and petals), the menorah is a symbolic tree of life, providing light in the Tabernacle at night.*

Layers of woven cloth are used to cover the Tabernacle, and wooden planks form its outer walls. Separating the inner and outer courts is the parochet (a hanging tapestry).

The outer courtyard has the sacrificial altar at its very center. The altar is to be square, with hornlike protrusions at each corner. The parashah ends with instructions for making the enclosure for the outer courtyard.

Where Is Love?

Sefer Sh'mot, the book of Exodus, is arguably the most important single story in all of Jewish history. The tale of the liberation of the Israelite slaves from Egyptian oppression, of God's role in freeing the Jews and leading them to the base of Mount Sinai, the revelation of the Ten Commandments and the beginnings of Jewish law constitute the very core of what it means to be a Jew.

If the book of Exodus is so central, it might be worth our while to stop for a moment to reflect on its central theme. What exactly in the message of Exodus is distinctive to modern Jews? From its inception, the book of Exodus is clearly a book about *hesed*—best translated by the English word "grace." Grace is a particular kind of love, that which is undeserved, spontaneous, and unconditional. Often, love betrays the egocentrism of the lover—the object of affection must continually earn devotion, or the lover showers love because of what that relationship allows the lover to be. As common as such self-centered love may be, it is not *hesed*.

For love to be *hesed*, it must be given freely, without having been earned, in the words of the siddur: "Master of all worlds! Not upon our merit do we rely . . . but upon Your limitless love." Rare in the world of flesh and blood, it is that pure loving-kindness that establishes the theme of the book of Exodus.

Take a look at some of the relationships in this pivotal biblical book. It opens with the remarkable courage of the Egyptian midwives who demonstrate *hesed* for the Israelite baby boys. Then Yoheved and Miriam show *hesed* to the infant Moses by carefully building an ark and engineering his eventual rescue by Pharoah's daughter (who herself showers *hesed* on the baby).

As an adult, Moses's life takes a radical turn when he acts on his *hesed* for the Jewish slave being beaten by the Egyptian taskmaster, and Jethro and his daughters, in turn, meet Moses with *hesed* when he flees to Midian.

In every moment, the plot of *Sh'mot* advances because of undeserved love and kindness, the innate ability of one human being to empathize with and act on behalf of another (in the words of the Talmud, "Don't judge another until you have stood in their shoes"). Even God gets into the picture, liberating slaves who have done nothing to earn this special divine providence. That unearned grace continues at Mount Sinai, where God graciously extends an eternal *brit* to the Jewish people: "The Holy Blessed One desired to benefit the Jews, so God gave them the Torah with a multitude of mitzvot." The mitzvot themselves are examples of God's *hesed*.

The concrete symbol of that *hesed* is found in this parashah in the building of the *Mishkan*. God instructs the Jews to build this portable structure as a place in which the divine presence can dwell. In the midst of the Jews, God provides a tangible reminder of the special grace that has effected their liberation, has provided them with a path of living that is wise and harmonious, and has offered unparalleled access to the sacred and the holy.

The Tabernacle built in the wilderness reminded our ancestors of God's unqualified love. In turn, it stimulated them to redouble their own efforts to live up to God's estimation of the Jews as worthy of divine favor.

By opening our hearts to God's love, we build a tabernacle of the heart. By allowing God to dwell within our core, we respond to God's *hesed* with love. And by allowing that *hesed* to serve as a catalyst to greater observance and goodness, we take a portion of God's *hesed* toward us and offer it as our own gift of love to the rest of humankind.

Proximity, intimacy, and caring—these are the gifts of *hesed*, and they are its fruits.

Linking the Generations

We are born, so the Mishnah says, into the world against our will. No one consults with us before our arrival. We are born into a world that has already benefited and suffered because of the choices that other people have made. Where our parents live, their income and compatibility, whether we have a roof over our heads, beds to sleep in at night, and a full stomach every evening are all-important choices that we never make for ourselves.

The idea that our world and our options are already shaped and constrained by the decisions that others have made runs counter to the American insistence that an individual can control his or her own destiny. While there is certainly a great deal that individual initiative can accomplish, there is also a larger context that is not of our own doing. We are dependent on the foresight of those who have preceded us, just as our children will face the consequences of the choices we make—or postpone—today.

Parashat Terumah portrays the interconnection of the generations in a vivid way. As the Israelites are wandering through the wilderness of Sinai, God instructs them to gather material to build the *Mishkan*. Among the materials to be found are "gold, and silver, and brass, and blue and purple and scarlet yarn, and fine linen and goat's hair, and skins of rams dyed red, and skins of seals, and acacia wood."

Each of these supplies is subjected to rabbinic scrutiny, but none evokes such surprise as the *atzei shittim* (acacia wood). In his commentary, Rashi asks, "From where did they obtain this in the wilderness?" After all, there are no acacia trees in the desert. How could God expect the Israelites to have access to this kind of lumber? Rashi then quotes an answer from *Midrash Tanhuma* (fifth-century Israel): "Rabbi Tanhuma explained, 'Our father Jacob foresaw by means of the Holy Spirit that Israel was destined to build a tabernacle in the wilderness; so he brought cedars to Egypt and planted them and commanded his children to take them with them when they would leave Egypt.'"

According to this answer, the kind of foresight that Jacob showed is one of anticipating the needs of a future generation and then going out of his way to provide for those needs. He had no requirement for acacia wood, nor did he have any benefit from them. To the contrary, it must have seemed an unnecessary burden to his contemporaries. Yet Jacob knew that his descendants would need it, so he went out of his way to provide for them. Such foresight is so treasured that the Midrash attributes it to divine inspiration (*ruach ha-kodesh*).

In our own age, two parallels seem clear. The first is that if our generation does not provide for the care of the planet and all its inhabitants, then we will call into question the survivability of human life on earth. Like Jacob, we must measure our actions and our choices by their consequences seven generations hence—not by the yardstick of short-term comfort, but of long-term habitability. Jacob planted the trees that his children would need four hundred years later. How will our choices shape our descendants' lives in four hundred years? Will our choices today leave them with greater bounty and freedom or with constricted possibilities and compromised health?

Judaism provides the second forum where foresight is needed. Our children can only inherit what we ourselves possess. If we do not plant trees of living Jewish experience and passion now, they will not have the memories, values, or guidance to fall back on later in life. Our Jewish fidelity today will establish the Jewish possibilities of tomorrow. As with our ancestor Jacob, we too must rely on the *ruach ha-kodesh* as a source of insight, then translate that insight into action.

Tomorrow begins the moment today is finished. And the work we do today will shape our children's tomorrows.

Religion Is a Gift

A great deal of political energy and anguish has coalesced around issues like school prayer, teaching biblically based accounts of the Creation in biology classes, and allowing religious organizations to meet during school hours or on school premises.

Proponents of these policies argue that we have banished God and spirituality from public discourse, teaching that ethics and holiness are marginal to human development and civilization. These citizens argue that America was founded on biblical precepts, such as the notion that all people are created equal and that certain rights are endowed by our Creator. The mandates to feed the hungry, care for the poor, and shelter the homeless are all grounded in biblical understanding, a theology that forces us to look beyond self-interest, to care for each of God's creatures.

For these people, removing God from our schools and our politics means removing the very basis on which American democracy stands, the ethical fiber that binds all Americans together. How can we claim to educate our children and prepare them for the sacrifices that citizenship entails unless we also teach them to look inward for the gifts of spirit and to answer "yes" when they perceive God's call?

Opponents of these same policies respond that there is no neutral way to present God, that any kind of prayer reflects a specific theology and worldview that would alienate those who do not share that specific faith. Since the vast preponderance of Americans claim to be Christian, many religious Jews, Muslims, Hindus, Baha'is, Buddhists, and others object to mandatory public prayer because they fear that such a forum would present Christian prayer as the norm, imposing a sense of second-class citizenship on Americans of other traditions. Even prayers without explicit references to Christianity or Jesus would retain the form of Christian prayer.

A larger concern is that whenever the state mandates religion, it is religion that suffers. The idea of separating church from state came not from a secular judge, but from Roger Williams, a minister of God. He intuited that only a religion unfettered by governmental edict could possibly function in a godly way; only a soul that responds freely to God's outreached hand can rise to meet its Maker. The state that he established (Rhode Island) pioneered the idea of religious freedom from any government regulation not for the sake of government but for the flourishing of religion itself.

The Torah offers a similar insight. By framing our relationship with God in terms of a covenant that is expressed through commandments, the Torah recognizes that we must be able to say "no" to God for our answer of "yes" to mean anything. It is because we could reject Sinai that our acceptance of Torah is worthwhile. You don't issue commandments to an automaton: God wants our voluntary obedience.

That same perspective emerges from *Parashat Terumah*. In speaking of the communal obligation to build the *Mishkan*, the Torah insists that contributions should come only from "everyone whose heart is moved." Participating in this most sacred of enterprises, making a place for God at the very center of Israel's existence, was a purely voluntary effort. Any coercion whatsoever would merely have made God into a more effective and intimidating version of Pharaoh.

The God of Israel doesn't desire slaves. Instead, the service of our God must come from the heart, as a gift. We freely give to God because of the overwhelming sense that we have been given more than we could ever demand—existence, loved ones, community, a sacred tradition, freedom. God didn't owe us these blessings, and our response must emerge not from any imposed obligation but as an offering of love and thanks.

To mandate prayer, to coerce piety, however well-intentioned, is to cripple religion before it can even begin. Only freed from governmental mandates, from social engineering, can the promise of religion and the holiness of Torah make their mark.

For the love of God, for the sake of Torah, we dare not impose what can only be given. Prayer means nothing unless it is "an offering from everyone whose heart is moved."

Tetzaveh/You Will Command
Exodus 27:20–30:10

Tetzaveh *begins with commands about providing fuel for illuminating the Tabernacle. Aaron and his sons are to set up olive oil lamps in the Ohel Mo'ed (the Tent of Meeting), where they will burn from evening to morning.*

The Torah now moves to establish the kahunah *through Aaron and his sons—Nadav, Avihu, Eleazar, and Ithamar. They are provided with special dress to distinguish them from the other Israelites and to mark them for sacred service.*

The kohen gadol *(high priest) is unique in his golden attire. He wears eight special objects:*

1. *The* ephod *(apron)*
2. *The* hoshen *(breastpiece), which uses twelve colored stones to signify the twelve tribes of Israel*
3. *The* Urim ve-Tummim *(devices used to discern the will of God)*
4. *A robe made entirely of* tekhelet, *the blue dye also found in one thread of* tzitzit *(the fringe on the corner of the prayer shawl), and with pomegranates on its hem*
5. *The* tzitz *(frontlet) bearing the words "Holy to God"*
6. *The* kuttonet *(tunic)*
7. *The* mitznefet *(headdress)*
8. *The* avnet *(sash)*

Ordinary priests wear four garments.

Tetzaveh *goes on to describe the installation ritual of the priests, a ceremony presided over by Moses, which lasts for seven days. The installation ceremony consists of sacrifices of both animals and grain, bathing and cleansing the priests' bodies, robing them, and anointing them.*

The parashah ends with a summary of the purpose of this elaborate rite: "I will abide among the Israelites and I will be their God. And they shall know that I, the Lord, am their God, who brought them out from the land of Egypt that I might abide among them, I, the Lord their God."

Knowing What God Wants

In every generation, some people are so certain that their view of what is right is absolutely right that they are not only ready to dedicate their own lives to their ideals, but they are prepared to coerce others to follow in their footsteps. Religious or secular, these ideologues assume that their opinions reflect the structure of the cosmos itself. To disagree is not only to differ, but to invite disaster and dire retribution.

No group is exempt from these dogmatists; organizations worthy and flaky, serious and trivial all suffer their share of implacable spokespeople. Certainty, while it provides real vigor and conviction, has also been the cause of tremendous human suffering. Far from bringing credit, erroneous or vicious certainty simply makes its proponents seem fanatical and harsh.

While Judaism also has its share of people who insist that they know exactly how all Jews should observe Judaism, this parashah offers an interesting insight into the kind of religious humility that a Jew ought to cultivate.

In the time of the First Temple, God's will was known absolutely. The tools that revealed God's perspective to the Jews were known as Urim and Thummim. According to the Talmud, *Urim* comes from the Hebrew for "light" and *Thummim* comes from the word for "complete." Illumination and wholeness were certainly the result of using the Urim and Thummim, as these devices allowed the priest to inquire of God and receive specific answers that prevented the possibility of error. The *kohen gadol* wore them inside his breastplate to be able to "carry the instrument of decision for the Israelites over his heart before Adonai at all times."

The Urim and Thummim were Israel's guarantee that the people would always act in accord with God's desires. A later passage in the Torah specifies that the *kohen gadol* "shall present himself to Eliezer the *kohen*, who shall on his behalf seek the decision of the Urim before Adonai. By such instruction they shall go out and by such instruction they shall come in, he and all the Israelites, the whole community."

Imagine the security of knowing that you and your community were doing exactly what God wanted! No doubts, no reason to compromise or entertain any other viewpoints but the received one; life would be simple, clear, and a bit rigid.

The Urim and Thummim were used by King Saul and were part of Israel's consciousness as late as the time of the return of the Israelites from Babylonian exile under Ezra and Nehemiah around 500 B.C.E. We are told that several of the returnees were unable to verify their priestly lineage and were therefore barred from eating the priestly tithes "until a *kohen* with Urim and Thummim should appear."

Note that this passage from the book of Ezra implies that the Urim and Thummim weren't available in the early Second Temple period. The ancient historian Josephus (first-century Israel and Rome) reports their demise during the time of the Hasmonaean *kohen gadol* John Hyrcanus (around 135 B.C.E.), whereas the *Mishnah Sotah* reports, "With the death of the first prophets, the Urim and Thummim ceased." The Talmud, in *Yoma*, insists that they were present in the Second Temple but that they didn't function as they had earlier.

What is the religious implication of the loss of the Urim and Thummim (which coincided with the end of prophecy)? Whereas biblical Israel could claim explicit verbal communication from God, thereby eliminating uncertainty and confusion, Jews of later ages cannot. We don't have explicit divine words to tell us which path to follow, and we don't have devices that can dope out God's will once and for all.

All we have are our inherited traditions; our sacred writings; the world around us; and the small, still voice that speaks within each one of us. Those four legs are the base on which we stand, the compass by which a Jew can chart a proper course in life, the path for us to walk. Our traditions, the mitzvot and *minhagim* (customs), translate lofty imperative and profound insight into concrete deeds, providing constant access to holiness and morality. Our sacred writings record our ancestors' encounters with God and their insights of what God wanted from them (and wants from us). The world around us is also a source for understanding God, since the same God that speaks to us through Torah fashioned creation as well. And finally, the God who created the world also made the human heart, giving us the ability to distinguish between good and evil. By learning to listen to our inner voice, we strengthen our ability to hear God speaking through our conscience too.

No one path alone can convey the full majesty and depth of God's will. All four together have provided the web that has secured our place since the end of prophecy and the revocation of the Urim and Thummim. While they can't tell us exactly what it is God wants, and they will be understood differently by different Jews, these four paths are the only way available to us.

In utilizing the gifts of tradition, sacred writings, the cosmos, and conscience, we must also know that we filter these insights through the wisdom and experience of the entire Jewish people, the prism through which God's covenant is established in each age and every generation. Without the Urim and Thummim, we cannot disdain the viewpoints of other honest and well-intentioned Jews who may differ from us in their understanding of the covenant or the way they seek to embody God's will. Instead, we can learn from each other, even in our disagreements, and encourage each other, even though we may follow different ways. In the end, it may be that God removed the Urim and Thummim because we could not resist the temptation to be a little too sure, a bit too certain, and a little too smug.

At least, that's my opinion.

Come on, Baby, Light My Fire

Preparing to wander in the wilderness for forty years, the Israelites know that they must provide not only for their physical requirements in the desert but for their spiritual needs as well. Of the furnishings of the *Mishkan*, none has received more attention than the menorah, used to illumine the holy of holies during the endless desert nights. This parashah opens with the instructions for maintaining that light. The Israelites are told "to bring . . . clear oil of beaten olives for lighting, for kindling lamps regularly."

But why would the Creator of the Universe—the source of the light of the sun, moon, and stars—need our light? The ancient rabbis were sensitive to this same question. In fact, they put the answer directly into God's mouth. In *Midrash Sh'mot Rabbah*, God says that the light is "not that I need them but in order that you [the Jews] may give light to Me as I give light to you." God's need for a love relationship with the people Israel produces this divine willingness to invent ways for Israel to show its love for God.

The rabbis compare this to a blind man who is accompanied home by a man who can see. After the blind man gets home, the sighted one asks his fellow to light a lamp for him, "so that you will no longer be obligated to me for having accompanied you along the way." The rabbis tell us that the sighted man represents the Holy One, who guides us throughout our lives, and the blind man represents the Jewish people. In response to God guiding us, we also shine a light on God's wisdom and caring in the world.

In a day when there is neither *Mishkan* nor Temple, how do we shine a light back on God? How, in gratitude for God's guidance in our lives, do we establish a pure, burning brightness that reflects credit to God?

The midrash continues, "Just see how the words of the Torah give forth light to those who study them. . . . Those who study Torah give forth light wherever they may be. It is like standing in the dark with a lamp in hand; when you see a stone, you don't stumble, nor do you fall into a gutter because you have a lamp in hand. . . . God said, 'Let My lamp be in your hand and your lamp in My hand.' What is the lamp of God? The Torah."

In our day, then, the lamp of God comprises the rich teachings of the Torah. God shines that light into the world, illumining the pitfalls and stumbling blocks along the way. Through the guidance and discipline of the mitzvot, God offers us a path of sanity, profundity, and morality.

Yet the Torah remains merely a book, its instructions mere words, if we don't translate them into living deeds. It is in our hands to take the teachings of the Torah and later rabbinic insight and to let them shine through our example. We shine a light back to God when we live by God's commandments. In the words of the psalmist, "In Your light we are bathed in light."

As the book of Proverbs observes, "The mitzvah is a lamp, and the teaching is a light." By living our lives in accord with the commandments, we fashion a light so bright that it can shine into the deepest recesses of the human heart, lighting the way back from the precipice of egotism, hedonism, or habit.

It isn't enough merely to build the menorah. Each of us must bring to it our own supply of clear, pure oil. It isn't enough to own the Torah nor even to read it regularly. Each of us must implement its teachings, demonstrating them in deeds to the four corners of our lives.

In that way, we allow God's light to shine on us, so that we in turn can shine our light on God.

Sanctified by God's Presence—and Ours

In a world so frenzied that we rarely have time to pause, contemplate, or connect, it is too easy to pass our lives without savoring the preciousness of our time on earth. Distracted by our tasks, burdened by a sometimes selfish and uncaring world, we struggle to maintain our balance, to preserve mindfulness amid the distractions, to cultivate gratitude with grace. This parashah offers us a tool to sustain that radiance in the commonplace.

The last chapters of the book of Exodus turn to the consequence of God's liberation. No longer slaves, the Israelites recognize that relationships entail action, that our connection to others must become visible in our deeds. Now covenanted to God through Torah, the Israelites need a concrete way to demonstrate their love for God and express their unity with each other. And God graciously accommodates that need.

In the aftermath of the giving of the Ten Commandments and after the lengthy legislation that fleshes out our *brit* with God, God also provides the structures in which that relationship can flourish and grow. God tells the people to build a *Mishkan* and provides for the *Ohel Mo'ed*, in which Moses and God can continue to articulate the detailed consequences and manifestations of the *brit*. Of the tent, God tells Moses, "There I will meet you, and there I will speak with you, and there I will meet with the Israelites, and it [the Tent of Meeting] shall be sanctified by My presence" (Exod. 29:42–43).

The *Ohel* is a locus of holiness, made sacred by the encounter that happens there. Jewish tradition makes explicit that such a meeting increases the holiness in the world. The ability to come together, to truly know each other, to encounter each other as we are—such a meeting leaves us different, ennobled, greater than before. But what aspect of the encounter generates holiness? On that point, the commentators differ.

Rashi explains the holiness as the result of God's presence: "For My Shechinah shall rest in it." In rabbinic parlance, the Shechinah is the manifestation of God's presence in the world. So Rashi reads that the tent is to be sanctified by the manifestation of God that is revealed there.

But Rashi doesn't let matters stop there. He also goes on to quote an earlier rabbinic interpretation: "An Aggadic Midrash says, Do not read this as 'My presence' but as 'My presences' through My honored ones." In other words, it is not God's manifestation that makes the Tent of Meeting holy, but the presence of Moses, Aaron, and other Israelites whose very goodness and seeking bear holiness in their wake. In the words of Rabbi Bahya Ben Asher, "God feels honored and glorified by those who draw near."

With that insight, we enter the inner core of real relationship—reciprocity. We perceive the sanctity of the Tent of Meeting when we encounter God there, and God reveals holiness in the tent when we are present. Each party to the covenant is honored and glorified by the presence of the other. Holiness emerges *between* God and Israel, *among* God and Israel. It comes into the world through our coming together, God and Israel in a mysterious, ancient relationship that has shed light across the millennia. Perhaps it is that sacred secret—the hidden power of coming together—that can decode our third and final explanation for the sanctity of the Tent of Meeting. "I will manifest Myself to the people of Israel when the Tabernacle will be erected and the celestial fire will descend," teaches Rashbam (Samuel Ben Meir, twelfth-century France).

The fire descends when there is One to send it. The Tabernacle is erected when there is one to build it. The fire is celestial when the two come together. It is what we do with (and in) God's presence that allows holiness into the world.

Ki-Tissa/When You Take

Exodus 30:11-34:35

Ki-Tissa *begins with a census of Israelite men over the age of twenty and the assessment of a half-shekel poll tax on each of them. This tax is seen as a ransom to God so the participants will escape plague. The rich do not pay more, nor do the poor pay less.*

God then instructs Moses to construct a copper and bronze laver to be used for washing the feet and hands of the kohanim *prior to their performing sacrifices. Next, God tells Moses to prepare a special aromatic oil and prohibits using it for any purpose other than anointing priests. The contents of the Tabernacle's incense are then detailed, and its use outside is prohibited.*

God appoints Bezalel and Oholiav, two artisans of great wisdom and skill, to do the actual work of building the Tent of Meeting, the Ark of the Covenant, and all the contents of the Tabernacle.

Just as the Tabernacle represents holiness in space, the Sabbath represents holiness in time. God reiterates its observance: "You must keep My Sabbaths, for this is a sign between Me and you throughout the ages, that you may know that I, the Lord, have consecrated you." Work is prohibited on the seventh day.

God then presents Moses with two stone tablets, inscribed by God.

Meanwhile, down below in the desert, the people are frantic because they don't know what has become of Moses. They demand that Aaron make them a god. Aaron takes their gold rings and casts a molten calf, the Egel ha-Zahav. *The people begin to worship it, and Aaron makes an altar, which the people use to make a burnt offering. God tells Moses to hurry down and threatens to destroy the people for being "stiff-necked." Moses talks God out of this destructive reaction, reminding him of his promise to Abraham, Isaac, and Jacob that their children would become a great nation. Moses then descends from Mount Sinai. As soon as he sees the calf, he smashes the tablets, grinds the calf into powder, throws it in water, and makes the Israelites drink* it. Moses calls out, "Whoever is for the Lord, come here!" The Levites rally to him, and they slaughter some three thousand people that day. Moses then returns to God to plead for forgiveness on behalf of the people. God relents but refuses to accompany the people any farther, at which they go into mourning.

Moses continues to meet with God face-to-face and pleads with him to resume leading the Israelites directly. God relents because he has singled out Moses by name. Taking advantage of this favor, Moses pleads to see God's presence. God explains that people cannot see the Divine and live, but agrees to make God's goodness pass before Moses. Moses carves two new tablets, and when the Holy One passes by, Moses proclaims, "The Lord! The Lord! A God compassionate and gracious, slow to anger, abounding in kindness and faithfulness, extending kindness to the thousandth generation, forgiving iniquity, transgression, and sin."

God then lays out the prohibition against idolatry and discusses proper worship, which includes the calendar of the Jewish holidays and festivals observed to this day.

The parashah concludes with Moses rewriting the Ten Commandments on the new tablets. When he descends from the mountain, his face is radiant with light, so he covers his face with a veil from then on, taking it off only for private conversation with God.

Judaism Lite

Our age is one of hand-wringing. We fear for the survival of the Jewish people and our ancient civilization, and we establish funds and committees devoted to the noble work of continuity. We read article after article predicting the extinction of the American Jewish community and chastising us for our lethargy, our tedium, and our mediocrity. Plans to turn our people around—through trips to Israel, use of Eastern meditation techniques, strict observance of Jewish law (or its entire elimination)—all promise to save us from our greatest contemporary enemy: ourselves.

Far be it from me to gainsay the wisdom of most of what is written on the subject. Great minds and caring souls have probed the demographics and the beliefs of our people, and many of their solutions are worthy of our careful deliberation.

But one notes with some alarm a very different kind of so-called solution: the repeated implication that Judaism has entered an age in which one's form of observance and content of belief doesn't really matter much. Do what you want, think what you want, so long as you call it Judaism and identify with the Jewish community.

Indeed, the mantra of this fuzzy, feel-good unity is itself an insistence that belief and practice don't matter much. Some amorphous identity called "Judaism," purged of a cogent and compelling doctrine, obligation, and implication, will replace the vigorous debates that enlivened Jewish denominational dispute over the past hundred years. And that will unite us for our own good.

While our respect for each other is indeed a crucial aspect of *derekh eretz* (decency and civility) and our common peoplehood, I would submit that a refusal to take ideology and practice seriously represents an unwillingness to take religion seriously. And the lack of passion about matters of Jewish belief and behavior will erode even that fuzzy, shallow Judaism-in-the-making.

What is the alternative to this lack of passion? *Parashat Ki-Tissa* speaks to this very subject through the interpretation offered by the rabbis of antiquity. Following God's gift of the Ten Commandments, the Torah notes, "God gave to Moses, when He had finished speaking to him upon Mount Sinai, two tablets of testimony, tablets of stone."

The rabbis note that the term used for "he had finished" is *ke-khaloto*. Fully aware of Hebrew vocabulary, they nevertheless use a pun to make a serious point. They know that *ke-khaloto* sounds a lot like *kalah* (bride). So they connect the giving of the Torah to that most passionate of Jewish commitments, a marriage: "When the Holy Blessing One gave the Torah to Israel, it was as dear to them as a bride is to her spouse."

When God and Israel met at Mount Sinai, it was with the trepidation, exhilaration, and love of a bride and a groom on their wedding day. In fact, rabbinic Midrash often speaks of what transpired on that momentous mountain as a marriage: the marriage of God and the Jewish people. In that scenario, the cloud of glory was our huppah, Moses was our best man, and the Ten Commandments were our *ketubbah*.

Unless we approach our Judaism with all the specific passion of a newlywed, it won't amount to very much. It matters with whom we're under the huppah and what the terms of the *ketubbah* are. The Torah is no quaint relic, but the very foundation of our relationship with God. And God is no mere concept, but a living presence that enters every moment of our lives.

Different groups of Jews disagree on precisely how we understand God, Torah, mitzvot, tradition. These differences are real and profound. To water them down into some homogenous mush is merely to continue to trivialize Judaism, something that no group would endorse. Instead of shallow sameness, let's celebrate vigorous diversity. One can be a serious Jew, regardless of how one interprets that Judaism, and still honor those serious Jews whose Judaism looks different.

Rather than seek some false unity by imposing the uniformity of indifference, let us encourage our fellow Jews to cultivate cogent beliefs and implement those beliefs in practice, even when we disagree with their content. If we really have faith in God and Torah, then we can afford to advocate our own best understanding of who God is and what God's Torah means. So long as we also embody the best values that our Torah implies—values of restrained speech and love for our fellow Jews—the debate well joined will do more for Jewish continuity than any stuporous removal of content ever could.

Care to join me under the huppah?

Knowing God

One of the dilemmas facing a modern Jew is the question of how to know God. Increasingly disappointed with our previous faith in progress and the power of reason to bring about salvation, we turn increasingly to some of the timeless resources of our ancestral faith, looking to Judaism to root our search for meaning.

For some contemporary Jews, the search is straightforward—the Torah comprises the literal words of God, so anything we want to know about God is to be found there. And if it isn't mentioned in the Torah, it means that we aren't meant to know it. That view has much to commend it—its simplicity, its certainty, and its clarity. For those

Jews who can believe that the Torah is literally true, it provides community and direction in great abundance.

For most American Jews, however, the claim that every word of the Torah and Talmud is literally the word of God doesn't ring true. Most American Jews affirm that the Torah is divine and reflects divine will, but not necessarily word for word. And most American Jews insist that life experience and secular learning also contribute to our knowledge of God.

Within that framework, just how much can we know of God's characteristics? Can we know God absolutely? This parashah suggests not. Moses asks God, "Let me see Your presence!" God's response, however, is "I will make all My goodness pass before you, and I will proclaim before you the name Lord, and the grace that I grant and the compassion that I show. But . . . you cannot see My face, for man may not see Me and live."

God tells Moses that there are intrinsic limits to how well a human being can comprehend divine nature. After all, God is infinite—beyond all description or limit. And human beings, finite as we are, can't possibly comprehend so vastly different an order of existence. We can relate to God, but we cannot encompass God with our minds.

The great medieval rabbi Maimonides (Moses Ben Maimon, or Rambam) says virtually the same thing in his magisterial code, the *Mishneh Torah*. There he explains that theology can only be taught to one person at a time—not to a class, but with one teacher focusing on one student. After selecting a student intelligent enough to grasp theological insights, Rambam adds an additional caveat: the student "is given [only the most] fundamental points [of theology], and an outline of the concepts is made known. He is expected to continue to contemplate until he reaches understanding with his powers of knowledge and knows the ultimate meaning and depth of the concept."

Rambam asserts that theological truths cannot be reduced to words without becoming distorted. Only the broadest outline of Jewish theology can be transmitted verbally. Then, the student must rely on prayer, meditation, and solitary contemplation to arrive at an understanding of God's nature.

This view concedes that any theology—however brilliant or satisfying—is only an approximation of a truth. Any verbalization necessarily trivializes and distorts the very meaning it tries to convey. In the words of the Maharal of Prague, "God is not merely beyond the limits of human knowledge; He is unknowable in essence."

While God may remain ultimately beyond knowledge, we can still strive to understand as best we can. We each must formulate our own understanding of God and learn to appreciate God's presence in our own introspection and silence.

Knowledge of God is a private affair. Living in the presence of God, however, is the proper business of Judaism and the Jewish people. It is that cornerstone of Jewish living, our *brit* with God, that commands the attention of the sages of every period of history and the realm that deserves our energies today.

The Holiness of Time

The culmination of the ancient Babylonian myth of Creation is the erection of a temple to the pagan deity Marduk. What that structure makes clear is that the holiness of space is primary; its crowning representation is the holy space where Marduk was worshipped. In stark contrast, the Torah's account of Creation establishes the capstone of the event not as any place in particular or even any space at all. Instead, the pinnacle of Creation is the establishment of holy time: Shabbat, the Sabbath day.

In a cultural milieu in which people were expecting the creation of the world to conclude with the creation of a holy place, the story of the Torah must have been shocking. Creating holiness in time became the pinnacle of Jewish religion and the primary contribution of Judaism to a world of harmony and peace.

That same emphasis continues in this parashah, and it is even less expected here. In *Parashat Ki-Tissa*, and in *Parashat Tetzaveh* as well, God instructs Moses about the building of the *Mishkan*. It served as the place where the Israelites could make their offerings and sacrifices in accordance with God's will, simultaneously providing a center to their camp. Wherever they were in the Sinai Peninsula, the center of their community was the *Mishkan*, both topographically and spiritually.

Given the importance of the *Mishkan* and the great attention to each detail of its construction, it is shocking to observe that the instructions pertaining to the Tabernacle come in six general units and that the seventh deals with Shabbat. Here, too, the pinnacle of holy space is holy time. The Torah relays God's words that "nevertheless you must keep My Sabbaths, for this is a sign between Me and you throughout the ages, that you may know that I, Adonai, have consecrated you."

God goes on to prohibit all *melakhah* (conventionally translated as "work") on Shabbat; the violation of this rule is a capital offense. Finally, God brings the verse back, full circle, to the very beginnings of the Torah: "The Israelite people shall keep the Sabbath, observing the Sabbath throughout the ages as a covenant for all time: it shall be a sign for all time between Me and the people of Israel. For in six days Adonai made heaven and earth, and on the seventh day God ceased from work and was refreshed."

Why is the law of Shabbat observance, of the requirement to refrain from all labor on Shabbat, inserted at the end of the details for building the Tabernacle? What is God trying to tell us?

It is clear that without a willingness to create holy time, our holy spaces will remain empty shells, mocking the very piety they were built to sustain. If we build lovely synagogues without also clearing the time to worship in them regularly, if we hire talented rabbis, cantors, and educators but don't make the time to learn from them and study with them, then all we have is holy space—and neglected space at that.

No matter how elegant the facility, regardless of how expensive its upkeep, there is simply no substitute for human involvement. Our presence is necessary to give our institutions life, and our involvement is necessary to preserve the ancient and wonderful way of life that Judaism provides the world.

Judaism understood from the start that holy space without holy time was a mockery of true religion. That's why the pinnacle of Creation is Shabbat. Six days were spent creating a place (the world and all it contains) in which holiness could be made real, but the fulfillment of the promise of place moves us beyond the tangible into the realm of time.

The point, then, is that even a religion as profound and as joyous as Judaism cannot hope to transform our lives, let alone our world, if we will not invest the time necessary to let it work its wonders on our hearts. If we don't sanctify the Sabbath day, if we don't regularly attend our synagogue's worship services, if we don't put aside time for Jewish learning on a regular basis, then we can't hope to realize the potential that Judaism offers.

Instead, we find it too simple to fall into the Babylonian fallacy—to regard a willingness to sustain a sacred place as sufficient to safeguard our values and our dreams. While contributing to the upkeep of Jewish institutions is indeed a necessary base, it is but a start. The task of the Jew, to establish the sovereignty of God in the here and now, takes much more than just a proper place. It requires a good deal of heart and soul. And cultivating those precious and evanescent virtues takes time.

Va-Yakhel/He Assembled

Exodus 35:1–38:20

Moses convenes the entire people. Just as the laws of the Tabernacle end with the laws of the Sabbath, so too the process of building it begins with a reiteration of the holiness of the Sabbath, mandating that the people refrain from work and from kindling fire on Shabbat.

Moses calls for contributions from the people and asks those with talent and ability to participate in the project. The response is so generous and enthusiastic that all the men and women whose hearts move them to bring anything for the work that the Lord, through Moses, commanded, do so as a freewill offering. Bezalel and Oholiav take the donations and begin to work. The donations are so bounteous that Moses has to order the people to stop giving.

The people join in the work of construction, sewing, and building, and Bezalel turns to fashioning the furniture and accessories of the Tabernacle: the ark, the table, the menorah, the altar of incense, the anointing oil and incense, the altar of burnt offering, the laver, and the enclosure.

Pekudei/The Accounts

Exodus 38:21–40:38

A tally is made of all the metals used in the construction of the Tabernacle: gold, silver, and copper. The instructions for making the priestly garments are implemented, and the people make the vestments just as God commanded.

When the work is complete, the people bring each item to Moses for inspection: "And when Moses saw that they had performed all the tasks—as the Lord had commanded, so they had done—Moses blessed them."

God now instructs Moses how to erect the Tabernacle, which is done on the first day of Nissan, near the second anniversary of the Exodus from Egypt. Moses does as God commands, and when he finishes the work, a cloud covers the Tent of Meeting, and the presence of the Lord fills the Tabernacle.

The people rest when the cloud is settled and move only when the cloud lifts, thus following God's initiative and leadership as they wander toward Eretz Yisrael.

Art Provides a Tool—or a Mask

Until very recently, common knowledge maintained that Judaism prohibited works of art. The Ten Commandments contains a prohibition against graven images, and the Torah forbids representation of any astral bodies. Modern Jews have assumed that Jews never made representations of people, animals, or divine beings because such art would violate our standards against idolatry. Christians make statues of their object of worship, but Jews don't. As a result, it is widely affirmed that we also don't make artistic representations of anything, whether or not in a religious context.

That assumption has been safely laid to rest. Through the work of scholars (such as Erwin Goodenough) and the publication of beautiful books of Jewish art, it is clear that Judaism cultivated a rich artistic tradition. Descriptions of Solomon's temple in Jerusalem attest to the delicacy of the artwork there, and the archaeological remains of ancient synagogues reveal rich mosaic floors and elaborately painted murals. Art played an essential role in the construction of the *Mishkan*, the *Aron*, and the menorah inside. Accordingly, Moses introduces the first biblical artist, "the Lord has singled out by name Bezalel . . . and has endowed him with a divine spirit of skill, ability, and knowledge."

Impressive credentials indeed! God directly inspires the artist, so that sculpture, architecture, music, and other forms of artistic expression provide a privileged path of religious expression. Art involves more than merely a desire to make pretty objects. Through the use of color, shape, movement, and sound, people articulate impulses, thoughts, and insights that words alone cannot convey. Art gives voice to those mute, inaccessible parts of our souls. Art allows us to share the private, to realize and develop inner visions and secret dreams.

Lurking underneath the claim that art can liberate is the more audacious claim that art can civilize. After all, we don't support opera and museums simply to ventilate an artist's inner longings. We participate in artistic projects because we hope to emerge as better, more sensitive human beings. Does art civilize?

Regrettably, no—or at least, not by itself. The Romans were among the most esthetically developed and sophisticated people in the world, and they were also the most ruthless. Europe developed a culture that valued painting and music and simultaneously murdered six million Jews. The same Americans who enslaved millions of African captives also built elegant plantations.

Our rabbis understood that art by itself can be either good or bad. Art permitted the idolatry of the golden calf and the sanctity of the *Mishkan*. In the words of *Midrash Sh'mot Rabbah*, "Israel sinned [with the golden calf], whereupon Bezalel came and healed the wound [by constructing the *Mishkan*]."

Art can provide a tool for a sensitive person to cultivate sensitivity. Or it can provide a mask for the callous to conceal abuse. As always, each human being must first make an existential choice: by what values do we live?

Having chosen, art will heighten the expression of that choice. It will either reinforce a lofty moral commitment, or it will distract us from the suffering of our fellow human beings, deaden us to their cries. Art will express the choice we have made, but it cannot substitute for the choice itself.

The Power of Passion

We live in an age of technical expertise and calm deliberation. Civilization functions so smoothly that there are forms for every occasion and dispassionate experts who keep the system going. What we seem to be short of is passion—caring deeply about an ideal, an individual, or a cause, and a willingness to devote our talents, energy, and minds to the service of that cause.

If anything, passion is often disparaged in our culture. Someone motivated by a dream is derided as an "idealist" as opposed to a "realist." Someone devoted to a cause is accused of "having an agenda," and someone devoted to an individual is a "groupie." We carry a pack of insulting terms to let us disregard passionate people and to seek advice and leadership from the bland, the opportunistic, and the practical. Then we resent our leaders for their indifference and their inability to get worked up. We seek the very passion we flee.

Having safely removed idealism and passion from public life, having separated caring from professionalism, we turn to fiction to fill the void. There we confront the opposite extreme; instead of purpose without passion, we have passion with no greater purpose. People blow each other up, murder each other, and have sexual escapades without any sense of a larger meaning to their lives or their deeds. Thrill becomes an end in itself. The only way to know we are alive is to watch actors pretend to be torn apart.

This ersatz living, releasing our passions in the darkened, anonymous space of the movie theater or living room, helps distract us from the emptiness of our own lives. There is no passion, there is no purpose, there is no belonging in the world we have made, so we retreat to our fantasies. Like the gladiator fights in ancient Rome, they may be barbaric, but at least they quicken the pulse.

Passion is precisely what streams just under the surface of this parashah. In speaking about the artisans who will fashion the *Mishkan* and its implements, God "proclaimed by name Bezalel, son of Uri, son of Hur, of the tribe of Judah. . . . [God] gave him the ability to teach, him and Oholiav, son of Ahisamah, of the tribe of Dan." They and "every wise-hearted man within whom God has put wisdom and understanding to know" are to "do all the work for the labor of the Sanctuary." This host of artisans was to build God's *Mishkan*, a place where Israel and God could meet, a way for God to dwell in Israel's midst.

So why, if all these craftsmen are at work on the *Mishkan*, is Bezalel given the credit? Why does the Torah state, for instance, "Bezalel made the Ark of Shittim wood"? Why not give credit to each participant?

According to *Midrash Tanhuma* and also recorded by Rashi in his famous Torah commentary, it is "because Bezalel devoted himself to the work more than the other sages, so it is called by his name." We have no indication that Bezalel was more talented than the other artists. We have no sense that he was in charge of the project. But according to this medieval midrash, Bezalel was unique in the degree of his devotion and passion for the *Mishkan*.

Bezalel, you see, wasn't motivated by his wages, nor did he consider this a good career move. Instead, his motivation was to serve God and his people at the same time. Bezalel hoped that his art would serve a purpose beyond aesthetics, that his skill would bring a measure of holiness and peace to the world. Inspired by a sense of mission, he was willing to devote endless hours to the many technical details that such fine artistry requires. Bezalel pressed himself for nothing less than excellence. He insisted that he give his all, since he was serving a higher cause.

It might have been true that no one would notice. But, after all, the One would notice. And being noticed by God and singled out by Torah was more than enough reward.

We need to rekindle that sense of purpose, passion, and service in the details of our own lives and jobs. Instead of seeing each assignment as a task to finish and cross off a list, instead of evaluating each option for what it can do for our own advancement, if we trained ourselves to see an opportunity for service in each new challenge, if we learned to speak the word *mitzvah* anytime helping another human being was a possibility, think what a world we could fashion.

It's almost enough to get excited about.

Linking Our Generations

Throughout human history, great thinkers, spiritual giants, poets, and doctors have devoted their best energy and strongest talents to defeating death. Occasionally, we celebrate minor victories in the skirmish against mortality—we find the cure for a once-fatal illness, a new diet allows people to live a little longer or a little better. But we win those battles knowing that the war will ultimately be lost forever. Each of us has to die.

Across the millennia, Judaism has attempted to straddle the difficulty of death with the hope borne of faith. Without claiming a definitive knowledge of what happens after death, Judaism has always asserted that something—we don't know precisely what—does continue beyond the grave. Each generation of Jews has struggled anew with the stark reality of our finitude as individuals, each seeking succor and courage from our heritage and our God.

One unlikely source of comfort emerges from the rabbinic discussion of this parashah. It opens by explaining, "These are the records of the Tabernacle, the Tabernacle of the Pact, which were drawn up at Moses's bidding."

The rabbis focus on the very first word of the sentence, *eleh* (these). Rather than understanding that word in its context, they choose to read beyond its superficial meaning and look at it as something independent of what follows. For them, the word *these* points to something more significant than finances for building the Tabernacle. For the rabbis, it signifies precisely what price it was that the Israelites had paid in the wilderness and what was coming to them as a result.

As their first stop in the wilderness, the Jews rested at the foot of Mount Sinai, where they received the Torah and all its teachings. According to *Midrash Sh'mot Rabbah*, "when God gave the Torah to Israel, they became exempt from the sway of the Angel of Death. . . . For as soon as Israel accepted the Torah, God adorned them with His own glorious splendor. . . . Rabbi Shimon Bar Yohai said, 'God gave them weapons on which was engraved the Ineffable Name of God, and as long as this sword was in their possession, the Angel of Death could exercise no power over them.'"

Along with the revelation of Torah, the Jews received immortality at Mount Sinai. But then, according to the midrash, they lost it when they created the golden calf: "When they sinned, God deprived them of all these good things." With their rebellion against God, the Israelites once again fell under the sway of death.

Even without taking this story literally, it is possible to understand it metaphorically as an insight of great worth. We live eternally to the extent that we can tap into something eternal, something that connects our most distant ancestors, ourselves, and our most distant descendants.

Judaism is that eternal something. In the stirring words of Rabbi Jacob Kohn (twentieth-century United States), a life of Torah provides "the unbroken faith that links our generations one to another." When we study the words of the sages, read the calls of the prophets, or chant the words of the Torah, we link ourselves to their lives. In the words of the mishnah, "their lips move from the grave." We grant them posthumous life through our study. And we connect ourselves to our descendants, who will also pour their souls into these insights.

When we translate the mitzvot from objects of study into living realities, we link ourselves to an aspect of *kedushah* (holiness) that stretches throughout and above time. Observing the mitzvot allows us to soar beyond the tyranny of linear time to enter the realm of the sacred and the timeless.

Finally, when we study our sacred writings, make the mitzvot the cornerstone of our lives, and let the values of Judaism shine through our deeds, we make our souls tabernacles in which God can dwell. By placing ourselves in the Eternal One's line of vision, we join the panoply of tzaddikim and sages who live eternally in God's eternity.

The truth is, the Torah still conveys eternal life in some significant ways. In values that pass from one generation to another, in deeds that transform our communities and the world, and—most precious of all—in making ourselves fit to be cherished by God, we live on as members of *Beit Yisrael* (the household of Israel).

Leviticus

Va-Yikra

———◦◦◦———

He Called

Va-Yikra/He Called
Leviticus 1:1–5:26

Located in the center of the Torah, the book of Leviticus exemplifies the distinctive fusion of ritual and ethics that has always been the way of Torah. At the center comes Chapter 19 of the Holiness Code, a summary of the entire ethos of a Jewish way of life. Before and after this pivotal section, Leviticus concerns itself with the regulations of the priesthood, the proper performance of the sacrifices, atonement, and righteous living. Each of these facets gives expression to the covenant linking God and the people Israel.

The book begins with three chapters detailing the main types of sacrifices. The olah (burnt offering) provides "a pleasing odor before God." The minha (grain offering) must be without leaven. The fat and blood of the shelamim (peace or whole offerings) cannot be consumed. These sacrifices serve many different purposes, communal and individual, required and optional.

Chapters 4 and 5 highlight a different kind of offering: the hattat (sin offering). The hattat is for the unintentional commission of a prohibited act by a kohen (community), the head of the community, or an individual. It is also the necessary ritual response for withholding testimony, touching something tamei, touching human tumah, or failure to fulfill an oath.

Finally, the asham (guilt offering) is for robbery or fraud, for me'ilah (the misappropriation of Temple property), and for the unintentional violation of prohibitions.

Speaking of Values

Admit it—it's fun to gossip. As entertainment, gossip is still the choice of millions because it's free, it's easy, and it's accessible. Besides, a little harmless fun can't hurt anybody, can it?

Or can it? We live in a culture that doesn't value words. Fewer and fewer Americans read, and our literacy rate is dropping with each passing year. Our politicians offer abundant promises during their campaigns, and most public opinion polls show that Americans don't expect any of these promises to be fulfilled. We lie in large ways and small; we shade the truth; we exaggerate. The web of distortions and subterranean insults bind us in an ever-tightening grip. It becomes harder and harder to see the best in each other and in ourselves. Words count.

Judaism knows that words matter. In permitting Adam to name the animals, the Torah acknowledges the power of words to identify and to mold character. Perhaps that's why God's name isn't really a word, but all vowels, like breath itself. Perhaps that's also one reason why Jewish tradition has always placed such a strong emphasis on *sh'mirat ha-lashon* (guarding our speech) and on preventing *l'shon ha-ra* (malicious gossip).

The very beginning of *Sefer Va-Yikra* (the book of Leviticus) outlines each different type of sacrifice made in the Tabernacle (and later in King Solomon's temple), who brings it, and how it is carried out. Yet even in the midst of this description of ancient Israelite worship, our sages saw evidence of God's insistence on using speech to heal and nurture.

The very first verse of *Va-Yikra* says, "The Holy One called to Moses from the Tent of Meeting, saying . . ." Why, the rabbis wondered, is that extra "saying" there? What is God trying to teach us by using a superfluous word?

"We learn that if you said something to your neighbor, that neighbor must not spread the news without your consent," says the Talmud. We learn an act of *derekh eretz* from this verse. Even though it was quite clear God transmitted this message to Moses so that Moses would pass it on to the children of Israel, Moses still needed God's explicit instruction before repeating these words to the Jews. Later Jewish tradition incorporated this stringent concern by insisting, in the words of the thirteenth-century *Sefer Mitzvot Gadol*, "If someone tells something to a friend, the friend is not allowed to tell others unless specifically instructed to tell these things to others."

In other words, we should see our conversations as private. Our assumption is that people will feel free to repeat our private conversations unless we specify that they should not. Instead of having to assure each other that "this is just between us," following this Torah law would mean that when we didn't mind something being repeated, we would indicate that to our confidante. And if we didn't, then we could be sure that the conversation would go no further.

As a rabbi, I often counsel people on very sensitive, painful issues, and I'm struck by the fact that they feel the need to tell me not to repeat their conversation to anyone. Even in the heart of a rabbi's study, people feel that their words aren't safe, that their most private revelations could become public domain. How sad! I imagine that this paranoia must keep a lot of painful secrets buried within, causing additional pain, shame, and damage. I can feel their relief when I assure them that our conversation is their property and they may do with it as they choose, but that I regard it as theirs, not mine.

If Moses needed God's explicit permission before repeating God's words—words about public matters issued in the Tent of Meeting— then how much should we care about the words of God's creatures, uttered in confidence to a solitary individual.

Ours is an age in which trust is a luxury few can afford and fewer deserve. Yet without that trust, that *emunah* and *bitahon* (faith and trust), decency becomes a sham and a cover for vindictiveness. If we hope to shine the healing light of Torah in a dark and dreary time, if we intend to live as God's ensigns in this war against pain and despair, then we had best be prepared to wage that war on the front lines—in our own harsh words and careless chatter.

Sha, shtill. God is listening.

Form and Substance

Every living thing exhibits a balance between alteration and continuity. A single cell takes in new substances (food, air, water) and remolds those building blocks to fashion its own form. At the same time that its constituents change, its shape remains the same. Persistence and change, it seems, are different phases of the same phenomenon, different faces of the same reality. One cannot successfully remain and thrive without an openness to change, and one cannot retain the energy and will to change without a commitment to something time-less and constant.

That same dynamic tension has characterized Judaism from its inception, allowing the ever-renewed energy and depth of Torah to reverberate throughout the ages. This parashah hints at this remarkable capacity for renewal and regeneration. *Sefer Va-Yikra* informs us that "the priest shall turn these [sacrifices] into smoke on the altar as food, an offering by fire to the Lord." Commentators have noted the odd choice of words the Torah uses to describe the sacrifices: *lechem isheh l'Adonai* (literally "bread of fire for God"). Why does God need bread? Why are we told to offer a sacrifice to God in the first place?

This use of *lechem* (bread) to denote sacrifices is not unique to this parashah—elsewhere in the books of Leviticus and Numbers, the Torah reflects the same archaic Hebrew. Rashi points out that *lechem* "denotes food" and Rabbi Abraham Ibn Ezra reminds us, "The word *bread* is often used in Hebrew to denote food in general."

This traditional understanding of *lechem* not as bread alone, but as all types of food, is confirmed by modern scholarship as well. The authoritative Rabbi Jacob Milgrom writes, "In the Semitic languages, *lechem* refers to the food of the country. In Arabic, it means 'flesh'; in seashore areas, it can mean 'fish.'" In his commentary on the book of Leviticus, Baruch Levine writes that the "Hebrew *lechem* not only means 'bread' but is a more general word for food."

Why does the Torah describe the sacrifices to God as food? Rabbi Jacob Milgrom reminds us that this archaic language of God's food "hearkens back to earliest times, when sacrifices were intended to feed the gods. But Scripture rejects this notion, and in the cultic texts this term can be characterized as a linguistic fossil." Professor Levine concurs, "In most ancient societies, it was believed that gods required food for their sustenance and relied on sacrifices for energy and strength. . . . The Torah codes, while preserving the idiom common to ancient religions, understand the process somewhat differently. God desires the sacrifices of . . . worshippers not because He requires sustenance but because He desires their devotion and their fellowship."

The Torah could have developed a completely new terminology to characterize the sacrifices offered. Instead, it used the languages of earlier and surrounding pagan religions, both to work from within the assumptions of its listeners and to elevate that worldview to a higher plane. Rather than breaking with the past in the form of its worship, Judaism employed existing forms to educate its followers to a truer understanding of God and God's desires.

Judaism isn't so much about shifting forms and timeless truths as it is about retaining timeless forms that allow for new interpretations. We deliberately go out of our way to reinterpret ancient ritual precisely to maintain the venerable quality so apparent in Judaism's sacred moments. Even when we can no longer share the original understanding of a particular ritual (breaking the glass under the huppah to scare away demons), we refuse to abandon the mitzvah, instead giving it an interpretation that allows us to retain it and pass it on to the next generation unchanged.

Throughout the ages, Jews have retained loyalty to the commandments and customs that make Judaism distinctive, awesome, beautiful, and effective. And in each age, sages and scholars have provided new insights and readings that allow each new generation to reclaim those practices as their own, still reverberating with God's holy voice.

The continuity of Judaism lies in its forms, rich and fertile symbols capable of bearing a rainbow of meanings across time. With each new midrash and each new reading our sages teach, we harvest the Torah anew. And that process is to be found in the Torah itself.

Human Dignity: For the Birds?

With the book of Leviticus, we return to the heart of the Torah, to remarkable passages that translate the lofty values of Sinai into the concrete practices of everyday life, passages that instruct how to infuse the most mundane of deeds with the glow of sanctity and how to invest every moment of our day with the intimacy of God's presence. Through the detailed descriptions of the rituals of the *Mishkan* and later the *Beit Ha-Mikdash* (the Temple), the Torah provides observant Jews with the guidelines that shape our lives, our communities, and our religious practice to this very day.

This parashah opens by describing the most ancient of the sacrifices performed in Israel, the *olah*. The *olah* could be taken from a herd of cattle or from a flock of goats or sheep. These animals were quartered and then offered in flames as a way of expressing joy before God or contrition and *teshuvah*. They required unblemished, male animals.

Imagine just how expensive such an offering must have been. Considering the cost of meat today, think about purchasing an entire cow and then burning it without getting to take any of it home. The *olah* must have been possible only for the very wealthy.

Here the Torah provides for the needs of Israel's poor by allowing the offering of a turtledove or young pigeon as well. This *olah* would have been well within the reach of any Israelite, expressing the democratizing impulse that motivates much of the Torah and traditional Jewish belief.

The rabbis of antiquity and the medieval period recognized this sacred inclusiveness in the *olah* of birds. The Torah comments that once the pauper hands over the bird, "the *kohen* shall tear it open by its wings, without severing it." Why, the rabbis wondered, are the wings to remain on the bird? And why aren't the feathers removed before burning the bird's remains? The cow, lamb, or goat offerings had their skins removed. Why not in this case as well?

Rashi paraphrases the insight of Rabbi Yohanan in *Midrash Va-Yikra Rabbah*, observing that "it is true that no one can smell the smell of burning feathers and not be nauseated. So why, then, does God say to sacrifice it [with the feathers]? So the altar should satisfy and adorn the sacrifice of the poor."

Rashi understands that people attach great significance to appearances. We can't help but compare our own achievements against the accomplishments of others. We judge our homes or apartments, our status and our wealth, by referring to the people around us. Imagine, then, how badly an impoverished worshipper must have felt offering a tiny bird when some ancient fat cat had just offered an enormous bull. Hezekiah Ben Rabbi Manoah Hizkuni affirms that the reason the feathers are left intact is "because it [the bird] is small, and if you sever it, there will be only small pieces, and it won't be seemly to bring before the [divine] King."

That understanding is affirmed by modern scholarship as well. In his magisterial study of Leviticus, Jacob Milgrom writes that "its purpose may be to increase its size and give the appearance of a more substantial gift."

In deference to the potential embarrassment of the poor, the Torah insists that the bird's wings remain intact. Even though burning feathers smell terrible, the slight to the pauper—seeing the offering of the bird made even smaller—was far more offensive in the sight of God. In order to protect the dignity of even the least important Israelite, everyone in the Temple courtyard had to endure the stench of burning feathers. Our Torah is that passionate about the nobility of each human being.

In our own age, when most Americans give precedence to their own comfort at the expense of the homeless, the illiterate, or the unemployed, the stench of burning feathers should fill us with shame. Our God commands, and our ancestors' example inspires, a life of deference to simple human dignity.

Don't strip the feathers; endure the stench. Perhaps if the smell gets bad enough, we might become motivated to care and to act. The measure of our humanity is at stake in our response.

Tzav/Command

Leviticus 6:1–8:36

The first two chapters of Tzav *instruct the priests how to perform the rituals accompanying the sacrifices described in* Parashat Va-Yikra. *These chapters focus on the priests as officiants and emphasize the care required to maintain a state of* tohorah *(purity). A special focus of* Tzav *is the instruction that a portion of each sacrifice belongs to the priesthood and becomes the core of their sacred meals.*

Tzav begins with a discussion of the kodesh kodashim *(the most sacred offerings), which are four: the* olah *and the* minhah, *since both are part of the public ritual; the* hattat *and the* asham, *which are not part of the routine public ritual but result from private penitence.*

Afterward, the Torah describes the kodashim kallim *(offerings of lesser sanctity). These include the* zevah ha-shelamim *(peace or whole offerings), which are used in private worship, except for the specific* shelamim *offered at the festival of* Shavuot.

The Torah moves on to the hakhel *(gathering) of the entire community and the ordination and consecration of the altar and the priests over the course of seven days. The ordination includes sacrifice and the ritual of Moses taking some of the sacrificial blood and smearing it on Aaron's right earlobe, his right thumb, and his right big toe.*

The Worlds of Learning

The rabbis of the Talmud and Midrash were sensitive readers of Torah. They studied these sacred words day and night, always seeking new interpretations and novel implications of our special love relationship with God. In the process, they uncovered nuances and insights that continue to guide us on a path of righteous and holy living.

One of their remarkable insights was to notice the unusual wording found in *Parashat Tzav*. In speaking of a series of sacrifices to be offered on the altar in the *Mishkan*, the Torah says, "This is the torah of burnt offerings." Why, they wondered, did God use the word *torah*, which means "teaching" or "instruction," rather than saying "These are the rules"? Surely there must be some deeper lesson here, some significance worthy of consideration.

In the Talmud, the sage Resh Lakish asks the same question, "Why does the Torah say, 'This is the torah of burnt offerings'? In order to teach that if someone studies the laws of an offering, it is as though they had actually offered the sacrifice themselves."

Resh Lakish offers a remarkable notion: that study is vicarious action, that reading about something with sufficient imagination and identification constitutes doing it. Upon that idea—the power of the mind to create images that are as forceful as life itself—the entire enterprise of Judaism stands and thrives.

Think for a moment about some particularly vivid dream or fantasy you have. Now think back to a distant memory. Does one seem more real or vivid than the other? Chances are your fantasy feels a lot like a memory. Perhaps one of the key characteristics of human beings is our ability to use imagination to extend our experiences beyond the limits of our own bodies, our own vision, and our own knowledge. Through the use of our minds, through the integration of reading, art, and conversation, we expand to encounter people long dead, places we've never been, and ideas that other people have thought and articulated.

This ability to transmit abstract ideas, to cultivate belonging to a community that transcends time and place and sustains the timeless gift of values and virtues, is a key human function, perhaps our most godlike trait.

Judaism recognizes the power and necessity of cultivated imagination and projected identification. To be able to make a fantasy live requires the ability to identify with its characters, to place oneself amid its action, and to grow in exposure to its values. Far more than the memorization of facts or repetition of concepts, this kind of learning can take place only with the right creativity, sympathy, and receptivity.

This kind of learning is "talmud torah," study that is not simply a matter of satisfying curiosity or expanding skill (although it can certainly do both), but that teaches us something about God, something about what it is God wants from us, something about God's creation, or something about our partnership in the establishment of God's sovereignty.

When we study the Torah simply as an interesting document from the ancient Near East, then Torah study becomes merely academic learning. But when we study even the functioning of an automobile engine or read a good comic as an expression of God's bounty in the world or of the godlike capacity of the human soul to create and touch another soul, then even the Sunday funnies can be a source of talmud torah. Talmud torah is not what we study, but how we study.

Ha-Shamayim m'saprim k'vod El (The heavens declare the glory of God). Looking at the sky with the proper *kavvanah* (intention) can reveal something significant about God and creation, about what it means to be a person and a Jew. The special trick of rabbinic Judaism is to teach us to see all things as a sacred text waiting to be read and studied in our constant search for God and holiness.

In that search, there are no finer tools than the sacred writings of the Jewish people throughout the ages. Trained in spiritual openness, rooted in a culture that translated God's will into living words, the sages, prophets, poets, and philosophers compiled a library of insight, profundity, elevation, and exultation.

And when we study their words, when we engage in talmud torah, thereby making their words our own, it is as though we ourselves performed the sacrifices with a whole heart, as though we ourselves split the sea, received the Torah, or sat in the great Sanhedrin.

Through the miracle of talmud torah, we transcend any one age or place, making ourselves one with eternity and everywhere, binding ourselves with the One who invites us to participate in thinking the thoughts of the Divine.

Relevant to Whom?

The highest praise a rabbi hears is that her or his sermons and classes are always relevant, by which the generous congregant means that the topics pertain to everyday life and are not arcane or archaic in content. But another way to translate that praise is to hear that the rabbi didn't stretch the congregant's sense of what pertains to modern living. If *relevant* means "something the congregant already has an interest in," then a rabbi who restricts teaching to those areas prevents the congregant from a broader interest in the world, in human history, and in the history of the human spirit.

I've often been tempted to add another perspective, to inquire, "Relevant from whose perspective?" Maybe some topic seems removed to the listener but contains great insight and wisdom nonetheless. Maybe the lack of interest by the congregant is simply a defense against hearing something disturbing but necessary for spiritual growth. Or maybe some detail isn't relevant to the life of the congregant (yet) but is something God would have us consider and integrate.

Calling something "irrelevant" often reveals more about the listener than it does about the subject. Nothing Jewish is irrelevant. There is no "Jewish Trivial Pursuit," because no part of Judaism or Jewish history is trivial. But we do need to work to demonstrate its relevance, and we need creativity and energy to illumine its significance. If a student of mine sees something I teach as irrelevant or trivial, it means I haven't presented it well enough.

Parashat Tzav, as well as *Sefer Va-Yikra*, is often called "irrelevant." Reading the list of sacrifices to be brought to the *Mishkan* in the wilderness and the Temple in Jerusalem, the modern reader is confused by the staggering amount of detail and is often horrified by this catalogue of animal killing. But the primary charge against reading all those sacrifices is "irrelevance." After all, the last Temple was destroyed some two thousand years ago, and there have been no authorized sacrifices in Judaism since that time. So why spend all this time reading about something we can no longer do (and which many of us would not desire to do even if we could)?

Midrash Va-Yikra Rabbah, compiled two hundred years after the destruction of the Second Temple, faced a similar dilemma, and the rabbis provide valuable insight into why we continue to read about sacrifices. Rabbi Aha said in the name of Rabbi Hanina Bar Papa, "In order that Israel might not say: 'In the past we used to offer up sacrifices and engage in the study of them; now that there are no sacrifices, is it necessary to engage in the study of them?' The Holy Blessing One said to Israel, 'If you engage in the study of them, I account it to you as if you had offered them up.'"

What Rabbi Aha offers here is the importance of imagination and sympathetic study as a religious value. While we no longer offer animal sacrifices, our ancestors derived great comfort from that practice. We can learn of their sense of loyalty, obedience to divine fiat, and their intimacy with God by studying their piety and their practice. When we read the parashiyot about the sacrifices, when we learn the rabbinic expansions of those laws, we become like actors given a challenging script. Just as great actors make themselves feel what their characters would feel, Jews—through talmud torah—train ourselves to share our ancestors' piety and passion. We infuse our souls with the drive to make God's will our own and tingle with the thrill of responding to God's needs.

By reading about the sacrifices, we learn to shift the center of our spiritual gravity away from self-gratification toward meeting the needs of others and the Divine Other. By placing God's agenda at the center of our lives, by allowing God and the Torah to define relevance in their own context, we dethrone our despotic egos and learn to place the needs of our family, neighbors, community, and faith at the center of our own agendas.

And in displacing our voracious selves, we discover not only our true selves, but God.

Wholeness and Human Dignity

Ours is an age in which human dignity has taken a beating. We place our faith in money, allowing financial interests to dictate how we treat our people and our planet. This pernicious notion that anything cost-effective is proper and anything that is not efficient is to be abandoned is used to pollute our air, starve our working poor, and dismantle our schools. We have reduced ourselves to a lonely collection of cynical, self-centered consumers. We no longer think of ourselves as citizens or as souls, let alone as God's stewards for the planet.

In the past, there was a very different measurement of worth and wisdom: the intrinsic dignity of the human soul. While there was always a gap between the ideal and its implementation, the religious conviction that we are each made in God's image provided a powerful vision for those who took the God of Israel and the Bible seriously.

The holy scripture makes clear that the Holy One is a God who liberates slaves, loves all creatures, and asks that we respond to God's loving call to fashion a world of spiritual profundity and social justice.

In this parashah, the rabbis recognized the Torah's obsession with goodness, with justice, and with righteousness. One of the sacrifices mandated by God in the Torah is the *Zevah Shelamim* (whole offering, or peace offering). The Hebrew word Shelamim is related to the word *shalom*, which means "peace," "wholeness," "tranquillity," and "completeness." That *shleimut* (wholeness) was an inspiration for a series of remarks in *Midrash Va-Yikra Rabbah* about *gadol ha-shalom* (the greatness of peace). After all, the sacrifices were to bring peace between a fallible, striving humanity and our forgiving, empowering Parent in heaven.

The greatness of peace inspired this story. One of the greatest of the tannaitic rabbis (sages from the time of the Mishnah) was Rabbi Meir. His lectures and discussions were extremely popular and always well attended. One woman, in particular, loved his talks and was sure to participate whenever the great rabbi spoke. One evening, she was so inspired by his class that she stayed late and arrived home after her husband's food had grown cold. He was so incensed that he told her she could not enter their home until she had spit in the rabbi's face.

You can imagine how outraged and crushed she was: to be denied the chance to learn Torah, to be kicked out by her husband, forced onto the streets because she loved learning and mitzvot! And to add insult to injury, she now had to publicly humiliate her teacher if she hoped to live in her own home again.

Weeks passed, during which time the woman didn't return to her own home or attend any of Rabbi Meir's lectures. In a limbo caused by her husband's denigration and her unwillingness to harm her rabbi, this poor woman had literally no place to go, nowhere to be recognized. Miraculously, Rabbi Meir discovered the cause of her isolation and misery. Elevating her well-being above his own concerns for dignity and recognition, he approached her and told her that he was suffering from an eye ailment whose only cure was to have someone spit in his eye seven times. Since she was such a trusted student, he knew that he could ask her to perform this odious task that so few others would be willing to do.

Of course, she was delighted by this fortuitous turn of events. She spit in his eye and was able to return home. When asked how he could allow someone to spurn a rabbi's dignity in this way, Rabbi Meir was clear: God allows the divine name to be erased for the sake of an accused wife, so how could he do less?

Human dignity is no mere secular imposition, no relativism. Indeed, *k'vod ha-briot* (human dignity) is a supreme religious value, the logical consequence of a God who loves creation and wants all creatures to see the divine image in each other.

True dignity, the kind that allows people to cherish each other's differences and live with each other as a community, is an unimpeachably biblical value. Great, indeed, is such *shleimut*.

Shemini/Eighth

Leviticus 9:1–10:47

Parashat Shemini *begins with the first celebration of sacrifice after the seven days of ordination. This sacrifice on the eighth day marks the first time that the altar is used for a sacrifice on behalf of the people Israel. Moses underscores the purpose of sacrifice when he says, "This is what the Lord has commanded that you do, that the Presence of the Lord may appear to you." Aaron and his sons follow the instructions of Moses and perform the sacrifices exactly as God has commanded. Then Aaron lifts his hands and blesses the people. God's presence appears to all the people, and a fire from God consumes the burnt offerings. The people respond by rejoicing and worshipping.*

Joy turns to tragedy as two of Aaron's sons offer alien fire, rather than performing the sacrifices in accordance with God's command. As a result, a fire from God consumes them, and they both die instantly. Aaron is silent in the face of God's power and his sons' death, and Moses tells Aaron and his remaining sons not to engage in public displays of mourning. Instead, he instructs the entire community to mourn for the burning. Moses then instructs the priests to refrain from wine or other intoxicants when performing the sacred service. He lays out God's instructions for the role of the priesthood: "You must distinguish between the sacred and the profane, and between the unclean and the clean, and you must teach the Israelites all the laws which the Lord has imparted to them through Moses." The Torah then provides the laws of kashrut, reflecting the conviction that what and how one eats has spiritual consequence, creates strong communal bonds, and reinforces important religious insights.

The first examples listed are permitted land animals: those with fully cleft hooves that chew their cud. Other land animals are prohibited. Of water creatures, the permitted animals are those with both fins and scales. Prohibited birds are listed without any broad principle of explanation. Most winged swarming creatures are prohibited, except for four types of locusts. These form the core of the kashrut system still observed by Jews today.

The reason for these kosher laws is offered by the Torah: "For I the Lord am your God: you shall sanctify yourselves and be holy, for I am holy. For I the Lord am He who brought you up from the land of Egypt to be your God: you shall be holy for I am holy."

Seek, Though You Won't Find

Imagine the excitement in the air as the children of Israel gather around the newly constructed sanctuary! The *Mishkan* is promised to them as the central structure of their encampment, and God promises to be present in that place. All of the people come together to donate their jewelry, to contribute the wood, the gold, the yarn, the skins. Each person with artistic and practical skill joins in the labor, and the *kohanim* and Levites are consecrated for holy service. Then, as all gather for the initiatory celebrations, Moses announces the good news, "Today the Holy One will appear to you."

This is a curious promise. If God is incorporeal, if God is beyond all limitations and restrictions, then what can it possibly mean to see God? This perplexity is not merely the result of deep theology, but comes from the Torah's words themselves. At the end of the celebration, when the divine presence consumes the sacrifice, we are again told, "Fire came forth from before the Holy One and consumed the burnt offering and the fat parts on the altar. And all the people saw, and shouted, and fell on their faces." What did the people see? They saw the fire, and they saw the sacrifice consumed. Yet they aren't told they will see God's acts, they are told they will see God. Why?

Rashi explains God's appearance to mean "to rest God's Shechinah in the work of your hands." God's presence isn't a fact that the eyes can see or data that the mind can analyze. Rashi insists that God's appearance is through our emotions and our actions; God enters the world when we orient our lives in harmony with God's presence, when we sanctify creation and create meaning by living the mitzvot.

That same profound insight—preventing us from reducing God to a mere fact, forcing us to perceive the divine presence with our hearts, with our minds, and with our deeds—has animated Jewish faith through the ages. The great sage Rambam cautions us that biblical sightings are "prophetic visions and parables" meant to teach us life lessons rather than create visual records. The philosopher and poet Shlomo Ibn Gabirol (eleventh-century Spain) tells God, "You are light that is eternal. The intellect's eye yearns for You and catches only glimmerings. Endless is the extent of Your vision but all of You cannot be seen (*Keter Malkhut*)."

Seeing God is not a physical activity. These sources and the Torah itself remind us of what every believer knows—that God is the ground of our being, that there are values that emerge immediately from a relationship with the divine. We "know" God by being, through the mindful exultation of life itself. Perhaps that's why the Israelites respond to the fire with shouting and worship. They do not respond by quantifying; they respond with life.

Our minds cannot master God, but the quest is essential nonetheless. As the ancient philosopher Philo (first-century Egypt) reminds us, "Though the clear vision of God as God really is denied us, we ought not to relinquish the quest. For the very seeking, even without finding, is felicity itself."

To find God is beyond human attainment and probably represents a distortion of our own existential possibility. But to seek God, to yearn for holiness, and to strive for righteousness—these orient our lives as a magnet positions the needle of a compass, providing us purpose, direction, and hope. "What grander or holier house could we find for God in the whole range of existence than the vision-seeking mind?" asks Philo.

What grander house indeed! May our visions be liberating on every level; may we see ourselves crossing the sea into our truest reality; and may we experience that quest as an experience of the divine that continues to shine light into our souls and dazzle our days.

Kashrut and Conquest

Human beings are bloody animals. For millennia, we have cultivated the brutality of warfare, calling the process of killing each other in large numbers an "art" or a "science." As each new century gives way to another, our warfare becomes more devastating, our technological skills harnessed to the challenge of ever-more-efficient ways of killing of ever-larger numbers of people. While almost every author on the subject regrets the existence of warfare in theory, each and every war has enjoyed thoughtful and enthusiastic supporters on both sides. We hate warfare but love wars. And so our killing continues unabated.

Perhaps we don't hate wars as much as we say we do. Maybe we like the thrill of the slaughter, the passions that warfare unleashes, the triumph of victory and even the resentment of defeat. Could it be that killing is a primal human lust?

If that is true, then the question facing us is how to channel and contain that lust so that it does the least possible damage. From experience, we know that denying lust can often result in its eventual manifestation without restraint. The great genius of Sigmund Freud was to counsel the sublimation of drive, redirecting an impulse into a less harmful mode of expression.

Living in the twenty-first century, we rarely link our all-too-human lust for blood with our desire to eat meat. After all, there is an entire industry whose sole purpose is to disguise our food so we don't have to consider its origins. Meat is cleverly wrapped and displayed so it doesn't look like the animals it once was. Blood is kept to a minimum behind crisp, clean plastics. Our very language masks what it is we devour—to speak of "carcasses," "death," or "corpses" in the context of food is prima facie evidence of extremism.

Yet in earlier centuries and in many other parts of the world today, people are only too aware of the sources of their food. That awareness pervades this parashah as well.

Parashat Shemini provides a lengthy list of animals that are permitted and prohibited for Jewish consumption. One of the pillars of kashrut involves restricting which animals may be used for food. All vegetation is permissible; the restrictions of kashrut apply to meat. Those restrictions teach a reverence for life, not by prohibiting the consumption of animals, but by forcing a consciousness of the choices we make. A kosher Jew cannot eat meat unaware.

But back to the subject of aggression. Anthropologists today affirm the biblical rabbinic link between eating and aggression. In fact, rabbinic tradition affirmed that a *shokhet* (ritual butcher) was but one step removed from a killer. And in a passage from *Midrash Va-Yikra Rabbah*, Resh Lakish explicitly linked the two: "If you will prove yourselves worthy, you will consume; but if you do not prove worthy, you will be consumed by the nations." Resh Lakish uses the same verb, *tokhelu* (to consume), to apply to a Jew sitting down to eat and to the oppression of despotic and bloody nations. His message is that we choose the kind of world in which we live. If we live in fidelity to God's laws, then we can contribute to a world of trust, compassion, and peace. If we respond only to our own drives, including our lust for blood, then we will pay the price for those choices by living in a dangerous climate.

Lest we think that this link between eating meat and aggression is merely rabbinic, Rabbi Aha supports his colleague Resh Lakish by quoting the biblical prophet Isaiah: "If you are willing and obedient, you shall eat the good of the land; but if you refuse and rebel, you shall be devoured by the sword."

Both the Tanakh and the rabbis recognize eating meat as an attempt to redirect humanity's bloodlust away from the slaughter of other people. Kashrut goes beyond that sublimation to impose a restriction on the free expression of that craving.

Kashrut has a vital role to play by teaching us to live our lives in accordance with the Torah. If we are able to shape our eating to the sacred values of our God and tradition, then we might be able to fashion acts of piety and goodness in other endeavors as well. Kashrut is a tool in the arsenal of civilizing humanity toward gentleness, empathy, and restraint.

So before you take another bite, give it some thought. God is waiting on your decision.

Hesed: A Traditional Value

We live in an age of vigorous political debate, as liberals and conservatives present their views of the world and their prescriptions for how to redress our problems in books, articles, and speeches all over the country. Perhaps because the stakes are so high, perhaps because there is no real consensus, how we understand the issues confronting us has important ramifications for the future we leave to our children. Within the Jewish community, Jewish progressives and Jewish neo-Conservatives offer competing assessments of how Jews ought to act politically.

No one argues with the recognition that American Jews are a very liberal group. Liberals insist that this progressive stance has deep roots in Jewish moral and religious values. Conservatives insist that this liberal posture may once have served Jewish self-interest, but it is no longer beneficial to us and no longer moral.

One of the points of contention between the political factions is looking out for number one. On the one hand, there are those who argue that our attempt to care for other people is an effort we cannot afford financially and is in opposition to our own self-interest. As Jews, we are the butt of the hatred and bigotry of the rest of the world. No one cares about our safety and our welfare, and no one lifts a finger to come to our aid. When the Jews were in trouble in World War II, the nations of the world turned their backs on us. And whenever the State of Israel is in need, the rest of humanity is willing to sit on its hands and let Israel sink. In such a world, Jews had best look out for themselves by looking out only for themselves.

In opposition to that stance, Jewish progressives insist that looking out for justice for all and making special efforts to care for the poor and provide opportunities for ethnic minorities and women is the best way to protect Jewish self-interest and reflect Judaism's traditional moral concerns. In times of financial straits, resentment, and animosity, the Jews are among the first to become scapegoats. If we expect others to treat us with justice, we must be sure to treat others as we would be treated ourselves. On a purely practical level, looking out only for ourselves will put us in a precarious position with the majority culture.

But from the perspective of morality, these progressives argue, there is an even more compelling point. The answer to Cain's selfish question, "Am I my brother's keeper?" is a resounding "yes." The law most frequently repeated in the Torah is that "you shall have one law for yourself and for the stranger who dwells in your midst." Legislation that enforces setting aside tithes for the poor is at the cornerstone of Torah law. We are commanded to provide for the widow and the orphan. We established the world's first universal public education system (for males). Not merely our modern history, but our Torah legislation impels placing the concerns of others high on the Jewish agenda.

The ancient rabbis understood this parashah to suggest that same point by listing those animals that are not kosher and may not be eaten: the pig, the rabbit, shellfish, the stork, and forbidden insects. The Talmud notes that the word for "stork" is *hasidah*, which they read as relating to the word *hesed* (loving-kindness). They note that the stork was given this illustrious name because it makes a point of sharing its food. Why then, if this bird is so praiseworthy, is it not kosher? Because it would only share food with its own kind.

Our *hesed*, if restricted only to providing for the needs and interests of our own kind, is *treif* (improper). To truly reflect God's attribute of *hesed*, we must be willing, as God is, to seek the welfare of all God's creatures and to pursue justice and peace for all humankind.

Tazria/Delivery

Leviticus 12:1–13:59

The next two parashiyot detail issues of tumah and tohorah.

A woman is tamei for seven days if she gives birth to a son and fourteen days for a daughter. The boy is to be ritually circumcised on the eighth day. There is a subsequent period of tumah for either a boy or a girl, and then the mother brings a sacrifice to restore her tohorah.

Tzara'at is an eruption that affects human skin (and has often been confused with leprosy). The Torah speaks of four different categories regarding tzara'at: (1) tzara'at in humans, (2) tzara'at in fabrics and leather, (3) a ritual to restore the purity of a person healed of tzara'at, and (4) tzara'at in plastered or mud-covered building stones. The role of the kohen is strikingly nonmagical: he doesn't "cure" anyone of the illness; he merely diagnoses it and, when it is already cured, restores the person's ritual wholeness. In cases of acute tzara'at, the sufferer is banished from the camp for the duration of the illness, often for life.

Metzora/The Leper

Leviticus 14:1–15:33

Metzora continues the discussion of the ritual response to tzara'at. The parashah opens with the rites for restoring the tohorah of a person who has suffered from acute tzara'at. These elaborate rituals are similar to those performed for a person who comes into contact with a corpse. Like the ordination of priests, this ritual takes a full seven days plus one (marking a new creation or rebirth of the individual). Also like the ordination of priests, the person has sacrificial blood smeared on his right earlobe, right thumb, and right big toe.

Within Eretz Yisrael, this plague also affects homes. The home is then cleared prior to the priestly inspection. If it is indeed infected, the home is shut up for seven days. At the end of this period, the priest inspects it again, and the affected stones are removed from the home (and the town). The plaster inside the home is scraped off, and new plaster is applied. If tzara'at breaks out again, the home is demolished. The ritual for purging a "healed" home is almost the same as for a healed individual.

The parashah now moves to consider discharges from sexual organs, male or female. These discharges result from illness or infection and do not include menstruation or normal seminal emissions. As with much of Leviticus, illness is subsumed under the category of tumah, making illness a religious concern and equating healing with tohorah. Abnormal male and female discharges are both referred to by the same term: zav. The philosophy underlying this religious attention is expressed at the end of the parashah: "You shall put the Israelites on guard against their uncleanness, lest they die through their uncleanness by defiling the Tabernacle, which is among them."

Religious Humility on Life's Journey

Modern men and women like to pretend that we have a direct pipeline into reality; that we know, in an absolute and ultimate way, about ourselves, about the world around us, about true wisdom. Forgetting that previous generations were equally sure about their "truths"—that the earth was flat, that the universe was a few thousand years old, that women were inferior to men—we presume that our most cherished verities will last forever. We confuse our grasp of reality with reality itself, our understanding of humanity with humanity, our self-confidence with truth.

Take, for example, the book *The Bell Curve*, which claims that general intelligence corresponds to income levels and race. By assuming that IQ and other standardized tests accurately measure some innate ability called "intelligence," this book confuses test results with creativity, insight, memory, and control. Based on this blithe (and demonstrably false) assumption, the authors then claim that blacks are less intelligent than whites, that Ashkenazi Jews are the brightest of all. Confusing the map with the territory, the authors' absolute certainty reveals an insolence at once false and dangerous.

Confusing our grasp of reality with reality itself isn't unique to modern men and women. But its pernicious effects are heightened by our secularity, a general assertion that humanity is the measure of all things and the ultimate arbiter of good and evil, right and wrong. Such superficial smugness is directly challenged by Jewish religious sources, particularly by *Parashat Metzora*.

This parashah speaks of a variety of afflictions that mar the skin and home. Such illnesses produce a state of ritual impurity, with dire consequences for the sufferer and the community. Declaring the *tzara'at* to have officially commenced was a religious obligation of the highest significance and was assigned to the local *kohen*.

God instructs Moses and Aaron, "When you enter the land of Canaan that I give you as a possession, and I inflict an eruptive plague upon a house in the land you possess, the owner of the house shall come and tell the *kohen*, saying, 'Something like a plague has appeared upon my house.'"

The ancient rabbis notice that "something like a plague" is pretty tentative language—striking for a culture in which such epidemics were events of great moment and consequence. Notice also that the Torah mandates this line. As the Mishnah notes, "Even if he is a Torah scholar and knows for certainty that it is a plague-spot, he shall not declare outright, 'It is a plague-spot,' but 'Something like a plague-spot.'"

This tentative phrasing is particularly noteworthy because the Torah doesn't hesitate to make definitive statements when it can. Pure and impure, kosher and *treif*, permitted and prohibited are the lofty standards that any lover of the Bible integrates as a way of seeing the world and of navigating a path of righteousness. So why the hesitation here?

I think that the Torah is teaching a kind of religious/intellectual humility to its followers. We are not God, and we are far from perfect. The way we acquire knowledge and wisdom is limited by our own five senses, our own life experiences, and our own subjective intuition. We do not observe from some neutral or privileged place. Instead, each of us can only see what our eyes will see, only understand by building on the analogies of what we already know. Human wisdom and judgment is, of necessity, limited, imperfect, and provisional.

As we continue in life, we learn new facts, new ways of thinking, new experiences, all of which allow us to revisit our own convictions and beliefs, to challenge our own insights and dogmas. While we continue to assert our own understandings, the Torah is suggesting that we do so with the humility that our most passionate conviction may be erroneous or based on something we will come to reject later on. This religious humility and the consequent courage to fashion a life of meaning based on a provisional fix on timeless truth is the highest form of saintliness, blending as it does the courage of one's convictions with the recognition that good people may not share those convictions and may not be wrong. Because of our limited vision, we may all have only a partial truth, so that different and conflicting perceptions may each be partially true and partially distorted by our finitude.

As the ancient midrash *Otiot de-Rebbi Akiva* notes, "Truth has legs." Scurrying as it does, truth eludes final capture or complete possession. We are all seekers along the way, all wanderers in the wilderness, never quite making it into the Promised Land but struggling to come closer to our sacred home.

Out of our Torah-mandated religious humility can emerge the recognition that we need each other's insights, even where we disagree strongly, to come to know God and God's will in the fullest way possible.

Can we help each other on the journey?

The Miracle of Birth

In a sense, the thrust of *Parashat Tazria* and *Parashat Metzora* is to restore peace of mind and spiritual wholeness after the disruption and terror of disease. The opening lines of the joint portion speak of something different, of birth: "When a woman at childbirth bears a male, . . ." While rabbinic Judaism has volumes to say about *tumah* and *tohorah*, the rabbis of the ancient midrash *Va-Yikra Rabbah* use this reference to childbirth to consider what a miracle birth really is.

First, the rabbis consider the medical marvel that pregnancy entails: "If a person holds a bag of money with the opening downward, don't the coins scatter? But the embryo has its residence in the mother's womb, and the Holy Blessing One guards it that it does not fall out and die." The miracle of the female body's ability to retain the fetus within is heightened by the fact that human beings stand erect and walk on two feet: "It is the way of a beast to walk with its body in a horizontal position, and its embryo is in its womb in the form of a bag, whereas a woman walks erect while the embryo is in her womb, and the Holy Blessing One guards it that it should not fall out."

How marvelous that, as a rule, women have the capacity to carry the fetus to term, and that the human body is capable of such wondrous feats!

Consider another marvel of pregnancy: "If a person were to stay in hot water for one hour, wouldn't that be fatal? Now a woman's womb is at boiling temperature, and the embryo is in the womb, and the Holy Blessing One takes care of it." And one final miracle of pregnancy: "All the nine months that a woman does not see [menstrual] blood, she really should do so; but what does the Holy Blessing One do? God directs the blood upward to her breasts and turns it into milk, so that the fetus may come forth and have food."

These rabbinic observations may make us smile at their simplicity and their lack of anatomical sophistication. But that really misses the remarkable profundity of what the sages are trying to note: we take for granted the complex processes that insemination, pregnancy, and birth require. Yet the impediments facing an egg and a sperm combining, flourishing, and producing a healthy baby are so daunting that the end product is no less miraculous in our eyes than it was in the view of our ancestors. How striking that the human baby (and the mother) fights gravity for the duration of the pregnancy. Reflect on the fetus's complete reliance on its mother for temperature control, nutrition, and other necessities, and the wondrous nature of birth is overwhelming. Or consider that the rabbis didn't have dissections and autopsies, didn't know why the blood stopped flowing and the milk started production. But they were sound enough empiricists to note that the two events happened at approximately the same time and so must be linked to the same cause. It is a miracle that most mothers produce their baby's first food.

All of this wonder is limited to the physical and biological side of pregnancy and birth, a side that certainly justifies our sense of awe and marvel. But the rabbis were also physicians of the soul, and they paused to note the miracle that babies are born with distinct personalities, ready to unfold and express themselves to their parents and the world. That ready-formed character is a sign that God establishes a unique relationship with each new baby, so that his or her place in the world is irreplaceable from the moment of birth:

> It is natural that, if a man is confined to prison with no one giving him attention, and someone comes and kindles a light for him there, the former should feel gratitude toward the latter. So too is it with the Holy Blessing One. When the embryo is in its mother's womb, God causes a light to shine for it there. Is this not a matter for praise?

It is indeed.

Leaders Who Serve

Our leaders often have a sense of their own dignity and self-worth that is far removed from the estimation of common folk. The trappings of power form a temptation so great that few are able to resist. Small wonder, then, that leaders of all stripes inflate their own worth with the homage paid their positions.

The Torah offers a corrective insight into the proper attitude of a true leader. In *Parashat Tazria*, the Torah explains how a *kohen* is to examine an Israelite suffering from *tzara'at*: "When a person has on the skin of his body a discoloration, a scab, or a shiny mark, and it develops into a scaly affection on the skin of his body, it shall be reported to Aaron, the *kohen*, or to one of his sons, the *kohanim*. The *kohen* shall examine the affection on the skin of his body."

In addition to posing a medical trauma, the *metzora* (sick person) also entered a state of ritual impurity. Medicine was the purview of others in the biblical view, perhaps of the prophets. But even when healed of the illness, the *metzora* still required the religious attention of the *kohen*, who would examine him or her and supervise the steps leading back to the person's full participation in the community.

Midrash Va-Yikra Rabbah records surprise that someone as august as Aaron, the first *kohen gadol*, is expected to dirty his hands and sully his status by poking around the sores of a *metzora*. Rabbi Levi transmitted in the name of Rabbi Hama Ben Rabbi Hanina, "Moses was extremely aggravated by this matter, saying, 'Is this the honor of Aaron, my brother, that he should be the examiner of the sick!?'" Moses, it seems, is taken by his family's status and authority. The most humble person in the entire biblical panoply, he succumbs to the perks of his office. It strikes Moses as unbecoming that his brother should have to perform such indecorous tasks.

Yet God's response to the great leader is instructive for our generation as well: "Said the Holy Blessed One to Moses, 'Doesn't Aaron enjoy the twenty-four donations to the priesthood?'" God reminds Moses that Aaron doesn't complain about all the benefits he derives from his work, so he can hardly complain about added expectations either. The price he pays for extra benefits is extra responsibilities.

That balance between perks and obligation is noted in the Midrashic proverb: "One who eats the palm heart will be whipped with the dried palm." The added rewards come because of heightened expectations; social prominence emerges from social responsibility. The Talmudic observation that the Messiah can be found bandaging the wounds of those afflicted with *tzara'at* is therefore no surprise. True greatness is manifest in a willingness to serve.

This reality has not changed in our day either. Leadership, the Torah teaches, involves a willingness to extend oneself, to take on the onerous tasks to ensure that all Jews have access to their Judaism, that all humanity can enjoy the fellowship of other human beings.

In that regard, we are all called to be leaders. Roll up your sleeves; there is much to be done.

Aharei Mot/After the Death

Leviticus 16:1–18:30

After the death of Aaron's sons Nadav and Avihu, God tells Moses to tell Aaron that he and his remaining sons are to enter the shrine only when performing the sacrifices in a fashion commanded by God.

Chapter 16 discusses the rituals for Yom Kippur (the Day of Atonement). The purpose of these rituals is to remove the tumah of the Israelites, the priests, and the altar, transferring them onto the goat of Azazel (the scapegoat), which is then driven into the wilderness. The biblical purpose of the Day of Atonement is to purify the sanctuary, allowing God to dwell in the midst of the Jewish people and maintain the efficacy of the Temple ritual. Later Jewish thought shifts the focus from restoring the sanctuary to atoning for the people. This shift is reflected in the Torah in the words, "On this day atonement shall be made for you to cleanse you of all your sins; you shall be clean before the Lord."

The unit from Leviticus 17:26 is known as the Holiness Code because its dominant theme is the holiness of the people Israel. The constant refrain "You shall be holy, for I, the Lord your God am holy" becomes the vocation of each individual and the entire people. As a result, the laws of this section pertain to all Israel, not just to Moses or the priesthood. The code begins with a prologue that outlines the proper mode of worship and concludes with an epilogue consisting of blessings and curses.

After the prologue, the Holiness Code moves on to the commandments pertaining to forbidden sexual practices, which are designated as to'evah (abominations) inconsistent with priestly purity. The overarching principle of this section (and the following sections) is God's injunction: "My rules alone shall you observe, and faithfully follow My laws: I am the Lord your God. You shall keep My laws and rules, by the pursuit of which a person shall live: I am the Lord."

Kedoshim/Holiness
Leviticus 19:1–20:27

Kedoshim *contains a distillation of the essence of Torah instruction. Chapter 19 lays out the duties of the people Israel and presents representative teachings from the broad range of the mitzvot. This was already recognized in antiquity, as* Midrash Va-Yikra Rabbah *records, "Most of the essential laws of the Torah can be derived from it." A list of imperatives ("you shall") and prohibitions ("you shall not"), this chapter blends what we would call ritual requirements with ethical mandates in a way that is characteristic of the Torah's genius.*

These commandments are directed toward the entire community, beginning with the peroration, "You shall be holy, for I, the Lord your God, am holy." These laws often echo the Ten Commandments in content and form, and they lay out an agenda of ritual profundity, ethical sensitivity and rigor, and a passion for social justice.

Chapter 20 moves into a reformulation of laws on the subject of incest and forbidden sexual activity. Whereas Chapter 18 is in apodictic form ("Do not" or "You shall") without listing any penalty, Chapter 20 is causal ("If . . . , then . . ." or "When . . . , then . . ."). Both chapters assume a connection between pagan religion and sexual immorality, and both recognize that nexus as a reason for exile.

The penalties in Chapter 20 deal with capital offenses and those that carry the penalty of karet *(banishment from the community). The goal of these laws is that "you shall possess the land, for I will give it to you to possess, a land flowing with milk and honey. I the Lord am your God who has set you apart from other peoples, so you shall set apart the clean from the unclean. . . . You shall be holy to Me, for I the Lord am holy, and I have set you apart from other peoples to be Mine."*

Holiness Takes Many Forms

With *Parashat Kedoshim*, we begin what the rabbis of the Midrash recognized as "the section dealing with holiness." In this estimation, they anticipated modern scholarship, which also recognizes a distinct Holiness Code within the various strands that comprise our Torah. Characteristic of this portion of scripture is the repeated injunction, "You shall be holy, for I, the Lord your God, am holy."

I can think of no more sublime religious imperative. Yet its lofty elegance and moral rigor notwithstanding, it also raises a problem for us, as it did for our ancestors. In repeating the instruction to be holy, the Torah tells us *what* to be without telling us what that attribute entails. What exactly does being "holy" mean?

In *Midrash Va-Yikra Rabbah*, different rabbis perceive different definitions for this enigmatic term. Rabbi Shimon Bar Yohai links holiness to a sense of justice, quoting the prophet Isaiah that "the Lord of hosts is exalted through justice." Rabbi Judah reads a notion of distinctiveness into the term *holy*, saying, "The distinction You [God] conferred in Your world is eternal." Rabbi Levi understands holiness as inextricably connected to the unique status of the Land of Israel or—like Rabbi Judah—to distinctiveness. Thus, Rabbi Levi quotes God as saying to the Jewish people, "My children, as I am separate, so you be separate; as I am holy, so you be holy." While this ancient rabbinic debate about holiness shows no sign of slowing down in our own time, one ancient discussion about holiness bears particular relevance to the reality of Jewish life in America.

Much grief and regret is expressed in print and in rabbinic sermons about the abysmal level of Jewish learning in America. Through the loving blur of nostalgia, Jews look back to the "good old days" of Eastern Europe, when every male was a *yeshivah bochur* (a rabbinic student), everyone was pious, and everyone was observant. Time and again, we are scolded that all Jews must be learning Jews, and that American Jewry is only a pale imitation of "real" Jewish life, meaning one in which every Jew is a Torah scholar of sorts.

As laudable as that goal may be, it never represented the reality of Jewish living. Nor, according to the rabbis of *Midrash Va-Yikra Rabbah*, does it represent the only way to embody holiness. Recognizing that holiness comes from the Torah, they notice that the Torah itself says, "She is a tree of life to them that hold fast to her," and they understand the "she" in question to be self-referential. They are quick to recognize that the Torah doesn't claim to be a source of life only for those who study it or even just for those who observe it, but rather for all who *hold fast* to it. Anyone who contributes, in whatever way they can, to the relationship between the Jewish people and the Torah merits inclusion in our ultimate redemption. Rabbi Huna is explicit on this point:

> If a person feels weighed down by transgression, what action will merit life? If accustomed to read one page of Scripture, let that person read two pages. If accustomed to study one chapter of Mishnah, study two chapters.
>
> But what if that person was not accustomed to read Scripture or to study Mishnah at all? What then should that person do to merit life? Such a one should get an appointment as a communal leader or as an administrator of *tzedakah* and will thereby merit life.

Rabbi Huna and his colleagues, our sages of blessed memory, recognize that not everyone is able to study our sacred writings. That deficiency does not sunder a Jew from our collective heritage of Torah. Rather, the rabbis instruct, let those who cannot study perform acts of charity to support Jewish institutions, thereby perpetuating the values and learning of our ancient heritage. Let those who cannot learn assist other Jews by strengthening our synagogues, our religious and day schools, our rabbinical schools and universities. Let those who cannot learn volunteer their time to serve on committees, boards, and organizations that keep the Jewish people coherent and vibrant.

Not being able to study Torah does not sunder a Jew from membership in the Jewish people. Any Jew who supports Jewish living and Jewish community, who makes Torah study possible for others, or who devotes time to protecting the interests and needs of the Jewish community remains inseparably linked to our ancient covenant with God.

May all of us, joined in a single band, soon merit the redemption of our people, of all humanity, and of all the earth.

What Can We Learn from a Mother?

The consecration of the *Mishkan* has barely been completed when Aaron's sons, Nadav and Avihu, violate the established rules for the service of God and willfully impose their own offering and their own mode of offering. In response to their "alien fire," God engulfs the two men in a fire from heaven, striking both down.

What makes this story particularly gripping is that it comes at what ought to be the high point of their father's life. Aaron served God and the Jewish people by working as Moses's mouthpiece before Pharaoh. In the wilderness, he offered all sacrifices and ran the sacrificial worship in the *Mishkan*, and his offspring were promised similar roles in the Holy Temple in Jerusalem. The crown of the priesthood was his and his children's forever, and the celebration of that signal honor was to occur after the construction and dedication of the *Mishkan*.

With great pomp and solemnity, before the eyes of the entire people, Aaron and his sons were to perform sacrifices to atone for themselves and the priestly clan, and then they were to provide similar offerings on behalf of the entire people. At that cherished moment, with Moses and the house of Israel gazing on in awe, Aaron's sons perform their act of rebellion, and before the entire gathering, an enraged God executes both men.

After the death of his sons, Aaron silently accepts God's judgment as just, returning to perform his sacrificial duties with deference to the verdict against his children.

While the parashah highlights a world of men and public ritual, of fathers and sons and rebellion and punishment, it completely omits one key player: Aaron's wife, the mother of Nadav and Avihu. What of Elisheva Bat Aminadav? Does she also accept God's punishment in mute obedience and humble resignation? Is she so taken by her family's prestige that she accepts her sons' fate as the consequence of social prominence?

Where the Torah is silent, the Midrash fills in the gap. *Midrash Va-Yikra Rabbah* tells us that "Elisheva Bat Aminadav . . . witnessed five crowns in one day: her brother-in-law [Moses] was like a king; her brother [Nahshon] was like a prince; her husband was a *kohen gadol*; her two sons were both deputy high priests; and Pinhas, her grandson, was a *kohen* appointed for war."

This is a woman who has risen as high as any female can aspire to do in a patriarchal age. Every one of her male relatives has achieved high office and weighty responsibility; each one is respected and revered. Surely, such a woman would be unassailably happy with her status. Yet the Midrash tells us, "[She] did not enjoy happiness in the world. . . . When her sons entered to offer incense and were burnt, her joy was changed to mourning."

Perhaps Elisheva's response is no different than that of any other human being, but I can't help thinking that her training as a woman helped shape her priorities: titles, social station, and prestige may be nice, but the only real significance in the world is the love, health, and well-being of those we love. Elisheva knew that the high station of her family meant nothing once her children were dead. She knew that even this highest honor of the Torah was a shallow ghost, a mockery in the face of her grief.

Perhaps that is why the Torah passes over her in silence, behind a veil. Grief such as hers and a sense of priorities that values one's children over one's status has little place in public annals or professional accounts. Wisely, then, the Torah leaves her out of a public tale, and equally wisely, the rabbinic sages of the Midrash lift the veil so we can gain insight from this wise woman, our ancestor Elisheva.

Just as Aaron, her husband, exemplifies the wisdom of accepting what we cannot change, Elisheva demonstrates the priority of people over position and relationships over status. Her unwillingness to be happy after the death of her sons is an act of emotional loyalty and a summons for her descendants—male and female—to emulate her passionate and stubborn loyalty toward each of our children and toward the family of humanity.

Identity Rooted in Illogical Laws

Most of us like to think of Judaism as a religious tradition that values reason and open debate as a signal value. We point to the Torah's frequent recourse to providing reasons for its laws, to the rabbinic tradition of providing ta'amei ha-mitzvot (reasons for the commandments and the pervasive discussions and logic throughout the Talmud), and the flowering of philosophical rigor in the medieval period.

We also characterize our religion based on its values: love of learning, passion for justice, and yearning for God and a life of holiness. The paradox, however, is that these virtues are not the monopolies of Jewish tradition, and lots of other peoples and cultures cherish them as well. If we are not distinct by virtue of our values, then what makes us distinct as a people and a tradition?

Within a few concise chapters of the Holiness Code (particularly Chapter 19), the Torah lays out a way of life and guidelines for living unparalleled in any other time or place. And that section opens with God's charge to the Jewish people: "You shall keep My laws (*hukkotai*) and My rules (*mishpatai*), by the pursuit of which you shall live." Ever attentive to the subtle nuances of the words of the Torah, the rabbis inquire, "What is the distinction between a *hok* and a *mishpat*?" God wouldn't waste precious Torah space on mere synonyms, so there must be some significant meaning that each term possesses. "What," they wonder, "is that distinction?"

Rashi answers their question by noting that the *hukkot* have no logical basis; they are rules simply because they are found in the Torah. Thus, not eating pork, not wearing linen and wool together, bringing sheaves of the barley harvest to the Holy Temple in Jerusalem each day between Pesach and *Shavuot*, these practices don't emerge naturally from logical premises. We do them because they are commanded and, after the fact, try to understand what symbolic meaning they have.

The second category, the *mishpat*, is a rule based on logic and needed to make society function. Thus, honoring parents or refraining from murder, having compassion for animals, and loving one's neighbors—these laws, while profound and marvelous, could have been derived from reason had not the Torah saved us the need for that ratiocination. While we often root our pride in our Jewish heritage in precisely these *mishpatim*, they are actually found in many traditions the world over.

If they're not uniquely Jewish, then what makes them Jewish at all, and what makes Judaism distinctive? There are two ways that a practice can be a "Jewish" practice. In the category of the *mishpat*, it's not that the action is exclusively practiced or valued by Jews, but rather it is the context in which that deed is embedded. A Buddhist might also value compassion for all living things but wouldn't connect that value to several of the mitzvot in the Torah and to the rabbinic mitzvah of *tza'ar ba'alei hayyim*. We might share similar notions of how to implement this universal value, but where we get it and how we contextualize it are different. So one form of distinction lies not with the value itself, but with how we derive and sustain it.

With the *hukkim*, however, the distinctiveness is more thorough. These practices exist solely because they are found in biblical or rabbinic writing. Even if we can't think of any persuasive explanation for them, they don't lose their authority as mitzvot or as components of what it means to be a Jew. Whether or not separating linen and wool makes sense, whether or not it provides a spiritual high or a deepened sense of wonder, its value lies at a deeper level: it roots us in a practice that is uniquely Jewish, and it trains us to respond to Judaism on a different basis than simply satisfying our own desire, need, or individuality. Performing a *hok*, precisely because we don't understand it, is an act of loving obedience, pure and simple.

There is yet one more distinguishing connection, one that links the *hok* and the *mishpat*. Sometimes we begin to take on a mitzvah without necessarily understanding it or its ramifications. Then, as we grow in our study of Judaism and our practice of that mitzvah, its logical basis becomes apparent over time. What was once a *hok* now becomes a *mishpat*. That process of spiritual growth and maturation can only happen, however, if we are willing to let our deeds exceed our grasp. Only by doing a mitzvah (prior to understanding it or connecting to it spiritually) can we put ourselves in a position to cherish and feel enriched by it.

Just as our ancestors had to do at the foot of Mount Sinai, we must be willing to commit to the practice of mitzvot before understanding each one. Our ancestors recognized that their ability to live as Jews and transmit their Judaism to another generation required cultivating the *hukkim* no less than the *mishpatim*. That reality is no less true today.

Our behavior precedes our comprehension, and our spirituality is a consequence of our actions. Do first, and the feelings will follow. Wait for the feelings first, and you may never get to the next mitzvah.

Emor/Speak
Leviticus 21:1–24:23

The beginning chapters of Emor deal with laws of the priesthood, including laws of purity and priestly contact with the dead, marital restrictions for the priests, bodily wholeness, and rules governing which animals may be sacrificed and eaten. Just as priests must be physically without blemish, so must the animals used as sacrifices be physically free of defect.

The end of Chapter 22 deals with rules pertaining to the sacrifices offered by Israelites. The sacrificed animals must be whole of limb, without mum (blemish), and they may not be sacrificed when they are younger than eight days old nor on the same day as their mothers. Finally, the Torah lays out the regulations for a todah (thanksgiving offering).

The Torah flows naturally from a consideration of the sacrifices of the Temple to the calendar of sacred times—holy days and festivals—which mark the key moments in the history of God's covenant with the people Israel. "These are the fixed times of the Lord, which you shall proclaim as sacred occasions."

First is the holiest day: the Sabbath. The Torah repeats the prohibition on work during the Sabbath. Then it proceeds to the other sacred occasions of the year: Passover and the Feast of Unleavened Bread; Sefirat Ha-Omer (counting the new barley grains each night for forty-nine nights); Shavuot; the first day of the seventh month (now celebrated as Rosh Hashanah—the New Year); Yom Kippur; and Sukkoth.

The parashah continues with a collection of miscellaneous laws pertaining to lighting the menorah and to placing the showbread in the sanctuary, then a tale of the son of an Israelite woman who blasphemed against God's name. He is imprisoned while Moses speaks with God to determine what to do, and God commands his execution. Afterward, the general law prohibiting blasphemy and murder is explained, along with the famous "eye for an eye" declaration. Finally, the parashah concludes with the remarkable assertion "You shall have one standard for stranger and citizen alike, for I the Lord am your God."

Beyond the Letter of the Law

One of the defining features of traditional Judaism is its careful attention to matters of halakhah (Jewish law). While broader issues of theology and ethics form a significant backdrop to Jewish thought, primary attention is paid to the mitzvot and to the kinds of debates lawyers enjoy. Is something *muttar* (permissible) or *assur* (prohibited)? Is something *hayyav* (obligatory) or *reshut* (optional)? These kinds of evaluations are the typical vocabulary of rabbinic discourse, profoundly molding the culture and the worldview of the Jewish people.

Small wonder, then, that many people conclude that Judaism isn't a very spiritual enterprise at all. Trained by exposure to Christianity, Buddhism, and New Age faiths to define spirituality as an inner sensitivity to the awe and marvel of being alive, a sense of unity with all that is and with its source, many seekers give Judaism a brief opportunity to prove itself (often during services on Rosh Hashanah and Yom Kippur). Hearing talk about how a sacrifice is to be offered, enduring explanations of how the *kohen gadol* used to immerse himself and bow, and listening to the endless repetition of a fixed and archaic liturgy seems to many to be hollow, pointless, and futile.

In part, that problem is one of inadequate preparation. Without prior study, a Shakespeare play or a great painting will seem lifeless and stilted. Achievements of real depth require some training to be able to experience the wisdom they encode. And part of the problem is adopting a foreign definition of spirituality so that it precludes the strongest element of Jewish spirituality—building a community that sees solidarity, transformation, and transcendence as its highest expression of faith.

But those answers only explain part of the problem. To some extent, traditional Judaism has always recognized that just reducing all of Judaism to halakhah represents a betrayal of the fullness of Torah. The great Rabbi Abraham Joshua Heschel used to call this idolatry "pan-halakhism," reducing Judaism to a set of rules. As central as halakhah has always been (and must always be), the contours of Torah extend well beyond issues of permitted and prohibited.

Parashat Emor speaks to that religious realm beyond the reach of law. Much of righteous living cannot be reduced to simple rules. Prohibitions and mandates don't instill values such as kindness, selflessness, and charity. Above and beyond the rules is Judaism's insistence that we live our lives in a way that testifies to God's goodness and justice and love. Such a way of living is called *kiddush ha-Shem* (the sanctification of God's name). Any deed that makes God's sovereignty visible, any action that bears witness to God is *kiddush ha-Shem*, the highest value within the orbit of Jewish values.

This parashah is understood as the source of this mitzvah. God tells the Jewish people, "You shall not profane My holy name, that I may be sanctified in the midst of the people of Israel."

Life presents us with a simple choice: how we live our lives can either heighten a sense of God in the world, or it can diminish it. There is no neutral, middle ground. By treating our fellow human beings with generosity, we bear witness to God's generosity. Acts of greed and selfishness make that bounty harder to perceive. By speaking out against oppression and bigotry, we affirm God as the righteous judge, the One passionate about justice. To remain silent in the face of such suffering is to eclipse God's justice. By extending a basic trust to our fellows, we make it easier for them to feel God's willingness to trust them, to affirm the goodness of creation.

In everything we do, we can help other people to know that there is a God; we can bring credit to the God of Israel and to God's Torah. Far more than simply arguing about rules, the essence of Jewish piety is the compassion and love that the rules embody. As the great nineteenth-century rabbi Israel Salanter said, "Compassion is the foundation of belief. For a person who isn't compassionate, even the belief in God is a kind of idolatry."

In hell, legal philosopher Robert Cover noted, there will be only rules, and they will be strictly enforced. We make heaven here on earth; we sanctify God's name and God's Torah by using them to express God's values of love, compassion, holiness, and justice. We are what we do, and to be a holy people, we must live each moment as an opportunity to serve God.

That's *kiddush ha-Shem*.

This Little Light of Mine

In an age that struggles with the paradoxes of fabulous abundance and global poverty, of power great enough to alter the climate but a seeming inability to prevent the recurrence of slavery, democracies that can't inspire constituents to bother voting, and totalitarians who won't permit their people's will to surface, *Parashat Emor* offers some insight. Instructing the Israelites on the laws of priestly conduct and the calendar cycle, God then speaks to Moses, "Command the Israelite people to bring you clear oil of beaten olives for lighting, for kindling lamps regularly." Here is the divine instruction for establishing the *Ner Tamid*, the eternal light found in every synagogue before the *Aron Kodesh* (ark containing the Torah scrolls).

The rabbis of *Midrash Va-Yikra Rabbah* were quick to note a paradox: why would God need our light? They exclaim, "Who is like You? . . . You give light to the celestial and the terrestrial beings. You give light to all who come into the world and yet you crave Israel's light!"

What our tradition wrestles with here is how a paltry human being can even hope to make a worthy contribution to the God who is the Source of All Life, to the Creator of the Universe. What can we give to the God who has everything? What is it that God expects of us?

The rabbis see the *Ner Tamid* as an allusion to the centrality of the individual human soul and to the effort that every one of us can make to transform our own little corner of the world. The Talmudic sage Bar Kappara explained, "The Holy Blessing One said to humankind, 'Your lamp is in My hand and shall My lamp be in your hands?' . . . The Holy Blessing One said, 'If you light My lamp, I shall light yours.'"

There is a reciprocity to our relationship with God, a religious way of saying that ultimate meaning and ultimate justice require the constant exertions of the average man and woman. Our individual efforts, small though they may seem, are the indispensable building blocks of a society founded on righteousness and compassion. Without an ability to trust our fellow citizens, without a willingness to rely on each other for decency and assistance, no law, no military, and no government can hope to stand. Instead, expecting all the light to shine from above, we will each remain in our armed fortresses of ignorance, hatred, and violence. The drawbridges are up; the swords are unsheathed.

Only if we each contribute our own little light can we hope to illumine the darkness that threatens to engulf our world. Your little candle of hope, of goodness, of decency may not be much by itself. But with mine, and with those of our neighbors and the stranger down the road, we can build a blaze that will light our paths, incinerate our biases and misunderstandings, and forge an unbreakable bond of brotherhood.

All we're waiting for is your light.

What Is the Authority of the Torah?

Each Sunday morning, some TV preachers hold up Bibles and presume that ultimate authority can be lifted straight out of that book. They argue that the Bible says it, so that settles it. Many Jews have adopted that same approach, insisting that "Torah" Judaism is one in which the Torah has the final word—specifically that the *p'shat* is final. Thus, anyone who acts against the *p'shat* of the Torah is violating the will of God and going against the teachings of Judaism.

Yet that assessment of how we should live the Torah is really an act of assimilation, taking on the standards of one type of Christianity as though it were all of traditional Judaism. In reality, Judaism has always insisted that the Torah means what the rabbinic sages say it means and that the *p'shat* may be interesting from the perspective of study and scholarship (that is, to find out what the Torah meant in its ancient Near Eastern context), but the *p'shat* is virtually irrelevant to what the Torah means for us today. For that relevance, we have always turned to the *drash*—the Torah as it is read by each generation of Jews. Not only is that nonfundamentalist Judaism traditional, it is a necessary implication of a belief in *Torah sheh be-al peh* (an oral teaching that parallels, elucidates, and implements the written teaching). The written Torah means what the oral Torah understands it to mean.

One need not look far for examples in rabbinic writings. The Torah specifies that one cannot exempt oneself from a vow, yet the rabbis disregard the *p'shat* of the Torah to allow for rabbinic annulment of unwise vows. The Torah specifies the death penalty for certain crimes, but rabbinic interpretation virtually reads capital punishment out of existence—in disregard of the biblical view. The Torah prohibits touching the corpse of an animal that is *tamei*, yet Jewish law permits it. These are not acts of rebellion, but an assertion that the Torah "is not in heaven"; it is ours to interpret and align with the moral insights of each age. It is a way of continuing to hear the voice of the living God through its words.

In this parashah, we find a similar willingness to violate the *p'shat* of the Torah in the service of the spirit of the Torah. God instructs Moses and Aaron that no *kohen* "shall defile himself for any [dead] person among his kin, except for the relatives that are closest to him: his mother, his father, his son, his daughter, and his brother, also a virgin sister." A *kohen* may participate in the funerals of his closest relatives—parents, siblings, and children.

What about his wife? The clear *p'shat* of the Torah is that a *kohen* may not defile himself by participating in his wife's funeral. Rabbi Shimon Ben Meir, the master explicator of *p'shat*, correctly notes, "No husband from among the kinship [of the priesthood] may defile himself for his wife."

We are not the first generation of Jews to be troubled by that restriction. The rabbis of antiquity and the Middle Ages found it intolerable and unworthy of a loving God. If the Torah is a reflection of God, and if God is the loving source of morality, then any reading of the Torah that is unloving or immoral must be reinterpreted. So they imposed their own interpretation.

Rashi, quoting from the *Sifra* (an ancient midrash on Leviticus), understands "relatives closest to him" as only meaning "wife," and Rabbi Abraham Ibn Ezra asserts, "We have seen that our rabbis interpreted [the verse as] he shall defile himself for his wife." Most detailed of all are the words of Maimonides, who says, "As regards the wife of the priest—one must render himself impure, even against his will. . . . The scribes gave her the status of 'a dead person who one is commanded to bury.'"

The power of the rabbinic sage is supreme in traditional Judaism. In defense of the Torah as the preeminent vehicle for perceiving the will of the living God, the sage must be willing to read his or her interpretation back into the Torah, sometimes in violation of the contextual meaning of the Torah itself. To refuse to assert this authority demotes the Torah from a living guide into a brittle fossil, incapable of refracting God's love in the current age. To refrain from that traditional posture is to assimilate an unrabbinic view held by fundamentalist Protestant theology.

Etz Hayyim Hee (The Torah is a living tree). It is up to each new generation to water and fertilize the tree, to prune it, and to harvest its fruit. The gardener, not the plant, is the ultimate arbiter of what shape that tree will assume.

God cannot be restricted to the space between the covers of a book—any book. The rabbis of each age, not the book, are the ultimate deciders of what the Torah will mean for that generation of Jews. So pick your rabbi carefully.

Be-Har/On the Mountain
Leviticus 25:1–26:2

Be-Har *begins with an entire chapter dealing with use and ownership of land, the rights and obligations of landowners, and the process of selling and mortgaging real estate. It contains laws about both indebtedness and becoming an indentured servant as a way of repaying debts through work. The chapter also establishes the remarkable practice of* Shemittah *(sabbatical year), allowing the land to lie fallow every seven years, and the* Yovel *(jubilee year), adding an additional cycle of rest every half century.*

Providing coherence to these practices is God's assertion that "the land is Mine; you are but strangers resident with Me." Since God is the land's only true owner, our task is to maintain the land on his behalf. As a sign of God's dominion, the people are commanded to "proclaim liberty throughout the land, and to all the inhabitants thereof."

Be-Hukkotai/In My Statutes
Leviticus 26:3–27:34

This parashah constitutes an epilogue to the Holiness Code. Composed of neither legal nor ritual language, Be-Hukkotai expands on *the blessings that are experienced by the community that adheres to the teachings just concluded, the curses that emerge for those who violate these teachings, and a conclusion.*

The blessings for the observant community include peace and prosperity, a bountiful population, and victory over the nation's enemies. The blessings conclude with an affirmation of the covenant binding God and the Jews, as well as the eternity of that covenant: "I will establish My abode in your midst, and I will not spurn you. I will be ever present in your midst: I will be your God, and you shall be My people."

The curses follow, an outpouring of ever more dire consequences. Each cycle of disobedience unleashes a heightened cycle of consequences—military defeat, disease, ravages by wild beasts, famine, death, and exile. At its height, the cycle is broken by hope and love: "Yet, even then, when they are in the land of their enemies, I will not reject them or spurn them so as to destroy them, annulling My covenant with them: for I, the Lord, am their God."

After this powerful conclusion, Chapter 27 appears like an appendix, dealing with the important issue of funding the sanctuary, its services, and its clergy.

The book ends with an affirmation: "These are the commandments that the Lord gave Moses for the Israelite people on Mount Sinai."

Blessings and Curses

Leviticus is the book of priestly holiness, enjoining the people Israel to become a nation of priests and a holy people. At the end of the series of laws, the book ends with a series of blessings for those who obey the teachings of *Va-Yikra* and an even longer series of curses for those who disregard its instructions.

Our ancestors read these curses with dismay. Those curses helped shore up their determination to live in a godly way, even though for childish reasons. Those curses fill us with dismay of a different sort. We know that the world doesn't work that way, that many people abide by the teachings of the Torah and still suffer accidents, illness, and tragedy; just as many violate the mitzvot and prosper with both wealth and health. While the *tokhakhah* (reproof) may have functioned to keep our ancestors in line, with us it is mostly a stumbling block, tripping us up with its primitive sense of a punishing God.

Moses Ben Maimon, the Rambam, recognized that this was a troubling verse too. He explained it by comparing it to the way a child is taught. Imagine a small child who has been brought to his teacher so that he may be taught the Torah, which is for his ultimate good because it will bring him to perfection. However, because he is only a child of limited understanding, he does not grasp the true value of that good, nor does he understand the perfection he can achieve by means of Torah. So his teacher, who has acquired greater perfection than the child, must bribe him to study with things the child loves. Thus, the teacher may say, "Read and I will give you some nuts or figs. I will give you a bit of honey." With this stimulation, the child tries to read. He does not work hard for the sake of reading itself, since he does not understand its value. He reads in order to get the food. As the child grows and his mind improves, what was formerly important to him loses its sway, while other things become precious. The teacher will stimulate his desire for whatever the student wants then. The true value of learning is beyond the grasp of most children, so a good teacher will find some hook to inspire students to study. In time, they will see that the reward was a mere lure to prompt them to pursue a worthy end.

The same is true here; the rewards and punishments offered by Leviticus pale to insignificance compared to the true worth of living a life of Torah. Limited as we are, we fail to see the Torah's true worth. God's children still need the artifice of reward and punishment to encourage us to behave in our own best interests. As the Rambam explains,

Now all this is deplorable. However, it is unavoidable because of people's limited insight, as a result of which they make the goal of wisdom something other than wisdom itself. . . . A good man must not wonder, "If I perform these commandments, which are virtues, and if I refrain from these transgressions, what will I get out of it?" . . . Our sages have warned us about this. They said that one should not make the goal of one's service to God or of doing the commandments anything in the world of things. Antigonos of Sokho meant precisely this when he said, "Do not be like the servants who serve their master for the sake of a reward, but be like servants who serve their master without expecting a reward." . . . However, our sages knew that this is a very difficult goal to achieve and that not everyone could achieve it. Therefore, in order that the masses stay faithful and do the commandments, it was permitted to tell them that they might hope for a reward and warn them against transgressions out of fear of punishment.

The Torah utilizes the language of *berakhot* (blessings) and of *tokhakhah* to provide an artificial inducement toward righteousness. In every phase of our lives, we alternate between doing the mitzvot because we know it to be the right thing to do and because we believe we can make a deal with God ("I'll be good, and in exchange, You will protect me and my loved ones from all mishap"). While it might be nice for the world to work that way, the grown-up in each of us knows that it isn't so. But the childlike part of our souls needs the comfort and incentive of blessings and curses.

There is a deeper response as well. In truth, sin literally does have negative consequences—just not for each individual nor for each particular sin. A culture in which people live by greed, cruelty, and force, in which compassion and doing good are belittled as idealistic and foolish, is one in which there will be less trust, more violence, more pollution, and more hostility. There are curses that accompany the choice not to live by God's laws, and they are as inexorable as the night following the day. But they are true for the community as a whole, not for each individual within the community.

Perhaps, then, we need to see our every deed as swinging the balance. If we dedicate ourselves to living God's will, to doing the mitzvot, we can swing society toward goodness, toward justice, toward kindness. And then God's blessings will flow on everyone. Or we can choose to elevate the pursuit of our own private happiness to our highest ideal and continue to watch as our society and our planet erode.

As always, the choice is ours: blessing or curse. What's it going to be?

Invisible in Our Midst

Toward the end of *Parashat Be-Har*, the Torah speaks of our need to redeem Israelites who became slaves due to poverty. These specific commands are quite consistent with the Torah's commandments elsewhere. God says, "For it is to Me that the Israelites are servants. They are My servants, whom I freed from the Land of Egypt, I, the Holy One, your God" (Lev. 25:55).

Nothing shocking there. The Torah once again proclaims a teaching noble and uplifting and consistent with its message of human dignity and freedom for all. What strikes me in looking at that passage is that it precedes another paragraph that condemns idolatry, a topic that appears irrelevant to the one at hand. Without transition, the Torah launches an attack against idolatry and an insistence on observing the Sabbath: "You shall not make idols for yourselves, or set up for yourselves carved images or pillars, or place figured stones in your land to worship upon, for I, the Holy One, am your God. You shall keep My Sabbath, and venerate My Sanctuary. Mine, the Holy One" (Lev. 26:1–2).

It is not exactly news that the Torah condemns idolatry nor that it commands us to set aside a sacred time (the Sabbath and the festivals) nor that we should create space in which to encounter the Holy One. But I would like to tweak a Talmudic question: *Mah etzel herut l'avodah zarah* (What is the connection between freedom and idolatry)? Why would the Torah place those two concerns adjacent to one another? What's the link between liberty and false worship? Between freedom and holy space/time?

Here, I believe the Torah is making three points through the juxtaposition, and they are points that I commend to all of us.

The first point is that if a religious life does not stand on a basis of human concern—specifically, a concern for other people—then it has no basis whatsoever. Notice that the *pasuk* does not speak about our obligation to liberate ourselves. It is human nature, naturally, to focus on oneself and make one's concerns the primary object of our own attention. Precisely for that reason, the Torah insists that the liberation of others must be our most pressing concern. Indeed, that concern is the very consequence of God's having liberated us from slavery. We are summoned as Jews and human beings to work for the redemption of the enslaved, those suffering in our midst, both as a reflection of *ani Ha-Shem* ("I am the Lord") and *asher hotzeiti otam me-eretz Mitzrayim* (as a consequence of having been brought to freedom).

The second point is that idolatry is not a matter of simply putting the wrong name to or associating the wrong image with the Divine.

Idolatry is a matter of missing the Divine entirely, of elevating to worship that which is unworthy of our devotion. God's very nature is radical freedom—a freedom that explodes into space and time, a freedom that liberates slaves, and a freedom that brings people to their promised home. It is easy to confuse idolatry with an intellectual or theological error. But the God of Israel is not simply a different shape or a different structure. One cannot erect a visual image of God. One cannot, in our tradition, lightly and casually utter God's name. Instead, our Torah creates a link to remind us that God is beyond all visualization, beyond all representation. Judaism, as a religion, trains us to focus on the invisible, beginning precisely with the person who is invisible in our midst.

In the Talmud, in Tractate *Haggigah*, we are told a wonderful story. Rebbi and Rabbi Hiyya are journeying. They arrive in a certain town and ask the people there, "If there is a rabbinical scholar here, we would pay him a visit to do him and his Torah honor." The inhabitants of the town say, "There is indeed such a scholar here, but he is blind." Rabbi Hiyya, always concerned for the dignity of Rebbi's high office, says, "You stay here. I will go and visit this person, and I will pay respects on your behalf." Rebbi refuses to listen, and the Talmud tells us "he bests Rebbe Hiyya" and goes along. When they are finished with their meeting with this blind, anonymous scholar, he gives them a blessing: "You came to pay your respects to one who is seen but does not see. May you merit to pay your respects to the One who sees but is not seen." Rebbi then turns to Rabbi Hiyya and says, "Had I listened to you, you would have prevented me from receiving this blessing."

Attending to the invisible is the job of each of us. An invisible God, invisible causes, invisible people—people whom we choose to make invisible or simply overlook. It is precisely from these invisible ones that our blessings are to be derived.

The third point made by the Torah is that true worship of the Divine is the institutionalization of freedom, placing our concern for each other at the center of our spiritual life and rising to a life of service and gratitude. We know that we are worshipping the true source of holiness when there is no wall of separation between the redemption of our brothers and sisters and *et Shabbtotai tishmeru* (the marking of sacred time) and *mikdashai tira'u* (the reverence of sacred space).

The prophets of Israel, I remind you, do not condemn ritual. They condemn any ritual that is divorced from morality, quarantined from inclusion, or severed from service. And they condemn it in the strongest language as an offense against God.

The Torah and its traditions are tools designed to render the invisible in our midst visible. The God of Israel bids us see those who are unseen and ignored in our presence so that we may all feast together at God's table.

Then and only then will we fulfill the Torah's mandate of redeeming the captive.

Then and only then will we refrain from making ourselves into idols of stone.

Then and only then will we truly observe the Sabbath of rest and wholeness.

Only then will God's sanctuary be rebuilt.

"*Ani Adonai* (I am God)." We will find God only when we are able to see each *ani* (individual) who stands before us as an eruption of God into the world.

That is our task. And this is my charge to you.

Slavery and the Torah of Love

In the famous description of the Woman of Valor, the book of Proverbs praises her by saying that "she opens her mouth with wisdom, and on her tongue is a Torah of love." High praise indeed, but it raises a curious dilemma. If she speaks a Torah of *hesed*, does that imply that there is a Torah that is *not* a Torah of love? Is there a Torah of hate?

If we understand the Torah as a book, a finite text given on a specific day, then it is hard to avoid that there are parts of it that cause serious ethical problems for a sensitive and enlightened reader. In *Parashat Be-Hukkotai*, for instance, we read of the laws of slavery, both for an *eved Ivri* (a Hebrew slave) and an *eved K'nani* (a Canaanite slave). The Hebrew slave is a kind of indentured servant—limited in the duress he must endure and also to a finite term of service. But the *eved K'nani* enjoys none of these prerogatives. The Torah allows the master to put onerous burdens on this slave and prohibits the master from ever liberating the slave or the slave's children.

If God's revelation is a book, then this part of the book forces us to ask, what kind of God would allow slavery as part of an eternal revelation? What kind of God would mandate the ownership and permit the objectification of another human being?

There are many Jews who understand the notion of *Torah min ha-Shamayim* (Torah from the heavens) literally, and they construe God as having dropped the Torah from the sky. They grapple with such a text and try to interpret it in as humane a way as possible (often by insisting that the Jewish slave laws weren't as harsh as in other cultures).

For many other Jews, however, such an apologetic reading seems forced and untenable. It still puts God in the position of mandating slavery and permitting the ownership of another human being. Are we forced to simply concede that this passage is a Torah of hate? Is it the most that we can do to condemn it and try to move beyond it? What, then, of Torah and its holiness? What, then, of God and our covenant?

I would propose that our solution is to be found in another traditional understanding of the idea of *Torah min ha-Shamayim*. This understanding is less literal and requires a more dynamic way of reading the Torah. One can understand Torah not just as a particular *book*, but as a *process* of God reaching out to us. That process started at Sinai, resulting in the Torah, but it continues with full force in the writings of the prophets, the rabbis, and medieval and even contemporary sages. God's voice cannot be contained between the covers of any book (or set of books). Just as each wave on the shore leaves a new mark in the sand, each holy book marks another refraction of God's Torah, so that *Torah min ha-Shamayim* describes a process that is very much alive and electric.

How, with such an approach, can we understand the painful presence of slavery in the book of Torah? Seen as a process, the issue is not what is in Leviticus, but how Jewish tradition insists on reading that presence. How does the *process* of Torah deal with the existence of slavery in the *book* of Leviticus? For it is the process, not the book, that is authoritative, in which God's voice is to be found. As the *Zohar* recognizes, "Just as wine must be in a jar to keep, so the Torah must be contained in an outer garment. The garment is made up of the tales and stories, but we, we are bound to penetrate beyond."

Let us penetrate beyond the outer garment, the book of Leviticus, to uncover the process of Torah within. Let us look at one authoritative reading, that of the great Rabbi Moses Ben Maimon:

> It is permitted to work an *eved K'nani* with rigor. Though such is the law, it is the quality of piety and the way of wisdom that a man be merciful and pursue justice and not make his yoke heavy upon his slave or distress him, but give him to eat and to drink of all foods and drinks. The sages of old let the slave eat of every dish that they themselves ate and they fed . . . the slaves before they themselves sat down to eat. . . . Thus also the master should not disgrace them by hand or by word, because Scripture has delivered them only to slavery and not to disgrace. Nor should he heap upon the slave oral abuse and anger, but should rather speak to him softly and listen to his claims.

The Rambam accepted the fact of the law—slavery was technically permissible, and one could oppress one's slave. Yet the values of Torah make it a religious obligation to be merciful and just toward slaves. In fact, Ben Maimon insisted that one ought to share the same foods and allow the slaves to eat first as a demonstration of compassion. A good master is one who speaks softly and listens to what his slave has to say. In short, a Jewish master is one who affirms that his slave, like he himself, is made in God's image.

Verses in the book that are morally problematic call upon us to have the religious courage to read against the grain so that we can hear God's voice in the process of reading. In that process, we make God's gift of Torah our own and affirm our status as *b'nei rachamim* (the merciful children of a merciful god).

numbers

Be-Midbar

In the Desert

Be-Midbar/In the Desert
Numbers 1:1-4:20

The book of Numbers begins in the wilderness of Sinai. The people are organized into a military camp, which requires taking a census. Moses, Aaron, and the chiefs of the tribes register all the men over the age of twenty. The total comes to a little more than six hundred thousand. The Levites are not included in the census with the other Israelites.

Each Israelite is told to camp in military divisions by tribe, each tribe assuming an assigned position around the Tabernacle. The Levites are assigned to be attendants to the priests, and the priests are given sole responsibility for performing the rituals of the sanctuary.

In the wilderness near Mount Sinai, God tells Moses to perform a census of the Levite males; their total was twenty-two thousand. In lieu of God requiring the sacrifice of the firstborn among the Israelites, the Levites are now pledged to divine service. There follows a second census of the Levites, this time counting only those between the ages of thirty and fifty, to determine the workforce available to transport the Tabernacle.

Torah Gone Wild

Judaism in antiquity was a rugged, grounded faith. Poised between wandering in the wilderness and entering a promised land, the spirituality of biblical Judaism was one of creation as a sign of God's greatness and munificence, of learning to love a particular land as our inheritance and as God's gift. Biblical festivals and holy days pulsated to the cycles of agriculture and the seasons, recalling not only the great events of Israel's past but also the way the earth could adorn itself and provide for its denizens throughout the year. Small wonder, then, that the exultant book of Psalms—arguably the world's greatest collection of poems—is one that sees God in the rising of the sun, the way the birds get their food, the way the sea and its breakers roar.

Something happened along the way. Perhaps it was our recurrent conquest at the hands of foreign powers or the natural response to being denied a place among the peoples of the world. But for whatever reason, Jewish spirit turned inward, away from mountains and fields, into the more portable and modest realm of the study hall and sanctuary. The model Jew became one who sat in a dimly lit room, eyes focused on the folio of a book. In a world of violent desire, Judaism heard the voice of God in restraint and sublimation. In a world of might and suffering, Judaism heard God's will to mandate compassion. In a culture that denigrated intellect and celebrated athletics, Judaism elevated the life of the sage to the highest possible form of spiritual life.

That shift served us well, preserving the Jewish people in a difficult era and retaining our focus on acting as God's witnesses. But when the Torah became domesticated, something of its burning brilliance was reduced.

In our own age, what we need is a Torah not only of books and restraint, but also of sun and field and sea. At a time when Jews live in democracies as equals or have returned to our own land, it is time to summon the resources of that grounded Torah of land and life and seasons.

Parashat Be-Midbar is one such resource. The book of Numbers begins by recording that "God spoke to Moses in the wilderness of Sinai, from the *Ohel Mo'ed*." Why does the Torah, so cautious in using extra words, bother to tell us that God spoke to Moses in the wilderness? What is it about wilderness that can serve as a medium for conveying God's true voice?

Moses Ben Maimonides understood the connection as an antidote to moral depravity: "If all countries you know or hear of follow evil ways, as is the case in our time, then one must go out to the caves, the clefts of mountains, and the wilderness." When the values around us have gone haywire, when the distance between what people profess and how they behave is insurmountable, the way to restore spiritual balance and sanity is to escape the confines of civilization and head to the wilderness.

You see, society has a way of accepting its own particular assumptions as self-evident truths. Each culture assumes that the way it sets priorities and the choices it presents are the way the world ought to be. To question those priorities, to even be able to think outside of the constraints of popular assumptions, can be quite difficult in the thick of it all.

Wilderness is not tailored to human standards and does not contour its character to fit human foibles. Returning to real wilderness means returning to a place in which people are visitors and guests, where our will and arrogance don't parade as the measure of all things.

In the wilderness, the world reflects the grandeur of the God who made it. The wilds still pulsate with the novelty of creation, with the unbounded energy of life and of living things. There, the richness of life is sufficient purpose for the myriad creatures and the indifferent majesty of forest, desert, and swamp. They neither need nor seek a human purpose or benefit to justify their existence.

Returning to the wilderness reminds us to consider value not simply in terms of our own gratification, but by the standards of how well creation continues to demonstrate the power, wisdom, and goodness of God. The wilderness reminds us of the true source of all values, our own included.

That may be why God's voice is heard in the wilderness. That may be why Torah was given on a stormy mountaintop and why we need to look beyond the tops of our books more than occasionally. The Torah, you see, is wild.

Turning Our Backs

Contemporary humanity is marked by its relentless assertion "I've got to be me." If there is a conflict between us and someone else, then the presumption is that the other person is in the wrong. If our own urges conflict with communal interests, we assert our individual drive above the needs of the community.

This tension between individual self-interest and the needs of the community is not unique to this generation. It stretches back to the very beginnings of humankind. What is new is our smug comfort with one extreme perspective, that of the individual above all else, without a trace of tension or validity to what a community might legitimately demand of its members. "I want it all now" has too often replaced "What does the Lord require of me?" as the measure of all things.

Parashat Be-Midbar offers a subtle hint in that same direction, nudging us back to the *derekh yesharah* (the straight path balancing personal and social interests in a more fruitful balance).

The opening verses of the book of Numbers speak of the census of both the Israelites and the Levites as they prepare to resume their wanderings in the wilderness. Yet the rabbis of antiquity note that the words used to mandate both counts are not the same. When God orders the Levites to be numbered, "Moses recorded them at the command of the Lord, as he was bidden." But when the census of the normal Israelites is done, the Torah records, "Moses recorded all the firstborn among the Israelites, as the Lord had commanded them."

What's the difference? When Moses counts the firstborn Israelites, God is not actively involved; rather, Moses does as God "had commanded" in the past. When Moses records the numbers of the Levites, he does so in partnership with God, "at the command of the Lord." It is almost as though the two of them conducted the census together.

Why would God be more involved in the Levites' census than the counting of the firstborn Israelites?

Midrash Be-Midbar Rabbah responds, "The Levites were righteous and had not taken part in the incident of the calf, but risked their lives for the sanctification of the Divine name." The Levites had refused to follow the idolatrous urges of their own hearts. However desirable it might have felt to construct and worship the golden calf, they felt a communal obligation and responsibility to God. The Israelites, on the other hand, had put their individual pleasure before the needs of the community.

The midrash continues, "The Holy Blessing One therefore said, 'They [the Levites] associated themselves with Me, I also will associate Myself with them, by numbering them Myself and in My own glory.' The firstborn, however, withdrew themselves from the Holy Blessing One and offered sacrifices to the calf. So the Holy Blessing One withdrew from their census."

The obsessive focus on themselves, their refusal to elevate the community's needs above their own self-expression, reflected an idolatry, not of any statue, but of themselves as the measure of all things. They were so full of themselves that there was no room for loyalty, for discipline, for self-sacrifice. They were so full of themselves that there was no room left over for God. How can God dwell in a human heart that is completely absorbed with its own self-interest?

Too often, we follow the precedent of the firstborn rather than emulating the more humble, self-effacing Levites.

Tzorkhei tzibbur (valuing the needs of the community) is the bottom line of meaningful Jewish survival. Our connection to each other is our shared history, our common destiny, and our shared *brit* with God. There can be no progress on social justice, on supporting each other through times of crisis and of joy, if we are not willing to sublimate our own self-interests for those of our community and our people, if we are not ready to shoulder the yoke of the kingdom of heaven rather than bow only to our own insatiable idiosyncrasies.

As the readings approach the festival of *Shavuot*, which celebrates the gift of the Torah at Mount Sinai, it is worthwhile recalling that the revelation was a public event and that Torah can only be received and transmitted if there is a commanding sense of communal belonging and responsibility.

The voice of God is heard through the many voices of the Jewish people as a whole, through the collective sense of the community, even as it was at Sinai.

Equal, Yes—but Not Identical

One of the most deeply cherished beliefs of the American people is the equality of all human beings: "We hold these truths to be self-evident, that all men are created equal." With those stirring words, the founding document of the United States asserts that God made everyone of equal worth and that this assertion is so obvious as to require neither proof nor argument. The equality of all people is self-evident.

That ideal still thrills with its promise of a world transformed. Imagine if we took to heart that no one was of greater worth than any other, that all people have an equal claim to dignity and fundamental rights. What a world that would be.

One way that this noble ideal is subverted is simply to hold that people are not of equal worth or that individuals do not possess intrinsic worth. A distribution of benefits based on income or lineage ends up looking like we don't accept the equality of human beings; some seem more equal than others.

The second way is to insist on the sameness of all, and that silly notion has gained proponents of late: not only is everyone of equal worth, but no one should have access to anything that another person doesn't. No idea is better than any other idea; no value system is superior to any other system; I'm okay, you're okay; this is right for me, and that's right for you.

Parashat Be-Midbar suggests a different approach. While still insisting that all people are made in God's image, the Torah shows special consideration for the Kohathites, one of the Levitical clans assigned specific tasks in the maintenance of the *Mishkan*. The Torah records God's special solicitude on their behalf: "Do this with them, that they may live and not die when they approach the most sacred objects."

The rabbis of *Midrash Be-Midbar Rabbah* ask, "What reason did the Holy Blessing One see for commanding greater care in regard to the other families?" Shouldn't equal worth translate into identical treatment in every area of life?

Their answer is no, that our equal worth is a potential available to everyone. But some people, through diligence, persistence, sacrifice, and character, are able to shoulder greater responsibility than others.

And with responsibility comes privilege: "There is some superior virtue in the tribe of Levi and in the families of Kohath which is wanting in the rest of Israel. . . . All the other tribes were not concerned for the vessels of the Tabernacle, but the tribe of Levi carried the vessels. . . . Israel walked about shod in sandals, while the tribe of Levi, who carried the vessels of the Tabernacle, moved about barefoot. . . . The ordinary Levite would place his burden . . . upon wagons, but the Kohathites bore their burdens upon their shoulders."

The Levites distinguished themselves from other Israelites by their willingness to serve God and the community, even at personal sacrifice. God was merely reciprocating their intense devotion. And as much as the Levites excelled above the average Israelites, even more did the Kohathites exceed the piety and service of the Levites. Without that added measure of devotion and responsibility, the Israelite religion—indeed the Israelite people—would never have survived, never taught the world the intrinsic dignity of every person, never given the world the Ten Commandments or the lofty standards of justice embodied in the book of Leviticus and the words of the prophets.

In every age, some Jews were willing to shoulder more in order to serve God and the Jewish people. And in every age, the Jewish people reciprocate by cherishing and honoring those leaders.

In our day as well, there is a need to honor sacrifice and to recognize those who preserve our heritage, our identity, and our link with God. Everyone is equal, but no two people are the same. To the extent that we take on responsibility for our community and our covenant, we earn the special solicitude of our people and our God.

You can excel, and the world needs your excellence.

Naso/Take

Numbers 4:21–7:89

Parashat Naso *begins describing the duties of the Levitical clans, focusing on the duties of the Gershonites and the Merarites. Chapters 5 and 6 interrupt the preparation to march through the wilderness to lay out several laws designed to preserve the ritual purity, and remove any impurity, from the Israelite camp, thus allowing God to remain there.*

The first instruction is to remove any person with a bodily discharge or who has been in contact with a corpse and is thus ritually impure. The Torah then lays out the laws for an asham *for one who has made a false oath.*

If a husband suspects his wife of committing adultery but there is no proof, he may bring her before a priest. The priest makes her drink a mixture of sacred water, dust from the sanctuary, and parchment containing a curse that mentions God's name. If her body becomes distended, then she's guilty. If not, she's innocent.

In biblical Israel, there was no way for an ordinary person to live a life of full-time religion. The remedy for this was to provide for the Nazirite. The Israelite (man or woman) makes a vow, for a finite period of time, to abstain from intoxicants or any grape products, to grow the hair long, and to avoid contact with a corpse. During this Nazirite period, the individual serves in the sanctuary in consecration to God.

One of the duties of the priest is to bless the people Israel. The Torah here lays out the words of the priestly benediction. This benediction is still recited by kohanim *during the Days of Awe and the festivals and often by parents to their children on Friday night as Shabbat candles are kindled.*

The interruption now concluded, the finishing touches for the impending march make the Tabernacle ready for use. The chiefs of the tribes supply gifts, the menorah is completed and lit, and the Levites are placed in service. At the end of this elaborate preparation, the sanctuary can function as the site where God and humanity meet. "When

Moses went into the Tent of Meeting to speak with God, he would hear the voice addressing him from above the cover that was on top of the Ark of the Covenant between the two cherubs. Thus God spoke to him."

What We Really Own

I still recall, as if it were yesterday, when my last grandmother passed away. A week or so after our period of mourning ended, my mother sent me some of my grandmother's furniture, figuring (correctly) that my wife and I could use it in setting up our home. As the movers carried in the furniture, I had an eerie sense that something wasn't right. This, after all, was hers, not mine. I realized then, in a more concrete way than before, that we really never own the things around us. We borrow them for a while, and ultimately we return them. Either we no longer need them, or they cease to function—in which case, we return them to nature and the natural order.

Given that we can never really own anything, our lives and how we choose to apportion our time seem especially perverse. Modern men and women spend their most productive years in relentless pursuit. We pursue careers and ownership of cars, homes, clothing, appliances, artwork, stock options, pension plans, life insurance, and a staggering variety of other possessions. We are rich beyond belief in the accumulation of things.

Paradoxically, we don't feel rich inside. Few of us have a sense of inner fullness, of an ability to derive emotional nourishment from within. Plagued by unease, by a foreboding disquiet, we know we lack some essential ingredient; we just don't know what it is. So we buy another suit, join another club, eat another restaurant meal, seeking frantically to satisfy our eternal craving for we know not what.

Maybe that confusion over priorities and goals also accounts for why so many find *Parashat Naso* boring. The Torah recounts, at great length, the gifts the tribal chieftains brought to the newly constructed *Mishkan*: "The chieftains of Israel, the heads of ancestral houses . . . bound their offering before the Lord. . . . The chieftains also brought the dedication offering for the altar upon its being anointed."

For the next twelve days, each tribal chief brought offerings to dedicate the new altar, and for twelve paragraphs, the Torah simply lists everything they brought. Even the most diligent of readers begins to glaze over by the third day. Why would the Torah, normally so terse, so concise, and so dramatic, go on at such length with the dedication gifts of Israel's tribes?

In *Mishnah Pirkei Avot* (Teachings of the Sages), Rabbi Elazar instructs us, "Give God what is God's, for you and yours are God's." This thought is also expressed by King David: "For all things come from You, and we give You only what is Yours" (1 Chron. 29:14).

Rabbi Elazar understands that there is nothing wrong with owning things or enjoying their use. But possessions are, at best, tools for better living, never goals in themselves. No thing can bring happiness, security, or peace. The spirit of each human being soars above the concrete limitations of his or her possessions, crying out for something more essential, something more eternal, something more *neshamah*-like (soul-like) to meet it face-to-face.

Today's environmental philosophers translate Rabbi Elazar's wisdom into secular language when they tell us that we humans only have the power to take something out of the cycles of nature for a short time, but that sooner or later we must return it. We can either return the borrowed item in a way that lets the natural cycle continue to support a thriving biosphere, or we can return it in a way that threatens the continuity of life: "You and yours are God's."

We do not have ultimate possession of anything material. All that we own we owe, as Rabbi Abraham Joshua Heschel reminds us.

What we do acquire and own forever is our own character, our own deeds of loving-kindness and justice, our own piety. We own eternally the love we feel for others and their love for us. And we own, as Jews, an ancient and a sacred tradition that makes us God's lovers, God's partners, and God's children.

In those possessions, and not in mere things, a soul can hope to find contentment.

God's Healing Angels

Every culture identifies insiders and outsiders—those elect few who represent communal ideals and the despised few whose differences make them seem threatening to the rest of us. For the vast majority of us, straddling between the ideals and the rejects, life is an effort to seem more like the former and to distance ourselves from the latter.

A universal human weakness, this drive to demonize as a way of feeling better about ourselves is not some recent innovation. Rather, it is found in all societies and even in our holy Torah. What is surprising is not that it is there, but how an enlightened Jewish tradition responded to the temptation to label and expel.

In *Parashat Naso*, the Torah relates God's command to the Israelites "to remove from camp anyone with an eruption or a discharge and anyone defiled by a corpse. Remove male and female alike; put them outside the camp so that they do not defile the camp of those in whose midst I dwell."

This passage contains a troubling thought—that we should respond to those with physical differences or troubles by banishing them from the midst of the community. Does God really want us to expel these people to the fringes of our communities? Can we blame them when they walk away from their Judaism if their experience of Judaism is one of rejection and expulsion?

This topic is explored in *Midrash Be-Midbar Rabbah*, the ancient rabbinic commentary to the book of Numbers: "When the Israelites came to the wilderness of Sinai, God said, 'Is it consonant with the dignity of the Torah that I should give it to a generation of cripples?'" The modern reader can't help but cringe at the portrayal of a God so callous. Is this the God of compassion and mercy and love we pray to on Shabbat and our holy days? In fact, the midrash sets us up to expect God to justify their expulsion.

Yet that's not what happens. The midrash continues, "What did God do? God bade the angels come down to Israel and heal them." Rather than expelling the Israelites who were disabled, God cured them and reintegrated them into the community.

We too need to find ways to deal with our propensity to judge on appearances. Like God, our primary efforts must be to assist people in not having to be defined by a physical disability. By providing the funds for research and for distributing the necessary aids, we can allow more people to learn, to work productively, to dream and live their dreams. We can make ourselves God's healing angels.

But there will doubtless remain people who cannot live "normal" lives, others who won't look like everyone else, and still others whose disabilities prevent them from melting into a crowd. So the task of becoming God's healing angels, while always a priority, cannot be our only task. The other priority must be to learn to see the individual, not his or her appearance, as paramount. No one should be defined by an illness, a challenge, or an affliction.

Here, our Torah again points the way, offering us a collection of heroes who were disabled and glorious—Jacob with his limp, Moses with his speech defect, and Miriam with her skin disease. All offer examples of human giants who were not viewed through the prism of their disability. It's not that those disabilities weren't real or a continuing part of who they were, but their generation was able to see those disabilities as but one aspect of complex and truly wonderful people.

The Mishnah tells us, "Don't look at the flask, but at what it contains." In teaching ourselves to see the inner sparks that light a person's soul—rather than merely glancing at the casing that holds those precious assets of personality, aspiration, and caring—we can act like God in the wilderness, healing when we can and transcending limits when we cannot.

Sotah: Trial by Ordeal

One of the most troubling facets of the Torah is its apparent acceptance of the dominant patriarchy of the ancient world (and much of the modern world too). The Ten Commandments are clearly addressed specifically to men ("Don't covet your neighbor's wife"), as are many of the mitzvot; the preponderance of heroes are men; and even God is addressed primarily in masculine terms. Of late, that male focus has become a stumbling block for those who would look to the Torah for vindication of the notion of the equal worth of men and women. In fact, an entire school of interpretation—feminist Bible interpretation and theology—has emerged as a result of this tension, producing some powerful and surprising rereadings of familiar texts.

No parashah of the Torah has caused more consternation or anguish than *Parashat Naso*. There the Torah recounts the procedures whereby a jealous husband who suspects his wife of having committed adultery may bring her before the priests to submit to a trial by ordeal. In this trial, the accused woman is forced to drink a potion made from sacral water, dirt from the Tabernacle floor, and the written curses containing God's name (which are dissolved in the water itself). After accepting the priest's curse, the woman must drink the potion. In theory, her guilt is established if her belly distends and her thighs sag, "but if the woman has not defiled herself and is pure, she shall be unharmed and able to retain seed."

We read about this accused woman and wonder why her paranoid husband isn't forced to take such a test. Why is it the woman who is the only one who must endure the humiliation and public trauma of the *Sotah* ritual?

The sages and rabbis of the Talmud and Midrash shared the same concern. For that reason, the rabbis took the biblical verse now translated as "The man shall be clear of guilt, but that woman shall suffer for her guilt" and transposed its meaning to a more egalitarian "If the man is clear of sin then that woman shall suffer her guilt" (*Sifre Be-Midbar*). That same midrash quotes the prophet Hosea in support for its novel interpretation: "I will not punish their daughters for fornication, nor their daughters-in-law for committing adultery. For they [the men] themselves turn aside with whores and sacrifice with prostitutes." The rabbis of the Talmud (*Massekhet Sotah*) therefore limit the *Sotah* trial's effectiveness to the case in which the accusing man is himself innocent.

Even this move toward equalizing the *Sotah* trial wasn't sufficient for all, and under the jurisdiction of Rabban Johanan Ben Zakkai, when the Second Temple still stood, he eliminated the trial entirely. According to the Mishnah, his motivation was the rampant frequency of male adultery, which made punishing the woman alone ludicrous. *Tosefta Sotah*, a collection of tannaitic (early generations of Mishnaic rabbis) statements rejected for inclusion in the Mishnah but often found in the Talmud, adds a more cynical reason: the adultery of the *Sotah* period was performed in secret, in shame. By the time of the rabbis, adulterers were more brazen, seeing no reason to hide their deed. As a result, the use of a trial to ferret out adulterers was neither necessary nor a deterrent.

A modern scholar, Rabbi Jacob Milgrom, suggests yet another way to read the imbalance of the *Sotah* trial. In a world controlled by men, in a society in which a woman was transferred from the authority of one man (her father) to the authority of another man (her husband), a woman who had an affair was in danger of being lynched. By turning her over to the priests and explicitly stipulating that her only punishment was physical disfigurement, the Torah specifically precludes her execution. As Rabbi Milgrom notes, "The answer . . . is inherent in the ordeal. It provides the priestly legislator with an accepted practice by which he could remove the punishment from human hands and thereby guarantee that she would not be put to death."

In this reading, the priests of the Torah were looking for ways to mitigate the rampant patriarchy of the ancient world. Their willingness to do so in their age ought to empower and encourage us in our own to continue their precedent, to create a society that truly recognizes the divine image in each and every human being.

Be-Ha'alotekha/In Your Lighting
Numbers 8:1–12:16

Once God speaks to Moses from the holy of holies, Moses receives the final instructions about the menorah and its operation.

The parashah then discusses the purification of the Levites, who are charged with building and dismantling the Tabernacle, but must do so in a state of tohorah. *Levites older than age thirty are inducted into this sacred labor. The Levites also serve Aaron and his sons. Finally, the book of Numbers establishes an age limit of fifty for active duty, after which the Levite may still perform guard duty.*

Two years after their departure from Egypt, the Israelites prepare to move on from the wilderness of Sinai. Once again, they offer the Pesach sacrifice, but some of the men are in a state of tumah *and cannot participate. God authorizes a second Passover offering one month later for those who were* tamei *during the first one. Non-Israelites are explicitly permitted to offer a paschal sacrifice.*

Once the Tabernacle is built, a cloud hovers over it by day, and it looks like fire by night. It moves as a sign that God wants the Israelites to proceed, so they march whenever the cloud moves forward and camp whenever the cloud settles down.

Trumpets are used to mobilize the people for marching, to call out the soldiers in defense of Israel, "that you may be remembered before the Lord your God and be delivered from your enemies." The trumpets blow for Israel's festivals and new moons, as "a reminder of you before your God."

The Israelites resume their march from Sinai toward Jordan. Moses invites his father-in-law (here referred to as Hobab) to join them as their guide through the wilderness. The ark guides them.

The people begin to complain, first at Taberah, where a fire breaks out amid the people in the camp, then at Kibrith-Hattaavah, where they cry out for meat. God is furious with them, and Moses feels the full burden of his leadership, so God agrees to divide his load among

*seventy elders and to provide the people with meat. Moses expresses
doubt that God will be able to feed so many. God's spirit rests on
the seventy elders, who speak in ecstasy whenever this happens, even
Eldad and Medad, who aren't physically near the other elders. Moses
is delighted. "Would that all the Lord's people were prophets, that the
Lord put His spirit upon them!" God provides the people with quail
until they feel sick.*

*The parashah closes with Miriam and Aaron complaining about
Moses because he has married a Cushite woman. They claim that God
also speaks through them, and God gathers them together and asserts
the uniqueness of Moses. Miriam is afflicted with white scales, and
Moses offers the Bible's shortest prayer on her behalf: "El na refa na la
(God, please heal her)." After seven days, Miriam is restored and the
people set out from Hazerot to the wilderness of Paran.*

The *Pintele Yid*

When I first came to Congregation Eilat, in Mission Viejo, California, fresh out of rabbinical school, many of my congregants were
struck by how young I seemed. How, they wondered, could this kid
be our rabbi? Others responded by trying to help me in the areas of
my deficiencies, one of which is my lack of knowledge of the Yiddish
language. One congregant in particular made it his business to teach
me important Yiddish expressions. He was certain that these phrases
captured the essence of Jewish wisdom.

I gratefully accepted his willingness to educate this greenhorn and
will now share with you the very first term he taught me: a *pintele Yid*.
The phrase is said with a finger pointing toward one's heart. It means
that no matter how distanced one may become, there is always a Jewish point deep within, some small spark waiting to be ignited when
the time is right. Every Jew has this *pintele Yid*, and therefore every
Jew is worth the effort to bring him or her back to a life of Jewish
wholeness and holiness.

I love that concept, since I love the Jewish people and spend much
of my time trying to help Jews gain access to the depth of their own
traditions. I see myself as their steward, maintaining in good order
what is really their possession—the Torah, the mitzvot, the Jewish

values and traditions. The notion of a *pintele Yid*, a spark within every Jew that can blaze up with the light of Torah, means that we must never give up on anyone.

But where did this strange phrase come from? That was a question that my congregant couldn't answer. I found the answer in a note from my colleague Rabbi Maurice S. Kaprow. In *Parashat Be-Ha'alotekha*, God describes Moses as "very meek, more so than were all the men upon the face of the earth." The Hebrew word for "meek" is *anav*, which is normally spelled with four Hebrew letters: *ayin-nun-yud-vav*. In this instance, however, the Torah spells the word *ayin-nun-vav*. The *yud* is missing.

The ancient rabbis surmised that the missing *yud* was a sign of Moses's meekness. Why? Because *yud* is the first letter of God's name, and Moses left it out when he was transcribing God's description of him to avoid even the appearance of comparing himself to God.

Where did that missing *yud* go? It is buried deep within the soul of each and every Jew: hence the *pintele yud*, which became the *pintele Yid*.

That transformation makes the phrase even more extraordinary. Moses left out the *yud* to avoid saying that there was a divinity within. Yet Jewish tradition transformed the *yud* (the letter signifying God's name) into *Yid* (meaning a Jew). God is not only within each Jewish soul, but God's name becomes, in effect, each Jew—no matter how nonobservant, no matter how far removed from a life of holiness or mitzvot.

Indeed, each person is a new expression of godliness, a new rendition of God's name. Each of us reflects God in a way that no other person ever did or ever will. That *pintele Yid* is our reminder that holiness attends everyone. Our sense of self, our inalienable dignity and worth, is rooted in the sacred spark inside every human being.

And that spark takes a special kind of attention to reignite it into the full flame of Sinai. Through careful cultivation and the ability to blow fresh air on the sparks (not too hard and not too little), the steward of the heart can hope to excite an unlearned Jew with the wealth that Judaism and Jewish tradition offer. Not through sermons, but through experience, a soul can come to know the beauty of Shabbat, the power of *davvening*, the reward of *bikkur holim* (the mitzvah of visiting the sick). By offering the pathway of the mitzvot, the spiritual guide can hope to lead his or her ward to the deep pools of inner peace and true wisdom. Ultimately, the notion of a *pintele Yid* means we don't have to push too hard because we can trust the inner depths of our students to bring their own resonance to the Torah we offer. In holding out the wisdom of Torah and mitzvot, we know that our students will see a mirror of themselves.

That *pintele Yid* is still dozing, waiting for your prodding, your caring, your example.

Make Yourself a Trumpet

This is the age of vicarious virtue. All of us prefer to continue living our lives in much the same way we always have, and all of us want our leaders to adhere to the standard of our words. In that way, we get to enjoy our own laxity while still claiming credit for the morality of our ideals. Our mouths tout one thing, and our deeds blare a different, gaudier tune.

When we insist on doing our own thing, our music becomes discordant and self-indulgent. Simultaneously, the distance between our ideals and our actions grows wider with each passing day, so our frustration mounts. We lash out when the pressure gets too high, striking at wherever the pinch hurts most—each other, our religion, our politicians. But the fault, if fault is to be found, lies with our own lazy acceptance of ourselves as we are—our elevation of self-expression to the level of idolatry.

Parashat Be-Ha'alotkha speaks of the *Mishkan* built in the wilderness. There the Israelites were to assemble to serve God, and the Levites were selected to perform the sacred rites and sacrifices of biblical worship. God tells Moses and the Jewish people, "Have two silver trumpets made; make them of hammered work." These trumpets will be used to summon the community to assembly, to initiate communal journeys, to march out to wars of defense, to announce festivals and *Rosh Hodesh* (new moon) days, and when making sacrifices on the altar. Says God, "They shall be a reminder of you before your God: I, Adonai, am your God."

The rabbis of *Midrash Be-Midbar Rabbah* noticed an ambiguous Hebrew form for this instruction: the Torah records, *"Aseh lekha shtei hatzotzrot"* (literally, "Make yourself two silver trumpets"). What, ask the sages, is the purpose of this superfluous *yourself*? What does it mean to make yourself a trumpet?

A beautiful trumpet, even in the midst of producing music, doesn't draw attention to itself. It is the music, not the horn, on which people focus. So too, say the sages, by making ourselves trumpets, we focus attention on the God in whose service we delight. Our music is the sacred deeds we perform.

The sages illustrate this point with a charming midrash about King Solomon. As he was bringing the ark into the newly built Temple, he sang to the gates of Jerusalem, "O gates, lift up your heads . . . so the King of Glory may come in!" The doors, thinking that Solomon was referring to himself, were appalled by his arrogance. At once they "threatened to sink down on him and crush his head." They asked, "Who is the king of glory?" and fortunately for him, Solomon answered, "The Lord of Hosts is the King of Glory." The midrash tells us that "thereupon they paid God honor and lifted themselves up, and the ark entered."

Solomon was as wise, as rich, and as powerful a Jew as has ever lived. Yet he knew that the credit for his wisdom did not lie with himself. He was but a trumpet in the hands of a master musician. The notes, however beautiful, were his to emit but not to own.

We too work hard to produce some beautiful notes—by raising our children to be mensches, by studying and praying in our synagogues, by volunteering in our communities, by working with integrity and diligence, and in countless other ways. But our work becomes more than merely prudence, more than self-gratification, when we do it in the spirit of glorifying our Creator, our Commander.

Our goodness is the earthly reflection of God's divine *hesed*. Our performance of mitzvot is our eager gratitude for the gift of life. Our passion for Judaism is our joyous delight in God's bounty and the beauty of our heritage. We are the trumpets, but God wrote the score.

So the next time you want to toot your own horn, go ahead. But remember to play God's tune.

A Cloud by Day, a Fire by Night

One of the most famous of ancient Israel's symbols of God's presence is the bush that was aflame yet would not be consumed. That startling image has been taken both as a representation of a living faith and of the unquenchable spirit of the Jewish people. The burning bush has become the logo for countless Jewish institutions and adorns innumerable Torah mantles in synagogues all over the world.

No less striking a biblical symbol is the pillar that led the Israelites through the wilderness. As the Torah explains, "On the day that the *Mishkan* was set up, the cloud covered the Tabernacle, the Tent of the Pact (the Tent of Meeting); and in the evening, it rested over the Tabernacle in the likeness of fire until morning." Every evening, the fire would settle down, showing the Israelites where to pitch their camp, and in the morning, the cloud would move forward, pointing the way they were to proceed.

The Torah points out that this miraculous fire/cloud was the very locus of God's presence—the voice of Adonai spoke from amid the flaming smoke—and it was this combination of fire and cloud that was a permanent sign that God was the ultimate leader of the Israelite tribes throughout their wandering. According to the biblical scholar Jacob Milgrom, the fire was in the center of the cloud and became visible in the dark or when God wanted to summon Moses to a special audience. The fire was known as God's *kavod* (God's glory). It appeared to only three of Israel's leaders—to Moses, to Aaron, and to Samuel—conferring a high level of distinction on each of them.

This perplexing symbol doesn't adorn any Torah mantles and hasn't been adopted by any Jewish organization. It is rarely represented graphically. Yet the Midrash is filled with references to it that give it a postbiblical life that is quite illuminating in its own right:

• The *Mekhilta* points out that God's *kavod* played a special role in defeating the Egyptian soldiers when the Israelites were escaping to freedom; the fire made the ground so hot that the chariots stuck in the melting mud, trapping the soldiers so the slaves could make it to freedom.

- The *Midrash Kaneh* states that the cloud performed an additional miracle—the two Hebrew letters *yud* and *he* appeared in its depths. These two letters spell one of God's names, the name through which God created the world. The letters would point the Israelites in the proper direction each morning.

- *Melekhet ha-Mishkan* notes that the cloud would proceed when and where God wanted it to, but as a courtesy to Moses, it would stop in front of him and await his actual instruction to depart or return. Moses would shout *"Kuma Adonai* (Arise, God)!" and *"Shuva Adonai* (Return, God)!" and the cloud would respond to his words. We use these same words in our Shabbat Torah service in the synagogue.

- According to the *Midrash Yalkut*, the radiance of the fire/cloud was a brilliant purple, which shone like the sun and the stars. Heathens who saw it from a distance were frightened of the Israelites and were also moved to praise God for this miracle. The miraculous robes the Israelites were given by the angels were made in material of the same beautiful purple, so that they shone like God's *kavod* as they paraded through the desert.

- The *Midrash Sifre* notes that it was the *kavod*—the fire and cloud that waited while Miriam was recovering from her bout of *tzara'at*—that forced the Israelites to wait for her too. Thus the cloud of glory lent special dignity to this worthy prophet.

By adding these fanciful details to the raw majesty of the pillar of cloud and fire, the Midrash connects the pillar to the creation of the world, to the miracle of *Yetziyat Mitzrayim* (the Exodus from Egypt), to the authority of Moses (and hence to the entire Torah and the revelation at Mount Sinai).

Thus all the major strands of Torah theology—the marvel of God's Creation, the passion of God's liberation, and the gift of God's revelation—are combined in this wonderful symbol: a pillar of cloud and fire.

In a place where words cannot go, our path is illumined for us by the radiant light of God's *kavod*. Shine on.

Sh'lah Lekha/Send
Numbers 13:1–15:41

God commands Moses to send spies, one from each of the tribes, and to report back on the land and the people there. The spies find grapes so large that a single cluster requires two men to carry it, and they name the location Eshcol in honor of the enormous bounty. After forty days of scouting, they return, reporting that the land "does indeed flow with milk and honey." But they also report that the land is fortified by the Caananites, who are strong. In fact, the spies insist that they are too strong, that Israel will not be able to conquer them. Only Caleb affirms faith in God's promise of the land.

Hearing the spies' evaluation, the people burst into tears, saying it would have been better to remain slaves. Joshua and Caleb continue to insist that God can bring about the gift of the land, but the people try to stone them, and only the appearance of God's presence saves them. God threatens to destroy the people and to make a new chosen nation out of Moses and his descendants. Moses dissuades God, pleading for pardon on the Israelites' behalf. God insists that none of the naysayers (nor the Israelites of that generation) will live to enter Eretz Yisrael. God redirects their steps by way of the Red Sea. Frantic and too late, the Israelites gear up and attack the Amalekites (against the instructions of God and Moses), and they are routed at Hormah.

A chapter that provides some laws that will take effect when the children of the wilderness generation enter the land now interrupts the narrative. These laws include the libation accompanying meat sacrifices, the challah (dough) offering, expiation for unintentional error (either by individuals or the group), the punishment for a man who gathered wood on Shabbat, and the commandment to wear tzitz with a thread of tekhelet on the corners of their garments.

Facts and Values, Inseparable and Entwined

The task seems explicit: Moses instructs a select group of tribal leaders to conduct a scouting expedition into the Promised Land. There they are to observe carefully and return with the factual data that will allow Israel to plan the best approach to entering the land. Twelve individuals are selected—the spies, in later nomenclature. And Moses enumerates the facts they need to amass: "Go up there into the Negev and on into the hill country and see what kind of country it is. Are the people who dwell in it strong or weak, few or many? Is the country in which they dwell good or bad? Are the towns they live in open or fortified? Is the soil rich or poor? Is it wooded or not?" (Num. 13:17–20).

The assignment calls for compiling extensive lists of information. But something gets confused in the process. Instead of sticking to the facts, the spies return with an assessment: "The country we traversed and scouted is one that devours its settlers. All the people we saw in it are men of great size; we saw the Nephilim there—the Anakites are part of the Nephilim—and we looked like grasshoppers to ourselves, and so we must have looked to them" (Num. 13:32,33).

God and Moses are simply asking for information—just the facts. In the words of the Rashbam, "All this kind of information was needed so that they would know to take with them the tools needed to lay siege to fortresses, for example." But the spies allow their opinions to intrude. That the land devours its settlers isn't an objective measurement; it's an opinion. That they looked like grasshoppers to themselves and must have to the inhabitants too demonstrates subjectivity and sentiment designed to dissuade the Israelites from further advance.

Or so it has appeared to many generations of readers. Fact versus opinion, objective versus subjective, "is" versus "ought." The spies cross the line by offering the latter (opinion, subjective, "ought") when what is called for is the former (fact, objective, "is").

In reading the spies through this filter, we stand on the shoulders not only of great Torah commentators, but also of two of the greatest Western philosophers, David Hume and Immanuel Kant. One of the great tools developed by modern philosophy is a distinction, suggested first by Hume and made a cornerstone by Kant, between facts and values. The dichotomy of fact versus sentiment (for Hume) or the distinction between synthetic and ethics (for Kant) was elevated to a metaphysical principle—Hume's famous insistence that you can't derive an "ought" from an "is." He used this principled dichotomy to delegitimize religion, theology, and any attempt to make ethics rigorous or normative. Kant used the same dichotomy to save ethics for respectable conversation—at the price of content-filled revelation or ritual.

More recently, some prominent philosophers have begun to dismantle this wall of separation. It's not that there aren't some statements that are factual and some statements that express feelings; it's just that the two categories are rarely mutually exclusive or as hermetically sealed from each other as we once imagined. The philosopher W. V. Quine notes, "The lore of our fathers is a fabric of sentences. In our hands it develops and changes, through more or less arbitrary and deliberate revisions and additions of our own, more or less directly occasioned by the continuing stimulation of our sense organs. It is a pale gray lore, black with fact and white with convention. But I have found no substantial reasons for concluding that there are any quite black threads in it, or any white ones." Rather than admitting a principled dichotomy that separates fact from convention (values, ethics), Quine argues for their interplay and fusion.

A philosopher of the next generation, Hilary Putnam, has insisted, "Valuation and description are interdependent." Too many twentieth-century thinkers attempt to portray the world in two distinct columns: *objective*, which they equate with reality, facts, and truth; and *subjective*, which they see as beyond any norms, discussion, or evaluation. Putnam opposes this dichotomy: "It is clear that developing a less scientistic account of rationality, an account that enables us to see how reasoning, far from being impossible in normative areas, is in fact indispensable to them, and conversely, understanding how normative judgments are presupposed in all reasoning, is important not only in economics but—as Aristotle saw—in all of life."

Let's revisit Moses's instructions through this new/old prism, which insists that the very act of identifying and articulating facts rests on interpretation, imagination, and emotion and that the process of intuiting emotion or imagination rests on information, reason, and sense perception. The objective and subjective meet and mingle in the human dance of thinking/feeling/doing. Each is a participating part of the dynamic whole. Each is reshaped in the process of contributing to the total shape.

The "facts" that Moses seeks are really expressions of comparison—relationships between things, not things in and of themselves. People aren't strong or weak objectively, but only in comparison to other people. Few or many is a comparative assessment, depending against whom you measure. A country is good or bad only relative to other countries. And so it goes. Each of Moses's factual categories are inextricably mingled with values, relationships, and comparisons.

As Rabbi Menachem Mendl of Kotzk remarks, "What the scouts reported was factually correct, but it was not the truth. The truth is not necessarily as things appear, but stems from the depths of the heart, from the sources of one's faith. Truth and faith go hand in hand, and a person does not acquire truth easily and by a superficial glance."

Recognizing that human life is not a distillate of objective fact, but a swirling dance of fact and value, objective and subjective, outer and inner, intermingled and interpenetrating, allows us to recognize the proper relationship of brain to heart, of brain and heart to soul, of brain and heart and soul to body. All of them together form the unity that is a human being, and all of them together create the ways we come to know the world around us.

As we scout that world, as we explore the inner depths, the key is to bring unity to what seems disparate, to see in the many, One.

What Will *They* Think?

Upon hearing the terrifying message of the twelve spies, the people panic: "If only we had died in the land of Egypt! Or if only we might die in this wilderness! Why is the Lord taking us to that land to fall by the sword? Our wives and children will be carried off! It would be better for us to go back to Egypt!"

Given a choice between a difficult battle for freedom or an easy accommodation to slavery, the Jews choose slavery. Not much has changed in the past three thousand years. Given the choice between a difficult struggle to change our nation's way of living, our greed, callousness, and bigotry, most choose the slavery of materialism, convention, and conformity. No gain, maybe, but also no risk.

God, however, is furious and threatens to destroy the people instantly. A rejection of freedom, after all, is a rejection of God and God's mitzvot. Only after a passionate argument with Moses does God finally back down and agree to forgive the people. Even then, God exacts a strict penalty: they asked to die in the wilderness; very well, they will die in the wilderness.

But later commentators have been troubled by Moses's logic. At first, *Midrash Be-Midbar Rabbah* tells us that Moses tries arguing the merits of the people and their ancestors, but God won't hear it. So Moses shifts his argument, asking God instead, "When the Egyptians, from whose midst You brought up this people . . . hear the news . . . [they] will say it must be because the Lord was powerless." Is it possible that God backed down because of what the Gentiles might think? Is that divine?

Perhaps, though, we can learn from Moses's argument. The people who had been given freedom were on the brink of rejecting it. The nation that had been taught a sacred and just way of living were about to choose slavery, hierarchy, and oppression. If God responded the way Pharaoh would have in the face of a slave rebellion, wouldn't that response vindicate Pharaoh and the values he represented?

What Moses was telling God was that the final lesson of freedom and responsibility could not be imposed by threats, that the methods of the Pharaohs of the world could only produce more Egypts— places of great wealth and stifling poverty, places that treated people like chattel and reduced the sacred to empty form.

Moses was right, and God knew it. The battle for freedom constantly threatens to collapse—both because of its enemies and because of its would-be advocates. When we defend freedom by diminishing another's humanity, Pharaoh wins. When we defend freedom by labeling an intrinsically evil "them" against an always-good "us," Pharaoh wins. When we impose habit and conformity in order to stifle the really important questions or punish people for their differences, we drive God from our midst.

God forgives us because the Egyptians would look at that punishment and feel vindicated in their narrowness; their bigotry; their willingness to squash debate, free inquiry, or differences. After all, if God does it, then why can't they?

Not only the Jews, but God, stood at a crossroad. To use the methods of Pharaoh would simply have been to become the new oppressor. God forgave us in order to forever transcend the use of coercion.

You cannot teach freedom by fiat. You cannot bring people to the Promised Land through force. There is no "them." There is only us, and we are journeying toward freedom. Care to come along?

Are We Chosen? Are We Better?

One of the canards leveled against Judaism is that it holds Jewish people to be superior to all others. From early antiquity, in the writings of Josephus, we read of anti-Semites who accuse Judaism of cultivating a disdain for the rest of humanity. Because we claim that God has singled us out from among all the peoples of the earth by giving us the Torah, the charge goes, we also believe that we are better than the rest of humanity. Hence we try to keep separate from everybody else. Hence we only use other people for our own benefits and our own purposes.

It is tempting to simply write off these distortions of classical Judaism as absurd, the cloak that bigots use to cover their own hatred and ignorance. But aspects of its essence have been offered from within the Jewish community as well. Thus, the classical Reformers of a century ago asserted that the ritual practices of traditional Judaism serve only to divide Jews from other people and should therefore be discarded. The *Tanya*, a founding document of *Chabad* (a group within the Hasidic movement in Judaism), asserts that the souls of Jews are qualitatively different (and higher) than the souls of Gentiles. And the late Rabbi Mordecai Kaplan, founder of the Reconstructionist branch of Judaism, felt that the claim of "chosenness" led to ill will on the part of Gentiles and arrogance on the part of Jews, so he removed it from his version of the siddur.

The assertion that Judaism insists that Jews are special is true. But the claim that Judaism disdains the rest of humanity confuses the rich polyphony of diversity with the flattening deadness of homogenization. One can love being different and feel special because of that difference, while also admiring the distinctive traits that make other people different too. Judaism understands difference as distinctiveness (in fact, the ceremony ending Shabbat is called *havdalah*, which means "distinction."). But does distinction necessarily imply superiority or indifference?

To answer that question, let's look at a passage in *Sh'lah Lekha*. The Torah speaks of Israelites bringing sacrifices to God. Sacrifices were at the core of biblical worship, and the place where the sacrifices were made, the altar, was the defining implement of the *Mishkan* and of the Temple. Israel's holiest people, the *kohanim* and the Levites, busied themselves with the offerings and made these sacrifices in Israel's holiest building, the Temple.

If Israelites thought of themselves as the only people God cared for, then they might well have insisted that only an Israelite was permitted to make this most serious and sacred gesture, that only an Israelite could enjoy this most sublime privilege. But the Torah says, "When, throughout the ages, a stranger who has taken up residence with you, or one who lives among you, would present an offering of fire of pleasing odor to the Lord—as you do, so shall it be done by the rest of the congregation." Surely this passage alone would refute the terrible charge of misanthropy. Judaism doesn't neglect the spiritual treasure that each and every person represents. Indeed, its highest form of worship is available to all, Jew or Gentile, man or woman.

The Torah makes the point explicitly: "There shall be one law for you and for the resident stranger; it shall be a law for all time throughout the ages. You and the stranger shall be alike before the Lord."

Jew and Gentile are each precious to God. The Torah celebrates the rich diversity of human faiths and human beings by insisting that each has the right to the same level of legal protection. Without seeking to obliterate our differences, the Torah teaches a way to cherish and learn from each other. Celebrating diversity is the only true universalism. In fact, the false universalism that insists that everyone ought to be the same is really just the particularism of the dominant group, unable to see its own suffocating hold on the bouquet of cultures under its sway.

We are, each of us, precious. And the way to express that value is to maintain and cultivate our own diverse heritages without seeking to melt them into some all-embracing mush. With Jews growing in their Judaism and Gentiles walking in their own paths of wisdom and holiness, we have a chance of real spiritual growth.

You and the stranger who dwells in your midst—each different. And each holy.

Korah/Korah

Numbers 16:1–18:32

The theme uniting Parashat Korah *is the question "Who is allowed to approach the altar and perform sacrifices there?" Beginning with the rebellion of Korah against Aaron's priesthood, the parashah establishes that only* kohanim *descended from Aaron may offer the sacrifices, but that when they do, other Israelites may safely participate in the worship. The parashah ends by listing the benefits the* kohanim *and Levites receive for assuming the risk of guarding and tending the altar and the* Mishkan.

Korah, a Levite along with Datan and Aviram, rebels against Moses, as do 250 chieftains. Moses responds by asserting that God will clarify who is to speak on God's behalf and who has access to God's altar. Each is instructed to take his fire pan and put incense in it. Aaron does the same. Then, in front of the Tent of Meeting, God's presence appears, threatening to wipe out the entire community. The community pleads with God to punish only the guilty, and God agrees. Moses instructs the people to withdraw away from the abodes of the rebel leaders—Korah, Datan, and Aviram—and the earth opens and swallows them alive. Then a fire issues forth from God and consumes the 250 rebel chieftains as well.

God tells Moses to hammer the fire pans into plating for the altar as an eternal reminder. The community is infuriated at Moses and Aaron, and threatens to kill them. The two leaders repair to the Tent of Meeting, and Moses notes that a plague from God has already begun to strike down the Israelites. He tells his brother to take his fire pan and bring incense among the people to expiate them. Aaron is able to stop the plague in this way, although many people die.

Next, God has each chieftain inscribe his name on a staff, instructing Aaron to do the same for the tribe of Levi. All leave their staffs before the Ark of the Covenant, and the next morning, Aaron's has blossomed and borne almonds. His staff is to be displayed as a permanent reminder of the incident.

Finally, God instructs Aaron and his sons about their exclusive role as priests, establishing that they will be maintained from the sacrifices and offerings that the Israelites bring to the Mishkan.

The Guilty and the Innocent

The suffering of innocents raises one of the most painful and intractable moral dilemmas for people of faith: if there is a good God, then how can that God allow the innocent to suffer? A good God should be able to construct a just world, one in which people pay for their own evil but don't suffer as a consequence of wicked decisions or hateful actions that they did not formulate themselves. What a world that would be.

Life as we know it doesn't work that way. People whose worst sin is crossing the wrong street at the wrong time are routinely caught in the cross fire of gang warfare and pay the penalty for someone else's malice. Children born to absentee fathers or to drug addicts pay the penalty for their parents' self-indulgence. All Israelis pay a constant penalty for the venal politics of Middle Eastern despots, terrorists, and sheiks, and the civilians of Darfur and elsewhere are paying with their own bodies for the avarice and greed of ethnic strife.

The sad reality of life as it is lived is that the blameless often suffer at the hands of the guilty, and the upright bear the consequences of the wicked. Discrimination, it seems, is built into the structure of the universe as it exists in reality.

Parashat Korah refers to this sad reality with typical candor. After Korah and his band rebel, God commands Moses and Aaron to "stand back from this community that I may annihilate them in an instant!" Is it possible for the Creator of the Universe, the Source of Life and Torah, to obliterate the innocent along with the guilty?

The answer, both in daily life and in the honest literature of the Torah, is a firm "yes." As the *Mekhilta* recognizes, "once permission has been given to the destroyer to do injury, it no longer discriminates between the innocent and the guilty."

Why do the innocent suffer along with the guilty? Why would God condemn the entire community along with Korah?

Judaism affirms that our identity is formed not in "splendid isolation," but in relationship with others. From our earliest moments as babies, we learn who we are by interacting with someone else. We learn our own borders as we grow to recognize that we are not our mothers or fathers, but we also take their responses and intuitions on as our own. That dynamic creation of a self continues throughout our lives. Who we are is molded and guided by our families, friends, teachers, religion, and community. Each of us is inextricably linked to the others, and therefore, each of us shares some responsibility for what happens in our communities, even when we don't directly have a hand in those actions. Particularly, those of us who live in a democracy or whose religion is one of voluntary association share responsibility for our society's actions and its future.

Not only are we all interconnected and therefore responsible, but there is one other reason why the innocent often suffer with the guilty. One of the consequences of free choice, of the human ability to determine one's own actions, is that other people can impose their wills on us. If my neighbor decides to punch me in the nose (and I hope he doesn't), then my nose will get punched as a result of his choice.

Perhaps that is precisely what the *Mekhilta* is alluding to: our freedom curtails the freedom of other people, since our choices or lack of choices have direct implications in their lives.

Is there any resolution at hand? Notice Moses and Aaron do not accept God's inability to separate the innocent and the guilty. Instead, they act, knowing that there is no substitute for decisive human intervention: "They fell on their faces and said, 'O God, Source of the Breath of All Flesh! When one man sins, will You be wrathful with the whole community?'" As a result, God urges the innocent to distance themselves from the sinners and from their sin.

The lessons of this story, then, are twofold. First, we owe ourselves and each other our active intervention against bigotry, violence, and injustice. All it takes for evil to triumph is for good people to do nothing.

Second, our spiritual health requires us to distance ourselves from sin and from people who cause others to suffer. By associating with those who take the lofty values and sacred deeds of our tradition to heart, we will strengthen our own resolve as Jews and create a climate in which our interdependent self will be shaped toward good.

What better time to start than today? And what better place to start than your nearest synagogue?

The Staff of Aaron

In an age of uncertainty, when old truths seem to crumble a little too easily and new truths can't live up to the skeptical expectations of our generation, many Americans turn to religion to help cope with the trials of life. Jews too, in large numbers, look to our sacred traditions to establish priorities that will awaken us from the stupor of time. We look to Judaism to provide something ageless, something tranquil, and something profound.

Like us, our ancestors lived in trying times and turned to our Jewish traditions as a guide and a buffer against confusion or despair. In listening to the teachings of Judaism, we too may hear a voice of healing and of holiness. We too, by reclaiming their symbols and values, can create a link between heaven and earth.

In the aftermath of Korah's rebellion against Moses and Aaron, God seeks to establish Aaron's claim to the priesthood against the buffeting challenges of his impatient peers. God instructs Moses to take twelve staffs, one for each tribe, and to place them in the Tent of Meeting. Each tribe provides a staff, and the next day, they all see that the staff of the tribe of Levi, the one with Aaron's name inscribed on its length, has blossomed, producing the flowers and fruit of the almond tree.

Rather than simply reading this tale as history, the rabbis of *Midrash Be-Midbar Rabbah* sought to establish a timeless value, linking this staff and its message of religious reliability to the needs and fears (and rebelliousness) of every generation of Jews. In pursuit of profundity, they sought to provide a deeper identity for that staff:

"Some say that it was the staff that had been in the hand of Judah." That staff had passed from Judah to Tamar and then back to Tamar. It had been part of the incident that proved Judah mature enough and compassionate enough to found the preeminent tribe of the Israelite confederation, and it had witnessed the birth of Perez, ancestor of King David (and one day, of the Messiah).

A second midrashic view was that Aaron's staff was made when Moses "took a beam and cut it into twelve planks, saying to each of the princes, 'Take your stick, every one of you from the same beam.'" Because each staff came from the same wood, no one could claim that any of them was intrinsically holier than another. Not its inner nature, but its service on behalf of Aaron, its fulfillment of the will of God, rendered Aaron's staff holier than the others.

A third and final view asserts that "that same staff was held in the hand of every king until the Temple was destroyed, and then God hid it away." The descendants of King David who ruled over the glorious days of the First Temple, who witnessed the preaching of the prophets and the glory of Jerusalem, held on to that staff as a reminder of the mission of the Jews: to testify to God's glory and involvement, to order their lives in response to our *brit* with God.

Finally, the Midrash teaches that "that same staff also is destined to be held in the hand of the King Messiah." The same staff that saw the beginnings of our people under Judah, reminded the tribes in the wilderness of the religious core of Jewish identity, and inspired the kings of Israel to implement the lofty teachings of the Torah—that same staff would connect our ancient past to our hopeful future.

In that time when all humanity lives in peace, when the Jews are able to live freely in accord with our sacred ways, when the beauty of mitzvot permeates our ways—even then the staff we used to march through history will blossom with the flowering of our piety and the fruits of our good deeds.

God of All Breath

There is a place beyond which words cannot go. Words can only allude to our most deeply felt emotions: wonder, marvel, awe. Designed to help us communicate about ideas, facts, and values, words lose their power when it comes to the depths of human feelings, to an almost mystical connection to other living things and to life itself. Words get us to the shore, but to move to the depths, we have to discard our words for other modes of expression.

If powerful emotions are always deeper than words can express, then how much more so is something beyond human comprehension and limitation? God, the source of all emotion, the creator of life and of the universe, is far beyond the ability of mortals to comprehend, let alone describe. Our words fall flat when trying do describe the One beyond human understanding who is our source, our master, and our meaning.

Yet speak of God we must. Since human beings are able to communicate across the generations and around the world through the medium of language, we rely on words to carry an insight they cannot completely explicate. The words become the outer garment that shows the form and the motion of the invisible spirit within. We must use words, yet we must remember that the words are only helpful in pointing to a reality that begins beyond the place the words cannot go.

This understanding of language as expressing what eludes containment is fundamental to a Jewish approach to God. There is no chain of being leading from inanimate through single-celled plants to simple animals to humanity to God. God isn't simply at one end of the spectrum with molecules and atoms at the other; God is off the spectrum. In the words of the hymn "Adon Olam," "Peerless and unique is God, with none at all to be compared."

Since God is beyond all comparison, and since words correspond to human experiences and perceptions, it follows that no word or set of words can fully express God's nature. Hence, within Judaism, we rely on many different words to highlight several different aspects of God. God is called the Merciful, the Sovereign of the Universe, the Creator, the Holy One, the Ancient of Days, and much more.

These different names help provide a label, giving us a handle to know yet another way that God relates to us, to humanity, and to all creation. *Parashat Korah* uses an unusual phrase to describe God—*El Elohei Ruhot* (Source of the Breath of All Flesh).

What a powerful metaphor! God is the source of breath, that reliable, cyclical in-and-out of air on which our lives depend. Nothing makes us feel quite so refreshed as a deep, clear breath of air, and nothing can make us miserable quite so quickly as troubled breathing. Beyond the air itself is the way our bodies feel while breathing; the filling up as our lungs expand conveys a sense of health and well-being. When we're angry or frightened, a few deep breaths can fortify us and calm our mood.

God is the potent source of that ethereal energy. As we breathe in and out, we rely on the divine inspiration (and exhalation) that connects us with God as the source of breath.

But we can take this image of God one step further. The four-letter name of God, the one that is never pronounced, is made of four Hebrew letters, corresponding to *Y* and *H* and *W* and *H*. Those four letters are all vowels in biblical Hebrew. So the most potent name of God, the one revealed to Moses at the burning bush, is simply vowels, the sound of breathing itself.

God is not only the source of breath, but breath itself. Our breath—like our God—is something we cannot see or touch, but it is our very essence. Our connection to life is through this intangible but constant presence. With breath, we can run, learn, love, and live. Without it, we cannot live.

Taking in and breathing out, we share with other living things in their visible participation in the rhythm of life. God is never farther away than the next breath. And never less reliable than the air that we breathe.

Hukkat/This Is the Statute

Numbers 19:1–22:1

Hukkat *begins with one of the most complex and puzzling rituals in the Torah, that of the red heifer. This cow must be completely red, and its ashes are used to remove the most severe degree of* tumah, *contact with a corpse.*

The Israelites resume their journey, this time to the wilderness of Zin, at Kadesh. There, the prophet Miriam dies and is buried. There is a drought, and the people begin to rebel against Moses and Aaron once again. God instructs Moses and Aaron to take the rod, gather the people, and order the rock to produce water as a miraculous sign of God's providence. Instead of doing as God instructs, Moses strikes the rock twice. Water gushes from the rock, and the people drink and water their animals. God is angry with Moses for lacking sufficient faith to speak to the rock and therefore ordains that Moses will not enter Eretz Yisrael. The place receives the name Meribah, meaning "quarrel."

Moses contacts the king of Edom, requesting permission to pass through his land, but the king refuses the request. Edom sends out an army to attack the Israelites, so they turn away, seeking another route toward their goal.

At Mount Hor, Aaron dies and is mourned by the entire people. His son, Eleazar, becomes the new kohen gadol.

The king of Arad attacks the Israelites in the Negev, near Atarim. Israel emerges victorious and renames the place Hormah, meaning "destruction."

As they continue on their march, the people again complain about God and Moses. As punishment, God sends serpents that bite and kill many of the people, who plead with Moses to intercede. God tells him to construct a copper snake statue, called Nehushtan. When people look on it, they are immediately healed.

The march continues to the border of Moab on the east; to Be'er, where there was a famous spring of water; and finally to Pisgah. Moses sends messengers to Sihon, the king of the Amorites, requesting permission to pass through his land. Instead of acceding, Sihon launches an attack, and he is routed. The lands of the Amorites and the town of Heshbon are now occupied by the Israelites. A similar encounter with Og, king of Bashan, leads to a second Israelite victory. The parashah ends with the Israelites victorious and encamped on the very borders of the Promised Land, across the Jordan River from the city of Jericho.

The Torah: Can You Still Dig It?

Gathered at Be'er, the Israelites and Moses celebrate God's gift of a flowing well of water by singing to the well:

Spring up, O well—sing to it—
The well which the chieftains dug,
Which the nobles of the people started
With maces, with their own staffs.

This song is particularly strange since it interrupts the march of the Jews through the Transjordan, and then the narrative resumes without missing a beat. *Tractate Rosh Hashanah* of the Talmud relates that it was the practice when the Temple stood in Jerusalem to recite this song every third Shabbat afternoon, alternating with the more famous Song of the Sea.

Times change, and as they do, the needs of the community shift as well. With each passing generation, Jews have turned to the Torah and read new wisdom and new insight into it to renew and reclaim our timeless *brit* with God and to harvest the radiant blossoms of new interpretations.

In the age of the Torah itself, the Jews were governed by an aristocracy of tribal leaders and judges. Small wonder, then, that the Torah attributes the digging of the well to the chieftains and nobles, just as contemporary bedouin poetry credits their tribal leaders with digging the local wells.

After the destruction of the First Temple in 586 B.C.E., the Jews went into exile in Babylon and returned with a new social structure. No longer separated by tribe (since all of them, except for *kohanim* and Levites, were descended from the tribe of Judah) and no longer under the rule of a Davidic king, power now shifted to the priests, the sages, and the military leaders. Certainly by the time of the destruction of the Second Temple in 70 C.E., Jews were more under the sway of religious authorities than they were answerable to any Jewish aristocracy. What meaning, then, could a song glorifying the nobility hold for those Jewish communities?

The way Jews make the Torah relevant and allow it to continue to convey God's commanding will throughout the ages is through interpretation, or midrash. In this case, the rabbis noted the use of the term *mehokek* for "maces" or "staffs." Rather than sticking to this literal image, the Jews of the early rabbinic period interpreted it as a metaphor. The rabbis understood *mehokek* to mean "the one who ordains *hukkim*." In that reading, the one who teaches is God, the one who digs is Moses (or the sages of each new generation), and the staff used for digging is the Torah itself.

This revised reading, which clearly flies in the face of the *p'shat*, extended beyond the borders of the rabbinic community and found a home in the community that fashioned the Dead Sea Scrolls. Thus, one of these scrolls reads,

> The well is the Torah. They who dug it are penitents of Israel.
> . . . God named them "chieftains" because they sought Him and their fame was not disputed by any mouth. The *mehokek* is the interpreter of the Torah. The "nobles of the people" are those who come to dig the well with their staves [*mehokekot*], which the lawgiver [*ha-mehokek*] instituted [*hakak*].

The rabbis and sages of antiquity were willing to subvert the *p'shat* of the Torah for the sake of the Torah, to keep it capable of transmitting something sacred and precious across the ages. Through the power of interpretation, our tradition was able to reach across the millennia and provide the unshakable grounds for a renewed encounter with God. Sinai could still thunder its truths precisely because the lawgiver and the laws were placed in the hands of sages courageous enough to read the laws, stories, and poems through the insights and needs of each new age.

In that regard, Judaism has no new agenda and has only a new agenda. Each generation must dig its own wells, must establish its own midrashim. Each Jewish community, under the guidance of its rabbinic sages and Torah scholars, guided by the consensus of caring congregants, can reveal yet a new word of Torah, a new spark of the Divine that can light up our darkened age.

All it takes is Torah and Jews, openness and courage, caring and passion and faith.

And that is all it has ever taken.

Flying Snakes and Soaring Imaginations

The Torah is probably the world's most influential book—the all-time bestseller. We look to it for timeless truths and lofty principles to guide us through our lives and to fashion just and sacred communities. Reading the Tanakh through Western and rabbinic eyes, we expect the Bible as a whole, and the Torah in particular, to reflect a pure and sublime monotheism untainted by any magic, idolatry, or superstition.

Imagine our shock, then, to come across the story of fire-breathing, winged snakes in *Parashat Hukkat.* How do we make sense of this? God punishes the people by a scourge of terrifying snakes. The Hebrew verb *saraf* means "to burn." But we know from elsewhere in Israelite and ancient Near Eastern writings that the *Seraf* is a winged snake that stands upright and that this story has plausibility. From the area of Timna, archaeologists have uncovered the statue of a copper snake from around 1200 to 900 B.C.E. This snake is from the same region as Moses's snake and from the same period as well. Archaeologists have also uncovered a bronze bowl in the royal palace of Nineveh, the ancient capital of Assyria. Hebrew names are engraved on the rim of the bowl, and the figure of a winged snake is perched on a standard, just as the Torah describes the snake statue of Moses.

The strange figure of the *Seraf,* a healing snake, reverberates in later Jewish tradition as well. Thus, the prophet Isaiah speaks eloquently of seraphim who chant that God's "presence fills all the earth," and their repetition of the trisagion ("Holy, holy, holy") fills the Temple with smoke and rocks its very foundations.

The Tanakh recalls that later generations set up this snake statue in the Temple itself, naming it Nehushtan (a pun on the Hebrew word for "snake," *nahash*, and on the Hebrew word for "copper," *nehoshet*). Other relics from the age of Moses—the rod of Aaron, a flask of manna—were kept in storage in the Temple, but Nehushtan was erected publicly in the Temple courtyard. Because the Torah establishes that looking at the statue could heal a person, it is probable that Israelites would make their offerings and gaze upon the statue in hopes of a similar miracle.

What are we to make of this conundrum: a statue of an animal that clearly seems to violate the commandment against making a graven image, the idea of Israelites resorting to what looks like magic to counter a divine punishment and erecting this statue in the Temple itself?

Several responses come to us from antiquity. King Hezekiah, the great reformer king of ancient Israel, "broke into pieces the copper snake that Moses had made, for until that time the Israelites had been offering sacrifices to it" (2 Kings 18:4). Associating snakes with fertility in Canaanite religion and recalling the healing power of Nehushtan, the Israelites may well have begun to offer their sacrifices not to God but to the snake. Small wonder, then, that King Hezekiah destroyed it despite the fact that it was built by Moses and ordered by God.

A later ancient response viewed the building of the snake as a way for the Israelites to prove that they would, in fact, obey God's commands: "Only for a while were they thrown into disarray as a warning, possessing as they did a symbol of Your salvation to remind them of the commandment of Your law. For whoever turned toward it was saved not by the sight beheld, but through You, the savior of all" (Wisd. of Sol.). Having violated God's command and shown gross ingratitude for God's liberation, the Israelites now had to demonstrate a willingness to do as God said, even if that meant looking at the statue of a snake.

As the rabbis of the Mishnah remind us, "Could the snake slay or the serpent keep alive? It is, rather, to teach you that whenever the Israelites directed their thoughts on high and kept their hearts in subjugation to their Father in heaven, they were healed; otherwise they pined away."

We too need to fix our hearts on heaven to find the added resolve, virtue, and piety needed to heal our shattered souls.

A Religion of Life

Ours is a religion that celebrates life. Our toast at a *simcha*— *L'Hayim!*—means "To life," and it expresses the love of this life that our faith inculcates. God said that creation is *tov me'od* (very good), and we Jews affirm God's judgment by celebrating the gift of life each day and every moment.

Even as we rejoice at being alive, we also turn to our religion for solace and structure in our times of grief. During illness, Jewish tradition provides community and support through the mitzvah of *bikkur holim*. With the death of a loved one, Jewish tradition offers loving guidance through deepest grief and a gradual return to the living, through the mitzvot of *menachem aveilim* (comforting mourners) and *kavod ha-met* (providing dignity to the deceased). The wisdom of Jewish law is nowhere more apparent than in the way the traditional funeral affirms the reality of the loss while simultaneously offering hope and haven for the bereaved.

So we have a religion that focuses on life as a gift and a celebration. We expect our religion to walk with us in the valley of the shadow of death as well. Isn't that a paradox? A religion of life for the moment of death? That paradox gets even more complex when you consider how little the Torah or the Tanakh speak of life after death (it's there, it just isn't mentioned much). And that paradox becomes positively enormous when you consider just how difficult the laws of the Torah make it for people to have contact with the dead.

Consider *Parashat Hukkat*. In laying out the laws of *tumah* and *tohorah* for the Israelites to follow, God tells Moses and Aaron, "Whoever touches one that is slain with a sword in the open field, or a dead body, or a bone of a man, or a grave, shall be *tamei* seven days." Now to get a full sense of what that injunction entails, remember that the central religious event in an Israelite's life was the ability to bring a sacrifice to the Temple. This was the final step in the process of *teshuvah*. After the Israelite had repented, rectified the wrongdoing, and received the forgiveness of the aggrieved party, bringing a sacrifice was the way to free the altar from the taint of Israelite sin. God's ability to dwell among the Israelites was preserved by the constant offering of sacrifices. To become *tamei* by touching a corpse was to no longer be able to bring those sacrifices, to no longer be able to participate in public communion with God. For a full seven days, the Israelite was cut off from worship with other Jews.

The separation of life and death, so apparent in this restriction, was even more severe for a *kohen*. The *kohen* was not permitted to become *tamei* by participating in a funeral or burial at all, except for those of his parents, siblings, and children (the rabbis understood the Torah as including the wife as well). Only in that case could a *kohen* participate in a funeral or a burial at all.

What makes this prohibition so striking is our expectation that our own clergy—our rabbi and our cantor—will be there to comfort us and assist us at the loss of our loved ones. The clergy of biblical antiquity were not allowed to participate in any way. Why not? And why would the Torah require us to become *tamei* upon contact with a corpse, including that of a loved one?

Two possibilities suggest themselves: the first is historical, and the second psychological. In the realm of history, the Torah was locked in ideological combat with the pagan idolatries of the ancient world. In Egypt, death was the be-all and end-all of religion, used to justify the oppressive misery of thousands of slaves. While pharaohs and the nobility literally worked people to death, they justified their brutality with the constant hype that Egyptian idolatry lavished on the after-life. In contrast, the Torah wanted to insist that paradise could not be attained on the backs of suffering humans.

Justice, piety, and righteousness in the here and now is the certain road to *Olam ha-ba* (the coming world). To fix the focus of how we live our lives now, God prohibits Israel's clergy from participating in funerals in any way and quarantines those Israelites who do participate.

The second explanation, more psychological in nature, sees that quarantine as necessary for the well-being of the mourners. By being *tamei* for seven days, mourners were forced to attend less to public worship and more to contemplation and grief. Those seven days were devoted to the important work of grieving: to recognizing the loss that had occurred; mourning its finality; and building a new, inner relationship based on the abiding love that even death cannot destroy. By removing mourners from the bustle of work and public ritual, the Torah allows them the resources necessary to begin recovery.

That same wisdom is needed today and is embodied in the mitzvah of sitting shiva. Rather than rushing back to chores, employment, or socializing, Judaism gives us a time-out to regroup and regain our strength.

The paradox of Judaism, then, is a religion that cherishes life and embraces life even in death.

Balak/Balak
Numbers 22:2–25:9

Balak, the king of Moab, seeks to hire Balaam, a soothsayer of great repute, to curse the Israelites. When the elders offer this invitation to Balaam, he tells them to wait so he can inquire as to God's wishes. God tells him not to go with the Moabites nor to curse the Israelites, since they are a blessed people. The dignitaries return to Balak, who sends another delegation. Once more, Balaam inquires of God, and God permits Balaam to go with them but insists that "whatever I command you, that you shall do."

Balaam saddles his donkey and proceeds. But God is furious at Balaam and sends an angel with a drawn sword. The donkey sees the angel and swerves from the path, but Balaam beats it to force it to return. This happens again and again, until God causes the donkey to speak, berating Balaam for his lack of gratitude or vision. Then God allows him to see the threatening angel.

When Balaam arrives, he tells Balak, "I can utter only the words that God puts into my mouth." They make a sacrifice, and then Balak leads Balaam to a place where he can see some of the Israelite encampment. Balaam builds seven altars and offers seven bulls and rams. God tells Balaam what to say. This is a blessing that includes the famous description of the Jews: "There is a people that dwells apart, not reckoned among the nations. . . . May I die the death of the upright, May my fate be like theirs!"

Balak is distraught that the seer he hoped would curse the Israelites blesses them instead, so he tries again from another locale. A similar message emerges: "The Lord their God is with them, and their King's acclaim in their midst."

Balak attempts a third oracle, which offers the blessing, "How fair are your tents, O Jacob, your dwellings, O Israel!" At this final blessing, Balak sends Balaam back to his home. Before leaving, Balaam *offers a fourth oracle, unrequested, predicting Israel's victory against the enemy nations that surround it. He then returns home.*

While encamped at Shittim, the Israelite men are enticed by Moabite women to participate in the idolatrous cult of Baal-Pe'or. As a result, a plague erupts among the Israelites, and God commands Moses to impale the leaders of the rebellion. Before he has a chance to carry out God's grim decree, however, the priest Pinhas finds an Israelite man and a Moabite woman copulating near the sanctuary. Zealous on God's behalf, he impales the two with a spear during their copulation, and his action stops the plague.

Linked by a Shared Future

In one of the most gripping scenes in the Torah, the Gentile prophet Balaam ascends the heights of a nearby mountain to get a commanding view of Israel—all the better to curse them. Several times he attempts to curse the people, and each time he is overwhelmed by God's mandate to bless. Finally, in a moment of personal envy and hope, Balaam blurts out, "Let me die the death of the righteous. May my fate be like theirs!"

What do Balaam's words convey to us? We can ask that question on many levels. What did Balaam signify by his words? What deeper meaning does the Torah convey to us through them? And how have the sages of the Jewish people refracted God's light through them over the years?

In one reading, Balaam is asking to enjoy a death comparable to that of a Jewish saint. Lekah Tov (eleventh-century Germany) reads his words as "a request to share a portion with the patriarchs and the righteous of the world." The Midrash (*Be-Midbar Rabbah* and *Tanhuma*) sees this pious expression as an act of consummate hypocrisy. After coming to curse Israel, Balaam is caught by God and tries to mitigate his crime by saying something nice. The Midrash compares him to the story of a thief who attempts to steal and slaughter a cow belonging to the king. When he realizes he is about to be caught, he cleans out the cow's trough and brushes the cow's coat, hoping that these actions will diminish his culpability.

Later voices in our tradition note that Balaam asks to die like a pious Jew but doesn't ask to live like one. The *Hafetz Hayim* (nineteenth-century Lithuania) trenchantly observes, "It is no great feat to die a proper death. The real feat is to live a proper life." As important as an afterlife is to Jewish belief, the real emphasis remains on this world—the needs of our fellow creatures, the needs of our fellow human beings, and the imperative to pursue justice and embody compassion. The faith of a believing Jew promises a glorious reunion with those who have gone before, an eternity of joy and bliss. How easy to die such a death! But to live the life of a truly believing Jew—a life consumed by transforming every deed into a mitzvah, every encounter into an opportunity for service—such a life is weighty and difficult.

A second tradition reads Balaam's words as a desire to share in the destiny of the Jewish people. Rabbenu Bahya Ben Asher (thirteenth-century Spain) understands Balaam as saying, "May my ultimate destiny be like that of the Jewish people. . . . He thereby acknowledged that the people Israel would inherit the physical world of the future also." That same understanding underscores the words of a twentieth-century commentator, Rabbi Jacob Milgrom, who states, "It is a blessing to share [the people] Israel's fate."

Indeed, to be a Jew is to share a glorious and complex past, a history of achievement and spiritual depth despite great obstacles and suffering. But our past only presents the context and prelude to our future. The destiny of the Jewish people remains our charge and our purpose—to translate the words of Torah into living human beings; to elevate its teachings into communities of holiness and justice; to renew the world through the study of Torah, the observance of mitzvot, and the practice of good deeds.

Small wonder that Rambam summarizes Balaam's message as emphasizing the need for Jews to remain distinct in order to fulfill our mandate to all humanity and to God: "The general tenor of Balaam's prophecy was that God does not want us to be cursed and that we are a people dwelling alone, God's portion and God's people. We shall not disappear among the nations, and our end will be good, according to the way of the righteous."

May you be blessed to live a life of righteousness so that you may merit the death of the righteous. And may your deeds and integrity so illumine those whose lives you touch that your fate is linked to that of the Jewish people and their age-old mission to repair the world under the sovereignty of God.

No Longer a People Apart

Recent studies of the Jewish population have confirmed what common sense already knew: we are less and less different from the people around us. Our children attend the same preschools, the same public and private schools, the same dance classes and activities, the same high schools. On weekends, they participate on the same athletic teams, and they hang out at the same malls. When they select a college, their standards are pretty much the same standards as everyone else's, and their choices of professions don't differ much from those of our neighbors.

Small wonder, then, that a majority of marriages since 1985 have involved a Jew marrying a non-Jew, and approximately one million children with Jewish ancestry are being raised as Christians. The walls of discrimination have come tumbling down, and our future existence is imperiled by the fulfillment of our fondest dream—living in a society where Jews don't have to be different. It's killing us.

No one wants to be different. Line up any group of small children and ask them if they are different from anybody else. They'll confirm that we all have a deep-seated drive to be similar. Being different means being lonely, being hated, sitting apart. Yet that is precisely what our tradition knows is the essential prerequisite of Jewish survival.

In *Parashat Balak*, the Gentile prophet Balaam sees that role as necessary for Israel to be able to make a significant contribution to humanity. Looking over the Israelites assembled in the valley, he exclaims,

> As I see them from the mountaintops,
> Gaze on them from the heights,
> There is a people that dwells apart,
> Not reckoned among the nations.

For Balaam, our essential trait is that we dwell apart, that being Jewish means retaining and cultivating a distinctive identity.

A good Jew ought to be different, ought to stand apart from a crowd. Rashi recognizes as much. He knows that distinction is not a punishment, not some badge of shame to be worn with sorrow. Rather, he understands that "this is what their ancestors merited for them, to dwell alone."

Rashi sees our being different as something wonderful that we have earned through the merit of our ancestors—of Abraham and Sarah; of Isaac and Rebecca; of Jacob, Rachel, and Leah. Their piety, their goodness, and their integrity earned our right to be different.

But are we? Isn't it striking that we are the generation of Jews least different than our neighbors and at the same time least capable of transmitting our identity to our children? Most of us remember a *zeyde* (grandfather) who started each morning in tallit and tefillin and a *bubbe* (grandmother) who baked a challah and set out the wine for kiddush and the candles to *bentsch licht*. Will our children grow up with those beautiful building blocks to a healthy identity?

Starved for spiritual meaning, we run after fads and cults, so distanced from Jewish observance that we don't even consider the mitzvot as the real cure for our sense of loss and emptiness. At our best, we were a people apart, separated not by superiority, but by a passion for Torah, mitzvot, and *gemillut hasadim*, the three-fold path that has preserved us through the millennia and enabled us to become a beacon for the rest of humanity.

We abandon our distinction at our own peril and the impoverishment of mankind.

The Burden of Freedom

The Torah, Rambam insists, is based on the idea of human freedom. If we were not free to choose our future, to determine our own actions, then the idea of giving us commandments would make no sense, and rewarding or punishing us for our fidelity to God's ideals would be morally and logically preposterous. For the great medieval rabbi, human freedom is woven into the very fabric of creation.

The idea that we are free and therefore responsible for the consequences of our choices no longer musters universal support. Complicated by the impact of genetics (how free are we if our genes predispose us?), by the impact of social norms (how free can we be if habit and consensus limit and frame our choices?), it is no simple matter to insist that human choice, though bounded, is still fundamentally unfettered. We are, indeed, the captains of our souls and the masters of our own destiny.

That issue rises in *Parashat Balak*, as Balak sends a group of dignitaries to ask Balaam to curse the Israelites, and Balaam responds, "Though Balak were to give me his house full of silver and gold, I could not do anything, big or little, contrary to the command of the Lord my God." He then invites the dignitaries to spend the night so he can have time to confer with God and report back what God demands.

Balaam's piety may be feigned, or it may be sincere. He may be reflecting a belief in determinism (I can't choose anything other than what God has determined for me) or merely obedience (I won't choose anything other than what God demands). Our interest is not in his words, but in what God says next. God visits Balaam in a dream and tells the prophet, "If these men have come to invite you, you may go with them. But whatever I command you, that you shall do."

Baalam's dream is quite convenient, given that he's just been offered a fortune to go with the dignitaries, and in his dream God allows him to make that choice. Looking carefully at God's words, what is clear is that God basically says, "You, Balaam, get to make this call. Go if you want; stay if you want. But when it comes time to speak, please adhere to my wishes." In other words, "The choice is yours, human. You are free to decide for yourself." In the words of the Talmud, "A person is led the way s/he wishes to go."

Be-Midbar Rabbah, the ancient midrash to the book of Numbers, makes God's perspective explicit: "I [God] don't desire the destruction of the wicked, but since you [Balaam] are bent on following this path that will lead to your destruction, I will not prevent you from doing so." Rambam underscores this point when he teaches, "The Creator does not compel or decree that people should do either good or bad. Rather, everything is left to their own choice."

If in the Bible, where God's will seems so clear and God's voice resonates, free will is immutable, how much the more so is it in our world, where God's will is often more nuanced and God's voice more muted? Human freedom, however qualified by the limitations of biology, society, gender, or wealth, is still freedom. We are the authors of our actions, and we are responsible for our choices.

Of course, being free to choose does not make every choice equally valid. We are free to make the right choices, and we are free to make the wrong ones. Freedom to choose does not remove the consequences of our choices. Instead, we are free to pay the price for poor choices we have made or to harvest the benefits of well-made choices.

Balaam chooses badly and pays with his life for his poor choice. Every moment, we are faced with the choice—to enhance life, to nurture the divine image in our fellow human beings and all of creation, to add our voices to the call of shalom.

Choose wisely, you who are free.

Pinhas/Pinhas

Numbers 25:10–30:1

God bestows on Pinhas an eternal covenant of peace as a reward for his zeal on God's behalf. The Israelite who was killed, Zimri, was the son of a chieftain from the tribe of Shimon. The woman was Cozbi, the daughter of a chieftain of the Midianites, a group allied with the Moabites. God commands Moses and the Israelites to attack the Midianites because they lured the Israelites into idolatrous worship and apostasy.

The parashah continues with the rise of a new generation and preparation for the conquest of Eretz Yisrael. This new generation is characterized by fidelity to God and Torah.

At the end of the plague, God mandates another census of men who are over twenty years of age. Unlike the earlier census, this one is by tribal clans, and the total number is more than six hundred thousand males of fighting age. Once the number of people is established, God discusses allocating the Promised Land by lot and the size of each tribe.

The census confirms that the generation of the Exodus has died, fulfilling God's dictate that those rebellious Jews would die in the wilderness and their children would reach the land of Israel. The daughters of Zelophehad raise an issue with the justice of the inheritance system. Why, they ask, should their father's land allotment go outside the family just because he had no sons? Moses consults with God, who affirms the wisdom of the daughters and grants them the right to inherit. God tells Moses to ascend to the heights of Mount Avarim to view the land the Israelites will enter, after which he too will die. Still concerned for the well-being of the people, Moses asks God to appoint someone to lead in his stead, so that the Lord's community may not be like sheep that have no shepherd. God appoints Joshua, and Moses signifies the choice in a public ceremony.

God establishes the calendar of public sacrifices, the festivals and holy days of ancient Israel and contemporary Judaism. These occasions of public festivity mark the daily offering, Shabbat, *Rosh Hodesh, Pesach,* Shavuot, *Rosh Hashanah, Yom Kippur, Sukkot, and Sh'mini Atzereth (the Gathering of the Eighth Day).*

New Moon!

The calendar of the Jewish holidays is an introductory course in Jewish theology and history, complete in itself. Through the cycles of holy days, festivals, memorials, and fast days—all rich with traditions, readings, meditations, and rituals—a Jew can become familiar with the basic values, beliefs, and history that have sustained us as a people.

One celebration that used to be quite prominent in biblical times but has been relegated to a place of lesser prominence in postbiblical practice deserves another look: *Rosh Hodesh*.

In *Parashat Pinhas*, the festivals of the calendar are detailed at length. Particular attention is given to the sacrifices offered on each day. *Rosh Hodesh* gets the same number of offerings as the other major sacred occasions—a sure sign that it was of equal importance to those holy days.

To understand the context of *Rosh Hodesh*, it is worth recalling the place of the moon in ancient pagan religions. For many of them, the moon represented a powerful goddess, whose worship often affected fertility and sustenance. In a world in which people worshipped nature as though it were divine (pantheism or transnaturalism), the moon was an attractive and frightening divinity.

The genius of traditional Judaism was to refashion such powerful symbols, making it clear that divinity did not inhere in nature or in simple being but was a constant gift of the God who was and is the source of nature and of life. How the Torah and rabbinic Judaism made a place for the moon speaks a great deal for their gifted understanding of the human heart and their masterful ability as teachers and counselors.

The Torah marks the new moon as a significant occasion, when the people of Israel gathered and praised the God who fashioned the sun, the moon, the stars, and other astral bodies. Rather than see-ing the moon as a marvel in its own right, it is significant as a sign of God's steadfast love and creative bounty.

In that regard, the Torah offers a fascinating hint, calling for the sacrifice of "one goat as a sin offering to the Lord." But that ritual occurs for no other festival in the entire Torah. So why here?

As Rambam explains in his *Guide for the Perplexed*, "As it was appre-hended that the he-goat offered on the new moon could be imag-ined to be a sacrifice to the moon . . . it was explicitly stated that this goat was consecrated to God and not to the moon." In other words, a pagan ritual was now transformed to meet the purposes of ethical monotheism. The light of the moon now illuminated the riches of Torah and the sovereignty of the *Ribbono shel Olam* (the Commander of Space/Time). The new moon became a time to praise God for the reliable cycles of nature.

Thus, on the Shabbat prior to *Rosh Hodesh*, the synagogue resounds with a prayer that the new month should be marked by love of Torah and fear of sin. On *Rosh Hodesh* itself, the congregation chants the Hallel, the ancient collection of praises to God offered by the Lev-ites in King Solomon's temple. A few nights later, Jews gather for the ritual of *Kiddush Levanah*, sanctification in response to the new moon that consists of reciting a psalm that firmly establishes God as the author of the natural order, noting that the sun, moon, and stars do God's will reliably (and implying that we should too).

One Talmudic rabbi claimed that "one who blesses the new moon is regarded as one who greets the Shechinah." Blessing the new moon is like seeing God's face, because when Jews gather to bless the moon, we do so as an act of fidelity to the God who made the moon, who continues to pour supernal light on the world through the renewing moon, the rising sun, and the glistening stars of the night sky.

Surely that is a celebration worth renewing in our own troubled and doubting age.

The Blessing of Prayer

After the sin of Baal-Pe'or, when our ancestors began to worship an idol, God responded by unleashing a terrible plague. Sinners and innocent alike were stricken, and the plague was only stopped through the intercession of Pinhas. As remembered by the psalmist, "Then Pinhas stood up and *vay-falel*, and so the plague was stayed, and that was counted to him for righteousness to all generations forevermore."

What did Pinhas do to stop the plague? What is the meaning of *vay-falel*? Interestingly, two quite different words emerge from this common root. One means "to execute judgment," which is how this psalm is generally translated. But the *shoresh* (root of this verb), F-L-L, also means "to pray," as in the Hebrew word *tefillah*. The Radomsker Rebbe, a great Hasidic teacher, seizes upon this meaning to offer a different understanding. Pinhas intervened by praying, and it was his prayer that stopped the plague. Because of that intervention, God gave Pinhas his covenant of peace.

It would seem that intervention on behalf of God's people results in receiving a special blessing from God. The lesson we might draw from Pinhas's reward is that whenever our people are threatened, we must rush to their defense. Just as Pinhas intervened to stop their suffering (even though it was recompense from the hand of God), so we must not fail to intervene to prevent or terminate Jewish suffering.

But, the Radomsker notes, such intervention doesn't always result in blessing. Note, for instance, the fact that Aaron, the *kohen*, also intervened on behalf of God's people. After the sin of the golden calf, a plague also broke out among the people. Without hesitation, Aaron took the incense burner and ran out among the people, swinging the incense to block the epidemic. Aaron's intervention also worked—the plague stopped wherever he stood. But God remained silent. There was no eternal blessing or special covenant to reward Aaron for his diligence or his concern. Why not?

According to the Radomsker Rebbe, the difference between Aaron and Pinhas was that the former relied on incense, which was only available while the Temple stood, whereas the latter relied on prayer, which is always within our reach. Why didn't God grant a new covenant to Aaron? Perhaps because God wanted us to know that we need nothing more than prayer—turning our hearts to God in the full simplicity of our love to commune with our Creator. Perhaps God was concerned that we might attribute the miracle of the healing to the incense itself. Or maybe God needed to discourage using props when direct action would suffice.

The implication of both stories together is clear: God doesn't need fancy incense, lofty titles, or great drama. God needs nothing more than our need. As the Talmud puts it, "*Ha-Kadosh-Barukh-Hu liba ba'i* (God wants the heart)." If we give God our hearts, even just a little, then God will enter that space we offer, providing us with purpose, strength, and peace.

The key is that God cannot take the first step. We are, indeed, the captains of our souls, and God waits for an invitation to step in. Only after we call upon God in purity and wholeness, only after we have turned ourselves toward God, only then does the Holy One reach out to us. So perhaps the silence we sometimes hear, the absence we sometimes feel, isn't so much God's absence but our own.

God wants the heart. That little offering is actually the hardest gift to give. Our hearts yearn for so many things; much of what we desire is harmful to us, much of what we seek is petty or inconsequential. Underneath that distracting clamor lies our yearning for matters of true significance: love, truth, beauty, goodness, holiness. We bury those deepest desires under the gaudy, pushy calls of the superficial and the dangerous. And in acceding to this perverse hierarchy, we banish God from our hearts.

We need, as Jeremiah recognized, to circumcise our hearts anew— to be able to feel the fullness of our feelings, to transcend our wounds and our disappointments, to allow hope and faith to flourish as though we were babes. Our tradition teaches that we have only to reach out to God, and God will be there for us.

The first step is ours. Care to take it?

A Torah That Mirrors Real Life

After the Israelites sin at Baal-Pe'or, God lashes out in anger, ordering Moses to "take all the heads of the people and have them publicly impaled." Before Moses can act on God's command, a leading Israelite named Zimri and a leading Midianite woman named Cozbi enter the sacred site of the Tent of Meeting and there, before the entire people, begin to copulate. This arrogant escalation of sin inflames Pinhas, the leader of the Levitical guards, who grabs a spear and impales the two sinners.

While most modern readers are shocked and appalled by the bloodshed of this scenario, even more horrifying is God's response: the bestowal of an eternal pact of friendship (*briti shalom*) to Pinhas and his heirs. Why would God mandate the death of all the leaders, innocent and guilty alike? And why would God reward Pinhas for a violent and impulsive act of killing?

Jewish tradition offers small comfort to those in search of sweetness and elevation from religion. Unlike other religious traditions that emphasize only the positive or that seek to uplift by focusing only on the sublime, Judaism has always adhered to the reality principle: religion must illumine life as it actually happens, not some saccharine, edited version that would be useless in times of trouble.

Life can be bloody and unfair. Violence can sweep out of control and take the lives of the innocent in a twinkling. Our problem with the story of Pinhas is not that it doesn't resemble real life enough, but that it reflects reality too faithfully.

The truth is that we live in a world in which the innocent often pay for the deeds of the guilty. The Torah understands that truth and, because of that insight, provides stories and leaders capable of providing wisdom and guidance during the storms life can bring. The challenge of the Torah is the challenge of looking at life without blinders.

The rabbis understand as well. The *Mekhilta*, the ancient midrash to Exodus, comments that "once permission has been given to the 'destroyer' to do injury, it no longer discriminates between the innocent and the guilty." Once violence is unleashed, even if it was originally directed against evil, it cannot be directed with any pretense of precision. That insight is only too clear from a history of "just" wars and their innocent victims.

Rabbi Eleazar Ben Shammua made a similar point in *Sifre Be-Midbar*: "As it is impossible for a doornail to be taken out from the door without extracting some of the wood, so it is impossible for Israel to separate itself from [Baal-]Pe'or without losing souls." Because human beings live in society together, the good and the innocent regularly pay for the sins and selfishness of the wicked. The bicyclist breathes in the soot of the motorcyclist, and the *davvener* suffers the assault of a blaring radio.

In another explanation in *Be-Midbar Rabbah*, Rabbi Judah insists that all of Israel's leaders share the responsibility for the sin of Baal-Pe'or by virtue of their authority. If they had been truly righteous and diligent leaders, the Israelites would not have been tempted to sin.

In a democracy where all of us have the power to vote and to lead, we become responsible for the sins of our own society. The gap between rich and poor; the staggering rate of teen pregnancy and child poverty; violence against ethnic, religious, or sexual minorities; bias against women; pollution—all of these are our responsibility because we allow them to continue.

The violence of Baal-Pe'or, then, is a clarion call to become involved. We can turn to the Torah to reveal a picture of real life designed to empower us to realize holiness in the world. Or we can close the scrolls and try to keep our eyes closed, our ears plugged. In either case, the innocent are suffering. What are you going to do about it?

Mattot/Tribes
Numbers 30:2–32:42

This parashah begins with the issue of oaths and vows, establishing their binding nature for all men and for women, provided that the fathers of minor daughters or husbands of married adults don't retract the vow when they first hear it. The vow of a widow or divorced woman is precisely as binding as that of an adult man.

Moses needs to seek vindication from the Midianites for having drawn the Israelites into the licentious idolatry of Baal-Pe'or. He musters a force using soldiers from each of the tribes, and they vanquish the Midianites without losing a single Israelite warrior. In addition to executing the five Midianite kings, they slaughter Balaam.

The soldiers take booty from the Midianite settlements, including women and children, beasts, herds, and gold. Moses is outraged that the very women who led the Israelite men astray are spared, and he orders their prompt execution as well. Then he mandates that the soldiers undertake a seven-day period of purification prior to reentering the camp.

The booty that remains is divided equally among those who fought and the rest of the community, at God's command. The officers donate all their gold plunder to the sanctuary.

With the last battle of the wilderness behind them, Israel moves into a new phase: that of settlement. The two tribes of Reuben and Gad petition to settle on the eastern bank of the river Jordan rather than on the western bank. At first, Moses resists this proposal, but once he is assured that the two tribes will continue to fight along with their fellow Israelites, he consents.

Massei/Itineraries
Numbers 33:1-36:13

The final parashah of the book of Numbers recounts each of the forty-two camps of the Israelites, from Rameses to Sinai, from Sinai to Kadesh, and from Kadesh to the steppes of Moab. This listing of encampments is a joyous recollection of God's miracles along the way and a sobering reminder of Israel's many rebellions against God and Moses.

At the border of Canaan, God mandates the conquest and apportionment of the land. While Moses isn't allowed to enter the land, he is permitted to draw up the plans for its settlement and growth. He lays out the regulations for the conquest, the precise boundaries of the new Israelite home, and the authority of the tribal chieftains who will establish forty-eight towns for the Levites and the six Levitical towns of asylum for involuntary manslaughter.

The parashah and the entire book end with a follow-up from the family of Zelophehad, concerned that the women who will inherit family land will then marry into other families and their land will be lost. To address this concern, God mandates that the women must marry within their own clan.

The book of Numbers closes with this observation: "These are the commandments and regulations that the Lord enjoined upon the Israelites, through Moses, on the steppes of Moab, at the Jordan near Jericho."

Say What You Mean

Every four years, with each new presidential election, Americans come face-to-face with the unpleasant reality that we don't trust each other. Each candidate stands before countless audiences, solemnly promising what will happen under a new administration. Few voters bother to consider the campaign promises, let alone take them as any indication of how a president will actually perform.

The Torah posits a very different expectation, one in which a person's word creates an unshakable commitment, so great is the correlation between promise and deed. This parashah speaks of the vows made by an adult man, a daughter, a wife, and a widow. In each case, the Torah provides guidelines for how a vow may be made and when it can be nullified without the incursion of guilt for its violation.

The word *abracadabra* comes from the Aramaic (the ancient language of the Talmud) and means "he does as he speaks." What is now an expression of genies on sitcoms was once a morality that pervaded Israelite society. The world of the Torah and the Talmud is one in which words matter, in which what we say creates an enforceable obligation.

Vows were taken so seriously that the rabbis looked with great disfavor on making vows. The Talmud records the view that "if one makes a vow, it is as if one has built a *bamah* (forbidden idolatrous altar), and if one fulfills the vows, it is as if one had sacrificed upon it." The rabbis discouraged making promises that might not be kept.

They also extended their understanding of vows beyond the *p'shat* of the Torah itself; whereas the Torah seems to assert that only an adult man makes irrevocable vows, the rabbis extended the responsibility for vows to anyone whose intention matches their words. The Mishnah explicitly states that "a statement is not binding unless intention and expression agree."

An incident recorded in *Sifre Zuta* (a tannaitic midrash on the book of Numbers) illustrates that general principle. A child came before Rabbi Akiva and said, "Rabbi, I dedicated my shovel."

Rabbi Akiva asked, "Perhaps you dedicated it to the sun or the moon?"

The child answered, "Rabbi, do not worry. I dedicated it to the One who created them."

Rabbi Akiva said, "Go, my child. Your vow is valid."

Because the child's intention was grounded in an accurate knowledge of reality and the consequences of the vow, Rabbi Akiva considered the vow to be valid.

We have a lot to learn from the biblical and rabbinic treatment of vows. They share a lofty expectation of human responsibility, a recognition that we are held accountable for what we say, and our word is to be our bond.

Only in that context is it possible to take seriously what other people tell us. Just as our leaders must focus on finding a new way to address America's problems, they must also return to an old way of addressing our people. Like each one of us, they must mean what they say.

What Do We Prize Most?

There is no denying the consensus that it's better to be rich than to be poor. Or that money may not be able to buy happiness, but it can buy the things that buy happiness. While much of the world may deride Americans as being overly materialistic, few nations complain when their standards of living (always measured in material terms) rise, and few object to emulating the American way of life. Jeans, disco, and McDonald's remain strong export items all around the globe.

Even here at home, although many people criticize our obsession with "things," few are willing to deny their own desires. We may differ as to which objects are worthy of our efforts and sweat, but few individuals are completely indifferent to material reality.

While some other religions and schools of philosophy may cultivate a disdain for the physical, many voices within Judaism have asserted that possessions are neither intrinsically good nor necessarily evil. What matters is how we come to possess them (ethical business dealings), how we use them (*derekh ha-beinoni*—moderation and consideration of others), and how we discard them when we are finished (*bal tash'hit*—avoidance of waste and the concerns of ecology).

As *Midrash Tanhuma* remarks, "Three gifts were created in the world, and these are wisdom, strength, and wealth." Possessions, if come by honestly and used reasonably, if shared with others and harnessed to righteous goals, can enhance our lives and our society. While some Jewish leaders were ascetic in their approach, most of the prophets, rabbis, and sages recognized that physical comfort, pleasure, and security could strengthen our sense of being loved by God, in turn stimulating our love of God and our caring for each other.

This parashah, however, speaks of a case in which material desire gained an excessive prominence, where lust for property corrupted religious values and displaced social responsibility. The tribes of Israel were so close to their goal of entering the Promised Land, the land of Israel, that they could practically see their destination from where they stood. Most could hardly wait to take possession of the land.

Yet the members of the tribes of Reuben and Gad couldn't help noticing that the land they were standing on looked pretty good—green and lush and watered. It occurred to them that this land might meet their (material) needs perfectly, without their having to fight for the land of Israel. The Torah records of these tribes that "the children of Reuben and the children of Gad owned cattle in very great numbers."

Rather than affirming their loyalty to God, grazing their flock with the least effort became their supreme goal. So they asked Moses if they could remain where they were. *Midrash Be-Midbar Rabbah* describes them perfectly: "You find that they were rich, possessing large numbers of cattle, but they loved their money and settled outside the land of Israel. Consequently, they were the first of all the tribes to go into exile.... What brought it on them? The fact that they separated themselves from their brethren because of their possessions."

They placed their ease and wealth above all other values and commitments. Consequently, when they were threatened, their ease had dulled their ability to respond and their wealth made them a flashy and easy target.

While few would deny that wealth can be a great blessing, it can also be a person's undoing. When it becomes an obsession rather than a luxury, when it becomes a goal rather than a means to a goal, when it displaces the abiding sources of happiness and the Abiding Source of Meaning, wealth turns on its owner and becomes a snare and an enemy. As the rabbis so wisely observed, "If one is privileged to possess wealth, he has attained everything. When does this apply? When they are gifts of heaven and come through the force of the Torah."

Let our highest goals remain those of Torah—fidelity to God, passionate love of Jews and Judaism, and a resolve to make the world more just and compassionate—and let our wealth serve as a means to achieve those ends. Then and only then can we remain masters of our possessions rather than their slaves. And only then can our possessions move us toward a truer contentment and peace.

The Benefits of Camping

Several years ago, *Reader's Digest* produced a slimmer, improved Bible. The editors removed all the "begats" because no one wanted to slog through the long lists of names. They streamlined Leviticus and Numbers because no one wanted to bother with the ancient laws of priestly purity and sacrifice, and they got rid of the long stories describing the wanderings of the Israelites from one place to the next. After all, we don't know where any of those camps are, so we needn't trouble ourselves with endless lists of unknown places.

This new and improved Bible is still on the market. So, thank God, is the original. And in that Bible, the one that God gave and our ancestors treasured and shielded with their lives, those lengthy lists claim prominence of place. "These were the marches of the Israelites who started out from the land of Egypt," this parashah begins and then provides the names of each and every camp the Israelites established, used, and pitched. Names we see nowhere else occupy as much space as camps we still have stories about. Apparently, God thought that there was some valuable lesson to be derived from listing the names of the camps.

In *Midrash Be-Midbar Rabbah*, several reasons are given:

1. The names of the camps are listed so that we can remember all the miracles that God did for us during the precarious period of our wandering. For forty years, we marched through the wilderness with no source of food or water, no shelter, no fortress for protection. Our only shelter, our only sukkah, was God and our faith. Each name of a camp reflects yet another time that God secured our tranquillity. Thus, the midrash records God as instructing Moses to "write down the stages by which Israel journeyed in the wilderness, in order to know what miracles I wrought for them."

2. Another reason the camps are listed is to remind us of our own mistakes. We sinned plenty in the wilderness: hounding Moses and doubting his leadership, not appreciating Miriam when she was with us, repeatedly indulging in idolatry, murmuring against Aaron and Moses, kvetching about God, preferring to return to slavery in Egypt. Over and over again, we showed flawed

judgment and weak faith. We were unable to give ourselves over to trust in God, to be willing to let Moses take us where we needed to go. And we paid a stiff price for that stubborn cynicism. Recording each campsite is a caution to us against relying too much on our own powers to control nature and the world, to account for all variables, to wander away from our ancestral covenant with God. As the midrash notes, God says to Moses, "Recount to them all the places where they provoked Me."

3. A third reason for the lists involves two critical virtues that can enhance human life: God bids us to list the camps to teach the value of *hakh'nasat orehim* and gratitude. Just as God cared for us throughout the forty years, acting as gracious host to an unruly crowd, so we should be willing to host guests in our own homes and provide for those who need shelter in society at large. And just as we would expect our guests to show appropriate gratitude for our efforts to care for them and their physical needs, so we ought to be grateful to God for the lavish hospitality that God provided to us so we could be free. As the midrash notes, "Why were all the stations recorded in the Torah? In return for their having hosted Israel, the Holy Blessing One will give them their reward. Now if the wilderness is to be rewarded, is it not certain that one who hosts scholars or guests will be rewarded all the more?"

A list that looks superfluous and dull provides important lessons for us. Our lives are strewn with miracles that we lose if we don't remember them periodically; we have to remember our mistakes and learn from them; hospitality is a great mitzvah; and gratitude is the proper response to the bounty of being alive and to being God's guests in the world.

Making lists is how we organize our lives and keep our households in order. This list is an opportunity for moral and spiritual shopping, for timeless virtues, and for renewed gratitude.

I'll bet you never thought you'd get all that from camping!

Deuteronomy

Devarim

———◦◦◦———

Words

Devarim/Words
Deuteronomy 1:1–3:22

The fifth book of the Torah constitutes Moses's farewell address to the people Israel on the border of Eretz Yisrael. According to Jewish tradition, Moses's series of discourses took thirty-six days to deliver, beginning on the first day of Shebat and ending on the sixth day of Adar. Deuteronomy is portrayed as the time that "Moses undertook to expound this Teaching (ha-Torah ha-zot)." The purpose of this instruction is to convey law as well as teachings that must be studied and pondered, with the intention of molding character, establishing virtues, and making goodness and holiness habitual.

The first discourse describes the history of Israel from the liberation from Egyptian slavery up to this event some forty years later. The first section of the first speech offers a retrospective and culls important moral lessons for Israel to learn from its first half-century. The theme of this section is neatly summarized: "Adonai your God has blessed you in all your undertakings. God has watched over your wanderings through this great wilderness. Adonai your God has been with you these past forty years: you have lacked nothing."

Moses uses this opportunity to remind the Israelites of key lessons they will need as they enter Israel: a lack of trust in God and a lack of obedience result in defeat. God is the warrior who does battle on Israel's behalf. Moses relates how the disobedience and rebellion of the tribes led to their defeat by the Amorites and the condemnation of the first generation to death in the wilderness, and how the second generation's trust led to military victories over the enemy rulers King Sihon and King Og. The conclusion that Moses derives from Israel's liberation and early wanderings is this: "You have seen with your own eyes all that the Holy One your God has done to these two kings; so shall the Holy One do to all the kingdoms into which you shall cross over. Do not fear them, for it is the Holy One your God who will battle for you."

Have No Fear

The world can be a very scary place. Every time we pick up the morning paper or turn on the television, the media provides us with more evidence of just how terrifying life can be. Fires that rage out of control, brutal warfare abroad, incessant terrorist attacks, gangs and criminals who terrorize our streets, illness, death, unemployment, and a host of more private sorrows are the constant companions of the living. We are all wounded by the simple act of staying alive.

On every page of the Torah, we read of the challenges and torments that afflicted our ancestors—childlessness, sibling rivalry, murder, loveless marriage, rape, war. Even the greatest of all prophets, our rabbi Moses, encountered enough bitterness that he several times suggested that he would prefer death to the life he was living. So it becomes particularly noteworthy to listen to his farewell address, delivered on the border of the Promised Land with the people Israel attending their aged and unparalleled leader.

Twice in *Parashat Devarim*, he repeats the same idea: "Fear not, and be not dismayed" and "Have no dread or fear of them." In fact, Moses quotes God as saying, "I have delivered him [Canaan] into your hand." Note that the Torah doesn't promise "I *will* deliver him" but assures that the deed is as good as done.

What's going on here? Surely Moses, a man who has suffered so profoundly, knows that life is no bed of roses. So how can he offer this Pollyannaish advice of "Don't worry; be happy"? We have good reason to fear, so why is God adamant on this point?

Perhaps the Torah is teaching us the right attitude with which to face life's impediments. In a sense, our propensity to fear can be our worst enemy, more dangerous than the object of fear itself. In the face of the unknown, our fantasies are more ominous than our realities. In the face of life's challenges, giving way to our pessimism and our fear strips us of our will to fight. Fear is the ally of tragedy, transforming spirited humans into passive victims.

Half of the battle lies in a refusal to give in to fear.

Midrash B'raisheet Rabbah hints at the power of hope and faith in the face of danger and hostility. It offers three scenarios that justify the assurance that the Canaanites have already been delivered into Israel's hands. The first is that when Abraham was confronted by the plotting king and ancestor of the Canaanites, Og, Abraham continued the mitzvah he was engaged in—preparing food for a ritual meal. A second midrashic explanation says that the deliverance of the Canaanites into Israel's hands was assured when Og threatened to kill Isaac, and Abraham responded by going ahead with the mitzvah of brit milah. The third and final explanation concerns Jacob. Og sought to cast the evil eye on Jacob, and Jacob continued the mitzvah he was engaged in—blessing Pharaoh.

The power of Jacob's blessing was stronger than Og's evil eye. The mitzvah of celebrating our inner freedom was more conclusive than any threat of attack, and the continuity and holiness of celebrating the birth of a Jewish child was more compelling than Og's murderous intent.

Ultimately, the faith of the Jew is the resilience of hope. Refusing to give in to despair, the Jew musters the inner resilience that comes from spiritual depth and a vision of holiness that transcends time. It is not that we can avoid suffering entirely, but we can fashion our response to suffering. And just as our patriarchs responded to suffering with a renewed commitment to the mitzvot, to the Jewish people, and to God, we too can make our mark in the world by how we choose to confront pain and disappointment.

By living our lives in goodness, by cultivating a rich connection to our God and the mitzvot, and by alleviating the suffering of others, we vindicate Moses's insight and embody his remarkable courage. Fear not and be not dismayed.

In Praise of Moses

Many of the world's religions share a great deal: a sense of wonder and marvel at the simple fact of existence, the miracle of creation and life, the mystery of human consciousness, the awareness of the sacred and the profane, the love of our fellow human beings, and the pursuit of peace and of justice. Just as many of the world's religions trace their discovery of these traits to their founders, so Judaism sees many of its highest values embodied in Moshe Rabbenu (our teacher Moses).

The entire book of Deuteronomy is presented as Moses's farewell address. Standing at the border of the Promised Land, he is also on the border between life and death. At the end of his unparalleled career, he recounts the significance of his half-decade of leadership and charges the Jewish people with continued fidelity to God and to Torah.

As Moses begins his great speech, let's take a moment to consider the legacy that this great prophet leaves to us. What can we learn from the life and teachings of Moses?

• First and foremost, Moses teaches that holiness and ethics cannot be separated without doing serious harm to each. Unless religion is in constant communion with moral rigor, its own way of marking time and of accessing holiness can become a source of human hatred and suffering, a way to justify bigotry. On the other hand, ethics without ritual discipline quickly reduces to lip service. Absent the commanding voice of God, our values melt into mere preferences, like extended aesthetics. By fusing morality with religion, Moses fashions a powerful tool for moral uplift and spiritual depth. Mosaic religion is a profoundly moral spirituality; Mosaic ethics is intoxicated with God.

• Moses teaches us that decency is measured not by lofty pronouncements but by prosaic details of everyday living. Rather than presenting a complex philosophy or a systemic theology, Moses focuses on how to behave. The laws and teachings of the Torah don't impose a trickle-down goodness, one that relies on right thinking to lead to right behavior. Instead, by mandating proper behavior, the Torah expects deeds of goodness to construct an implicit theology— one built on the painstaking work of compassion, of caring, and of justice. By making our diets sacred, by infusing the cycles of our lives with holy days and holy times, we express our beliefs through our actions. And that theology has stood the test of time.

• Moses teaches us the power of passion. He loves his people irreducibly and his God without limit. Standing before the Jewish people, he argues forcefully for the God who brought them to freedom. Standing before God, he speaks on behalf of each and every Jew, defending his people before their Maker. Moses exemplifies the ability to love deeply and sustain multiple loyalties, while remaining true to an all-embracing integrity that unites one's loves in a higher expression of conviction. His passion for God and for Israel create the bridge that allow God and Israel to fashion a *brit* that expresses itself first in the Torah and unfolds in the ensuing commentaries and interpretations of each succeeding age. Passion can unite. Passion can change the world.

• Finally, Moses teaches us that love and faith must ultimately express themselves in a commitment to one's fellow human beings and to all living things. Faith in God as Creator and Lawgiver implies a dedication to God's creation. Moses exemplifies that capacity for empathy and the courage to transform the world. He works against the injustices he sees and creates a framework in which his descendants can continue to walk in his footsteps.

There is one key way in which Judaism diverges from other faiths. The founders of many faiths gave their names to the traditions of their teachings; hence, we have Confucianism, Buddhism, Christianity. Moses was convinced that the one who matters is God, that he was significant only as God's prophet. The fact that our faith does not bear his name, that we neither pray to or through him, that we don't recount his life's history as the embodiment of human perfection constitutes his greatest tribute.

His memory is a blessing.

Choosing Judaism

Once each year as a congregational rabbi, I and thirty eager people would drive to Laguna Beach. Not to play volleyball and not to bask in the glorious California sunshine. Our purpose was much more sacred and venerable than that. These thirty people were among the students who were converting to Judaism.

That process of joining the destiny and faith of the Jewish people is an ever-inspiring story. It takes great courage and persistence to study the teachings of Judaism, to take on the mitzvot as personal obligations, and to willingly join a persecuted people.

The steps of conversion are found explicitly in the Talmud, and the rabbis of antiquity traced one of the requirements for conversion to *Parashat Devarim*: "Hear out your fellow, and decide justly between anyone and a fellow Israelite or *ger* (stranger or convert)." The rabbis understood "decide justly" (*u'shfatem tzedek*) to establish the rule that "a conversion requires three judges." Building on that Talmudic base, Rabbi Yehudah established that "one who is converted by a beit din is indeed a convert; one who converted by himself is not a convert."

Thus the key to a traditional Jewish conversion is the interview before the beit din—the religious court of three observant Jews. After a ritual immersion in a *mikvah* (the ritual purifying bath) or the ocean, and after *hatafat dam brit* (taking a drop of blood to symbolize ritual circumcision) for the male convert, all converts must appear before the beit din to demonstrate that they are knowledgeable in Judaism and want to convert for sincere motives. Finally, each convert must explicitly accept the authority of Jewish law in its totality.

That last requirement is particularly ironic today, when so many Jews who are born to this wonderful heritage live much of their lives without reference to the mitzvot and the depth of the halakhah. While conversion to Judaism has always required explicit affirmation of the commandments, many people who are born Jewish don't even pause to consider the place of the mitzvot in their lives.

Several years ago, the Orthodox, Conservative, and Reform rabbis of Denver cooperated on joint standards to conversion. Those standards included (1) a commitment to regular Torah study as a continuing process; (2) certain minimal ritual practices (fasting on Yom Kippur, affixing a mezuzah on the doorpost, candle-lighting on Shabbat and festivals, regular attendance at communal worship on Shabbat and festivals, maintaining a level of kashrut); and (3) acts of loving-kindness (such as giving to *tzedakah* [charity], affiliation to and involvement with a synagogue, a commitment to the land of Israel, and a commitment to create a Jewish home in which all children receive a Jewish education).

Those standards were the minimum expected of converts who wished to be accepted into the Jewish people. Yet I wonder how many of us who were born into Judaism could rise to the challenge of those standards as our own?

In an age when people are free to abandon their Judaism at will, when so many Jews are raised without a Jewish education or experience of Judaism in the home, we are all—in a very real sense—potential converts. We each face a personal decision: whether or not to make Judaism central to our identities and our lives.

Like our ancestors standing at the foot of Mount Sinai, we have the power to affirm or spurn the gift God offers us. A legacy stretching across the millennia, a wise and joyous way of life that links the generations, a rich relationship with God, and a sacred way of life—these riches are our birthright if only we are willing to accept them.

Perhaps now is a time to rise to the standards of the faithful—the converts who bathe in the waters of Judaism for the first time *and* those steadfast Jews who continue to act as beacons of light and fidelity by living their Judaism.

Va-Et'hanan/I Pleaded

Deuteronomy 3:23–7:11

Moses exhorts the people to obey God's laws so that they might dwell securely in the Promised Land. In a sense, Chapter 4 introduces what follows: general themes that Moses will repeat throughout the book. Here Deuteronomy highlights relying on Israel's experiences of deliverance and wandering, of the threat of exile, and of God's forgiveness and teshuvah in the places to which they will be scattered. In this chapter, Moses highlights the commandment to worship only Adonai and to love God, prior to presenting the outlines of the mitzvot. This provides a model for later theology and law codes, such as the Mishnah Torah (legal code) of Maimonides.

These laws make it possible for Israel to dwell in the land with security and compassion: "Observe them faithfully, for that will be proof of your wisdom and discernment to other peoples." The Torah then warns against idolatry, recalling the gift of the Ten Commandments at Mount Sinai and calling on the Israelites to never give in to worshipping images of any corporeal being or astral body. Moses calls heaven and earth to witness against Israel, should the Jewish people transgress when he is no longer alive, and points out the penalty of exile should they sin. Yet he also assures his listeners that God will remain open to the possibility of teshuvah, "for Adonai your God is a compassionate God."

Moses then appeals to his listeners (and to us) to observe the commandments as a response to God's uniqueness and kindnesses to our ancestors and to us. "Know therefore this day and keep in mind that the Holy One alone is God in heaven above and on earth below; there is no other. Observe God's laws and commandments, that I enjoin upon you this day." Moses then establishes the three cities of asylum east of the Jordan.

The second address, the core of the biblical book, begins with a lengthy prologue in which Moses describes how God appointed him to lead the Israelites. He recapitulates the revelation at Mount Sinai, including the Ten Commandments and the people's selection of him as their intermediary with God.

Chapter 6 opens with the Shema, the core affirmation of Israel's faith in God's uniqueness and special relationship with the people Israel. We are to tell our children about our miraculous liberation from slavery and to remain distinct from the pagans in Canaan, faithful to our covenant with God, in the service of holiness and justice.

Love the Lord

What is the proper emotional attitude to take toward God? In our day, as in the past, religious people are divided into two general camps. Some argue that we must fear and venerate God, while others stress the need to love God.

Fear and love have a long history within Judaism. Both *yirat shamayim* (fear of heaven) and *ahavat ha-Shem* (love of God) find ample attestation in traditional and modern writings. While most Jews retain elements of both, individuals and communities tend to stress one tendency over the other.

The natural consequence of a stress on fearing God is to expect the human-divine relationship to work in one direction: God commands and people obey. Halakhah is immutable because people, including community leaders, are overwhelmed by a sense of their own inadequacy and insignificance. The highest form of human response becomes unquestioning acquiescence.

While fear of God may be important as a secondary value, a long precedent gives priority to loving God. *Parashat Va-Et'hanan* highlights the value of *ahavat ha-Shem*. Before the assembled tribes of Israel, Moses recalls the stirring moment at Mount Sinai when God gave the Ten Commandments. He then continues with the Shema, reminding us of God's unity and pledging our loyalty to God's exclusive service. Moses instructs, "You shall love the Lord your God with all your heart and with all your soul and with all your might." For Moses, the most important component of serving God is to love God.

In his Torah commentary, Rashi explains that Moses meant "Perform God's commandments out of love. One cannot compare a person who acts out of love to one who acts from fear, who serves a master out of fear. When the latter feels overburdened, he leaves and goes away." Rashi, a keen student of the human heart, knows that fear can motivate behavior only so long. As soon as the source of fear loses its strength, service stops. Those who serve God primarily through fear do so only as long as it "works" for them. Once they see their service no longer exempts them from the hazards and disappointments of life, their inducement for serving God also stops. Perhaps it was for this reason that Maimonides insisted that serving God out of fear is not "the standard set by the prophets and sages." At best, it is a useful educational measure "until their knowledge shall have increased, when they will serve out of love."

What was true then is even more true now. Modernity, with its insistence on the worth of the individual, on the ability of humanity to progress, has moved us beyond the utility of fear. If modern Jews want to draw close to God, they will do so out of love.

What is crucial, then, is to become open to perceiving that love. Through the beauty of nature, we can experience God's love as Creator. Through the profundity of our sacred Jewish heritage, we can integrate God's love as the *honen da'at* (the One who bestows wisdom). Through the performance of mitzvot, we can *takken olam bemalkhut Shaddai* (repair the world under the sovereignty of God). And through the acts of caring from those we love and our community, we can experience God as the *Gomel Hesed* (the One who bestows loving-kindness).

Is God Really Blessed by Our Deeds?

Surely the most famous passage from the Torah is the Shema, the verse from *Parashat Va-Et'hanan* that proclaims, "Hear, O Israel! Adonai is our God, Adonai alone." That verse is recited twice during public prayer and once in bed at night before going to sleep. Many synagogues emblazon those words above the *Aron Kodesh* or on the sanctuary wall. And traditionally those were the last words a Jew recited immediately before dying.

What does the recital of the Shema signify? The rabbis of *Midrash Devarim Rabbah* explain that the Shema "involves accepting the kingdom of heaven." In other words, the Shema is the Jewish Pledge of Allegiance; by reciting it, we renew our loyalty to God alone and affirm that we remain God's loyal servants in word and deed. Small wonder, then, that it brackets our day as our first words in the morning and our last words at night. From waking to slumber, the Jew is summoned to strengthen God's rule.

The ancient rabbis read this understanding into the liturgy by adding another line, *"Barukh Shem Kevod Mal'khuto Le-Olam Va-ed"* (Blessed is the name of God's glorious domain forever and ever), immediately after this one. Tractate *Berakhot* of the Talmud insists that worshippers whisper this line, almost silently. The sole exception to this is on Yom Kippur, the only time the congregation chants the affirmation as loudly as the Shema itself.

According to *Midrash Devarim Rabbah*, there are two ancient explanations for this puzzling practice. The first traces the origin of the Shema to Jacob's deathbed. As he lay dying, he gathered his children around him and expressed his fear that they would not continue to serve God alone. His children responded, "Hear, O Israel (Jacob's other name), only Adonai is our God," to which he weakly responded, *"Barukh Shem."* We imitate the dying words of our ancestor Jacob by affirming Jewish continuity in the service of God, and we also imitate his weakness, perhaps in recognition of our own finitude and the limits of each individual Jew. As individuals, we can only do a little, but as members of the Jewish people, as heirs to the *brit*, we are indeed testimony to God's sovereignty and greatness. Hence, the softness of our response is really an affirmation of God's covenant with the Jewish people.

A second midrash relates that Moses ascended to heaven and heard the angels above praising God by chanting, *"Barukh Shem."* When he returned to the Jewish people at Mount Sinai, he taught them to say this after they had recited the Shema. The midrash asks, "Why doesn't Israel make this declaration publicly (aloud)?" Rabbi Assi replies, "This can be compared to a man who stole jewelry from the royal palace and gave to his wife, telling her, 'Don't wear these in public, but only in the house.'"

Since Moses had "stolen" the praise that the angels used, he told the Jews to recite it silently. Our silence reminds us that we bear the burden of having to strive to imitate the angels while simultaneously recognizing that we are but impostors. We cannot attain the level of purity that is our goal, yet it remains our task to keep trying.

Why, then, do we recite the line out loud on Yom Kippur? Because, the midrash explains, "On Yom Kippur, when Israel are as pure as the ministering angels, they do recite publicly, 'Blessed by the name of God's glorious domain forever and ever.'" On the day that we transcend all bodily needs and focus exclusively on our spiritual responsibilities, our moral shortcomings, and our obligations to God, we most closely approximate the holiness of the angels. On that day alone we merit to use their lines without embarrassment.

The next time you whisper, *"Barukh Shem,"* remember your significance as a member of a covenantal people and your need to become a bit more angelic.

Searching in All the Wrong Places

This is a remarkable age to be Jewish. With access to modern education and the freedom to live as we choose, where we choose, we may well enjoy the greatest liberty and luxury of any generation of Jews in history. Yet our mood is far from exultant. Instead of rejoicing in our wealth and comfort, we live lives of dizzying busyness and seem as much the slaves of our professions and possessions as we are their masters. In the midst of unprecedented plenty, we sense a great big hole. Something is missing, but we don't know quite what that something is. Adding to the strange quality of this era, growing numbers of Jews are turning back to ancient wells of wisdom to restore a sense of sanity and balance to their lives. They are studying their sacred literature (and that of other traditions), reclaiming mitzvot that had long been discarded in their families, and renewing the contours of their ancient faith—all in an attempt to bring some measure of purpose and community into their lives.

How odd to see Jews who already have it all acting as though they are in need of something else. How inspiring to see the courage of people who are experts in their fields willing to become beginners once again. As striking as their spiritual quest is, it is hardly new. The truth is that it was anticipated many years ago. Consider this remarkable passage from *Parashat Va-Et'hanan*:

> Adonai will scatter you among the peoples, and only a scant few of you shall be left among the nations to which Adonai will drive you. There you will serve man-made gods of wood and stone that cannot see or hear or eat or smell. . . . But if you search there for Adonai your God, you will find God, if only you seek God with all your heart and soul . . . and in the end, return to Adonai your God in obedience.

Speaking across the millennia, this passage from the Torah seems to be addressing us directly. In your wanderings, you will pursue activities and passions that seem compelling at the time but ultimately cannot satisfy your deepest needs. The more these distractions fail to satisfy, the more desperately you will pursue them, until your own exhaustion and helplessness lead you to the recognition that you need to choose a different path. The man-made gods of wood and stone cannot satisfy, however tangible and attractive they may appear, however much our culture may extol them.

As pleasant as our possessions are, as much as they can add comfort and options to human living, they remain mute things "that cannot see or hear or eat or smell." Useful tools to our lives, they cannot provide love, belonging, or depth. Having attained the highest success our culture can measure—be it wealth or power or fame or high office—we are surprised to discover that having it all isn't enough. Despite our comfort and our apparent control, that persistent, subterranean disquiet constitutes our wake-up call.

There is a deep need within each of us to live a life of meaning and wonder. Far from accepting that our lifespan is merely time to occupy or that life is but a game to be won by amassing the most fame/wealth/power, we recognize an unshakable drive to find meaning and purpose in what we do and in how we spend our time. Not acquisition but connection moves the human heart. Not imposition but significance allows the soul to soar.

Perhaps it is time to hear the voice of Torah speaking directly to each one of us. In our wanderings through the wilderness, what gives us direction is the goal of the Holy Land. In our journey through life, what adds depth and satisfaction is the recognition of our deepest aspirations and self. That recognition, in fact, comes from knowing we have been recognized.

God is the one who recognizes each of us. In turning to God, we turn to the One who has always turned toward us, the One who has waited patiently for our own growing recognition that we need to be known.

That need to be known is really a call. There is One who can know us fully and who would know us if we would but open our hearts. Once we recognize what functions as our contemporary equivalent of idols for what they are—useful as tools, blasphemous as goals— then we are in a position to return to Adonai, our Creator, with open hearts, questing minds, and souls ready to receive the gift of being known, of being recognized, and of being loved.

Ekev/It Came to Pass

Deuteronomy 7:12–11:25

Parashat Ekev *opens with a reference to the blessings that will flow if the people live in harmony with God's rules. Moses reminds the Israelites that they do not have to worry about the Canaanites, despite their numbers or their power, since God is with the Israelites. Israel will thrive and prosper if it remains loyal to God and God's covenant, because "man does not live on bread alone, but on anything that the Holy One decrees."*

God is giving Israel a rich and bounteous land. Gratitude is the optimal response to that graciousness, including thanking God after meals for the food and the land.

Moses then shifts tone, instructing against attitudes of self-righteousness that Israel's victories and conquest might engender. Instead, the Jews are to hold on to humility as a safeguard against arrogance and smugness. Toward that end, Moses reminds his listeners of the sin of the golden calf and of God's resulting anger to that offense.

After that tragic incident, God renewed the covenant with instructions to craft a second set of the Ten Commandments and the selection of the Levites for service in the Tabernacle (and later, the Temple).

Chapter 10:12–19 contains a summary of religious faith second to none, starting with God's sovereignty and uniqueness, moving through God's selection of Israel and its fidelity to His commands, and ending with the need to bring justice to all peoples as the only proper fruit of faithfulness to God.

Chapter 11 exhorts Israel to love God and to observe God's commandments. Paragraphs from this chapter form the middle selections of the Kriyat Shema, *the daily recitation of the Shema in Talmudic and contemporary Judaism.* Ve-hayah im shamoa *speaks of the collective consequences of social greed and injustice, and of the need to teach and study these teachings repeatedly.*

Finally, the parashah concludes with the assurance that faith and fidelity to God will secure the success of the conquest of Eretz Yisrael.

Finish the Job

Years ago, when my children were almost three years old and had finally reached a stage in life where they enjoyed helping me and their mother prepare meals, they liked to help rip up the lettuce or mix the food in a bowl. As much as I appreciated their helpfulness, there was also a drawback to their voluntarism—they often didn't finish the job they had begun. If I didn't watch the process from start to finish, I'd return to find the food congealed rather than mixed or the lettuce still a great big clump on top of a few shredded leaves.

That drifting attention span is normal in young children. It isn't totally foreign to adults either. How often have people told you that they meant to call you or write or return a borrowed object and just never got around to it? The desire to do the right thing may be real, but that intention isn't enough. The bottom line is what we do, not how we feel.

The rabbis of antiquity derive a similar point from *Parashat Ekev*. Moses recounts God's command that "you shall faithfully observe every commandment (*kol ha-mitzvah*) which I command you today, that you may live and increase and be able to possess the land that the Holy One promised on oath to your ancestors." Noting that the phrase *kol ha-mitzvah* literally translates as "the entire command-ment," we are justified in asking why the Torah doesn't say observe *kol ha-mitzvot* (all the commandments)? What does this strange phrase teach?

In *Midrash Tanhuma*, Rabbi Yohanan notes that "whoever begins a mitzvah and afterward someone else comes and completes it, the mitzvah is credited to the one who completes it." Rashi makes the same point: "If you begin a mitzvah, finish it, for it is only credited to the one who completes it."

While good intentions are nice to have and may add meaning to a good deed, intentions are often overrated. When a beggar on the street asks for money, good intentions won't provide food or shelter. When a child cries out in fear, thinking good thoughts won't soothe or calm. A sick person isn't comforted by an intended visit that never materializes, and the loneliness of a shut-in isn't diminished by the intent to call. In such instances, good intentions are just a sop to appease a guilty conscience for its own failure to do the right thing. Sometimes the only thing that matters is what we do.

In the same way, we moderns often define religion as a branch of psychology, useful to the extent that it makes us feel good. We expect (demand?) God's understanding when we fail to live up to our own sense of what we owe religion, and we approach our faith with a pervasive sense of entitlement. Judaism should accommodate us and our desires.

We pay a price for that shift in focus. Demanding of religion that its highest purpose be to make us feel good, we fail to invest enough time, energy, or emotion to enable it to speak to our souls. Expecting an effortless reward, we often turn away at the first signs of effort, disappointed that we felt no rush, experienced no thrill. God grows ever more distant, and life feels ever more frightening and purposeless.

Perhaps that's why the rabbis insist that we finish each mitzvah we undertake. Having perceived a divine imperative in a particular deed, our failure to see it through is a betrayal of our own integrity and potential. Rather than creating a moment of spiritual breakthrough and growth, our easy distractedness can lead to stagnation of the soul.

Jewish tradition teaches that God only enters the heart that lets God in. Only our willingness to let holiness play a significant role in our lives makes it possible for God to enter. Only our willingness to entertain the discipline of the mitzvot will allow us to climb the ladder of holiness that Judaism offers. Anything less is just going through the motions.

When you have the opportunity to do a good deed, see it through. When you have the chance to do a mitzvah, stay the course. You may be surprised at the rich rewards you will reap.

True Power Is Compassion

I've often marveled at the designation "the Great" in the history books tracing the development of Western civilization. Consider the august individuals who carry that appellation: Alexander the Great, Herod the Great, Charlemagne (which means "Charles the Great"), Catherine the Great, Peter the Great. In truth, the only traits that link these people are their ruthlessness; their despotism; and the fact that they were responsible for the deaths of many, many innocents.

Think about what that says about the values of the people who wrote the history books we all used in grade school, high school, and college. The guardians of Western civilization seem to cherish wealth, power, and force. Little wonder that the world is in the sad shape it is, when the people we glorify are the most ruthless. The standards are pagan—reveling in raw power and the ability to impose one's will on other people whether they accept it or not. This is Friedrich Nietzsche's *ubermentsch* (superman) trampling through the annals of human history, glorifying in wealth, power, fame, and beauty.

Even as a schoolboy, I never understood why these people were great. "Terrible" seemed a better title for those who chose to initiate wars of conquest, who ruthlessly suppressed their subjects, and who made the lives and deaths of humanity the clay with which to sculpt their own memorials.

We may think we eschew that form of grandeur in its starkest form, but that would be a delusion. When U.S. President Gerald Ford was slipping in the polls, he attacked Cambodia and his popularity soared. Prime Minister Margaret Thatcher sent the British military to the Falkland Islands and enjoyed a remarkable increase in popularity. Iran's despotic Saddam Hussein invaded neighboring Kuwait, and his own people applauded. However "biblical" we think our morality may be, the sad reality is that we consider launching assaults that result in human deaths to be "presidential," and the more mundane and complex tasks of diplomacy and cooperation bore us and seem to be a sign of weakness.

Not so with God. In a remarkable passage in *Parashat Ekev*, Moses reveals what makes for true greatness. He describes the Holy One as "God supreme and Lord supreme, the great, the mighty, and the awesome God, who shows no favor and takes no bribe, but upholds the cause of the orphan and the widow and befriends the stranger, providing him with food and clothing."

How striking! A claim of greatness that has nothing to do with demonstrations of force, killing, or intimidation. God's greatness, says Moses, is based on moral rectitude, fairness, and compassion for the weakest members of society. As the Talmud wisely notes, "With God's might, you find God's humility."

True greatness consists of using our strength, our wealth, our wisdom, and our power to build communities of love, justice, and caring; to reach out to those who cannot fend for themselves; to build bridges with all humanity and all living things; to care for the earth and all who dwell upon it.

"Let not the wise glory in their wisdom, nor the powerful in their strength, nor the rich in their wealth," says the prophet Jeremiah. Rather, by training ourselves to recognize those attributes as loans, we recognize that they were lent to us for a specific purpose—not for our own private pleasures but to increase God's love and compassion in the world.

By harnessing our material blessings to concern for our fellow human beings, we make ourselves more godly. By learning that "what I own, I owe," we can teach ourselves to find contentment not in what can be lost, but in what is eternal—gratitude, camaraderie, love, and fellowship. By mastering the weakness within that causes us to lash out at individuals or strike at other nations to shore up our own sense of decline, we can heed the Torah's message: true might is demonstrated by humility.

Not by might and not by strength, but by God's spirit will we poor and contentious humans hope to bring a measure of healing and peace to this battered world.

Welcoming the Stranger

Well, the statistics are in, and the news isn't good. Hate crimes, it seems, are more popular than ever. Perhaps it's because we live in an age of rapid social change, and there are people who resent the changes and feel powerless because of them. Or perhaps there are simply people willing to do evil and lacking the self-restraint (or communal restraint) to stop themselves.

Beatings, bombings, hate mail, and intimidation are frequent—if not accepted—behaviors in the world today. We seem to live in a climate of militants in an age when people act viciously in public and think their zeal justifies their barbarity. Even at the funeral of then-President Bill Clinton's mother, a minister and his congregants picketed the president's "baby-killing, fag [sic]-loving" agenda. This kind of despicable, bigoted intrusion into a private, tragic moment would have been unthinkable a few decades ago.

Parashat Ekev has something useful to say about the nature of bigotry. In speaking of the conquest of the land by the newly liberated Israelites, the Jews are told, "Don't be afraid of the people already in the land, because God will send *ha-tzirah* (generally translated as 'a hornet')." Rashi quotes from the Talmud (*Massekhet Sotah*) to explain this peculiar word, saying the *tzirah* "is a type of flying insect that discharges poison into them and renders them sterile and blind."

Both Rashi and the Talmud weigh their words with great care to transmit a deeper meaning; they are unearthing a hidden perspective from the Torah about the price that bigotry exacts.

The Canaanite culture was one of rigid social hierarchy in which the rich dominated and the poor suffered. Living in fortress cities, the wealthy exacted their luxury from the sweat of the poor, an imposition that the Hebrew mind condemned as unjust and intolerable. The Israelites were a free people living by the rule of a profound legal system that bound all its members, rich and poor alike. Serving only God, the Israelites were explicitly told to fear no mere mortal, to treat all with the same standard of justice. Such an open and progressive society must have seemed extremely threatening to the despots of Canaan.

We can well imagine how those satraps justified their persecution of the poor and their hatred of the Israelites by repeating the same bigoted stereotypes one group uses to write off all the members of another group—they're lazy, they're not willing to work hard, they're dishonest, they smell funny.

Then as now, the mind-set of bigotry is tempting and deadening. Bigotry is tempting in that it allows a person to avoid confronting the humanity of a fellow human being, empathizing with suffering and pain, and getting involved in alleviating misery or fighting evil. But bigotry is also deadening; the inability to see a fellow human being is a terrible blindness indeed. A refusal to learn from the great majority of human beings and cultures is a sterility that can preclude all real creativity and growth. Perhaps that is why the poison of the *tzirah* is one that blinds and causes sterility among the bigots it attacks.

Canaanite culture was blind to the changing reality around it, unwilling to see the Israelites as anything other than a military threat and a peasant people. By responding with hostility and violence, the Canaanites doomed themselves to destruction and stagnation.

Imagine if they had responded to the Israelites by welcoming them instead. What might have happened if the Canaanites had been willing to learn from the Israelites and been willing to teach them as well? Instead of hundreds of years of conflict and hostility, with mutual stereotyping and violence on each side, both peoples could have become vital partners to each other.

Bigotry doesn't go away, and there are closet Canaanites in every group. How we respond to the newcomers in our midst may well reveal the Canaanite within each of us. "You shall have one law for yourself and the stranger who is in your midst, for you were strangers in the land of Mitzrayim."

True Israelites welcome the stranger.

Re'eh/Behold!

Deuteronomy 11:26–16:17

Moses's preamble to the laws ends with the basic premise of the Torah: "See, this day I set before you blessing and curse." The choice, then as now, lies entirely in our own hands. Attention shifts to the laws themselves, forming the longest section in Deuteronomy and the royal road to a life rich in meaning, goodness, joy, and belonging. Rather than attempting to present a comprehensive code, complete with every detail, Deuteronomy lays out general principles, relying on an unwritten oral tradition to enumerate practice.

Moses begins with the sanctuary and maintaining religious consistency and purity. Idolatrous sites are to be destroyed, and God is only to be worshipped at the Temple in Jerusalem. "Together with your households, you shall feast there before the Holy One your God, happy in all the undertakings in which the Holy One your God has blessed you."

While sacrificial meat may only be offered in Jerusalem, provision is now made for the secular consumption of meat, through the laws of kashrut, particularly removing the blood from any meat to be consumed.

Eating in a way that is "good and right in the sight of God," the Jews are then told to shun religious syncretism (mixing alien forms of worship with Judaism). Toward that end, if someone, even a true prophet, seeks to get Jews to abandon the covenant, give up the mitzvot, and worship anyone other than the Holy One, that person is being sent to test their fidelity and courage. Jews are to resist that enticement and to remove that prophet from their midst, "for he urged disloyalty to the Holy One our God to make you stray from the path that the Holy One your God commanded you to follow." This is the commanded response for prophet, individual, or entire town seeking to separate Jews from Torah and Judaism.

Laws of holiness follow, dealing with mourning and dietary laws. Jews are prohibited from gashing ourselves in mourning and from eating any land animals except those with cloven hooves that chew their cud, sea animals with fins and scales, and particular birds. Again the Torah prohibits seething a kid in its mother's milk.

The Torah lays out recurrent obligations: tithes owed annually and every three years, the Sabbatical year remission of debts, freeing the eved Ivri at the end of seven years (or arranging for permanent bondage if the servant so chooses), and the three annual pilgrimage festivals—Pesach, Shavuot, *and* Sukkot.

Answering the Missionary

Each and every day, we mingle with a dazzling array of non-Jews from every corner of the globe. By choice, we live in the world as a part of the world. Most of us want our children to be exposed to a range of human cultures, to learn to treasure the beauty in the vast literatures and faith traditions of all humankind. The benefits of that exposure aren't hard to see—an enlightened understanding of the human condition; an appreciation of the values of democracy, equality, and freedom; and a determination to fight bigotry whenever it rears its ugly head.

Harder to discern are the disadvantages of this triumphant universalism. The difficulty of living in such open proximity to different peoples and cultures is that it often becomes harder to maintain one's own way of life. Every ethnic minority struggles with how to retain and transmit its ancient ways, its writings, and its faith in the face of the blandishments and attractions of syncretism. How do we remain distinct in a culture that celebrates blending?

As Jews who love Judaism and the Jewish people, this issue is particularly pressing. One million children who have a Jewish parent are currently being raised as non-Jews or as nothing (by their own definition). The struggle to continue biologically is merely the first and most visible aspect of the challenge, since the purpose of Jewish survival has always been the service of God through our ancestral *brit*—the combination of Torah, worship, and deeds of loving-kindness that is the very goal of Judaism in the first place.

One of the greatest challenges to our continued faith and faithfulness is the challenge presented by those Christians who feel that their own faith requires them to persuade us to abandon ours. There was a time when Jews knew the Torah and the Talmud well enough that the slick quotations of zealous missionaries—always out of context and often mistranslated—were easily corrected and rebuffed. Today, however, we are hardly the people of the book.

Parashat Re'eh contains a lengthy passage that every Jew should carry around for just such confrontations. This passage gives a direct response to the claim that a Jew should abandon exclusive loyalty to Adonai and the Torah:

> If there appears among you a prophet or a dream-diviner and he gives you a sign or a portent, saying, "Let us follow and worship another god"—whom you have not experienced—even if the sign or portent that he named to you comes true, do not heed the words of that prophet or that dream-diviner. For Adonai your God is testing you to see whether you really love Adonai your God with all your heart and soul. Follow none but Adonai your God, and revere none but God; observe God's commandments alone, and heed only God's orders; worship none but God, and hold fast to God. As for that prophet or dream-diviner, he shall be put to death; for he urged disloyalty to Adonai your God—who freed you from the land of Egypt and who redeemed you from the house of bondage—to make you stray from the path that Adonai your God commanded you to follow. Thus you will sweep out evil from your midst (Deut. 13:2–7).

This crucial passage makes several points well worth our attention:

• We experience God through the miraculous liberation from slavery and from the many miracles of each day—the beauty of the sun coming up, the love of other people, the joy of simply being alive.

• God commands our devotion exclusively. The *brit* can only fit two parties—God and the Jewish people—just as only two people can be in a marriage at any one time. We must love only God, without any other claimant sharing that love or devotion.

• If someone urges us to abandon that love relationship, whether or not their prophecies come to pass, we are to disregard them and, in fact, to view their proposal as evil. God wants Jews to be Jews, loyal to the Torah and our sacred traditions as they are interpreted by the sages and faithful of each generation.

God may well have other paths for other peoples, and our staunch loyalty to our own religion doesn't imply that others are inferior or false, simply that God wants Jews to stay faithful to our ancestral covenant.

Let other peoples serve their own gods; we shall serve the Holy Blessing One, Creator of the Heavens and the Earth. Anyone who asks us to leave our covenant, our people, and our heritage is simply offering us an opportunity to affirm our love of God.

Kashrut: The Dietary Laws

It is a rabbinic dictum not to attempt to weigh the value of one mitzvah against another. Rather than saying that this mitzvah is more important than that one, we are to recognize that all mitzvot are grounded in our *brit* with the Holy One and derive their authority from our chosen response to God's will.

And yet it is hard to resist the temptation to create a hierarchy. So, at least in the popular mind, there are some mitzvot so central to Jewish identity that they are almost synonymous with Judaism itself. Lighting Shabbat candles is one of them. Wearing a *kippah* (head covering) is another. And a third is kashrut, the dietary laws. When you think of a religious Jewish home, it is a kosher home. So central is kashrut, in fact, that the term *kosher* has become the way to refer to any action or person that is moral, upright, and proper. In that sense, it has even entered the English language.

The dietary laws are simple in their larger principles: meat and meat products (fleishig) are strictly separated from dairy products (milhig). Vegetables, fish, and fruits may be served with either meat or milk. Only a small number of animals are permissible as possible food sources: fish with fins and scales, land mammals with cloven hooves that chew their cud, and a specified range of birds that fly. Additionally, those permissible animals must be slaughtered through *shehitah* (the least painful way possible to kill an animal). While the general principles of kashrut are simple to list, the details of their application fill volumes.

The most complex of those details pertain to the eating of meat. *Parashat Re'eh* elaborates on God's permission to eat meat: "When the Holy One enlarges your territory, as God has promised you, and you say 'I shall eat some meat,' for you have the urge to eat meat, you may eat meat whenever you wish. . . . You shall slaughter . . . as I have instructed you, and you may eat." Meat is a concession to human urges: if you feel compelled to take an animal's life for the sake of your hunger, you may do so, but only in this limited and supervised way.

What possible benefits does keeping kosher provide? What lessons does kashrut teach?

• Kashrut teaches us the value of responding to a divine command. God tells us to observe kashrut as a way of learning self-discipline and fidelity. Just as it did in the past, kashrut teaches that lofty lesson today.

• Kashrut, like vegetarianism, teaches reverence for life. Because it restricts the number of animals that may be eaten and then insists that the method of slaughter be strictly regulated, kashrut makes sure that the animal's death is as painless as possible. By forcing a kosher Jew to have to choose whether to eat meat or milk and then requiring a waiting period after any consumption of meat, it ensures that eating becomes a more conscious act, that we make ourselves aware of what we are doing and how that animal was transformed into food. Unlike vegetarianism, which elevates the value of animal life beyond the possibility of human consumption, kashrut represents a compromise that insists on humane slaughter and awareness but doesn't require as strict a commitment as does vegetarianism—a compromise more Jews can live with.

• The commitment to keep kosher and to maintain a kosher home is one that expresses and enforces solidarity with the Jewish people across time and around the world. Throughout the ages, Jews have hallowed our lives and nurtured a sense of community through observance of the kosher laws. By forcing us to make specifically *Jewish* choices about how and what and when we eat, kashrut reminds us of our larger Jewish commitments and privileges every time we sit down to dine. And by maintaining a level of kashrut, we ensure that Jews the world over can eat comfortably at home. Kashrut is a non-verbal reminder that Jewish values are practiced here.

• The Torah contains God's call to become a nation of priests. Just as the priests used the laws of purity and impurity to extend the service of God to every aspect of their lives, we can do the same. By observing kashrut, we make every snack, every meal, an occasion to serve God through one of our most basic and elemental acts.

The laws of kashrut remind us of who we are and what we may yet become. Observing the dietary laws is a response to God's will and a way of integrating an ancient wisdom into our lives. In the words of *Parashat Re'eh*, "Thus it will go well with you and with your descendants after you forever, for you will be doing what is good and right in the sight of the Eternal, your God."

Be Yourself

Social pressure to conform is a steady and soul-deadening force. With relentless enticements, cultures seek ways to impose a similarity of worldview, behavior, and even thought upon their members. In spite of its laudable commitment to individuality, contemporary society imposes subtle mandates through television, through movies, through advertisements, and in countless other ways. The truly free soul is rare. Indeed, for many who practice religion (and many who flee religion), conformity and habit are nowhere more imposing than in the realm of faith and ritual. Can it be that God wants us to conform?

Parashat Re'eh speaks with great joy of the three pilgrimage festivals of the Jewish calendar:

Three times a year—on the Feast of Unleavened Bread, on the Feast of Weeks, and on the Feast of Booths—all your males shall appear before the Holy One your God in the place that God will choose. They shall not appear before the Holy One empty-handed, but each according to his own gift, according to the blessing that the Holy One your God has bestowed upon you.

The Torah presents a fascinating threefold series of descriptions of our offerings: (1) we are not to appear empty-handed; (2) we are to give according to our own gifts; and (3) our gifts are to reflect God's blessing. What do these three qualifications tell us about our place in society, the place for our personality and distinctiveness in God's world?

On the surface, the statements are parallel, reiterating that we are to give in joy and to give within our means. As the medieval sage Sa'adia Gaon reminds us, they teach a person to offer "what his hand can afford, according to that which God has bestowed upon you." Similarly, the Talmud insists on limiting our charitable contributions: "If one wishes to spend generously, one should not spend more than one-fifth of one's income." The *p'shat* of the Torah, most traditional sources agree, intends to regulate our voluntary religious gifts so that they are given joyously and are within our financial capacities. This insight is no small advance. Imagine how differently we might celebrate *b'nai mitzvah*, wedding parties, and Jewish communal celebrations with these stipulations in mind.

As profound as this reading is, I'd like to explore a deeper approach. Perhaps these three guidelines are meant not only as synonymous phrases, but as three plateaus, each adding a layer of meaning to extend and complement its partners.

During our joyous celebrations, we must not come empty-handed. To celebrate in God's presence, we must not focus only on taking, on our own personal joy. To celebrate in the fullest sense is to harness our private triumphs to contribute to the repair of God's world. Whether that means using a party to feed the hungry or to link a personal milestone to some communal cause, we transform moments of celebration into occasions to heal wounds and to right wrongs (and to show true gratitude) when we connect our *simchas* to *tzedakah*, our parties to justice.

The second biblical qualification is that the offering we bring must be according to our own gifts. That is to say that no two people may bring precisely the same thing. Each must bring an offering reflective of his or her own special talents and passions, something that illumines his or her uniqueness. That gift should be, in the words of the Talmud, "in accordance with one's own acumen" (Gittin 59a).

The third qualification is that the offering be "according to God's blessing." Here the Torah recognizes that human individuality is a reflection of divine love and bounty. God's greatness is reflected not in some numbing conformity, but in the stunning diversity of human character, interest, and talent. As the Mishnah affirms,

> A single person [Adam] was created to proclaim the greatness of the Holy Blessing One, for when people stamp many coins from the same seal, the coins are all alike. But the Holy Blessing One has stamped every human with the seal of the first person, but no two descendants are alike. Therefore everyone is required to say, "The world was created for my sake."

Knowing that God wants us to be who we are—unique, special, and distinctive—can provide a desperately needed tool for fighting social conformity and thoughtless habit. We dare not appear before God empty-handed, but what we do bring must reflect our unique gifts and personalities if it is to reflect God's blessings and to bless the lives of others in turn.

Shoftim/Judges

Deuteronomy 16:18-21:9

Parashat Shoftim *deals with the primary arms of authority in biblical Israel: judges, monarchs, priests, and prophets. The Israelites are to appoint magistrates and judges in each settlement, and these are commanded to show impartiality toward all cases and petitioners, being scrupulous to avoid any bribes. "Justice, justice shall you pursue" was to guide their deliberations and their procedures.*

Three prohibited religious practices—setting up an asherah *(pagan wooden pillar), sacrificing an animal with a* mum, *and allowing an apostate to remain within the community—interrupt the discussion of judges, perhaps to indicate the importance of serving God properly as the cornerstone to true justice. The Torah provides a system of referral, from a local court to a high court, to handle cases that the local court cannot decide. This biblical grant of authority to "the magistrate in charge at the time" and the mandate to "observe scrupulously all their instructions to you" so that "you do not deviate from their verdict" forms the basis for rabbinic authority to this very day.*

The Israelites are permitted to establish a monarchy as they desire, but Moses places limits on the king's authority and power. The only responsibility that Deuteronomy explicitly assigns the king is to write and study a copy of the Torah. This monarchy was to be under the authority of the law and answerable to it. The king's wealth, stables, and harem were all limited so that "he will not act haughtily toward his fellows or deviate from the Torah."

The kohanim *are to receive the offerings and sacrifices, from which they are to support themselves. The Torah then lists the specific portions they may rightfully claim. Finally, a Levite no matter where in Israel he dwells may claim the right to serve in the Temple. The prophet looms large in the Deuteronomistic vision, and the book of Deuteronomy seeks to strengthen the authority and scope of the prophets. Alone of all biblical authorities, the prophet's basis is a quotation* from God, rather than Moses's own words. The prophet is the heir to Moses himself. The parashah then restates the laws of the cities of asylum, establishes the law regarding intentional murder, and discusses the inviolability of boundaries and the law requiring not less than two witnesses. Chapter 20 establishes the laws of just warfare, limiting the extent to which the military can strike against civilians, who may be drafted, and the treatment of surrounding agriculture. Chapter 21 deals with a case of unsolved murder.

When the Rabbi Sins

The year 2006 was a difficult time to root for rabbis. One rabbi in Israel made national news when he was accused by several women of sexual harassment and inappropriate exploitation of his position as counselor and teacher. Another rabbi was filmed on national TV in what seemed like a highly inappropriate encounter. A yeshivah teacher of many years was accused by several men of past child abuse. Yet another rabbi was charged with inappropriate sexual and financial dealings.

These rabbis come from all religious denominations within Jewry and from both congregational and academic life. While it can immediately be stated that rabbis are human, it must still be asked whether that is a justification for sinful behavior, an explanation for it, or an excuse.

If rabbis are human, then shouldn't they be allowed the same indiscretions and errors that other people routinely make? Rabbis are often held to a higher standard, so that the offenses others can get away with are more shocking (and more publicized) when committed by a rabbi. Is that fair? Is that right?

Parashat Shoftim speaks of the importance of establishing courts of justice in which true justice is administered. What is the result of true justice? "Justice, justice shall you pursue, that you may thrive and occupy the land that the Lord your God is giving you." A tannaitic midrash, *Sifrei Devarim*, expands on this point: "The appointment of honorable judges (literally, 'kosher judges') is sufficient to keep Israel alive and to return them upon their land."

In the time of the Bible, the judges were the sages and elders sufficiently learned in Torah law that they could apply it to the lives of ordinary Israelites. By the time of the ancient rabbis, some two thousand years ago, the term *judges* was understood to represent those qualified to rule in cases involving halakhah—in other words, the rabbis themselves.

Notice the significance, then, of "kosher" rabbis. Their presence and activities sustain the Jewish people, forming a lifeline that connects our people with the eternal Source of Life. Not only that, but honorable rabbis justify and make possible our return to Zion. Rabbis who embody the values and practices of Torah in an upright and compassionate fashion—who practice what they teach—ensure that Jews will care enough about Judaism and the Jewish people to make *Eretz Yisrael* a continuing priority.

When any Jew sins, somebody suffers. When anyone commits a crime or an ethical lapse, some victim is traumatized. That holds true for sinning rabbis too. But beyond the suffering that each rabbi's victim endures—which is the consequence of any human failing—the rabbi's act bears an additional consequence solely because of his or her position within the community. Sinning rabbis discredit the Torah and give other Jews an excuse for not taking Judaism seriously. Their sin severs the connection between many congregants and the Holy One of Israel, and it weakens the bonds needed to maintain Jewish community.

When a rabbi fails to embody the mitzvot by cheating on a spouse, violating Judaism's lofty standards of business ethics, or committing more subtle sins (engaging in gossip, failing to set aside time for regular Torah learning, neglecting to follow through on pledges to *tzedakah*), not only is that particular rabbi stripped of authenticity, but she or he discredits the Torah and even God. In the minds of most Jews, rabbis represent Torah. They are the walking embodiments of the Jewish ideal and of the ideal Jew. When a rabbi falls short of that mark or sins against it, Jews conclude that the Torah itself is fraudulent, that it cannot produce righteousness and integrity. Often their response is not simply that Judaism has failed in this instance, but that Judaism is a failure.

Our Talmud wisely notes that the highest praise one can offer a rabbi (or any Jew) is that "one's insides match one's outside," or that "one's actions should match one's words." Jews demonstrate their beliefs not by what they say, but by how they act. A rabbi whose actions are abhorrent demonstrates a lack of faith in God, in Torah, and in Israel. Such a person is still a person, still needs *teshuvah*, and can still bring good into the world. But that person is no longer qualified to hold a position of highest honor in the Jewish community.

Each of us has an obligation to embody the highest values of our tradition, to serve as ambassadors of Judaism to each other and to humanity. In that sacred task, we depend on the shepherds of Israel, our rabbis, to show us the way through their own example. Rabbis can help their fellow Jews aspire to righteousness by living as tzaddikim. And all Jews can create an environment in which the rabbi's efforts to act as a role model can be facilitated by their embracing those same goals.

In that eternal mission, we need each other.

Whole Before Your God

In his magisterial presentation of Judaism, *Guide for the Perplexed*, Rabbi Moses Ben Maimon explains that the purpose of the Torah is twofold: the welfare of the soul and the welfare of the body. Rambam points out that the welfare of the soul is more noble and greater, but that it comes only after the welfare of the body. He defines the welfare of the body both in terms of the individual (maintaining health) and of the body politic (fashioning a society of justice and compassion). Neither element can survive alone. The purpose of the Torah is to elevate both realms. Unless our relations to each other are guided by the highest values of Torah, we cannot proceed to perfect our souls. It takes both halves to produce a whole.

Parashat Shoftim speaks to this wholeness when it instructs us, "You must be *tamim* with the Holy One your God." The new Jewish Publication Society version of the Tanakh translates *tamim* as "wholehearted" and explains in its commentary to Deuteronomy that the term means to be "undivided in your loyalty to God." In that sense, *temimut* implies a high degree of devotion to God alone. There is no room for competing desires or distracting temptations. What God wants is the heart—all of it.

The great medieval commentator Rashi shifts the focus. He understands *tamim* as a degree of trust, rather than just loyalty. "Look ahead to God and don't seek after the future. Rather, whatever will come to you accept with wholeheartedness. Then you will be with God and will be of God's portion."

For Rashi, wholeheartedness is a matter of accepting both the good and the bad with equanimity. Accepting that being *tamim* implies something exclusive for God, Rashi argues that it is human nature to seek to force the future to conform to our desires, but that effort is both futile and desperate. Instead, he urges us to embrace whatever the future brings. Rashi recognizes the future as the portal to an encounter with the Eternal if we will only open our arms to the embrace.

He wisely counsels us away from a destructive desire to manipulate time, to squander our gifts in order to assert control in areas we cannot control. By advising us to accept what the future offers, Rashi opens us to life's possibilities as far transcending our own plans, ambitions, or scripts.

I'd like to extend the idea of God's embrace a bit beyond Rashi's. What is true of time is true of people too. Invisible to most of us, buried deep within our hearts, is a system for rating others—those who matter, those who don't; those who are worth attention, those who aren't. Perhaps being *tamim* involves a different way of looking at our fellow human beings—and ourselves as well.

Rabbi Yitzhak Elhanan of Kovno notes that in one other location, the Hebrew Bible uses the same term, *temimah* (perfect), as does our verse. In the book of Psalms, we read that "the Torah of the Lord is *temimah*." Rabbi Elhanan points out that what makes a Torah scroll ritually *temimah* is that it isn't missing a single letter. If the scroll omits even one Hebrew letter, the entire Torah is *pasul* (ritually unfit). So too if a single Jew is excluded from the community, then the entire community is, as it were, *pasul*.

At the beginning of the Kol Nidre services, we remind ourselves that we aren't a congregation if we don't include the sinners in our midst. If someone is left out, we are not whole, not *tamim*. We can only attend to our own repentance after we've truly welcomed all of the members of the community.

With our people besieged and assaulted, with anti-Semites no longer seeming to need to hide their poisonous hatred, can't *we* at least show love to the entire Jewish people? Can't we take the mitzvah of *ahavat Yisrael* (love of our fellow Jews) as seriously as we take the other mandates of Jewish values and Torah tradition?

Perhaps what the Torah is telling us is that if we aspire to be "with the Lord our God," we had better make room for the Jew next to us—the one whose politics/lifestyle/observance/faith/disability/orientation makes you squirm a bit. To be holy, we must be whole.

We Are All Responsible

Liberals and conservatives are locked in a passionate debate about whether criminals are merely bad people doing evil or there is a larger social context that can push people in one direction or the other. Of course, if criminals are just bad people, then the response is to restrain the wicked and punish them. That would be the end of the matter. But if the way we organize our society, our bigotry, and our economic divisions work to keep some people down and some groups suffering, then a reasonable person might suggest that we have to respond to the cause of the problem, not just to its most dramatic symptom.

Parashat Shoftim directly raises this issue. A corpse is discovered out in the open, on land that isn't part of any town. While such an occurrence may hit the evening news on a regular basis these days, in biblical times, we can presume that it was a rare event. Even today, it would constitute a shocking discovery to those who made it. What is the proper response to finding a dead body? Who is responsible for the deceased, and who is responsible for the death?

These are not idle questions. In every culture, there is a fine line between the responsibility of the immediate perpetrator of a crime and the extent to which the society as a whole must share in the responsibility. In biblical Israel, organizing a society along lines of righteousness and justice was an imperative if God was to continue to dwell in the people's midst. In contemporary America, we too have an interest in fostering justice and decency and holiness.

Back to the Torah. Upon discovering this corpse, the elders of the nearest town are called to offer a special sacrifice. They wash their hands over the sacrificial heifer and declare, "Our hands did not shed this blood, nor did our eyes see it done. Absolve, Adonai, Your people Israel whom You redeemed, and do not let guilt for the blood of the innocent remain among Your people Israel."

At first glance, it seems that the Torah takes a conservative line. After all, the elders insist that they are not responsible for what has happened, and this ritual allows them to establish their innocence before God and their communities. But a nagging question remains: if they are innocent, why did they need to make any declaration at all? If they are innocent, what is the guilt that requires absolution?

In fact, this ritual makes no sense unless it assumes that the elders of the town are somehow tainted and implicated in this gruesome tragedy, even if their hands were not directly involved in the death.

The late, great rabbi Abraham Joshua Heschel observed that "in a free society, only some are guilty, but all are responsible." The biblical elders may not have physically killed the deceased. But the Torah's ritual suggests that they could have done more to prevent such crimes in the larger social context, one in which anger can be resolved in peaceful ways and in which people don't feel compelled to take revenge into their own hands.

Today, we may not each be guilty, but we are all responsible. We are responsible for the fact that our country—to its shame—has the largest gap between rich and poor of any first-world country. We are responsible for the fact that our world has not created a level playing field on which racial identity is irrelevant for predicting social standing, income levels, educational advancement, or death expectancy rates. We are responsible for the homophobia that prompts gay teenagers to commit suicide in such high numbers and leads to gay bashing and bigotry. We are responsible for the fact that our nation consumes such a disproportionate amount of the world's natural resources.

The list goes on and on. We may not be personally guilty of each of these sins (although there aren't many who haven't participated in some of them), but we are responsible. As citizens in a democracy, as people capable of involving ourselves in the political process and in volunteering our time to worthy causes, we are responsible to making as great a difference as we possibly can.

Like the elders of that ancient town, we are God's hands in the world. If we do nothing, then evil triumphs. For the vindication of God's love and justice, we must be willing to act, and we must do so now.

Ki-Tetze/When You Go Forth

Deuteronomy 21:10–25:19

This lengthy parashah contains the final collection of laws in Deuteronomy, a miscellany dealing with private concerns. Here are laws dealing with the individual and family, communities, and neighbors, as opposed to matters of state or public authority.

The parashah begins with three family laws: laws limiting the prerogatives of a man who captures a woman in warfare, establishing the rights of a firstborn child in a polygamous family, and discussing the punishment of a ben sorer u-moreh *(a stubborn and rebellious son).*

Given that the body reflects the divine image, the Torah mandates respectful treatment for the corpse of an executed criminal.

Chapter 22 presents a series of laws on returning lost animals and lost property, assisting a fallen animal, maintaining gender distinction in dress, treatment of a mother bird and her eggs, and building a parapet on the roof. Laws follow prohibiting sowing mixed seeds in a single field, plowing with an ox and ass, and wearing clothing made of shaatnez *(linen and wool). Four-cornered garments require* tzitzit.

A series of laws about sexual misconduct deals with premarital sex, adultery, and rape. Chapter 23 continues the theme with a listing of forbidden relationships, then shifts to a discussion of who may or may not enter into God's assembly.

The remaining laws span a range of topics: the sanctity of the camp, asylum for escaped slaves, cultic prostitution. Lending on interest is prohibited, and the fulfillment of vows is mandated. One is allowed to eat in another person's vineyard.

Chapter 24 continues this eclectic listing, forbidding remarriage to an ex-spouse if she remarried in the interim. A man is allowed to postpone military service if newly married. There are laws on kidnapping, skin affliction, taking property to compel repayment on a defaulted loan, and prompt payment of wages.

Passion for God requires passion for justice, for "everyone who deals dishonestly is abhorrent to the Holy One your God." The parashah ends with the ultimate symbol of dishonest, cruel treatment, that of the Amalekites, who "cut down the stragglers in your rear." Israel is commanded, therefore, to blot out Amalek's memory.

Safety First

When we think about the mitzvot of Judaism, most of us are inclined to think first of the ritual commandments, of someone wearing tallit and tefillin, or of lighting Shabbat candles. We might also think of hosting a Passover seder or perhaps of blowing the shofar on Rosh Hashanah and at the close of Yom Kippur. These mitzvot, known as *bein adam la-Makom* (between a person and God), are important components of a religious Jewish life. But no less necessary, and by no means less important, are the *mitzvot bein adam le-havero* (interpersonal, or ethical, commandments). The realm of ethics, from a Jewish perspective, is an essential branch of religion. One can be an ethical person without being religious, but one cannot be a truly religious Jew without being ethical.

Parashat Ki-Tetze contains one such ethical commandment that is often ignored even among the strictly pious. In this parashat, God commands us, "When you build a new house, you shall make a parapet (*ma'akeh*) for your roof, so that you do not bring bloodguilt on your house if anyone should fall from it." This rule, from early on in Jewish history, was understood to pertain to more than just preventing people from falling off buildings. Echoing the ancient midrash *Sifrei*, Maimonides writes in his *Sefer ha-Mitzvot* that this commandment also mandates us "to remove any obstacles and traps from all your property and build a railing around all roofs, ditches or holes and their like, so that no one can fall into them and get injured. We must also make sure to remove all other hazardous objects that we might control."

In Rambam's masterful summary of the entire Mishnah Torah, he explicates this commandment in the section pertaining to "the Laws of the Murderer and the Preservation of Life." For Maimonides, then, the preservation of human life is at issue. Safety is a religious obligation, and negligence is not merely a crime, it's a sin. As Rambam reads this law, the Torah orders us to assure the well-being and health of those around us. Beyond merely telling us not to harm directly, it makes us responsible for ensuring that people can't easily be harmed by the property under our control.

What an interesting proposition—a religious Jew is not only punctilious in performing the required rituals of Judaism, but he or she understands the safety of other people as a divine obligation. How far removed such a thought is from our sanitized notion of religion as private faith or quaint ritual. The Torah doesn't countenance being restricted to the study hall or the synagogue. Instead, it is concerned with the fullness of life as it is lived, intent on bringing the healing touch of holiness to every aspect of human living.

A God who can be partitioned off from human life is no God at all. Far from being just a "faith" or a "religion," Judaism offers a way of living life that brings a sacred perspective to bear on all activities.

How we provide for each other is indeed a Jewish matter. That we might allow a potential danger to threaten another person is a betrayal of Judaism's most fundamental teaching: that we are, each of us, made in God's image and that all people are deserving of God's love as well as ours. Given the commitment of the God of Israel to liberate slaves, given the way our God insists on "one law for you and for the stranger who is in our midst" and tells us to "pursue justice," it must come as no surprise that the service of this God finds its loftiest expression in ensuring the health and safety of the other members of our community.

A religious Jew is called "observant." Perhaps we need to open our eyes, to observe the ways in which we can take better care of each other and secure each other's health and safety more completely. When we look out for each other, our observance is something beautiful to behold.

Take care.

The Positive and Negative of Social Justice

The rabbis of the Talmud established a method of reading the Torah that is embodied in the thirteen rules of Rabbi Ishmael (known as the

Yud-Gimel Middot) found at the beginning of the ancient midrashic collection the *Sifra*. These hermeneutical rules provided guidelines for transforming the text of Torah into a living and applicable document. Subsequent rabbis went further, providing for how to derive *halakhot* (specific laws) from the Torah's timeless legislation as well.

One of the rules they articulated pertains to punishment for a violation. In order for a violation of Torah law to result in punishment, it must be stated twice, once in its positive form ("You shall do X") and once in its negative ("You shall not do the opposite of X"). An example of this biblical practice is the mandate that meat be slaughtered only in Jerusalem according to the laws of *shehitah* and another verse that prohibits the consumption of *treifah* and *nevelah* (improperly slaughtered meat). The idea is that if something is significant, it should be both mandated in an imperative and its opposite should be explicitly prohibited.

That unique stance of Jewish law also finds its equivalent in *Parashat Ki-Tetze*, which offers a list of rules necessary to respect human dignity: how to treat prisoners of war, rights within marriage, proper care of animals, prohibition of sexual oppression, provision of refuge for slaves, denial of interest on business loans, prohibition of kidnapping, relations with the poor, and honest weights (to be honest in business dealings). In each of these instances, the Torah details important components of any positive effort to establish a just society. We are mandated to show compassion, responsibility, and sensitivity—positive virtues by anyone's standards.

But after providing all these heartwarming rules, affirming our common kinship with our fellow human beings, and insisting that we identify even with the powerless and the down-and-out, the Torah appends a strikingly different rule:

> Remember what Amalek did to you on your journey after you left Egypt—how, undeterred by fear of God, he surprised you on the march, when you were famished and weary and cut down all the stragglers in your rear. Therefore, when Adonai your God grants you safety from all your enemies around you in the land that Adonai your God is giving you as a hereditary portion, you shall blot out the memory of Amalek from under heaven. Do not forget!

Ostensibly, this passage is a call to nurse a grudge. Because of the heinous barbarism that the tribe of Amalek inflicted on the sick, the old, and the weak along the journey in the wilderness, we are to keep their memory alive until we are in a position of power. Once we have entered the land of Israel, once it is securely in our hands, then we are to "blot out the memory of Amalek from under heaven."

On first blush, this passage sounds grotesque and primitive. Why would someone as forgiving as God demand that we keep alive this ancient story of having been wronged and that we should use this memory in the service of vengeance? Isn't that a bloodthirsty and vicious kind of morality?

In truth, I think part of our discomfort is appropriate. Our first response to any call for bloodshed should be negative. Life—all life—is so precious that we must take great care to ensure that the passions of the moment don't lead us to do something that we later realize to be excessive, irreversible, and immoral. But beyond our laudable discomfort with violence, a part of our squeamishness has to do with an unwillingness to oppose evil strenuously.

You see, to resist evil means more than simply to advocate good. There are people in the world who are willing to resort to violence and force to impose evil on others. There are those who believe that the strong have a right to dominate the weak, to take what they desire. To limit our response to platitudinous condemnations and hand-wringing is simply a moral abdication. The unwillingness to use force in the battle against evil is nothing less than a passive partnership with that very evil. God knows (and knew) it took many deaths to liberate the Israelites from Egyptian slavery. Pharaoh wasn't moved by Moses's stirring oratory, however much we may be. Today's Pharaohs aren't much moved by speeches either—a mighty hand and an outstretched arm still have roles in the service of justice.

All those positive deeds we can do in the pursuit of righteousness mean nothing if we aren't willing to fight for it. Without the commitment to remember Amalek, the obligation to seek peace is simply an invitation to ruthless domination. Both commandments—the positive and the negative—are part and parcel of the overriding mitzvah of loving God.

As the psalmist says, "Those who love Adonai hate evil." Eternal vigilance is, indeed, the price of liberty.

The Torah and Transvestites

In an age of strident fundamentalism, many Jews assume that "Torah-true" is the most authentic way of being Jewish, and they understand that commitment as being whatever the Torah says, goes. Hence, even well-meaning Orthodox rabbis will publicly refer to non-Orthodox Jews as "less religious" rather than realizing that many passionate Reform, Reconstructionist, or Conservative Jews are deeply pious, but they understand the commands of God differently than do their Orthodox cousins.

Recognizing that there are religious and lazy Jews in every denomination, we still face the question, what does loyalty to the Torah imply? Does it mean that whatever the Torah says is law? Or might it imply something more elastic and flexible?

Parashat Kit-Tetze offers a classical example of how the authentic Jew of the past was not "Torah-true" in the fundamentalist sense of being bound by the literal meaning of a biblical verse. The Torah records God's command: "A woman must not put on man's apparel, nor shall a man wear woman's clothing, for whoever does these things is abhorrent (*to'evat*) to the Lord your God."

It's pretty hard to misunderstand that verse. In its *p'shat*, it clearly forbids wearing the clothing of the other sex, going so far as to call it an abomination. That forceful language is an expression of strongest repugnance and clearly seems to prohibit transvestitism.

Yet that is not how the tradition interpreted this verse. Rashi records a fascinating reading that restricts the application of the verse to a very narrow circumstance. Commenting on a woman not wearing men's clothing, he records the Talmud's explanation that she would do so "in order that she shall resemble a man, in order that she should go among men. For this is only for the purpose of immorality." In other words, the Talmud provides a specific narrative backdrop or context that shifts what the prohibition means. By understanding the motivation to wear a man's clothing so that a lusting woman could more easily mingle among men and find a sexual partner for an immoral purpose, Rashi (and the Talmud and *Massekhet Nazir*) reads the Torah as prohibiting cross-dressing when it is done for immoral purposes—but not necessarily in other instances.

In fact, the *Sifrei* is explicit in limiting the meaning of the biblical verse: "What does Scripture mean to tell you? That a woman may not wear white garments and that a man may not wear colored clothes? No . . . [only] something which results in abomination."

In the medieval period, Maimonides offered a different slant, arguing that the prohibition was to be understood in the context of pagan idolatry, which often required cross-dressing. For the Rambam, then, the Torah only prohibits cross-dressing for idolatrous purposes but not secular cross-dressing.

I don't want to imply that Judaism says nothing about transvestites. In fact, many sources (*Sefer Ha-Hinnukh* and *Sefer Ha-Mitzvot Ha-Katzar* of the *Hafetz Hayim*) record a blanket prohibition that covers all cases, regardless of motive or context. But I want to assert that traditional Judaism (as opposed to any single denomination today) has always had some rabbis who were strict constructionists and some who were not. Both types were faithful and pious and provided authentic ways to read the Torah and translate its teachings into life.

Today, as well, some rabbis look to what the Torah says on the surface, and some read it in the light of modern ethical imperatives and technological knowledge. Both are authentic approaches to revealing God's sacred will and valuable tools for harvesting Torah in our own age.

The Talmud teaches us that there are seventy faces to the Torah, so the Torah has a special revelation that is appropriate for each Jewish soul. Our job is not to discount each other's Torah, but to engage ourselves every day in revealing the one meant for us.

Ki-Tavo/When You Come In

Deuteronomy 26:1–29:8

Ki-Tavo *begins with the offer of prayers to be recited by farmers, one when bringing the first fruit offerings to the Temple and the other when giving the tithe to the poor every three years. These are the only examples of fixed liturgy addressing God, the words of which are established by the Torah.*

All of the details of the laws are now enumerated. Moses offers a conclusion to the lengthy series of rules completed. These are more than mere rules; they are the structure of a comprehensive relationship between the people Israel and God. In fulfilling these mitzvot, Israel "shall be, as God promised, a holy people to the Holy One your God."

There are three ceremonies to be performed once Israel has entered the land:

1. *Erecting stone tablets with the text of the Torah, building an altar, and performing sacrifices on Mount Ebal.*
2. *The standing of the tribes on Mount Gerizim and Mount Ebal, there to proclaim the blessings and curses that the covenant can evoke.*
3. *The listing of the punishments by the Levites when people sin in ways difficult to try in human courts; the people are to affirm those punishments.*

The parashah proceeds with a lengthy description of the blessings awaiting Israel if it obeys God's laws and an even more extensive treatment of the punishments that will follow the violation of the covenant.

This section concludes the second address: "These are the terms of the covenant which the Holy One commanded Moses to conclude with the Israelites in the land of Moab, in addition to the covenant which God has made with them at Horeb."

Moses's third address urges ratification of the additional covenant:
"Therefore observe faithfully all the terms of this covenant, that you
may succeed in all that you undertake."

Giving with a Smile

Even though we are aware of all the important services and goods our
tax dollars provide—from feeding hungry children to caring for the
elderly to maintaining roads to defending the nation—we still don't
like to pay taxes. We complain, we find ways to lessen our tax burden,
and we even make a political movement out of paying less.

Of all the taxes, aid to the poor is the one most resented. We feel
cheated of our hard-earned income and assume that the recipients of
welfare are living high at our expense. They are viewed as lazy, shift-
less, and selfish, and many a political career has risen on their backs.
In this contemporary debate, there are those who claim that the Bible
is linked to the "traditional" values of self-reliance and private charity. Proponents insist that "returning" to those values will restore
America's ethical rigor and national vitality. And the first step toward
such a restoration is to end the "culture of dependency" that keeps
the poor on the rolls and siphons off the money we would otherwise
use to invest in a booming economy.

What does the tradition present on this subject? *Parashat Ki-Tavo*
mandates providing special tithes for the Levite, the orphan, and the
widow, three groups in biblical Israel who had insufficient property
to provide for themselves. Are these tithes voluntary? No. Are they
mandated by the authorities? Yes. Are they legislated by a central
group? Yes. Looks like welfare is a traditional and very biblical idea.

Which makes perfect sense. Since the whole world is God's, and
God provides for us all out of divine bounty and love, we have an
obligation to care for those among us who need assistance. Since we
are merely God's caretakers, and God is the only true owner, we must
use the resources God places in our hands to care for all creatures,
particularly those least able to do so themselves. This responsibility
isn't optional, and it isn't private; *tzedakah* is a tax imposed by God on
behalf of the needy in our midst.

Not only do we have a Jewish duty to provide for the poor, but we're supposed to enjoy it! The Torah bids the donor to state "I have not transgressed any of Your commands, nor have I forgotten." Now it's easy enough to understand the first part of the phrase—in giving *tzedakah* to the poor, we show our recognition that God owns all and that we are obligated to use God's resources to care for the rest of God's children. But what does it mean to say, "Nor have I forgotten"? We already know that the donor has remembered to tithe for the poor, so the Torah must be teaching some additional truth. What is it telling us?

Rashi asked the same question, and his answer is instructive. We haven't forgotten "to bless You during the separation of tithes." Not only must we give, but we must thank God for the privilege of being able to do so. We have to pay our taxes gladly, with a spirit of gratitude.

Can the Torah really expect us to enjoy supporting the poor? Yes, and for two principal reasons:

• The Torah assumes that we are merely given permission to use what ultimately belongs to God. Given that God is the Creator and Possessor of All Creation, everything we own, we owe. How natural to show our gratitude to God for allowing us to use this bounty by sharing it with others. The Jew is expected to want to provide for the welfare of others so that they too can come to experience God's bounty directly.

• The Torah assumes that we are all God's children, equally deserving of care and support. Those who have more are obligated to share more because of that common humanity, because we are all children of God. If God doesn't hoard the riches of the earth, then by what right can we?

Traditional biblical law mandates transfer payments from the rich to the poor, legislating an obligatory tax that is an entitlement of those in need of care. Beyond even the requirements of the Internal Revenue, the Torah expects us to give and to give in a cheerful spirit.

Remember that next tax day!

Renewal

One of the sorry attributes of most adults is the routinization of the soul. We become complacent, taking for granted our daily routines, our closest relationships, and our familiar possessions. What we see frequently we fail to notice—an odd form of blindness indeed. So it is that even residents of the most luxurious mansions fail to marvel when they wake up in the same magnificent bedroom they have used for the past two decades, just as we all fail to be truly moved by the miracle of having a bed at all. There is a creeping callousness, a form of progressive illness that engulfs our ability to be enchanted. Our addictive need for novelty and replacement leaves us unable to appreciate what is already ours.

Take, for example, the chilling statistic that the average American owns a car for anywhere between two and four years. After four years, you are holding on to a clunker, something to exchange for a shiny, new model—even though there is nothing wrong with the car you own.

The desire for novelty, it seems, lies deep in the human psyche. Perhaps it is connected to our fear of finitude, the certainty that death will come one day, that leads us to seek renewal and new beginnings. But that need for newness exacts a price as well, causing us to waste the precious resources of the planet in our madcap rush for anything fresh. Friendships are easily discarded as they age; we shift our connections without regard to loyalty or the enriched depth that only time can add. That turnover poisons relationships in the workplace as well—corporations fire their employees without considering their length of tenure, and workers leave their firms without any loyalty to the people who trained them and gave them a chance in the first place.

Our addiction to innovation leads to an inability to trust the permanence of anyone or anything. We live in a pretty lonely world.

There is another way, one suggested by the way the rabbis of antiquity read a verse in *Parashat Ki-Tavo*. Moses says, "This day, Adonai your God commands you . . ." Attentive to every nuance in the Torah, the rabbis note that the ensuing commands were not actually issued on "this day" but rather had been given some forty years earlier. So what does Moses mean by "this day"?

Rashi summarizes earlier rabbinic commentary by recounting that "every day, they [the mitzvot] should seem new to you, as though on that very day you were commanded regarding them." While the mitzvot come from an age long gone, there is an existential sense in which we must make them fresh with each new encounter. Rather than languishing as some ancient inheritance, they can become electric vessels for an encounter with God and bring deeper wisdom if we recognize them as newly issued for each new opportunity.

Whenever we face the chance to do a mitzvah, it is as though that mitzvah is presented for the first time. Just as we are sometimes able to see a sunset as though we have never seen one before, we need to open our souls to perceive a holy act in that same original way. We can cultivate our capacity to be surprised, delighted, and enriched by actions we have performed in the past.

Take as an example parents facing the bat or bar mitzvah celebration of their second child. Even though they have witnessed hundreds of such celebrations—in the community at large and among their friends in particular—there is no doubt that they will feel marvel, profound emotion, and rich joy when their own child chants from the holy Torah. Cousins and close family friends will be touched deeply, not because the ceremony is any different this time, but because they have opened their heart to the power of the moment.

The key to a spiritual connection with the universe is to do the hard work necessary to remain open to the moment, to every moment. If we approach prayer the way we do a beach at sunset, if we perceive the mitzvot as we do a moment in a loved one's life, then we don't need constant novelty. Instead, the very predictability of the occasion—the fact that we witness a drama that recurs over and over again—provides the loom on which we can weave the woof of our loftiest aspirations and the warp of our fondest hopes.

Novelty is a cultivated art. It has more to do with our attitudes than our activities, more with our willingness to marvel than our need to be entertained. The power to renew lies within.

Choosing Torah

A remarkable revolution has hit the Jewish world. For the first time in its history, the federations and secular organizations acknowledge that Jewish education must be one of the highest priorities of the entire Jewish community. Funding that used to go to institutions whose Jewishness consisted primarily in the ethnicity of its top staff (rather than any distinctive programming or services offered) is now being reallocated for the explicitly Jewish concern of talmud torah (Jewish learning).

Why the shift? Because every study of the demographics of Jews in North America affirms the simple truth that without Torah there will be no Jews. Without a desire to serve God through mitzvot, to study and implement the Torah in our daily lives, there is simply not enough reason to put up with all the bother and separation that Jewish identity entails. This is no mere matter of partisanship—every Jewish religious denomination has been asserting this truth for at least a quarter of a century. Nor is it a retreat from universalism, but simply a recognition that any universalism that requires (or produces) our destruction as a distinct people is false, more akin to cultural imperialism than true human concern.

While Jews have been known as the chosen people from time immemorial, it is now essential that we become the "choosing people." It is time we choose the Torah anew—for our own survival and for the survival of our mission of exemplifying righteousness.

The idea of choosing to follow the Torah is rooted in ancient Judaism. *Parashat Ki-Tavo*, for example, lists a series of blessings for the Jew who follows God's commands and a series of curses for the one who rebels against divine dictates. The Torah records, "Cursed be the one who does not uphold the words of this teaching to do them, and all the people shall say, 'Amen.'"

What is striking is the plain sense that the Jews can choose whether or not to follow God's will; that God holds out blessings and curses to us implies that we have a choice. God doesn't coerce observance. Instead, through teaching, example, and incentive, God hopes to persuade us to elevate our behavior to incorporate the holy and moral code of Jewish living.

Rashi takes the notion of choice one step further: "Here [in these words] Moses included the entire Torah, and they [the people] accepted it upon themselves with a curse and with an oath." While there are certainly midrashim that view Israel's acceptance of the Torah as forced upon them, Rashi here identifies with the idea that the Jews of Moses's generation freely chose to be bound by the Torah.

In a sense, choosing Judaism is still what links the contemporary Jewish people, regardless of our denominational affiliations. An Orthodox Jew retains the power to choose to violate the words of the Torah and the traditions of Judaism and is expected to choose to adhere to Jewish law as it is propounded by contemporary Orthodox sages. So too a Conservative Jew is expected to choose to bind himself or herself to Jewish law as the Conservative movement in Judaism understands that law. And a Reform Jew is under a similar obligation—to freely choose to respond whenever he or she hears God's commanding voice in a mitzvah. Where they differ is in how they perceive Jewish law and its development and in who they think speaks authoritatively on behalf of Judaism, God, and their own spirituality. But all three movements affirm the need to listen for God's commands and respond, as our ancestors did, with *"Hineni."*

Our ancestors willingly chose the yoke of the Torah with its need for self-discipline, diligence, and study. As a result of their choice, we are here today, and the world is a richer and more compassionate place. We are now called to make a similar choice, to choose a life of Torah and mitzvot, and our choice can also transform the tomorrows yet to be.

As the parashah says, "Hear, O Israel! This day you become a people for Adonai your God. You shall listen to the voice of the Holy One your God, doing God's commandments and God's statutes which I command you this day." As always, we have the power to choose to listen or to shut our ears to that still, small voice.

Are you listening?

Nitzavim/You Stand

Deuteronomy 29:9–30:20

Moses summons all Israel—men, women, children, and strangers—to ratify the covenant. This new covenant reaches beyond those present at the time: "I make this covenant, with its sanctions, not with you alone, but both with those who are standing here with us this day before the Holy One your God and with those who are not with us here this day." He also points out the consequences of violating the covenant and how dire those acts will be, but he reminds his listeners that "concealed acts concern the Holy One our God; but with overt acts, it is for us and our children ever to apply all the provisions of this Torah."

In the midst of enumerating the disasters that disobedience will elicit, Moses asserts the saving power of God's love and of teshuvah: *"When you return to the Holy One your God, then the Holy One your God will restore your fortunes and take you back in love." He asserts that these teachings are not too complex or too distant, but rather "the thing is very close to you, in your mouth and in your heart, to observe it."*

Once again, Moses reminds us that this is about our own choices: "See, I set before you this day life and prosperity, death and adversity. For I command you this day to love the Holy One your God, to walk in God's ways, and to keep God's commandments. I call heaven and earth to witness against you this day: I have put before you life and death, blessing and curse. Choose life—if you and your offspring would live—by loving the Holy One your God, heeding God's commands, and holding fast to God."

Va-Yelekh/He Went

Deuteronomy 31:1–31:30

With Parashat Va-Yelekh, *Moses begins the epilogue, concluding the great series of addresses that are the book of Deuteronomy. He begins by announcing his own impending retirement and the transfer of leadership to Joshua. It will be Joshua who will lead the Israelites in the conquest of the land, and Moses exhorts them to "be strong and resolute, be not in fear or in dread of them; for the Holy One your God marches with you: God will not fail you or forsake you." Moses then transfers the mantle of leadership to Joshua by repeating his charge to Joshua in the presence of the entire people.*

Moses writes down the Torah and puts it into the care of the priests and elders, who are charged with its interpretation and its regular public recital every Shemittah. Strikingly, the public reading is for men, women, children, and the strangers who are now part of the confederation Israel.

God calls Moses and Joshua to prepare the transfer of leadership by directly appointing Joshua. God informs Moses that the Israelites are bound to disobey in the future. He instructs Moses to compose a poem-song that will warn the Israelites and serve as a witness to them about the punishment their disloyalty will incur. Only then does God actually install Joshua.

Moses then follows up with the Levites, informing them about the care of the Torah, and convenes the Israelites to hear the chanting of the Song of Witness.

Jewish Values, Jewish Deeds

Almost every Jew is familiar with the most terrifying moment in all of Jewish ritual practice. We prepare for it, knowing that it's inevitable. We study, chant, pray, sing. As the dreaded moment approaches, we break into a sweat and smile bravely as our heartbeat speeds up. Finally, the *gabbai* (ritual director of synagogue worship services) calls us up as one of the seven who are honored to recite the blessings before and after the reading of the Torah on Shabbat morning.

Where did the practice of reciting blessings over the Torah originate? Shrouded in history, the rabbis of *Midrash Devarim Rabbah* trace its roots to the practice of Moses as recorded in this parashah. After recording the history of Israel's wanderings in the wilderness, as well as summarizing many of the laws of the Torah, we read, "and this is the blessing that Moses, the man of God, blessed with the children of Israel."

According to Rabbi Samuel Ben Nahman in the name of Rabbi Jonathan, this verse "intimates that after Moses had repeated the law, he recited a blessing. Hence the blessing after it [the chanting of the Torah]."

There is more to the practice of reciting a blessing after repeating the Torah than simply beautiful ceremony. This practice implies that the teachings of the Torah and their implementation constitute our supreme blessing. Building on an unprecedented and revolutionary idea of ethical monotheism, Judaism implements this concept in the reality of day-to-day living. We call that process of implementation halakhah, and its particulars are the mitzvot. Without them, there is no Judaism and no Jewish people.

Often Jews will claim to love and practice the values of Judaism without practicing its mitzvot. By this, they mean that they cherish the morality but not the expression of Judaism, its premises but not its implementation. But can the two be separated? Why do we need the mitzvot? Why struggle with obedience to Jewish law? In short, why did Moses bless the teachings of the Torah, and why do we?

To be a good Jew ultimately means to accept the laws of the Torah as our own guides of behavior. Can we be good Jews without practicing Judaism? Commitment to a common definition of Judaism and a common practice unites the Jewish people across time and around the world. Generation to generation, the permanence of Shabbat, kashrut, our prayer book, our holy days, and countless other practices lead to stability that translates into belonging and identity. A Jew from Buenos Aires or Yemen can walk into a traditional congregation in the United States and follow along in its siddur because the contents almost exactly match the contents of his or her siddur back home. A traditional prayer book also resembles the siddur of a thousand years ago and of a millennium hence. Jewish law provides continuity.

Jewish law also moves Judaism beyond the realm of mere religion. Judaism is meant to transform those moments of our lives when we are not in a minyan—how we eat, how we treat other people and living things, how we live in the world. These are the grist of Judaism's alternate vision of a world redeemed from hunger, oppression, insensitivity, and violence. Refraining from Jewish practice is also a retreat from implementing Judaism's agenda of building sacred communities in the here and now. Jewish law provides involvement in the repair of the world.

Judaism opposes the separation of the human soul from our institutions, insisting that the two are inextricably linked. Too many political ideologies reduce everything to social institutions—class, the market system, race, or gender identity. When all issues emerge from social conditions, questions of character and integrity and compassion reflect mere luxury or distraction. Reforming the world requires reforming our personalities—not just what we think but also how we act. Jewish law provides for responsible sensitivity.

For all of these benefits—Jewish community and identity, social justice, and individual character-building—and for experiencing God's presence in every moment of our day, there is simply no substitute for the mitzvot, the building blocks of Jewish living, the colorful blossoms on the growing tree of Jewish law.

Just as we bless the Torah, so its teachings bless and enrich us, our communities, and our world.

Whose Torah? Your Torah

In one of its most sublime breaks with other religious traditions, the Torah records God's insistence that the sacred writings of Israel belong to the entire people, not simply to one holy caste or aristocracy. The Torah of Israel belongs to all Israel.

In *Parashat Va-Yelekh*, we recall that premise in stirring words: "Surely this Instruction which I enjoin you this day is not too baffling for you, nor is it beyond your reach. . . . It is not in the heavens . . .

neither is it beyond the sea. . . . No, the thing is very close to you, in your mouth and in your heart, to observe it."

While we may all be moved by these lovely words and their lofty sentiment, our community's stark ignorance of the Torah and the widespread abandonment of the path of living that the Torah represents should provoke us to ask the question, do we really still mean these words? Do we, the Jewish people, still possess the Torah?

Do we still want to accept the Torah as a gift of God's love and as our sacred duty? Or would we rather preserve the Torah exclusively on the level of a symbol—a scroll that stands for something else and therefore need rarely be unrolled, never read, and only sporadically observed?

One of the greatest challenges for those Jews who *would* like to learn more about our sacred heritage, who *would* like to lay claim to what is their birthright, is the sheer quantity of Torah and its offshoots in rabbinic traditions. The amount of writing, the depth of analysis, and the profundity of ideas is so vast that it can look too daunting for anyone but the specialist or the full-time student. Given our ignorance and lack of time, is it simply no longer possible for us to learn Torah?

While the problem may seem new to us, in actuality, it is not. Moses was impelled to insist that the Torah wasn't too hard or too lofty, implying that Jews in his day felt that Jewish study and observance was beyond them. Certainly by the Talmudic period (70–600 C.E.), the rabbis often had to encourage a reluctant Jewry to take the first steps in Jewish living.

One of the most effective ways to avoid learning Torah is to adhere to an all-or-nothing approach that devalues anything short of absolute fluency and mastery. Given the impossibility of attaining scholarly excellence, insisting on it as the only goal is a sure disenfranchisement of the Jewish people, a guaranteed way to sunder us from our heritage.

Midrash Devarim Rabbah pays eloquent testimony to the self-defeating attitude of someone who allows the sheer volume of Jewish learning to prevent that first step. The rabbis say, "The fool enters the synagogue and, seeing there people occupying themselves with the Torah, asks, 'How does one begin to learn the Torah?' They answer the fool, 'First, one reads from a Scroll containing a portion of the Torah, then from the Book itself, then from the prophets, and then *Ketuvim* (the third section of the Hebrew Bible). After completing the study of Scripture, one learns the Talmud and then the halakhot and then the *haggadot* (rabbinic legends).' After hearing all this, the fool says, 'I can't learn all this!' and he turns back from the gate."

The fool's mistake is to confuse the optimal goal—mastery of the entire corpus of Jewish learning—with a more reasonable and attainable first step. This step is simply to take that first step. Later on, there will be plenty of time to worry about the next step. In contradistinction to the fool, the wise person "learns one chapter every day until completing the whole law." That gradual approach—always making progress, always growing in learning and observance—is the only sound approach.

The challenge before us, then, is not to become either omniscient or saintly. It is to have the courage to become Jews.

The Trouble with the Jews

When I was the rabbi of a bustling congregation, I often had the opportunity to counsel young people who were considering or planning a wedding. When I asked them why they wanted a Jewish wedding, they often told me they were doing it because of an aged grandparent or some other relative or because their family went through the Holocaust. As a way of honoring their relative or their history, a Jewish ceremony seemed the appropriate thing to do.

What strikes me about that is how few responded with some personal connection solely from their own experience. Few told me they wanted a Jewish ceremony because that was what God wanted or because they found it the most moving or because it expressed best who they were.

At first, I was deeply troubled by this kind of response. After all, Judaism is not merely a history, it is also a *brit kodesh* (a sacred covenant that links every Jewish soul with the Holy Blessing One). As a rich path of spirituality and wisdom, Judaism has so much to contribute to the life of every Jew. So why, I wondered, didn't Jews ever respond in that context? Why always connect their personal celebrations to family, ancestors, Israel, or history?

As I've explored that commitment with so many couples over the years, however, my respect for their answer has deepened. I marvel at their intuitive recognition that Judaism is far more than just a religious path. They know that being Jewish is a destiny, a people, and a shared past as well.

Parashat Va-Yelekh speaks of that tenacious history in a fascinating way. Moses tells the Jews that they are standing, that day, before God. He urges them to "enter into the covenant with the Lord your God, that the Lord your God is concluding with you this day . . . to the end that God may establish you this day as His people and be your God."

Rashi comments on this verse from God's perspective: "To such an extent has God taken the trouble in order to establish you as a people in God's presence." It isn't easy being Jewish, and it never has been. What Rashi highlights is the difficulty and persistence that Jewish identity has always required. Even for God, the survival of the Jews takes great effort. And if God has to work at it, how much more so do we?

Think about the effort God put into Jewish survival: taking us from Egyptian slavery; bringing us through the wilderness to the land of Israel; establishing our homeland with Jerusalem as our capital; enabling our people to survive and even flourish in the many diasporas through which we have wandered; and creating the miracle of surviving the Nazi murderers, of the renewed State of Israel after two thousand years, of a reunited Jerusalem, and of a contentious and energetic Jewish community in North America and elsewhere.

As Jews, we train ourselves to see the hand of God in the commonplace. In the case of the survival of an ancient people and the tenacity and profundity of our ancient faith and way of life, it is virtually impossible *not* to acknowledge the hand of God.

And if God takes so much trouble for the Jewish people, surely God still has a purpose for our existence. God still needs Jews to embody a vision of sanctity and righteousness, of justice and compassion. God still needs Jews to perform acts of love and kindness in the world, to fashion sermons not of words but of deeds, and to testify thereby to the wisdom of the Torah and the greatness of God.

In an era in which sex no longer implies love and commitment and prestige has little to do with decency and wisdom, the world needs Jews to remain faithful activists on behalf of God, Torah, and righteousness. If God has taken (and still takes) such effort on our behalf, can't we also put some effort into the survival of Judaism and the Jewish people?

The world may depend on it.

Ha'azinu/Give Ear!

Deuteronomy 32:1–32:52

Ha'azinu is an extended poem that warns the Israelites of their future betrayal of God's covenant and the disastrous consequences that this disloyalty will entail. It begins with an invocation of heaven and earth as witnesses against Israel when the poet is no longer alive.

Then it moves through the history of God's relationship with the people Israel and of Israel's consistent lack of gratitude and loyalty in the face of God's saving acts. The poet declares that God will, indeed, punish Israel for its rebelliousness but will limit the severity of that punishment. He will ultimately turn divine anger against Israel's enemies, the tools of God's temporary anger against Israel.

Ultimately, God will deliver a repentant Israel, and Israel will sing in celebration of that eventual redemption and salvation.

Moses concludes, after the end of the poem, that the people must remain devoted to Torah, since "this is not a trifling thing for you; it is your very life."

The Heavens and the Earth—and Ears

What is the essence of human nature? Are we really creatures of spirit and mind, capable of forming ourselves at will to correspond to the highest conceptions of humanity possible? Or are we rather little better than the animals of the field and forest, driven by instinct and whim, incapable of modifying our behavior or our aspirations?

The question of whether we are little lower than the angels or simply standing, naked apes has preoccupied poets, philosophers, and sages from the dawn of time. In every age, cogent defenses of both positions volley forth from vociferous advocates, each deaf to the merits of the other's position or the flaws of their own.

On the one hand, it is remarkable what marvels humans have accomplished. With only the power of our minds, we have erected buildings that stand across the millennia and stretch up to the very skies. We have turned the desert into farmland and found ways to link people separated by thousands of miles through a vast array of communication and transportation networks. Having conquered a long list of malignant diseases, our scientists seem on the brink of winning the battle against illness, even as our educators perfect methods of conquering illiteracy. We are truly reflections of the divine, able to create worlds through our will and our words.

And yet.

Even as our accomplishments loom so large, our failures assume a still-more terrifying posture. Our scientific advances threaten to poison our air, render our water unusable, and leave our land blighted. Even as medicine advances, we grapple with plagues that remind us of our continuing frailty and our devastating impotence. Despite our tremendous wealth, the illiterate and unemployed, outcasts and hopeless loom ever larger, making a mockery of our smug self-satisfaction. Women are still underpaid and subject to assault. Terrorists and floods catch us ill-prepared. Blacks and Latinos are still underemployed and subject to assault. Gays and lesbians are still despised and subject to assault. Maybe we really are animals after all.

Jewish tradition rejects this simple dichotomy. Both angel and animal, human beings are unique precisely because we have the potential to develop in either direction, often both at once.

This parashah opens with Moses's stirring words, "Give ear, O heavens, let me speak; Let the earth hear the words I utter." The Talmudic and geonic (medieval Jewish authorities in Babylon) rabbis asked themselves why Moses felt impelled to mention both heaven and earth. Wouldn't one have sufficed as a witness?

In *Midrash Devarim Rabbah*, several answers all point in the same direction. Rabbi Tanhuma said, "Because God will redeem Israel only through the agency of them both." Another explanation posits that "the Torah was given only through the agency of them both." Or that "manna and the quails were given through the agency of them both." Or finally, that "God compared Israel to the stars of heaven and the dust of the earth."

Each of these answers insists that salvation comes only through the combination of heaven and earth, of the mundane and the spiritual, of the ideal and the concrete. Both lofty goals (often unattainable) and repair of the world (often prosaic) are necessary for the redemption of humanity and the establishment of a caring community.

Without a goal of complete social justice, our communities and the human family cannot attain a better world. But without a willingness to look after the little details—the individual homeless, poor, sick, or hungry—the goal will remain elusive and ethereal.

Without a sense of the mitzvot as a goal—seeking to incorporate God's will and a sense of the sacred into our lives—there is little hope of elevating our souls. Yet holiness can only enter our lives when translated into practical behavior, shaping how we eat, study, pray, rest, and celebrate.

Our destiny as a people, as the house of Israel in the modern age, integrates that same stubborn balance: a flesh-and-blood people still wrestling with an angel in the night, still insisting that holiness is possible and that righteousness must flow like a mighty stream.

By holding on to our own physical nature, we can hope to elevate the material world into something higher. By retaining our dreams, our vision, and our faith, we provide a direction for otherwise pointless business and dreary years.

All it takes is heaven and earth and the ability to listen. It hasn't changed since Moses first sang to us his song of love.

Always on a Journey

The great Jewish existentialist Franz Rosenzweig began his monumental philosophy of Judaism, *The Star of Redemption*, with these words: "All knowledge of the Whole has its source in death, in the fear of death." That abiding fear and the inescapable destination of all human lives (and of all human life) in death is a fact beyond appeal. There are no exceptions, no delays, and no negotiations with our ultimate end. "From dust you are, and to dust you shall return" is no empty biblical verse; it is the context within which we fashion our lives and attempt to establish some record of enduring worth.

Death threatens to reduce human life to an absurdity. If I am to die, then it doesn't really matter how I live my life at all. Whether we're righteous or selfish, generous or stingy, rich or poor, death will claim us all in the end. This fact is so staggering that it makes our lives appear irrelevant, like we're merely passing the time in the face of the inevitable.

Some seek solace from this terrible fact in the comfort of religion and the hope that death isn't really the end at all. Others seek to soothe their fear through philosophy, hoping that abiding value may emerge from clear thinking. Still others seek peace in a psychological approach, simply resigning themselves to eventual nothingness. Around the globe, some search for comfort in identification with the group, knowing that their own identity will continue through the existence of the group, even though they themselves will cease.

While each of these responses has some merit, none makes the fear subside completely. Regardless of what goes on in our hearts, our heads, or our souls, we still don't like dying, and we still feel sorrow and distress at its call.

All of us—from the greatest to the least—will die. But does that really render our lives irrelevant? Is it pointless to go to a party simply because we know in advance that the party must end? Do we avoid love because our lover may someday disappoint us? Is it absurd to rear children because they will one day move out?

Rather than retreating to some abstraction to save ourselves from the fear of death, we might look to the way we conduct our lives in the face of death. We live our lives in the belief that the journey itself has intrinsic, irreducible value. We fall in love because it is right for the moment; we raise children because it is delightful and meaningful to do so; and we party because there is so much in life to celebrate.

I know of no greater symbol of the ultimate value of living for its own sake than that greatest of all prophets, our teacher Moses. Knowing that the prophet's death is imminent, God tells Moses, "You may view the land from a distance, but you shall not enter it—the land that I am giving to the Israelite people."

Moses spends his whole life journeying toward the Promised Land. The great goal of his entire career is to bring the children of Israel from Egyptian bondage to freedom in the land of Israel. Yet even

Moses cannot enter his final destination; he can only approach it, only approximate it, only view it from the outside.

In this view, Moses resembles each of us—always on the way, never able to reach the final destination, but blessed with the vision to see what we cannot attain ourselves. *Targum Onkelos* (the ancient translation of the Torah into Aramaic) tellingly renders the passage as telling Moses that he cannot go "to the land, for I am giving it to the children of Israel." The ultimate goal is one that we cannot attain as individuals but is a gift to the ages—to our children and to all children. Perhaps it is for this reason that this parashah contains no mitzvot, no commandments that need doing. In the last stages of life, we turn our attention to conjecture, to seeing what we cannot experience individually. Our vision exceeds our grasp, and knowing that our children will continue our journey is a vision well worth having.

Perhaps this is the reason Rashi notes that God tells Moses, "I know that it is dear to you, therefore I say to you, 'Ascend, and see.'" Rashi knows that our ability to imagine, to conjecture, to anticipate is a step up from mere animal existence. By feasting our eyes on the path we have taken, we affirm our membership in something transcendent. Death for Moses constitutes an elevation, the next stage of his journey.

As Franz Kafka, a contemporary of Rosenzweig's, writes, "Moses fails to enter Canaan not because his life is too short but because it is a human life." Moses's humanity (and ours) is a finite measurement. Our limits are real and unavoidable. But our vision can soar above our bodies, and we can touch the heavens with our ability to imagine, to identify, and to affirm.

The Midrash asserts that what we do during our lives has meaning because we are weaving the fabric we will wear in the world to come. How we conduct ourselves now—the extent to which we study, embody, and transmit Torah—determines the nature of our influence on the world and on the future, inspiring the Eternal One to bestow some measure of eternity on the works of our hands and on our journey.

Barukh Ha-Shem (Praise the Lord)

It's always easy to distinguish the "insiders" from the newcomers at any synagogue service. The old-time regulars all know where to get the tallit and the prayer books; always seem to know when to stand and when to sit and when to turn around; and always seem to know what page the cantor is on, no matter how fast he or she is going. But the greatest mark of distinction, the high-water mark of mavendom (expertise), is that these regulars always know, in the middle of the prayers, when to rush and mumble *"Barukh hu u'varukh sh'mo* (Blessed is God and blessed is God's name)."

To the uninitiated, it may look like magic or like serendipity. After all, the tuneless chanting of the cantor is too fast for most to follow and is indistinguishable anyway. So how do these people know when to interject with their rushed phrase, and how do they always manage to say it in such a way that no one who doesn't already know it can possibly figure out what it is?

The answer to this dilemma lies in the middle of the lofty poetry of Moses's penultimate poem. In *Parashat Ha'azinu*, Moses proclaims, "When I proclaim the name of the Lord, Give glory to our God." He may well have meant this as a poetic preamble, preparing his listeners for the praises of God that were to follow. This poem is, after all, one of the most sublime in the Bible.

But our tradition has an interesting relationship to scripture. Often, those verses that were intended (on the level of *p'shat*) to be taken literally were actually interpreted and applied metaphorically. And equally often, those verses that were probably intended (as a matter of *p'shat*) to be understood metaphorically were given a tangible and practical meaning. It is as though the rabbis understood that poetry that remains on the level of sentiment can only rarely change people's lives. To truly alter the contours of the human soul, even poetry must find expression in concrete behavior.

Thus, with Moses's poetic exclamation, Rashi provides a concrete interpretation for a poetic passage: "When I will proclaim and mention the name of the Lord, you 'shall ascribe greatness unto our God' and praise God's name. Hence, our rabbis said that one must answer, 'Blessed be the name of God's glorious kingdom forever and ever' after the recital of a blessing in the sanctuary."

What the rabbis of the Talmud mandate is that every mention of God's name during a *berakhah* is itself worthy of an exclamation of praise. That phrase—*"barukh shem kavod mal'khuto le-olam va-ed"*—is inserted in our prayer service during the Shema. And during other *berakhot*, it is still customary to insert *"barukh hu u'varukh sh'mo."*

What is the point of all that individual mumbling during the prayer service? Doesn't it distract the worshippers from concentrating on their own spiritual needs or the flow of the prayers themselves?

In many ways, the honest answer is "yes." Having to take time out each time God's name is mentioned, having to stop the flow of the prayers to call out God's glory in a ritual fashion does indeed distract from attending to one's own inner strivings or the beauty of the service. Perhaps that is precisely the point.

In contemporary life, we tend to associate prayer with only one kind of praying—the spontaneous outpouring of the individual soul. We unburden ourselves of our hopes, disappointments, or pain, confident that God will hear our prayers and hopeful that God will respond the way we want. One step removed is to still see some artistic value in a service that is "performed" beautifully. The majesty of the prayers, when offered by a powerful cantor and a well-rehearsed choir, is incontestable. But are our needs or an appreciation of beauty the only—or even the primary—purpose of a prayer service?

There is always time to call out to God. According to the Talmud, "The gates of prayer are never closed." And the beauty and majesty of our service is an added bonus. But the purpose of organized prayer (as opposed to private prayer) is not to respond to our needs but to train us to try to respond to God's. By putting the Eternal One at the center, we struggle to remove ourselves as the sole or primary focus of our own attention. And as a tool for doing that, we call out God's praise each time someone chants the Divine name.

There is a time for all kinds of prayers. But sitting in a synagogue isn't directly intended to address our own needs. Instead, by learning to derive satisfaction from praising God, from cultivating a sense of gratitude for the gift of life and community and spirit, we do derive a benefit—the benefit of peace. Which paradoxically can only come when we stop looking for a benefit for ourselves and focus instead on making ourselves pure vessels to carry and reflect God's light.

Barukh ha-Shem!

Ve-Zot Ha-Berakhah/This Is the Blessing

Deuteronomy 33:1–12

The final parashah of the Torah ends on a joyous note; it is appropriately called "This Is the Blessing." Moses's final words to Israel are of benediction. Throughout his long leadership, Moses has shown the people his authority as lawgiver and his moral rigor as chastiser. Only now does he reveal to them what he has already shown God: his deep love for and loyalty toward the Jewish people.

Moses begins with praise of God's power and God's devotion to Israel: "Lover, indeed, of the people, Their hallowed are all in Your hand." God's sovereignty is placed in the hands of the Jewish people.

Moses then goes through each tribe, offering a vision of its future, its character, and its challenges. After reviewing each tribe, he again praises God's love of the entire people: "O Jeshurun (upright one), there is none like God, riding through the heavens to help you . . . O happy Israel! Who is like you, a people delivered by the Holy One."

After concluding his final blessing to his beloved people, Moses ascends Mount Nebo. Before dying, he gazes on the vista of the land that Israel will enter and in which it will shape the history of all humanity. Then he dies at the age of 120 years, "his eyes . . . undimmed and his vigor unabated."

The Torah pauses in its narrative to praise this "nursing father" of a prophet: "Never again did there arise in Israel a prophet like Moses— whom the Holy One singled out face-to-face—for the various signs and portents that the Holy One sent him to display in the land of Egypt, against Pharaoh and all his courtiers and his whole country, and for all the great might and awesome power that Moses displayed before all Israel."

Glossary of Terms

Abram. Abraham, patriarch and father of the Israelites.

Aharei Mot. Lit., "after the death"; parashah in the book of Leviticus.

ahavat ha-Shem. Love of God.

ahavat Yisrael. Love of one's fellow Jews.

Al tifrosh min ha-tzibbur. Don't separate yourself from the community.

Am Yisrael. The soul of Israel.

Amidah. The standing, silent prayer that marks the liturgical pinnacle of every Jewish worship service.

anav. Meek.

ani. An individual.

ani Ha-Shem. God's nature.

Aron. The Ark of the Covenant.

Aron Kodesh. The ark containing the Torah scrolls in every synagogue.

Aseh lekha shtei hatzotzrot. Make yourself two silver trumpets.

Aseret Ha-Dibrot. The Ten Commandments.

asham. Guilt offering; one of the main types of sacrifices.

asher hotzeiti otam me-eretz Mitzrayim. A consequence of having been brought to freedom.

assur. Prohibited.

atzei shittim. Acacia wood.

avnet. Sash worn by the high priest.

az. Assertion of the propriety of the Israelite conquest in the time of Joshua.

ba-kol. In everything.

bal tash'hit. To not waste and have concern for ecology.

Balak. Parashah in the book of Numbers; named after the king of Moab.

bamah. A forbidden idolatrous altar.

Barukh Ha-Shem. Praise the Lord.

Barukh hu u'varukh sh'mo. Blessed is God and blessed is God's name.

Barukh Shem Kevod Mal'khuto Le-Olam Va-ed. Blessed is the name of God's glorious Domain forever and ever.

Barukh Shem Kevodo l'olam va-ed. Praised be God's glorious sovereignty throughout all time.

Be-Ha'alotekha. Lit., "in your lighting"; parashah in the book of Numbers.

Be-Har. Lit., "on the mountain"; parashah in the book of Leviticus.

Be-Hukkotai. Lit., "in my statutes"; parashah in the book of Leviticus.

bein adam la-Makom. Charitable acts known only to the doer and God.

beit din. The religious court of three observant Jews.

Beit Yisrael. The household of Israel.

bekhor. Firstborn.

Be-Midbar. Lit., "in the desert"; parashah in the book of Numbers.

ben sorer u-moreh. A stubborn and rebellious son.

bentsch licht. Yiddish for "light candles."

berakhah. Blessing.

berakhot. Blessings.

Be-Shalah. Lit., "he sent"; parashah in the book of Exodus.

Bet Ha-Midrash. House of Study.

bikkur holim. The mitzvah of visiting the sick.

bitahon. Faith.

b'nai mitzvah. Responsible for the commandments.

b'nei rachamim. The merciful children of a merciful god.

Bo. Lit., "go"; parashah in the book of Exodus.

B'raisheet. Lit., "beginnings"; the book of Genesis; parashah in the book of Genesis.

brit. Covenant.

brit kodesh. A sacred covenant that links every Jewish soul with God.

briti shalom. An eternal pact of friendship.

bubbe. Grandmother.

Canaan. Ham, a son of Noah.

Chabad. Hassidic Jewish organization.

davven. To pray.

derekh eretz. Decency and civility.

derekh ha-beinoni. Moderation and consideration of others.

derekh yesharah. The straight path balancing personal and social interests in a more fruitful tension.

Devarim. Lit., "words"; parashah in the book of Deuteronomy.

drash. Inventive commentary.

drashot. Interpretation.

Egel ha-Zahav. The molten calf cast by Aaron.

Ekev. Lit., "it came to pass"; parashah in the book of Deuteronomy.

El Elohei Ruhot. Source of the Breath of All Flesh (God).

El na refa na la. God, please heal her.

elai. To me.

Emor. Lit., "speak"; parashah in the book of Leviticus.

emunah. Faith, trust (in God).

ephod. Apron worn by the high priest.

Eretz Yisrael. Land of Israel.

et Shabbtotai tishmeru. The marking of sacred time.

Etz Hayyim Hee. The Torah is a living tree.

eved Ivri. A Hebrew slave.

eved K'nani. A Canaanite slave.

gabbai. Ritual director of a worship service.

gadol ha-shalom. The greatness of peace.

Gehinnom. Hell.

gemillut hasadim. Good deeds.

ger. Stranger or convert.

goat of Azazel. A scapegoat.

Gomel Hesed. Lit., "the One who bestows loving-kindness."

Ha'azinu. Lit., "give ear"; parashah in the book of Deuteronomy.

Hafetz Hayim. *Lover of Life,* a book about gossip.

haggadot. Rabbinic legends.

Ha-Kadosh-Barukh-Hu liba ba'i. God wants the heart.

hakhel. Gathering.

hakh'nasat orehim. Hospitality; to welcome guests.

hakh'nasat orhim. To host guests; hospitality.

Ha-K'naani az ba-Aretz. The Canaanites were then in the land.

ha-mehokek. Lawgiver.

hametz. Leaven.

Hanokh. Enoch, patriarch and father of Methuselah.

Ha-Shamayim m'saprim k'vod El. The heavens declare the glory of God.

hasidah. Stork.

hatafat dam brit. The taking of a drop of blood to symbolize ritual circumcision.

ha-Torah ha-zot. This Torah.

hattat. Sin offering; one of the main types of sacrifices.

ha-tzirah. Lit., "hornet."

havdalah. Lit., "distinction"; the ceremony ending Shabbat.

Hayei Sarah. Lit., "the life of Sarah"; parashah in the book of Genesis.

hayyav. Obligatory.

hesed. Love that need not be continually earned, loving-kindness.

Hevra Kadisha. Holy society, group who supervised burial of the dead.

hil'kheta ke-vatrai. Principle holding that the law follows the most recent ruling.

Hineni. Lit., "Here I am."

hok. Law.

honen da'at. The One who bestows understanding and confers knowledge.

hormah. Lit., "destruction."

hoshen. Breastpiece worn by the high priest.

Hukkat. Lit., "this is the statute"; parashah in the book of Numbers.

hukkim. Laws.

hukkotai. God's laws.

Jeshurun. Upright one.

kahunah. Priestly families; the priesthood.

kal va-homer. Inference from a minor matter to a major conclusion.

kalah. A bride.

karet. Banishment from the community.

kavod. Glory.

kavod ha-met. The mitzvah of providing dignity to a deceased person.

kavvanah. Intention.

Kedoshim. Lit., "holiness"; parashah in the book of Leviticus.

kedushah. Holiness.

kehillah. Community; congregation.

ke-khaloto. Lit., "he had finished."

Keter malkhut. Crown of soveriegnty.

ketubbah. Wedding contract.

Ketuvim. The third section of the Hebrew Bible.

kiddush ha-Shem. Acting in a way that reflects positively on God.

Kiddush Levanah. A sanctification made in response to the new moon that consists of reciting a psalm that firmly establishes God as the author of the natural order, noting that the sun, moon, and stars do God's will reliably.

kippah. A head covering.

Ki-Tavo. Lit., "when you come in"; parashah in the book of Deuteronomy.

Ki-Tetze. Lit., "when you go forth"; parashah in the book of Deuteronomy.

Ki-Tissa. Lit., "when you take"; parashah in the book of Exodus.

kohanim. Priests.

Kohelet. Ecclesiastes.

kohen. The community.

kohen gadol. High priest.

kol ha-mitzvah. Lit., "the entire commandment."

kol ziknei b'nei Yisrael. All the elders of the children of Israel.

Korah. Parashah in the book of Numbers; named after a Levite who rebelled against Moses.

kriyat Shema. The daily recitation of the Shema in Talmudic and contemporary Judaism.

Kuma Adonai! Lit., "Arise, God!"

kuttonet. Tunic worn by the high priest.

k'vod ha-briot. Human dignity.

lechem panim. Showbread.

lehem isheh l'Adonai. Lit., "bread of fire for God"; phrase used to describe sacrifices to God.

Lekh Lekha. Lit., "take yourself, go forth"; parashah in the book of Genesis.

L'Hayim. Lit., "to life"; a toast.

Lo ra'u ish et-ahiv. A man couldn't see his brother.

l'shon ha-ra. Malicious gossip.

lulei. Unless, or "had not."

ma'akeh. A parapet.

Ma'aseh avot siman la-banim. The deeds of the parents become signs for the children.

Mah etzel herut l'avodah zarah? What is the connection between freedom and idolatry?

makom. "The Place"; name of God.

marror. Bitter herbs.

Massei. Lit., "itineraries"; parashah in the book of Numbers.

massekhet. A section of the Talmud.

Mattot. Lit., "tribes"; parashah in the book of Numbers.

mehokek. Lit., "maces" or "staffs."

Mei ha-Shiloach. An Hasidic commentary.

me'ilah. The misappropriation of Temple property.

Mekhilta. A midrash to Exodus.

melakhah. Work.

melekh ha-olam. Monarch of Space and Time; God.

Melekhet ha-Mishkan. The work of the Tabernacle.

menachem aveilim. The mitzvah of comforting mourners.

metzora. A sick person.

Metzora. Lit., "the leper"; parashah in the book of Leviticus.

middat ha-din. Virtue of judgment.

middat ha-rachamim. Virtue of mercy.

Midrash Be-Midbar Rabbah. The ancient rabbinic commentary to the book of Numbers.

Midrash B'raisheet Rabbah. The ancient rabbinic commentary to the book of Genesis.

Midrash Devarim Rabbah. The ancient rabbinic commentary to the book of Deuteronomy.

Midrash Sh'mot Rabbah. The ancient rabbinic commentary to the book of Exodus.

Midrash Va-Yikra Rabbah. The ancient rabbinic commentary to the book of Leviticus.

mikdashai tira'u. The reverence of sacred space.

Miketz. Lit., "at the end"; parashah in the book of Genesis.

mikvah. A ritual purifying bath.

minha. Grain offering; one of the main types of sacrifices.

minhagim. Customs.

Mishkan. Tabernacle.

Mishnah Pirkei Avot. The Teachings of the Sages.

Mishnah Torah. Rambam's encapsulation of the oral Torah.

mishpatai. God's rules.

Mishpatim. Lit., "ordinances"; parashah in the book of Exodus.

mitznefet. Headdress worn by the high priest.

mitzvot. Commandments.

mitzvot bein adam le-havero. The interpersonal or ethical commandments.

Moshe. Moses, prophet who led the Israelites out of Egypt and received the Ten Commandments from God at Mount Sinai.

mum. Blemish.

muttar. Permissible.

nahash. Lit., "snake."

Naso. Lit., "take"; parashah in the book of Numbers.

nehoshet. Lit., "copper."

Ner Tamid. The eternal light found in every synagogue before the ark containing the Torah scrolls.

neshamah. Self, soul.

nevelah. Improperly slaughtered meat.

Nitzavim. Lit., "you stand"; parashah in the book of Deuteronomy.

Noah. Parashah in the book of Genesis; named after the patriarch Noah.

Ohel Mo'ed. The Tent of Meeting.

olah. Burnt offering; one of the main types of sacrifices.

Olam ha-ba. The coming world.

Or Ha-Hayim. A seventeenth-century commentary to the Torah.

Orhot Tzaddikim. A medieval compendium.

Otiot de-Rebbi Akiva. An ancient midrash.

parochet. A hanging tapestry.

pasuk. Biblical verse.

pasul. Ritually unfit.

Pekudei. Lit., "the accounts"; parashah in the book of Exodus.

Pinhas. Parashah in the book of Numbers; named after the priest Pinhas.

pintele Yid. No matter how distanced one may become, there is always a Jewish point deep within, some small spark waiting to be ignited when the time is right.

poskim. Legal decisors.

p'shat. History or fact.

Rabbenu. Our rabbi.

rasha. Wicked person.

rav. Teacher.

razim. Secrets.

Re'eh. Lit., "behold"; parashah in the book of Deuteronomy.

reshut. Optional.

Reuven. Reuben, a son of Jacob.

Ribbono shel Olam. Commander of Space/Time.

Rosh Hodesh. New moon.

ruach ha-kodesh. Divine inspiration.

saraf. Lit., "to burn."

Sarai. Sarah, Abraham's wife.

Sefer Ha-Brit. The book of the covenant.

Sefer Ha-Hinnukh. A thirteenth-century Spanish listing of the mitzvot.

Sefer Ha-Mitzvot. A list and description of the 613 biblical commandments written by Maimonides.

Sefer Ha-Mitzvot Ha-Katzar. A book of the commandments by Chafetz Chayim.

Sefer Ha-Yashar. A pseudepigraphic work of mythic history from the Creation through the Exodus, dated to the eleventh, twelfth, or sixteenth century.

Sefer Mitzvot Gadol. A thirteenth-century compilation about the biblical commandments.

Sefer Sh'mot. The book of Exodus.

Sefer Va-Yikra. The book of Leviticus.

Sefirat Ha-Omer. Sacred occasion during which the new barley grains are counted each night for forty-nine nights.

Seraf. In Israelite and ancient Near Eastern writings, a winged snake that stands upright and heals all those who look upon it.

sha. Yiddish for "Quiet!"

Shabbat. Jewish Sabbath.

shalom. Peace, wholeness, tranquillity, completeness.

Shavuot. The Festival of Weeks.

shehitah. The least painful way possible of killing an animal.

shelamim. Peace or whole offerings; one of the main types of sacrifices.

Shemini. Lit., "eighth"; parashah in the book of Leviticus.

Shemittah. Sabbatical year.

Sheol. The realm of the dead.

Shevat. A month in the Hebrew calendar.

Sh'lah Lekha. Lit., "send"; parashah in the book of Numbers.

shleimut. Wholeness.

Sh'ma. "Hear!"; quintessential Biblical proclamation of faith.

sh'mirat ha-lashon. Guarding one's speech.

Sh'mot. Lit., "names"; parashah in the book of Exodus.

Shoftim. Lit., "judges"; parashah in the book of Deuteronomy.

shokhet. Ritual butcher.

shoresh. Root of a verb.

shtill. Yiddish for "Quiet!"

Shuva Adonai! Lit., "Return, God!"

Sifra. An ancient midrash on Leviticus.

Sifre Zuta. A tannaitic midrash on the book of Numbers.

Sifrei Devarim. A tannaitic midrash.

simcha. Joyous occasion.

Sotah. Trial by ordeal; a ritual in which a husband who suspects his wife of having committed adultery may bring her before the priests to determine whether she is guilty.

ta'amei ha-mitzvot. Reasons for the commandments and the pervasive discussions and logic throughout the Talmud.

tahor. Ritually permissible.

takkanot. Legislation.

takken olam be-malkhut Shaddai. To repair the world under the sovereignty of God.

tallitot. Prayer shawls.

talmid. Student.

tamei. Ritually impermissible.

tamim. Wholeheartedness; a degree of trust.

Tanakh. Hebrew Bible.

Tanya. A founding document of Chabad.

Targum Onkelos. The ancient Aramaic translation of the Torah.

Tazria. Lit., "delivery"; parashah in the book of Leviticus.

tekhelet. A special blue dye.

temimah. Perfect.

temimut. A high degree of devotion to God alone.

Terumah. Lit., "offering"; parashah in the book of Exodus.

teshuvah. Repentence.

Tetzaveh. Lit., "you will command"; parashah in the book of Exodus.

todah. Thanksgiving offering.

to'evah. Abominations.

to'evat. Abhorrent.

tohorah. Ritual purity.

tokhakhah. Reproof.

tokhelu. To consume.

Toldot. Lit., "generations"; parashah in the book of Genesis.

Torah min ha-Shamayim. Torah from the Heavens.

Torah sheh be-al peh. An oral teaching that parallels, elucidates, and implements the written teaching.

Tosefta Sotah. A collection of tannaitic statements rejected for inclusion in the Mishnah but often found in the Talmud.

totafot. Symbol.

tov me'od. Very good.

treif. Ritually impermissible.

treifah. Improperly slaughtered meat.

tumah. Ritual impurity.

tza'ar ba'alei hayyim. Compassion for the suffering of animals.

tzaddikim. Plural of "tzaddik." Righteous people.

tzara'at. A degenerative skin disease.

Tzav. Lit., "command"; parashah in the book of Leviticus.

tzedakah. charity.

tzedek. Righteousness.

tzitz. Frontlet worn by the high priest.

tzorkhei tzibbur. To value the needs of the community.

Urim ve-Tummim. Devices used to discern the will of God, worn by the high priest.

u'shfatem tzedek. To decide justly.

Va-Era. Lit., "he appeared"; parashah in the book of Exodus.

Va-Et'hanan. Lit., "I pleaded"; parashah in the book of Deuteronomy.

Va-Yakhel. Lit., "he assembled"; parashah in the book of Exodus.

va-yashav. To return; to repent.

Va-Yehi. Lit., "he lived"; parashah in the book of Genesis.

Va-Yelekh. Lit., "he went"; parashah in the book of Deuteronomy.

Va-Yera. Lit., "he saw"; parashah in the book of Genesis.

Va-Yeshev. Lit., "he dwelt"; parashah in the book of Genesis.

Va-Yetze. Lit., "he went out"; parashah in the book of Genesis.

vay-falel. Lit., "to execute judgment" or "to pray."

Va-Yigash. Lit., "he came near"; parashah in the book of Genesis.

Va-Yikra. Lit., "he called"; the book of Leviticus.

Va-Yishlach. Lit., "he sent"; parashah in the book of Genesis.

ve-hayah im shamoa. "If you listen"; a section of the Torah.

Ve-shim'u el Yisrael avikhem. Hearken to Israel, your father.

Ve-Zot Ha-Berakhah. Lit., "this is the blessing"; parashah in the book of Deuteronomy.

Yalkut Shimoni. A midrashic collection on the Torah and Tanakh.

yeshivah bochur. A rabbinic student.

Yetziyat Mitzrayim. Exodus from Egypt.

Yid. A Jew.

yiddishkeit. Jewish knowledge.

yira. Fear.

yirat shamayim. Fear of heaven.

Yisrael areivim zeh ba-zeh. All of us are responsible for each other.

Yitro. Lit., "Jethro"; parashah in the book of Exodus; named after Moses's father-in-law.

Yoma. A volume of the Talmud dealing with Yom Kippur.

Yovel. Jubilee year.

Yud-Gimel Middot. The thirteen rules of Rabbi Ishmael.

zav. An abnormal male or female discharge.

zekhut avot. Ancestral merit.

zemirot. Songs.

zevah ha-shelamim. Peace or whole offerings; one of the main types of sacrifices.

zeyde. Grandfather.

Zohar. Lit., "The Book of Splendor"; a mystical commentary to the Torah from thirteenth-century Spain, written by Moses de Leon.

Some of the Commentators and Commentaries Influencing *The Everyday Torah*

Ancient

Avot de-Rabbi Natan. A midrash on *Pirkei Avot*; second-century Israel.

Mekhilta. A halakhic midrash on the book of Exodus; first- and second-century Israel.

Midrash Rabbah. A collection of midrashim on each of the five books of the Torah: *B'raisheet Rabbah, Sh'mot Rabbah, Va-Yikra Rabbah, Ba-Midbar Rabbah,* and *Devarim Rabbah*; fifth through twelfth-century Israel.

Mishnah. The authoritative compilation of rabbinic law and tradition by Rabbi Judah ha-Nasi; second-century Israel.

Pesikta de-Rav Kahana. Sermons on the synagogue reading cycle; fifth-century Israel.

Philo. A philosopher whose comments on the Torah were often allegorical; first-century Egypt.

Pirkei de-Rabbi Eliezer. An Aggadic midrash; eighth-century Israel.

Sifrei. A halakhic midrash to the books of Numbers and Deuteronomy; fourth-century Israel.

Talmud. An extensive collection of rabbinic law, tradition, and narrative. The Jerusalem Talmud dates from the early fifth century; the Babylonian Talmud dates from the early seventh century.

Tanhuma. A series of midrashim about the weekly parashiyot, beginning in the name of Rabbi Tanhuma; fifth-century Israel.

Torat Kohanim. Another name for the *Sifra*, a midrash on the book of Leviticus.

Medieval

Ben Asher, Bahya. Thirteenth-century Spain.

Ben Joseph, Saadia (Saadia Gaon). Ninth-century Babylonia.

Ben Maimon, Moses (Maimonides or the Rambam). Twelfth-century Spain and Egypt.

Ben Meir, Samuel (the Rashbam). Twelfth-century France.

Bonfils, Joseph. Eleventh-century France.

Hizkuni, Hezekiah Ben Rabbi Manoah. Thirteenth-century France.

Ibn Ezra, Abraham. Eleventh-century Spain and Italy.

Kimhi, David Ben Joseph (the Radak). Twelfth-century France.

Levi, Aaron Ha-. Thirteenth-century Spain; *Sefer Ha-Hinnukh.*

Rashi (Rabbi Shlomo Yitzhaki). Eleventh-century France.

Sefer Ha-Yashar. Eleventh- or twelfth-century pseudepigraphic chronology of Creation to the Exodus.

Sforno, Ovadiah Ben Jacob. Fifteenth-century Italy.

Zohar. Mystical commentary to the Torah, authored by Moses de Leon; thirteenth-century Spain.

Modern

Alter, Robert. *The Art of Biblical Narrative, The Art of Biblical Poetry.*

Ben Attar, Rabbi Hayim. *Or Ha-Hayim.*

Freud, Sigmund. *Character and Culture, Totem and Taboo, The Interpretation of Dreams.*

Heschel, Rabbi Abraham Joshua. *God in Search of Man, The Sabbath, The Insecurity of Freedom, What Is Man?*

Levine, Baruch. *The JPS Torah Commentary: Leviticus.*

Milgrom, Jacob. *The JPS Torah Commentary: Numbers.*

Neusner, Jacob. *The Enchantments of Judaism.*

Sarna, Nahum. *The JPS Torah Commentary: Genesis, Understanding Genesis, Exploring Genesis.*

Index

Communication. *See also* Words
 heart-to-heart, 81–82
 listening, 76
Community, 44, 63
 individual self-interest vs., 216–18
 sense of, 16–18
Compassion, 95–96
Compromise, of dignity and honor, 51–52
Conformity
 and distinctness of Jewish people, 261–62, 302–4
 individual uniqueness vs., 306, 308
Contentment, 77
Convention, facts vs., 236–38
Conversion to Judaism, 284–86
Convictions, humility in, 183–84
Covenantal promises
 in Moses's speech, 323, 330
 of rainbow, 9
 in *Sefer Ha-Brit,* 123
 and Ten Commandments, 115–16
 through brit milah, 24
Creation, 2
 building of Tabernacle as, 129
 as history, 3
 of humanity, 6–8
 meaning and purpose of, 4
 Shabbat as pinnacle of, 148, 149
Criminal laws, 123
Curses, 203–6

Darkness, plague of, 105–7
Death, 155–56
 dealing with, 255–57
 of Hanokh, 5
 and meaningfulness of life, 341
 righteousness and, 5–6, 259–61
Despair, hope in, 98–100
Dietary laws (*kashrut*), 174–78, 180, 304–6
Dignity. *See* Human dignity
Disabilities, 224–25
Distinction of Jewish people, 261–62, 302–4

Dreams
 Joseph's interpretation of, 63, 64, 70
 meaning of, 67–69
 significance in, 61–62

Elders, 87–89
Empathy, 82
Equality of human beings, 218–20
Eternal life, 155–57
Ethical commandments, 317–18
Ethics
 and holiness, 283
 of questioning God's justice, 90–91
Evil, resisting, 320

Fact, convention vs., 236–38
Faith
 expression of, 284
 as leg of Judaism, 47–48
 passive vs. active, 112–14
Fame, enduring, 97–98
Fear, 281–82
 awe as, 92
 of consequences, 92
 of death, 341
 of God, 91–93, 288–89
 of heaven, 91–93
Festivals
 laws establishing, 123, 196
 pilgrimage, 306–7
 significance of moon in, 266–67
Fire, pillar of, 233, 234
Flood, 9, 10
Food
 kashrut, 174–78, 180, 304–6
 in sacrifices, 163
Freedom, 2
 to choose God's will, 328
 fear of heaven as step toward, 92
 hope of, 98–100
 and idolatry, 207–9
 rejection of, 239–40
 responsibility of, 262–64
Friendship, 39–40
Fulfillment, search for, 291–93

About the Author

Rabbi Bradley Shavit Artson (http://www.bradartson.com) is Dean of the Ziegler School of Rabbinic Studies and Vice President at the American Jewish University in Los Angeles, where he teaches Jewish Philosophy as well as Senior Homiletics. He supervises one of the nation's largest Introduction to Judaism/conversion programs. The author of six books—most recently, *Gift of Soul, Gift of Wisdom: A Spiritual Resource for Mentoring and Leadership*—and a weekly e-mail commentary on parashiyot that goes to almost fifteen thousand subscribers, he served as a congregational rabbi in Southern California for ten years. During that time, his synagogue grew from two hundred to almost six hundred membership units, and he helped more than two hundred people convert to Judaism. On the editorial board for several journals and magazines, Rabbi Artson has written more than two hundred articles and is a frequent lecturer and teacher. A member of the Leadership Council of Conservative Judaism, he is on the faculty of the Wexner Heritage Foundation and speaks frequently for the United Jewish Communities/Federation. He is a doctoral candidate in contemporary theology at the Hebrew Union College/Jewish Institute of Religion. Prior to rabbinical school, he graduated from Harvard and then served as a legislative aide to the Speaker of the California State Assembly. He lives with his wife, Elana, and their twins, Shira and Jacob.

If you would like to receive Rabbi Artson's weekly e-mail commentary, "Today's Torah," at no charge, please send a message to listserv@ajula.edu with the following in the body of the message: "SUBSCRIBE torah."